China in the Global South

Theodor Tudoroiu · Anna Kuteleva
Editors

China in the Global South

Impact and Perceptions

 Springer

Editors
Theodor Tudoroiu
Department of Political Science
The University of the West Indies
St. Augustine, Trinidad and Tobago

Anna Kuteleva
School of International Regional Studies
National Research University Higher
School of Economics
Moscow, Russia

ISBN 978-981-19-1346-4   ISBN 978-981-19-1344-0 (eBook)
https://doi.org/10.1007/978-981-19-1344-0

This Springer imprint is published by the registered company Springer Nature Singapore Pte Ltd.
The registered company address is: 152 Beach Road, #21-01/04 Gateway East, Singapore 189721, Singapore

Contents

Contributors

Johanes Herlijanto Department of Communication, Pelita Harapan University, Jakarta, Indonesia

Sergei Ivanov Palacký University Olomouc, Olomouc, Czechia

Anna Kuteleva School of International Regional Studies, National Research University Higher School of Economics, Moscow, Russia

Tara Mock Honors College, University of Alabama, Tuscaloosa, AL, USA

Pablo Sebastian Morales London School of Economics and Political Science, London, UK

Amanda Reshma Ramlogan The University of the West Indies, St. Augustine, Trinidad and Tobago

Henryk Szadziewski University of Hawai'i at Mānoa, Honolulu, Hawai'i, USA

Theodor Tudoroiu The University of the West Indies, St. Augustine, Trinidad and Tobago

Sabrina van den Bos Sydney, Australia

Yu Xiang Shanghai University School of Journalism and Communication, Shanghai, China

Mingyuan Zhang University of Oslo, Oslo, Norway

Chapter 1
Not the Relationship You Would Expect: China, Sub-National Actors, and Structural Factors

Anna Kuteleva and Theodor Tudoroiu

Abstract This chapter serves as a concise general introduction to the volume, which scrutinizes the frequently ignored agency of the Global South sub-national actors in their interactions with rising China. Far from being passive recipients of Beijing-constructed images and cooperation models, these actors are fully aware of their identity and interests and respond accordingly to China's increasingly visible presence in the Global South. At the same time, however, we acknowledge the importance of structural constraints at national, regional, and international levels. To analyze the diverse and, at times, surprising resulting combinations, we have chosen case studies that cover heterogeneous geographies of the Global South ranging from Papua-New Guinea to Argentina and from Madagascar to the Russian Far East. They are enriched by a multidisciplinary approach that brings together insights from International Relations, Political Geography, Government, Development Studies, Anthropology, Cultural Studies, Media Studies, and International Communication Studies. Moreover, the authors of individual chapters work on China in different regions of the world. Their various linguistic, cultural, and scholarly backgrounds and expertise are conducive to unique perspectives on China's global expansion. The chapter ends by discussing the content of each contribution, as well as its position in the volume's overall architecture.

Keywords China · Global South · Sub-national actors · Agency · Structural factors

Using a multidisciplinary approach and case studies based on fieldwork in nine countries scattered across Asia, Africa, the Caribbean, Latin America, and Oceania, this volume scrutinizes the frequently ignored agency of the Global South sub-national actors in their interactions with rising China. It analyzes how these actors respond to China's emergence as an increasingly consequential power in the Global South and

A. Kuteleva (✉)
National Research University Higher School of Economics, Moscow, Russia
e-mail: a.kuteleva@gmail.com

T. Tudoroiu
The University of the West Indies, Kingston, Jamaica
e-mail: theodor.tudoroiu@sta.uwi.edu

whether they are attracted by cooperation models proposed by Beijing or deterred by its newfound assertiveness. Each chapter of this volume identifies and fills a gap in the literature on China's rise by offering a nuanced perspective on its relations with the Global South that captures such variables as social context, intersubjective meanings, and identities. They also illuminate often neglected aspects of China's role in the international politics of development and identify emerging trends in South-South cooperation. Critically, the central argument of the volume is that the agency of sub-state and non-state actors in developing countries meaningfully influences the evolution of their interactions with China. Far from being passive recipients of Beijing-constructed images and cooperation models, these actors are fully aware of their identity and interests and respond accordingly to China's increasingly visible presence in the Global South. At the same time, however, we place our analysis in the context of the structure-agency debate that is at the core of constructivist approaches to international relations, and hence we acknowledge the importance of broader political, economic, social, and environmental conditions and institutions at national, regional, and international levels. China's interactions with countries of the Global South are shaped by diverse and, at times, surprising combinations of sub-national agency and structural constraints that the existing literature largely tends to ignore. To explore the variety of these combinations, we have chosen case studies that cover heterogeneous geographies of the Global South ranging from Papua-New Guinea to Argentina and from Madagascar to the Russian Far East. All case studies engage with two interrelated questions. What are the real economic, political, and social impacts of China's growing presence in the Global South? And, more critically, how do the state and societies of the Global South frame and interpret their interactions with China amid its rise?

From the beginning of this project, we set out to engage the most diverse range of contributors, convinced that the best perspective on China's relations with the Global South is provided by scholars from different fields who are spread out across the various continents and have firsthand experience with the central issue of the book. The volume brings together academics working on China in different regions of the world. Their various linguistic, cultural, and scholarly backgrounds and expertise are conducive to unique perspectives on China's global expansion. This diversity further enhances the book's ability to unveil and analyze seldom ignored aspects of this complex and multifaceted phenomenon.

All chapters are based on extensive fieldwork and intimate knowledge of spaces whose dynamics often seem complicated or obscure to outside observers. Building their analysis on firsthand empirical findings, each contributor provides an improved and nuanced understanding of China's interactions with diverse, frequently divergent, and complex state-society systems of the Global South. A multidisciplinary approach enriches the volume and allows us to bring together insights from International Relations, Political Geography, Government, Development Studies, Anthropology, Cultural Studies, Media Studies, and International Communication Studies. The value and importance of such an approach are highlighted in the next chapter by Anna Kuteleva that explores gaps in the existing literature on China's rise in the Global South and emphasizes the need to examine China's relations with the countries of the Global South as a discourse and as a practice in the context of the structure-agency dialectic.

Following Kuteleva's detailed introduction of the volume's aims, the first cluster of chapters—*China's Image and Its Reception in the Global South*—provides an overview of different readings of China's rise in the Global South and highlights limitations of China's public policy in the Global South. It opens up with Tara Mock's chapter that explores the construction of China's national brand in Africa as a mani-festation of its far-reaching geopolitical interests on the continent. The chapter pays particular attention to how the Chinese state builds its image in Africa through the use of cultural artifacts representative of not only China but Africa as well. Drawing on the analysis of official speeches, magazine covers, editorials, and advertisements, the chapter critically unpacks the semiotic messaging and rhetorical intent of artifacts indicative of China's national branding. By doing so, Mock's chapter captures the contours of China's brand across the continent, critically examining broad themes and outlining overarching discursive patterns. Deconstructing the hegemonic Africa-China narrative reproduced by the Chinese state or enterprises affiliated with it, this chapter shows how "brand-China" evolves into a powerful geopolitical tool. Mock brings to the fore questions about China's strategic self-presentations in Africa and convincingly argues that both African leaders and ordinary citizens should pay greater attention to how their states engage in various performative practices. Mock's study sets the stage for the two case studies on how local audiences respond to China's self-promotion.

Yu Xiang's chapter explores the discursive politics in China's relations with Africa further, pointing out that, as confrontation between China and the West escalates, China has to seek the Global South's approval for the globalization model that it proposes through such projects as Xi Jinping's Belt and Road Initiative. Her chapter explores how China's national-branding strategy attempts to create a new discursive hegemony in Africa by examining the attitudes of African students in China to media content produced by China Global Television Network (CGTN). Similarly, the chapter of Pablo S. Morales examines how CGTN's region-specific content is perceived in Latin America, with a focus on Mexican and Argentinian audiences. Based on series of focus groups and individual interviews with news-watchers from Africa and Latin America, both chapters provide nuanced and critical perspectives on the appeal, tools, and success of China's public diplomacy.

Overall, Part I shows that China brings to the Global South not only much-needed investment but also new discourses of development, reframing patterns of the South-South cooperation and promoting the so-called China model. Chinese media carefully customize narratives of "win–win" cooperation for different audiences of the Global South and multiply images of China as a new global leader and trendsetter. These self-representations are rigid, monolithic, and almost seamless. On the contrary, responses coming from the Global South to China's growing self-confidence and assertiveness are dynamic and unbounded. As a result, the success of China's public diplomacy in the Global South is questionable.

The volume's second part, *China as a Dividing Factor within Countries of the Global South*, presents three case studies of developing countries where China's increased influence provoked multilayered tensions. Henryk Szadziewski's chapter explores such tensions between civil society and the state in Papua-New Guinea mainly triggered by concerns about environmental degradation and neo-colonialism. Heated, at times, debates take place in the context of a typical "development for resources" deal centered on Chinese investment at the large Ramu Nickel Mine. Szadziewski shows that both supporters and opponents of this investment have constructed their claims on specific understandings of the concept of self-reliance. The state actors present Chinese investment as an alternative to and autonomy from Papua New Guinea's traditional donor, Australia. In contrast, the civil society demonstrates agency by rejecting China's "neo-colonial" attitude toward local natural resources. These self-reliance discourses translate into different practical outcomes. On the one hand, Chinese financing enables the state to demonstrate new assertiveness regionally and on the global stage, especially regarding critical issues such as the climate crisis. On the other hand, civil society makes modest gains from Chinese companies. Tensions in responses to Chinese investment from the civil society and the state reveal different visions of the future for Papua New Guinea that are relevant to the entire Oceania region where China increases its aid and investment. The chapter suggests that Chinese future interventions will have to consider local interests more carefully and even negotiate with sub-state actors.

The contribution by Theodor Tudoroiu and Amanda Reshma Ramlogan expresses considerable skepticism for the possibility of such a change. It focuses precisely on China's lack of willingness to take into consideration the interests of societal actors using as a case study Trinidad and Tobago, a small state that is representative of the entire Commonwealth Caribbean. There, an important political elites-citizens gap has developed due to the negative economic, social, and governance effects of the Chinese presence. Trinidad has the highest connectivity with China in the English-speaking Caribbean and is a major recipient of Chinese foreign aid. As elsewhere in the region, the latter mainly takes the form of large infrastructure projects loan-financed by Beijing. Critically, these projects represent the so-called tied aid: all contractors, materials, and workers have to come from China. Trinidad's political leaders welcome the projects, which they use to increase their political legitimacy and electoral support. However, the tied aid has important negative socio-economic consequences that have triggered contractors and labor large-scale frustration and protests. Moreover, the secret negotiation of projects imposed by the Chinese side damages good governance. All this leads to a rather dark picture of what is officially presented as a Sino-Caribbean solidarity-based, win–win cooperative relationship. It is unlikely that the gap between Trinidadian political elites and the society at large will diminish. The elites fully accept the harmonious image of China-the-benefactor. But common citizens reject this image and perceive the pro-Beijing actions of the political elites as detrimental to the interests of their own country.

Finally, Johanes Herlijanto's chapter analyzes a similar split within the very elites of a Global South country impacted by the increasing Chinese presence. It examines how the interplay of the old and new knowledge about China shapes the way Indonesian elites perceive current interactions with the regional great power. The old perception of China as an expansionist power that intends to intervene in Indonesia's internal affairs is combined with new knowledge regarding Beijing's capability and recent international behavior, which some Indonesian elites regard as assertive. The result is the prevalence of negative perceptions of China, which are especially held by non-governing elites that are critical toward President Joko Widodo and his administration. Meanwhile, positive views of China are present among governing elites, as well as non-governing elites favorable to the President. In fact, on specific topics, concerns and caution are present even among the members of these latter groups. But, overall, a major split can be identified between pro-presidential and anti-presidential elites, which is illustrative of China's uneven reception among Indonesia's most privileged groups.

The examples of Papua-New Guinea, Trinidad and Tobago, and Indonesia presented in Part II show that sub-national actors in the Global South develop unique understandings of China's multifaceted presence that often diverge considerably from the official policies of their states. The ability of these actors to change the key aspects of the bilateral relationship varies widely, but this is perhaps less important than the fact that the self-serving image constructed and projected by China as discussed in Part I encounters serious difficulties in imposing itself among the diversified Global South audiences. Furthermore, the agency of sub-national actors is not the only factor shaping the actual impact of the Chinese persuasive efforts. The volume's Part III scrutinizes the structural factors that are equally at work. It shows that, in some cases, China's acceptance or partial rejection by a potential partner in the developing world is a function of that country's specific features and institutional settings.

The chapter by Sabrina van den Bos analyzes the surprising failure of China's first engagement with Colombia. Initially, the bilateral relationship seemed to follow the triumphal pattern visible in the case of most Latin American states. In particular, two-way trade went from zero to multibillion dollars within a decade. However, despite a host of widely publicized diplomatic initiatives, Chinese petroleum companies failed to win a single bid for the development of Colombian oil fields. Bilateral Free Trade Agreement talks proved futile. Colombia received almost no overseas foreign direct investment from China, despite a crying need for infrastructure development. For Beijing, Colombia became a Latin American anomaly. The chapter argues that it was Colombia's uniquely antistatist approach in the promotion of its liberal values complemented by a deep aversion to left-wing politics that left little room for government-backed initiatives. It brings to light historically motivated structural and ideational factors that influence state capacity and create specific constraints, which are incompatible with the patterns of action adopted by China in its first Colombian 'desembarco.'

Anna Kuteleva and Sergei Ivanov's chapter also focuses on structural factors, exploring intersections between Russia's China policy and the Far Eastern development strategy. The venue of Kuteleva and Ivanov's case study is Primorye, a province located on the very outskirts of Russia's vast empire. The distance between its capital, Vladivostok, and Moscow spans seven time zones and 5,770 miles. China, on the other hand, is right on Primorye's doorstep. The province's strategic location near the key Asian markets, coupled with its three major ice-free ports and valuable natural endowments, motivates Moscow to maintain strict control over local resources and international dealings. At the same time, in the mid-2000s, Primorye and, specifically the city of Vladivostok, became a showcase for Russia's "turn to the East." The chapter illustrates contingencies, complexities, challenges, and paradoxes that underpin the development of China-Russia relations and identifies the implications of closer ties between Beijing and Moscow for the development of Primorye and the Russian Far East at large. Firstly, the chapter discusses the position of the Russian Far East and particularly Primorye in Russia's "turn to the East" and explores the logic of the most recent regional policies. Secondly, it examines patterns of formal and informal cooperation along the China-Russia border over the past ten years. The analysis shows that Moscow constrains the region's cooperation with China and highlights contradictions in both the "turn to the East" policy and the new regional development strategy. Finally, the chapter examines how politicians, entrepreneurs, public intellectuals, and experts in Primorye perceive China and how they envision the future of China-Russia interactions on the local level.

Together, the two chapters of Part III show that unique combinations of sociocultural features, integrative normative settings, and other structural variables such as the dynamic of regional politics and policy-making define the outcomes of China's engagement with the countries of the Global South. Connecting these insights with findings from the first two parts, we argue that China's relations with the Global South are ultimately a result of the triangular interaction between China's normative power, the local agency, and structural factors. This idea is developed in detail in Theodor Tudoroiu's closing chapter that constructs a unifying conceptual framework for the volume.

Tudoroiu's chapter argues that China's increasing influence in the developing world represents a projection of normative power that uses a specific set of norms to shape understandings of "what is normal" in accordance with Beijing's views and interests. However, this is not a one-way, unopposed action. Political elites in power do align their views—and their states' policies—with Chinese local, regional, and global interests. This is the consequence of a very effective process of Chinese international socialization based on normative suasion and role playing. But numerous other socio-economic groups in the target countries are not socialized and resist Beijing's actions that are detrimental to their own, independently constructed interests. Cognitive and institutional structural factors in target countries further influence the acceptance or rejection of Chinese actions. The chapter's conclusion is also that of this volume: the future of the complex relationship between China and the countries of the Global South is open and will be to a large extent shaped by the agency of diverse and often competing sub-national groups.

Anna Kuteleva is a post-doctoral research fellow at the School of International Regional Studies at the National Research University Higher School of Economics in Moscow. Anna received her PhD in Political Science from the University of Alberta (Canada) in 2019. Previously, she obtained a Master's degree in World Politics (Shandong University, 2010) and a Master's degree in Comparative Politics (Peoples' Friendship University of Russia, 2010). Her research is located in a broad constructivist tradition of IR and focuses on the nexus between politics and sociocultural contexts in international relations, with particular interests in politics of security and international energy politics.

Theodor Tudoroiu is a Senior Lecturer at the Department of Political Science of the University of the West Indies, St. Augustine campus. He earned his Ph.D. in Political Science from the Université de Montréal and an M.A. from the College of Europe in Bruges, Belgium. His China-related publications include *The Myth of China's No Strings Attached Development Assistance: A Caribbean Case Study* (Lexington Books, 2020), *China's International Socialization of Political Elites in the Belt and Road Initiative* (Routledge, 2021), and *China's Globalization from Below: Chinese Entrepreneurial Migrants and the Belt and Road Initiative* (Routledge, 2022).

Chapter 2
Images and Models of China-Led South-South Cooperation: What Does Rising China Offer to the Global South?

Anna Kuteleva

Abstract Gaining stature and influence in world affairs, rising China is becoming a test for the existing rule-based liberal order in the Global South. How does China's rise reshapes the development of the Global South? And what model of South-South cooperation does China promote? This chapter sets the stage for the discussion of China's presence in the Global South by exploring the so-called "China model" and the discursive politics of China's development finance programs. Identifying several gaps in the ongoing debates, the chapter highlights the need to examine China's relations with countries of the Global South as a discourse and as a practice, with a specific focus on how sub-state and non-state actors in these countries experience China's rise and respond to it.

Keywords China model · Development · Development aid · South-South cooperation

2.1 Introduction

How does China's rise reshapes the development of the Global South? And what model of South-South cooperation does China promote? By answering these questions, this chapter sets the stage for the further discussion of China's presence in the Global South in this volume. It critically engages with the literature on the so-called "China model," explores the discursive politics of China's development finance programs, and contributes to the debates on China's role in the transformation of the traditional architecture of international aid over the past two decades. Identifying gaps in the literature, the chapter highlights the need to examine China's relations with the Global South as a discourse and as a practice, with a specific focus on how sub-state and non-state actors in countries of the Global South experience China's rise and respond to it.

A. Kuteleva (✉)
National Research University Higher School of Economics, Moscow, Russia
e-mail: a.kuteleva@gmail.com

2.2   Reshaping Development: The "China Model"

In the mid-2000s, China's rapid economic growth brought it to the center of international intellectual debates about the meaning of development and turned it into a new prototype. The first attempt to present China's development experience as a transferable model was John Cooper Ramo's Beijing Consensus. In 2004, Ramo used the term to describe China's development trajectory as a viable alternative to the Washington Consensus. The original concept combined "three theorems about how to organize the place of a developing country in the world:" the need to introduce "bleeding-edge innovations," the focus on improving living standards, and the commitment to financial and military self-reliance (Ramo, 2004: 11–12). While many scholars criticize Ramo's concept for being analytically incoherent and inaccurate (e.g., Ambrosio, 2012; Kennedy, 2010; Naughton, 2010; Ortmann, 2012), his attempt to conceptualize China's development provoked heated debates among academics and practitioners that further intensified in the early 2010s after China has smoothly survived the global financial crisis of 2008.

The ideologically neutral term "China model" has quickly replaced the controversial term "consensus." According to Kennedy (2010: 474), this term was originally employed to "distinguish China's gradualist reform strategy from the 'shock therapy' approach adopted by post-Communist states of central Europe" rather than to challenge the superiority of Washington Consensus. Such an approach connotes two interlinking Chinese concepts: the concept of "socialism with Chinese characteristics" (*Zhongguo tese shehuizhuyi*) and the concept of "socialist market economy" (*shehuizhui shichang jingji*). The leadership of the Communist Party of China (CPC) and lately Chinese scholars use these concepts to explain the shift from class struggle to market-based development, while at the same time legitimizing the continuity of the CPC's rule. For example, Hu Jun and Han Dong (2010: 16) claim that one of the distinctive features of the "China model" is the way the CPC operates with long-term and short-term targets:

> [The CPC] always blends long-term goals and current targets. It produces practical decisions out of the idealized long-term goals following present-day common interests, which corresponds with the public ideal of socialism with Chinese characteristics. Meanwhile, the major task at the current stage of development is the complete realization of the long-term goal of comprehensive and unrestrained individual development of all members of society.

Further, Hu and Han (2010: 19)—like many other Chinese scholars (e.g., Wang, 2013; Xiong, 2009)—emphasize that the defining feature of the "China model" is that it is based on a "socialist market economy" rather than on a "capitalist path" and "conventional market system."

Many scholars outside China, however, focus the discussion of China's development on contrapositions between Beijing and Washington and provide polarized portrayals of the competition between state capitalism and neoliberalism. They argue that the "China model" is no more than rhetoric that justifies, maintains, and legitimates an authoritarian regime. For example, Lo Bobo and Lilia Shevtsova (2012: 40) define the "China model" as "the archetypal example of authoritarian capitalism."

They claim that the notion of development that is at the core of the "China model" rationalizes "tyranny under the cloak of local traditions and culture" and benefits "the narrow interests of self-serving elites while depriving ordinary people of basic freedoms" (Lo & Shevtsova, 2012: 32). Similarly, Matt Ferchen (2013: 404) reduces the "China model" to "the Party-sponsored critique of the Washington Consensus and neoliberalism more generally" that articulates opinions of the "New Left" group.

In contrast, according to David Harvey (2005) and Giovanni Arrighi (2007), the fact that China does not follow conventional neoliberal prescriptions makes its development trajectory more viable rather than problematic. Arrighi (2007: 17) recognizes "the chasm between official discourse in Beijing […] and the reality of unbridled capitalism" and admits that "socialism with Chinese characteristics" is an ideological oxymoron designed to disguise the reality that China no longer follows a socialist path. Yet, in his opinion, even though China chooses a market-based development path, it does not replicate a neoliberal logic and thus does not belong to the Western capitalist cohort. Harvey (2005: 120), on the contrary, maintains that after Deng Xiaoping "opened-up" China in the early 1980s, its development is best understood in terms of "neoliberalism with Chinese characteristics," that is "a particular kind of market economy that increasingly incorporates neoliberal elements interdigitated with authoritarian centralized control."

Overall, examining the "China model," scholars both inside and outside China often operate with the broad categories of dichotomist dualism, defining it in opposition to abstract "Western model(s)" of development. They do not critically engage with concepts and understandings of development that underpin Chinese socioeconomic policies but explain China's experience through the prism of Western approaches to development. As Chen Minglu and David S. G. Goodman (2012: 172) put it, "the Cold War may have been resolved more than 20 years ago but the views expressed by many of the authors involved in discussion of the China Model have their roots in those much earlier debates." Hence, the focus too often shifts from China's development per se and possible implications of China's experience to whether economic growth in a non-democratic country could be qualified as development. In such a perspective, what the "China model" entails becomes less important compared to what it does not (Breslin, 2011: 1324).

Such scholars as Martin Jacques (2009), Barry Naughton (2010), and Chen Minglu and David Goodman (2012) reject attempts to constrain China's development choices to the binary opposition of the China-West dichotomy. They claim that China's approach to development is formed by highly specific circumstances, particularly China's size, scale, the continuation of culture and history, and unique features of social and political organization. In this respect, although certain lessons might be extrapolated from China's experience, the fundamental differences between China and other countries will significantly limit their potential replicability. Following this logic, attempts to generate a model out of China's experience are meaningless because China's development strategy cannot be reproduced elsewhere. Indeed, "nobody else is so big, possesses such a unique comparative advantage, or operates a remotely similar political system" (Naughton, 2010: 439). Nevertheless, when China's development strategy is deconstructed as a set of interconnected socioeconomic policies pursued by a strong developmental state, "Chinese characteristics"—however they are identified—start to represent a national exceptionalist narrative rather than an essence or objective explanation of China's developmental success (Breslin, 2011; Haan, 2011).

Bruse Dickson elaborates a procedural definition of the "China model" that combines elements of market economic policies and political regime characteristics. According to Dickson (2011: 41), a replicable "China model" includes five key policies: liberalizing the economy, rejecting the central planning system in favor of the market, importing foreign capital and technology, (re)orienting on exports, and maintaining an authoritarian regime to guide economic reforms. Further, he expands this definition emphasizing that China updated its development by creating "national champions" within different areas, stimulating the growth of the middle class, improving the quality of governance, and providing more public goods (Dickson, 2011: 42). In sum, the "China model" has a strong bias towards macroeconomic development. As Zhao Suisheng (2017: 10) emphasizes, "linking the legitimacy with its ability to deliver rapid growth, the Chinese state put political imperative over economic, social and environmental reasons to pursue growth single-mindedly for almost three decades."

In the mid-2000s and the early 2010s, amid the debates on the sustainability of the "China model" and potential threats that its success poses to Western liberal traditions, China's representatives largely distanced themselves from the concept and argued that China's domestic development strategies cannot be equated with its policies abroad. Between the early 1980s and the early 2010s, China has consistently identified itself as a developing country and a part of the Global South. More recently, however, Chinese public intellectuals, scholars, and politicians have nuanced this claim, stipulating that even though China has "typical attributes" of a developing country, it must be rightfully recognized as an exceptional rising power, an independent player, and a prospective leader of the Global South (e.g., Liu, 2014; Yan, 2014; Zhang, 2018). Importantly, China's confidence in the triumph of its development path and the newfound assertiveness in presenting this success as a model overlaps with the change in its approach to the Global South.

2.3 Exporting the China Model and Promoting South-South Cooperation "with Chinese Characteristics"

According to China's representatives, China is surrounded by "friends" and "brothers" in the Global South and is ready to share with them the fruits of its development through "win–win cooperation" (Liu, 2014; Wang, 2014). Narrating China's relations with the Global South, they emphasize that China—like all other countries formerly designated as the Third World—advanced its modernization from a low historical starting point and hence its modern rejuvenation is bound to be a long process. Chinese scholars (e.g., Liu, 2008) and diplomats (e.g., Liu, 2014) alike emphasize that together with other developing countries China suffered from invasions and colonization of Western powers. Accordingly, the rapprochement between China and diverse regions of the Global South is presented as simultaneously "the inevitable result of historical logic" (Liu, 2008: 88) and a conscious political choice based on "common long-term strategic interests" (Shu, 2010: 87). Following this logic, Chinese researchers frame South-South cooperation as a form of opposition to imperialism, colonialism, and hegemonism (Shu, 2010: 86).

According to Chinese scholars, the countries of the Global North tailor their global development strategies to serve their geopolitical ambitions. For instance, Sun Zhe (2009: 63), a deputy director of the American Studies Center at Fudan University, claims that the US uses development aid to create "a foundation of social legitimacy for [its] global hegemony." Therefore, the US and its allies "spend billions of dollars buying" the support of Asian, African, and Latin American countries (Sun, 2009: 63). China, on the contrary, relies on shared experiences of catch-up development and ideological legacies of the third-wordism. In this context, "the national renaissance of the Afro-Asian world" (Luo, 2009: 65) and more recently the establishment of "communities of common destiny" in other regions of the Global South (Liu, 2014: 9–10) become cases in point for the success of China-led South-South cooperation. For instance, Chinese scholars maintain that new alliances between China and African countries signify "the process of rejuvenation, mutual solidarity, and collaboration" that alters "the traditional structure of the international system established in the fifteenth century within which the Western developed world is at the center and the Asian and African underdeveloped worlds are at the periphery" (Luo, 2009: 68, see also Shu, 2010; Zhang, 2018). Along similar lines, China's official representatives reconstruct China's rise not as an exceptional phenomenon but as an inseparable part of the broader process of Asian revival. Liu Zhenmin (2014: 3), an experienced diplomat and a former Vice-Minister for Foreign Affairs of the PRC, explains that "Asia was at the forefront of the Cold War between the US and the Soviet Union" and, as a result, was divided between "the two camps of the East and the West." Regional economic growth and cooperation, according to Liu, took off only after the end of the Cold War when China and other Asian nations united. Using the concept of "community of common destiny" popularized by Xi Jinping, Liu concludes that China's success presents opportunities rather than threats to other members of Asian tightly-knit networks and developing countries in other parts of the Global South.

In the late 2010s, China started to promote South-South cooperation by building its national brand around the superiority of the "China model". Xi Jinping set China's experience as an example for the rest of the world, adding Chinese exceptionalism against Western values into the discursive politics of China's development (Zhao, 2017: 5–6). However, this political shift does not imply that China encourages its partners in the Global South to introduce marketization and competition without privatization, welcome FDI, or focus on stimulating "national champions" similar to Alibaba, Tencent, and Huawei. Quite on the contrary, the discursive politics of South-South cooperation backgrounds the policy content of the "China model" and emphasizes political imperatives behind it. As a case in point, at the 19th National

Congress of the CPC in 2017, Xi proclaimed that "China moving closer to center stage" and held out China as a model for other developing nations, emphasizing that China had raised without imitating the West. According to Xi (2017a), "socialism with Chinese characteristics" provides "a new trail for other developing countries to achieve modernization" and offers "a new option" for those of them "who want to speed up their development while preserving their independence." Consequently, currently China's leadership discursively centers the China model on the ideas of self-reliance (*zili gengsheng* or *zige*).

Assuring confidence in China's achievements and emphasizing the preeminence of the development path set four decades ago by Deng Xiaoping's reforms, Xi Jinping reframes China's relations with the Global South. Today, China is not "hiding capabilities and keeping a low profile" (*taoguang yanghui*) but "takes initiative" (*zhudong jinqu*) (Xi, 2013) and "actively goes in" (*jiji zuowei*) (MFA of the PRC 2014). To secure China's leadership position in the global multipolar game, Xi Jinping binds the Global South more closely to China through economic diplomacy under the banner of the Belt and Road Initiative (BRI) launched in 2013 and a complex web of loans and investments.

In the mid-2010s, China set up development banks that challenge the dominance of the World Bank and the IMF. The China Development Bank, the Export–Import Bank of China, the New Development Bank (known as the BRICS bank), and the Asian Infrastructure Investment Bank help China to win loyalty, strengthen friendships, and secure contracts for its companies in the Global South. As well as China's "policy banks," state-owned commercial banks (e.g., the Bank of China, the China Construction Bank) play an increasingly more prominent role in China's overseas development finance program and, particularly, in funding BRI projects. According to AidData, the number of projects worth $500 million or more approved each year by China's state-owned lenders tripled over the first five years of BRI implementation (Malik et al., 2021: 28). In addition to this, offering generous loans to Argentina, Venezuela, Russia, and other resource economies of the Global South during the 2014–2015 commodity price fall, China proved itself as a lender of last resort—the only one that will keep the money flowing when others turn away.

2.4 Conditions, Political Implications, and Contradictions of Chinese Development Finance Programs

In the framework of the liberal world order, newcomers and aid recipients are expected to make changes concerning their human rights performance, good governance, or environmental issues. In contrast, China does not attach such policy and political conditions to South-South cooperation. Over the past two decades, China's growing bilateral aid and state loan programs have challenged the traditional architecture of international aid (e.g., Bräutigam, 2011; Kersting & Kilby, 2014; Strange et al., 2017; Woods, 2008). China employs tied aid (Mawdsley, 2012), but it is routinely assumed that, unlike Western donors, China lends and invests abroad without attaching any specific policy conditions (e.g. Kaplan, 2016; Tan-Mullins et al., 2010).

Political conditionalities imposed by traditional Western donors are characterized by "the allocation and use of financial resources to sanction or reward recipients in order to promote democratic governance and human rights" (Molenaers et al., 2015: 2). In contrast, China is indifferent to democracy and does not have good governance as an objective or a condition of development financing. It also does not set explicit policy conditions that target structural adjustments of the recipient economy, such as privatization, financial liberalization, or incorporating environmental and social protections into projects. In other words, China, as *The Economist* (2018: 14) puts it, "has a genius to befriending those in need of options."

China's discursive politics of development cooperation emphasizes the solidarity with the South and projects an image of China as a pragmatic and anti-imperialist power. China contraposes itself to traditional Western donors by articulating "an alternative set of relations between sovereign states to those associated with colonial and post-colonial hegemonies and hierarchies between North and South" (Mawdsley, 2012: 265). In Deborah Bräutigam's terms (2011: 150), "non-interference in internal affairs is China's 'brand' as a donor." This, however, does not mean that China's bilateral aid and state loans are politically unconditional.

Adhering to the "one-China principle" is enshrined in all diplomatic agreements that precede China's lending activities and investment in the South. Consequently, those states that receive bilateral aid and loans from China are expected to formally recognize Taiwan as its inseparable part and support Taiwan's diplomatic isolation. Recent studies of the development of China's relations with African and Latin American countries convincingly demonstrate that those of them who maintain diplomatic relations with Taiwan receive little or no aid, loans, and investment from China (Dreher et al., 2018; Tuman & Shirali, 2017). Mikael Mattlin and Matti Nojonen (2015: 707) highlight several instances of China's government threatening to terminate or reduce aid to its partners who refused to "isolate Taiwan from multilateral international organizations and venues where membership or attendance is based on sovereignty."

China's conditionalities also include denying support to independence movements in Tibet and Xinjiang. Along with Taiwan, these two frontier regions are listed as "core interests" (*hexin liyi*)—the non-negotiable bottom lines—in key strategic foreign policy documents (Odgaard & Nielsen, 2014; Zeng et al., 2015). Even though most of the recipient countries take for granted that support for China's "core interests" goes along with China's loans and development assistance (e.g. Copper, 2016; Stallings, 2016), there is also evidence of China assertively mobilizing support for its political agenda abroad through aid and investment (Tudoroiu, 2019: 98–101).

Elites and governments of countries that cooperate with China are not only vulnerable to self-censorship regarding China's policies in Taiwan, Tibet, and Xinjiang but also are forced to take China's side in various domestic and international public opinion battles. China's leadership is becoming increasingly concerned about China's international image and pressures the Global South to support the CPC's attempts to protect it. Sarah Cook (2013: 9), a senior research analyst for East Asia at Freedom House, argues that in different regions of Asia, Africa, and Latin America government officials "have taken steps to restrict or punish reporting damaging to China's reputation" in local non-Chinese language media. According to Cook, such censorship is ensured "either at the behest of Chinese representatives or to preemptively avoid tensions with a large donor and trading partner."

Finally, BRI is a case in point for the controversies related to China-led South-South cooperation. China's media and official representatives present BRI as neither a new Marshall Plan nor a version of the Eastern Bloc but as a practical development strategy that can be tailored to serve the specific needs of individual participants. They promise that China will break development "bottlenecks" by improving "policy, infrastructure, trade, financial, and people-to-people connectivity" along the BRI route (Xi, 2017b). While BRI is supposed to offer new opportunities for developed and developing countries alike, the Global South is often highlighted as the key beneficiary of the China-led "win–win" globalization under its banner (Liu & Dunford, 2016). Importantly, BRI is portrayed as a novel multilateral project, and Chinese observers emphasize BRI is fundamentally different from its Western counterparts. For instance, *China Daily*'s featured piece claims:

> No doubt China is at the center of the BRI, sitting in the driver's seat. But it acts as no hegemon to impose its will on others, which is not its cultural gene. *Chinese* multilateralism as reflected therein contrasts *American* multilateralism, whereby the US as a missionary society is ready to convert others. (Gu, 2020, emphasis in original)

Nevertheless, the evidence suggests that the financing that comes to the Global South through BRI adds extra pressure on fragile debt-ridden economies (Tudoroiu, 2019: 51–53), brings limited direct benefits to the locals (Rowedder, 2020), and exacerbates the "governance problems" in those states that still struggle with corruption and low transparency standards (Cooley, 2016; Malik et al., 2021: 65–72). Consequently, China's no-strings-attached financing not only generates opportunities for development breakthroughs by enhancing national policy autonomy, as some scholars suggest (Dunford, 2020; Kaplan, 2016), but also creates long-term political challenges in recipient countries of the Global South.

2.5   International Responses to China's Attempts to Lead South-South Cooperation

Against the backdrop of controversy encountered by high-profile BRI projects in Pakistan, Sri Lanka, Lao, Kyrgyzstan, and some other countries of the Global South, international observers voice their concerns about the future of China-led South-South cooperation. Following Indian expert Brahma Chellaney (2017), China's most vehement critics describe BRI's development finance programs as "debt-trap diplomacy." In this view, China is purposely overloading its partners in the Global South with unsustainable loans and then uses these loans to seize their assets and manipulate their politics. Chellaney (2017) cautions the Global South countries "not yet ensnared in China's debt-trap" to "take whatever steps they can to avoid it." Elsewhere, he (2018) praises India for taking a "brave, principled stand against BRI" and being "the intellectual leader that helped shine a spotlight on BRI's financial and security risks."

Despite statements by Chellaney and other Indian experts, India's official position on BRI is more ambiguous: Narendra Modi's government neither fully rejects China's invitation for cooperation nor openly endorses it. India became one of the founding members of the Asian Infrastructure Investment Bank and holds a 7.65% vote share in it. At the same time, India's chief concern is that China will increase its economic presence in South Asia. One notable example is the so-called China-Pakistan Economic Corridor. Indian officials on multiple occasions rather bluntly emphasized that the inclusion of this project in BRI reflects China's unwillingness to take into account India's concerns about sovereignty and territorial integrity (Sachdeva, 2018: 287–289).

Another BRICS country, Russia, also is hesitant to support the expansion of BRI in its backyard and, particularly, China's dealings with Belarus and Kazakhstan. Russian proposal of "linking up" of the Eurasian Economic Union (EAEU) and BRI announced in 2015 is "strategically designed to allow Russia to affiliate itself with BRI on its own terms, without sacrificing its symbolic leadership positions in the Eurasian regional order," and represents "an internal compromise based on defensive reasoning" (Kuteleva & Vasiliev, 2021: 600).

The most aggressive critique of BRI and other China's development finance programs is coming from the US. High-profile officials provide assessments of BRI that are rooted in the "debt-trap diplomacy" and "predatory loans" discourses. Furthermore, they see in BRI a deliberate attempt to undermine US global influence and a threat to US economic, political, and security interests. Former Secretary of State Michael Pompeo (2018) argued that

> when China shows up with bribes to senior leaders in countries in exchange for infrastructure projects that will harm the people of that nation, then this idea of a treasury-run empire build is something that […] would be bad for each of those countries and certainly presents a risk to American interests.

Similarly, former Vice President Michael Pence cautioned participants of the 2018 APEC CEO Summit in Papua New Guinea against accepting foreign loans that jeopardize their sovereignty and emphasized that the US "do not offer a constricting belt or a one-way road." Accordingly, American core allies in the Asia Pacific region turn their backs on China. For example, in 2021 Australia's Prime Minister Scott Morrison blocked an agreement under BRI's brand between the state of Victoria and China, claiming that such an agreement contradicts Australia's national interest and is "inconsistent with the Australian government's policy" (Grattan, 2021).

Such a harsh criticism triggers China's equally harsh response. Unlike his predecessors, Xi Jinping takes on a more confrontational approach to China's critics. Proclaiming China as a frontrunner, he asserts the international acknowledgment of its development success and ramps up his efforts in narrative competitions in the Global South.

2.6   Conclusions

From a China that could only say "yes" to the "easy to join and hard to overturn" Western liberal order (Ikenberry, 2008), we now see a China that can—and even wants to—say "no." China is crafting a new space for itself in the international system and becoming more assertive in its relations with other countries. China's discursive politics of development cooperation emphasizes the solidarity with the Global South and projects an image of China as a pragmatic and anti-imperialist member of the developing countries community. Chinese representatives as well as many observers outside China argue that China offers unconditional financing for diverse development projects in the Global South. As Michael Dunford (2020: 133) puts it, "instead of adopting western liberal norms and values, China asserted its right to promote its own values and vision of mutual benefit, mutual respect and responsiveness to developing countries' perception of their own needs." However, here I argue that it is not the lack of political and social conditionalities but their nature, objectives, and application that distinguish China from traditional Western donors. Recipients of development aid, loans, and investment must respect China's "core interests," support the idea of China's "peaceful rise," and most recently are also encouraged to look up to the China model by Xi Jinping. The China-led South-South cooperation becomes a fertile environment for these political conditionalities.

The discursive dominance of the "win–win" cooperation and "no-strings-attached" financing narratives does not imply that countries of the Global South perceive China's development finance programs and ambitious cooperation projects such as BRI as politically neutral. As diverse contributions to this volume demonstrate, the agency of sub-state and non-state actors in countries of the Global South influences in a complex and meaningful way the evolution of their interactions with China. Far from being passive recipients of Beijing-constructed images and cooperation models, these actors are fully aware of their identities and interests and respond accordingly to China's rise. Hence, to understand and evaluate the impact of China's rise on the Global South, we need to examine China's relations with the Global South not from a bird's eye, as it is typically done in the mainstream literature, but as the emergent outcomes of local interactions and identity negotiations pertaining in various ways to the changing dynamics of global politics.

References

Ambrosio, T. (2012). The rise of the 'China model' and 'Beijing consensus': Evidence of authoritarian diffusion? *Contemporary Politics, 18*(4), 381–399.

Arrighi, G. (2007). *Adam Smith in Beijing: Lineages of the twenty-first century.* Verso.

Bräutigam, D. (2011). Aid "with Chinese characteristics": Chinese foreign aid and development finance meet the OECD-DAC aid regime. *Journal of International Development, 23*(5), 752–764.

Breslin, S. (2011). The 'China model' and the global crisis: From Friedrich list to a Chinese mode of governance? *International Affairs, 87*(6), 1323–1343.

Chellaney, B. (2017, January 23). China's debt-trap diplomacy. *Project Syndicate.* https://www.pro ject-syndicate.org/commentary/china-one-belt-one-road-loans-debt-by-brahma-chellaney-201 7-01

Chellaney, B. (2018, October 29). Belt and roadblocks: India's China stance vindicated. *The Economic Times.* https://m.economictimes.com/news/defence/belt-and-roadblocks-indias-china-stance-vindicated/articleshow/66410247.cms

Chen, M., & Goodman, D. S. (2012). The China model: One country, six authors. *Journal of Contemporary China, 21*(73), 169–185.

Copper, J. F. (2016). *China's foreign aid and investment diplomacy, Volume I: Nature, scope, and origins.* Springer.

Cook, S. (2013, October 22). *The long shadow of Chinese censorship.* A Report to the Center for International Media Assistance. https://www.issuelab.org/resources/16238/16238.pdf

Cooley, A. (2016). *The emerging political economy of OBOR: The challenges of promoting connectivity in Central Asia and beyond.* Center for Strategic & International Studies. https://www.csis.org/analysis/emerging-political-economy-obor

Dreher, A., Fuchs, A., Parks, B., Strange, A. M., & Tierney, M. J. (2018). Apples and dragon fruits: The determinants of aid and other forms of state financing from China to Africa. *International Studies Quarterly, 62*(1), 182–194.

Dickson, B. J. (2011). Updating the China model. *The Washington Quarterly, 34*(4), 39–58.

Dunford, M. (2020). Chinese and Development Assistance Committee (DAC) development cooperation and development finance: Implications for the BRI and international governance. *Eurasian Geography and Economics, 61*(2), 125–136.

Ferchen, M. (2013). Whose China model is it anyway? The contentious search for consensus. *Review of International Political Economy, 20*(2), 390–420.

Grattan, M. (2021, April 22) Morrison government quashes Victoria's belt and road deal with China. *The Conversation.* https://theconversation.com/morrison-government-quashes-victorias-belt-and-road-deal-with-china-159480

Gu, B. (2020, June 17) BRI is not revival of ancient China's tributary system. *China Daily.* Available at: https://www.chinadaily.com.cn/a/202006/17/WS5ee98711a310834817253a08.html

Haan, A. (2011). Will China change international development as we know it? *Journal of International Development, 23*(7), 881–908.

Harvey, D. (2005). *2005.* Oxford University Press.

Hu, J., & Han, D. (2010). Zhongguo moshi de shizhi, tedian he mianlin tiaozhan [The essence, characteristics and challenges of the "Chinese model"]. *China Review of Political Economy, 1*(4), 13–23.

Ikenberry, G. J. (2008). The rise of China and the future of the West-Can the liberal system survive. *Foreign Affairs, 87*(1), 23–27.

Jacques, M. (2009). *When China rules the world: The end of the western world and the birth of a new global order.* Penguin.

Kaplan, S. B. (2016). Banking unconditionally: The political economy of Chinese finance in Latin America. *Review of International Political Economy, 23*(4), 643–676.

Kennedy, S. (2010). The myth of the Beijing consensus. *Journal of Contemporary China, 19*(65), 461–477.

Kersting, E., & Kilby, C. (2014). Aid and democracy redux. *European Economic Review, 67*, 125–143.

Kuteleva, A., & Vasiliev, D. (2021). China's belt and road initiative in Russian media: Politics of narratives, images, and metaphors. *Eurasian Geography and Economics, 62*(5–6), 582–606.

Liu, W., & Dunford, M. (2016). Inclusive globalization: Unpacking China's belt and road initiative. *Area Development and Policy, 1*(3), 323–340.

Liu, H. (2008). Zhong-Fei guanxi 30 nian: Qiao dong Zhongguo yu waibu shijie guanxi jiegou de zhidian [Thirty years of Sino-African relations: A pivot in reshaping the Structure of China's relations with the outside world]. *Shijie Jingji Yu Zhengzhi, 11*, 80–88.

Liu, Z. (2014). Jianchi hezuo gong ying xieshou dazao yazhou mingyun gongtongti [Adhere to win-win cooperation: Jointly creating a community of common destiny in Asia]. *Guoji wenti yanjiu, 2*(5), 1–10.

Lo, B., & Shevtsova, L. (2012, July 1). *A 21st century myth—Authoritarian modernization in Russia and China.* Carnegie Moscow Center. http://carnegieendowment.org/files/BoboLo_Shevtsova_web.pdf

Luo, J. (2009). Ya-Fei fuxing shiye xia Zhongguo yu fazhan zhang guojia guanxi: Lishi bianqian yu shijie yiyi [China's relations with developing states amidst Afro-Asian renaissance: The transition of history and significance to the world]. *Journal of Contemporary Asia-Pacific Studies* (4), 68–83.

Malik, A., Parks, B., Russell, B., Lin, J., Walsh, K., Solomon, K., Zhang, S., Elston, T., & S. Goodman. (2021). *Banking on the belt and road: Insights from a new global dataset of 13,427 Chinese development projects.* AidData at William & Mary.

Mattlin, M., & Nojonen, M. (2015). Conditionality and path dependence in Chinese lending. *Journal of Contemporary China, 24*(94), 701–720.

Mawdsley, E. (2012). The changing geographies of foreign aid and development cooperation: Contributions from gift theory. *Transactions of the Institute of British Geographers, 37*(2), 256–272.

Ministry of Foreign Affairs of the PRC [MFA of the PRC] (2014). *Waijiao bu buzhang Wang Yi jiu Zhongguo waijiao zhengce he duiwai guanxi huida Zhong-Wai jizhe tiwen [Foreign Minister Wang Yi answers questions from Chinese and foreign journalists on China's foreign policy and foreign relations].* March 08, 2021. https://www.fmprc.gov.cn/chn//pds/wjb/wjbz/xghd/t1135388.shtml

Molenaers, N., Dellepiane, S., & Faust, J. (2015). Political conditionality and foreign aid. *World Development, 75*, 2–12.

Naughton, B. (2010). China's distinctive system: Can it be a model for others? *Journal of Contemporary China, 19*(65), 437–460.

Odgaard, L., & Nielsen, T. G. (2014). China's counterinsurgency strategy in Tibet and Xinjiang. *Journal of Contemporary China, 23*(87), 535–555.

Ortmann, S. (2012). The 'Beijing consensus' and the 'Singapore model': Unmasking the myth of an alternative authoritarian state-capitalist model. *Journal of Chinese Economic and Business Studies, 10*(4), 337–359.

Pence, M. (2018, November 16). *Remarks at the 2018 APEC CEO Summit.* Port Moresby, Papua New Guinea. https://trumpwhitehouse.archives.gov/briefings-statements/remarks-vice-president-pence-2018-apec-ceo-summit-port-moresby-papua-new-guinea/

Pompeo, M. (2018, October 26). Interview with hugh Hewitt. *Hugh Hewitt Show.* https://2017-2021.state.gov/interview-with-hugh-hewitt-of-the-hugh-hewitt-show/index.html

Ramo, J. (2004, March 4). *The Beijing consensus.* The Foreign Policy Center. http://fpc.org.uk/publications/TheBeijingConsensus

Rowedder, S. (2020). Railroading land-linked Laos: China's regional profits, Laos' domestic costs? *Eurasian Geography and Economics, 61*(2), 152–161.

Sachdeva, G. (2018). Indian perceptions of the Chinese Belt and Road initiative. *International Studies, 55*(4), 285–296.

Shu, Y. (2010). Zhongguo dui Fei yuanzhu: Lishi, lilun he tedian [China's aid to Africa: History, theory and characteristics] *Journal of Shanghai Normal University (Philosophy and Social Sciences Edition), 39*(5), 83–89.

Stallings, B. (2016). Chinese foreign aid to Latin America: Trying to win friends and influence people. In *The Political Economy of China-Latin America Relations in the New Millennium* (pp. 77–99). Routledge.

Strange, A. M., Dreher, A., Fuchs, A., Parks, B., & Tierney, M. J. (2017). Tracking underreported financial flows: China's development finance and the aid–conflict nexus revisited. *Journal of Conflict Resolution, 61*(5), 935–963.

Sun, Z. (2009). Meiguo baquan de fazhan weidu——Aobama zhengfu quanqiu fazhan zhanlue Pingxi [A developmental perspective of American hegemony: Critics on president Obama's strategy for global development]. *Shijie Jingji Yu Zhengzhi, 11,* 55–53.

Tan-Mullins, M., Mohan, G., & Power, M. (2010). Redefining 'aid' in the China-Africa context. *Development and Change, 41*(5), 857–881.

The Economist. (2018, July 28). China has a vastly ambitious plan to connect the world. https://www.economist.com/briefing/2018/07/26/china-has-a-vastly-ambitious-plan-to-connect-the-world

Tudoroiu, T. (2019). *The myth of China's no strings attached development assistance: A caribbean case study.* Lexington Books.

Tuman, J. P., & Shirali, M. (2017). The political economy of Chinese foreign direct investment in developing areas. *Foreign Policy Analysis, 13*(1), 154–167.

Wang, X. (2013). Jiexi zhonggong lingdao ren guanyu "Zhongguo moshi" de lunshu. [Analyses of the CPC leader's discourse of "the China model"]. *Dangdai zhongguo shi yanjiu, 3*(115), 23–36.

Wang, Y. (2014). Jianding bu yi zou heping fazhan daolu wei shixian minzu fuxing Zhongguo meng yingzao lianghao guoji huanjing [Adhere to the path of peaceful development and foster a favorable international environment for the great rejuvenation of the Chinese nation]. *Guoji Wenti Yanjiu, 1*(11), 8–23.

Woods, N. (2008). Whose aid? Whose influence? China, emerging donors and the silent revolution in development assistance. *International Affairs, 84*(6), 1205–1221.

Xi, J. (2013, December 31). 2014 *Nian Xinnian Heci* [*The 2014 New Year's Greetings*]. The Central People's Government of the PRC. http://www.gov.cn/ldhd/2013-12/31/content_2557924.htm

Xi, J. (2017a, October 18). *Secure a Decisive Victory in Building a Moderately Prosperous Society in All Respects and Strive for the Great Success of Socialism with Chinese Characteristics for a New Era,* Xinhua News Agency [PDF file] http://www.xinhuanet.com/english/download/Xi_Jinping's_report_at_19th_CPC_National_Congress.pdf. [Accessed 20 March 2021].

Xi, J. (2017b, May 14). *Work together to build the silk road economic belt and the 21st Century Maritime silk road.* The opening ceremony of the belt and road forum for international cooperation. http://www.xinhuanet.com/english/2017-05/16/c_136287873.htm [Accessed March 18, 2021].

Xiong, B. (2009). Guanyu Zhongguo fazhan moshi zai xikao [Rethinking of Chinese Development Mode]. *China Development, 9*(4), 44–48.

Yan, X. (2014). From keeping a low profile to striving for achievement. *The Chinese Journal of International Politics, 7*(2), 153–184.

Zeng, J., Xiao, Y., & Breslin, S. (2015). Securing China's core interests: The state of the debate in China. *International Affairs, 91*(2), 245–266.

Zhang, C. (2018). Xin shidai Zhongguo yu fazhan zhong guojia guanxi de tiaozhan yu yingdui [On theory and practice of China's diplomatic relations with developing countries in the New Era]. *Pacific Journal, 26*(7), 1–13.

Zhao, S. (2017). Whither the China model: Revisiting the debate. *Journal of Contemporary China, 26*(103), 1–17.

Anna Kuteleva is a post-doctoral research fellow at the School of International Regional Studies at the National Research University Higher School of Economics in Moscow. Anna received her PhD in Political Science from the University of Alberta (Canada) in 2019. Previously, she obtained a Master's degree in World Politics (Shandong University, 2010) and a Master's degree in Comparative Politics (Peoples' Friendship University of Russia, 2010). Her research is located in a broad constructivist tradition of IR and focuses on the nexus between politics and sociocultural contexts in international relations, with particular interests in politics of security and international energy politics.

Part I
China's Image and Its Reception in the Global South

Chapter 3
Manufacturing Sameness: Reconstructing Brand-China in Africa

Tara Mock

Abstract National image has long been an important component of China's (Beijing, PRC) identity. National Imaginary constructions influence the PRC's efforts to manage its domestic population as strongly as it does its ability to nurture relationships with foreign nations and nationals. Chapter three, "Manufacturing Sameness", outlines construction of the PRC's nation brand image on the African continent. The chapter pays particular attention to how the Chinese State constructs its image in Africa using cultural artifacts representative of not only China, but Africa as well. Using speeches, magazine covers, editorials, advertisements, and newspaper editorials as the population of communication, the chapter critically unpacks the semiotic messaging and rhetorical intent of artifacts indicative of brand-China. In this way the chapter examines the dialectical contours of China's brand across the continent, revealing broad themes emerging from the analysis. Focusing specifically on the reiteration key aspects of the Africa-China narrative crafted by State or State-owned or state supported enterprises, the author demonstrates how brand-China is wielded as a powerful geopolitical tool. By debating the significance of these images to China's continued rise on the continent the author hopes to prompt a reconsideration of the discursive power mechanisms exercised in and through national image making.

Keywords Africa-China relations · Nation branding · Soft power · Diplomacy · National identity

Abbreviation

PRC	People's Republic of China
FOCAC	Forum on China Africa Cooperation
SOE	State-owned Enterprise

T. Mock (✉)
Honors College, University of Alabama, Tuscaloosa, AL, USA
e-mail: tmock@ua.edu

The Western approach sees individual people as the units through which the world is understood and tends to think in absolutes, that is, good versus evil. The self is identified with God;
the other is the heathen and an irreconcilable enemy. In contrast, Chinese thought supposes
many kinds of other and suggests methods to reconcile that other into a harmonious existence.
Here, the other can become the self. (Wang, 2008: 262)

3.1 Introduction

On May 31st 2017, the Madaraka Express (*Madaraka*), a China Road and Bridge
Corporation constructed standard gauge railway, embarked on its maiden voyage
from Mombasa's Miritiri Station to the Nairobi Railway Station. One of several
planned China (Beijing, PRC) constructed railway lines in Africa, the railway
replaced the infamous Kenya-Uganda "Lunatic Express" (1903–2017), a holdover
from British colonial occupation.[1] *Madaraka* was designed to connect the Kenyan
capital with its eastern coastline, bisecting Tsavo National Park to ease the conges-
tion of slow-moving passenger journeys by cutting the route by matatu or car in
half. Completing the railway, on time, was a key priority and campaign promise
for Kenya's President Uhuru Kenyatta, for whom *Madaraka* represented a "new
era of autonomous rule on the continent" (Kenyatta, 2017b). Kenyatta, like many
leaders across Africa, has long heralded the benefits of Chinese-led projects; yet,
despite presidential support, the line opened to mixed reviews.[2] The pageantry
surrounding *Madaraka*'s inauguration wrought an onrush of rebuke from critics
questioning China's presence in Africa but also waves of nostalgia from supporters
reminiscent of the first Chinese-backed railway in Africa—the Tazara "freedom railway" (1976).[3] A study in continuity and change, whilst some detractors argued that
Madaraka is overpriced, as it accounts for more than five percent of Kenya's total
gross domestic product; others were disgruntled because the railway project was
adjudged emblematic of creeping Chinese cultural intrusion on the continent.

Subtle messages observed during the line's inauguration–pamphlets marking the
occasion written in Mandarin, visitors greeted by staff donning red and gold uniforms,
and a stone image of admiral Zheng He, the "Chinese Columbus", overseeing pedes-
trian traffic on the platform—underscored thinking that although *Madaraka* was a
Kenyan possession, it was still very much Chinese owned.[4] The image *Madaraka*
conjures of Africa-China is further undermined by the types of programming inter-
rogated in Yu Xiang's Chapter in this text on cultural imperialism. Negative press
and competing images which chronicled the railway's opening from a decidedly
Chinese point of view, ad exemplum, were heavily featured in CCTV's 2018 Annual
Spring Festival Gala "Celebrating Together". Broadcast in Mandarin to an audience
predominated by Chinese nationals, "Celebrating Together" featured Chinese actors
in blackface, caricaturing the vagaries of Kenyan life.[5] The presence of a solidarity
Africana actor (in the scene) donning a monkey costume was most concerning,
however, further complicating the narrative of Sino-African unity concomitant with
the official message of Madaraka. The performative practice of these artifacts in the

theatre of Africa-China is far more complex than simply signifying the inauguration of the PRC's latest infrastructure project. *Madaraka*, alongside the pomp and circumstance of its opening ceremony, plays an important role in the everyday politics of Africa-China. It is a role symbolic of the strength of the Chinese state and its global ambitions but, also one that serves as an ever-present visual reminder, at once exalting and decrying China's image as a development model, friend, and brother to Africa.

Efficaciously, in this sense, the Madaraka Express becomes connected with the *longue durée* of Africa-Chinese relations fomented pre-European conquest through 'giraffe diplomacy,' nurtured by diplomatic relations during the Bandung Conference of 1955, strengthened by Beijing's solidarity with African liberation movements and, ultimately, fortified contemporarily through the economic, social, and diplomatic might of FOCAC. Curating an image of Afro-China established through the mutually beneficial exchange of gifts, historical friendship, and cultural propinquity reinforces the notion that if not for the 'twin evils' of the transatlantic slave trade and colonialism, Africa and China would have remained consistently close 'friends, brothers, and partners' for more than 600 years (Xi, 2016). More importantly, the storyline mirrors ongoing attempts to transform domestic and international viewpoints of China, its interactions with African nations, and how that interface is inhibited by the tension between official and personal accounts of *brand-China* and Africa-China as "Celebrating Together" demonstrates.

How states view themselves and choose to communicate those visions to domestic and foreign audiences—which of their attributes to showcase and which to secrete is shaped by their national imaginary. Do states imagine themselves as industrial powerhouses? Tourist destinations? Military hawks? Peacekeeping forces? The Chinese State utilizes an array of performative symbols as it constructs its nation brand across Africa. Official narratives of Africa-China are reinforced through billboards depicting China Southern Airlines' new service from Nairobi to Guangzhou; Chinese cartoons broadcast in Antananarivo; diplomatic speeches during the opening of China Europe International Business School (CEIBS) in Accra, and editorials in Kenya's premier independent newspaper, *The Daily Nation*. Collectively, those and other artifacts convey curated messages of *brand-China* to observers old and young across the African continent.

Consistent with what Wang (2008) deems winning the struggle over public opinion (*dui wai xuan chuan* or *wai xuan*), *brand-China* often acts innocuously through seemingly nonthreatening messages of an Afro-Chinese weltanschauung legitimated within speeches, newspaper editorials, magazines, and advertisements. And the idea of intentionally creating a desired image of self for broad dissemination is nothing new to Beijing. The Propaganda Department of the Chinese Communist Party was established during the same year as the founding of the Party itself (1921), underscoring an understanding of the importance of messaging as an instrument of nation-building. Li Hongmei (2010) contends that the very same principles were adopted during the transition from imperial China to Communist China, and again, during the transition to neoliberal China. The State performed elements of nation branding to deconstruct the old and construct the new national imaginary

through state media. Demonstrably, Afro-Chinese solidarity posters (see https://hdl.
handle.net/10622/N30051002357652?locatt=view:level3), which became the principal format for promoting official discourse on Africa-China during the African
Liberation period, document this point (Fennell, 2013). Contemporarily, the discursive frameworks introduced during earlier eras continue to promote China's national
imaginary, its contemporary view of Africa-China, and spread its message for
consumption across the continent (Fig. 3.1).

At its core, this is a chapter surpasses the conversation of national imaginaries,
national identities, and national brands to pinpoint precisely how each is rhetorically
constructed and sustained. It explores how the Chinese state establishes images of
difference from the West and similitude with African people within its nation brand;
how *brand-China* is framed to align the Chinese historical experience as a community with Africa's distinct socio-historical marker(s); and whether and how African

Fig. 3.1 China Southern Airlines Billboard, NAIROBI (2015) image captured by author

producers co-create Africa-China in promotional discourse. Although the chapter historicizes the use of nation branding and propaganda within Afro-Chinese relations, using continued references to and re-imaginings of the 'Bandung Conference', 'Colonialism', 'Neo-Imperialism', and 'Globalization' as a cynosure guiding the analysis, ultimately, the goal is to discern the specific nature of *brand-China* in Africa, viewing contemporary depictions of the Chinese national imaginary within the historical frameworks of previous Afro-Chinese encounters. The principal concern is with how the Chinese state and state-owned or supported enterprises (SOEs) utilize nation branding to construct the PRC's image on the African continent. The chapter is organized along the following lines: It began with a brief outline of China's national imaginary in Africa by exploring Afro-Chinese relations from a nation branding perspective. The chapter continues by outlining the analytical methods underpinning the analysis before detailing the empirical core of the research and concluding with a summary of findings and closing thoughts.

3.2 Marketing China

Within marketing literature, brand image is a symbolic association with the brand—real or imagined—long-held in public memory after the brand experience is over. The image consumers maintain a given brand relies not only on the ocular but the sentient, auditory and abstract aspects of the product or services rendered. In this manner, the brand is not something the consumer can grasp, but something he or she perceives. Consumer perception is what the mechanics of branding strive to influence through advertising, marketing, and public relations. The eponymous Tiffany blue box, the fact that M&Ms "melt in your mouth, not in your hands," Macintosh's Apple, Starbucks' Siren, and McDonalds' Golden Arches are all brand images that evoke specific consumer perceptions. In Naomi Klein's excoriating account of brand culture, *No Logo* (1999), she notes that strong brands surpass the physical product; filling the space between with whatever image the consumer conjures. Be it positive, negative, luxury, family-oriented, or dependability, the image evoked represents the overall mental picture consumers possess of the brand's qualities relative to other brands.

Branding as an intentional practice is not limited solely to the corporate domain. As feudalism gave way to the nascent formation of the nation-state, the country was regularly constructed symbolically through folkloric dress or the lore of triumphant conquest or the obelisk of Axum, each sculpted symbols of wealth, power, and mystery. It is in this way that nations also branded themselves, using these and other national symbols to demonstrate who they were as a collective and what values they held most dear and wanted to communicate to others about themselves. Simon Anholt (2005), proposes that the branding of nations does not differ greatly from the branding of products or corporations. Corporate branding attends to the import of image within the private sphere; whilst nation branding is, likewise, concerned with image, though in this instance replacing the corporation with the city or nation-state as the unit of inquiry. Peter Van Ham (2001) scholarship on the rise of the 'brand state' underscores Anholt's argument and is often cited to justify state practices of adapting branding approaches to foreign policy and public diplomacy. With the emergence of *brand-states*, van Ham identified a paradigm shift, whereby the 'modern world of geopolitics and power is being replaced by the postmodern world of images and messages'.

A nation's brand can be 'organic' in that it exists without effort, as each country conveys a certain image to its publics, be it strong or weak, current or outdated, clear or vague. Ask anyone about Spain, for example, and the question might conjure up positive images of beach vacations in Ibiza, Gaudi architecture in Barcelona, Bosch paintings at the Prado Museum, tapas, bullfighting, or flamenco. To others, however, the same question might elicit negative responses about beach vacations in Ibiza, slavery, bullfighting, and separatist movements. Fan (2010), explains that ultimately, the associated image of each nation is situational. *Madaraka* demonstrably provides a glimpse into how the brand can function simultaneously at both levels and the danger of negative messaging. Brand narratives influence and speak to relations between nations at the elite economic and diplomatic levels, but also of a desire to direct conversations regarding these relationships and how the states within them are consumed at the popular social and cultural levels. In this instance, context matters.

Although context does matter, nation branding remains concerned with the country's whole image on the international stage. Global image becomes necessary because nations are economically, culturally, and politically diverse and projecting a single, positive overall image of each is a difficult task. Thus, the brand is comprised of the total sum of all perceptions of the nation in the minds of international stakeholders and exists with or without conscious effort. The underlying goal is to make the nation consequential in a world where borders and boundaries appear increasingly obsolete.

Establishing the nation as a differentiated identity with targeted international audiences through the use of specific, constructed 'image-signs', namely the state's name, logo, and other branding elements, has gradually become an important aspect of global competition. Diverse images of the United States– the Statue of Liberty, the "Real Housewives" franchise, President Donald Trump's escalating trade war with the Chinese, the United States' occupation of Guantanamo Bay, Exxon, and Marvel's the "Black Panther," resonate differently with the intersectional identities and experiences of those who consume them. Taken as a whole, such images affect public thoughts and opinions (both domestically and internationally) of the United States. Based on what one already knows about America's brand—its trustworthiness, characteristics, reliability, and so forth—consumers can make assumptions and form reasonable expectations about what they may *not* know. If consumers recognize, are knowledgeable of, and positively respond to a nation's brand, it lowers resistance to people, products, and services originating from that nation. This is why negative perceptions and stereotypes can be so invidious. The objective of nation branding, therefore, is to project a positive overall image that resonates with consumers. Although some aspects of the brand footprint may be negative, when consumers possess a cohesive, favorable overall nation brand image, the brand's messages have a stronger influence on their decision-making than competitors (Hsieh & Li, 2008).

3.3   Critical Discourses

Building on James Paul Gee's (2014) scholarship on the relationship between language and structures of power, the chapter makes use of critical discourse analysis. An array of cultural artifacts produced by the People's Republic of China as heuristic vehicles. Specifically, the author engaged in a visual and content analysis of speeches, magazine covers, editorials, and advertisements, which narrate the story of not only Africa-China, but the PRC as well, through a Chinese lens. The artifacts demonstrate how Beijing is discursively constructed within *brand-China* for African ingestion. The objective was to locate artifacts available for both popular and elite consumption, utilizing those objects within the same corpus of analysis. The population of communication for the analysis drew from official speeches delivered by Chinese and African officials during such seemingly benign events as book launches in Sierra Leone, magazine covers depicting rice shortages in both China and Africa, newspaper interviews rebuffing western claims of neocolonialism in Botswana, and advertisements enticing Kenyan consumers to select *Wechat Pay* or *Alibaba* rather than *Mpesa* for their money management needs.

An analysis of the March 2014 cover of *ChinAfrica* Magazine, demonstrates the coding and analytical processes undertaken for each document.[6] The artifact's header features the magazine's title, *ChinAfrica*, in both English and Mandarin, set against a red background. The decision to highlight English and Mandarin in the title, rather than Swahili, Wolof, isiZulu, or any other African lingua franca perpetuates cultural dominance and the exclusion of African people from the rights of representation within their own spaces, by promoting Chinese cultures as equal to the English-speaking west, while demoting nee silencing Africa. The title, *ChinAfrica*, privileges China ahead of a nameless globule of African nations, lumped together under the moniker *Africa*. The web address, *chinafrica.cn*, utilizes a Chinese domain name, situating the artifact as a solidly Chinese entity despite its South African geographical location. Finally, the use of red color, symbolic of good fortune, happiness, celebration, and joy, holds cultural significance within Chinese cosmology and underscores the magazine's attention to a Chinese aesthetic.

The artifact's header further reveals themes of "culture", through a focus on both the Chinese film industry and "the year of the horse'; as well as "security", by focusing on the global crackdown on wildlife crime, demonstrating the PRC's strength and its commitment to law and order. Finally, the magazine's feature image, highlighting food security, simultaneously reinforces and corrodes *brand-China*'s resonance on the continent. The image features a pair of chopsticks and a bowl of rice beneath the words, "Enough to Eat: Safeguarding food security a top priority in China and Africa". The implication is one of a shared need for food security, but also implicit is thinking that African states and China are at similar developmental and experiential stages. The image also centers on China and Chinese needs through the use of chopsticks, a uniquely Asian utensil, as well as the decision to feature rice, the most popular grain in Asia and one of the principals and most costly food imports to Africa. With hindsight, there is no expectation that everyone reading *ChinAfrica* will arrive at precisely the same conclusions, and this is especially true of the untrained eye, but there is a reasonable expectation that within any analysis of the same cover themes semantically related to some aspects of *Culture, Sameness, Security, Centering China,* and *Development* should emerge.[7]

Critical discourse analysis of the 337 artifacts selected for inclusion in the study yielded 88 unique nodes; including *Benevolence, History, Poverty, Solidarity, China Dream, Shared Marginalization, Science and Technology, Security* and *Mutual Benefit* amongst a litany of others. Some nodes were utilized more frequently than others, with many, such as *Education* and *Gender Equality*, mentioned only sparingly within one or two artifacts. The nodes were grouped into seven distinct thematic categories encompassing issues of *China as Developmental Model, Sovereignty, Friendship, Eurocentrism, Sameness, China as Developmental Partner*, and one wide-ranging category containing a miscellany of other references, such as the narrative of *Peacefulness*. An initial review of coding categories revealed the most frequent references to nodes surrounding themes of *Sameness, China as a Developmental Model, Friendship*, and *China as a Developmental Partner*. Collectively, these themes accounted for three-quarters (73.8%) of the variation in how *brand-China* is intentionally constructed in Africa. The most frequently referenced messages are discussed in turn and collectively serve as the foci of the remainder of this chapter.

3.4   China as Brother (Sameness)

Read any major newspaper on the continent of Africa and it will likely feature at least one story on China and its engagement with the continent's diverse band of leaders, markets, and people. Even more predictably embedded within these narratives, often-times deeply, are stories recounting some iteration of the sentiment that 'Africa and China are brothers'. Vera Fennel writes that following the Bandung Conference the CPC directed its propaganda network to deepen mutual understanding between China and Africa and other states of the Third World to create ideologically-inspired solidarity of brotherhood through which they could act as a political block in global politics. Print media, specifically posters, newspaper articles, and propaganda reels of the time promoted the official discourse on Sino-African brotherhood, emphasizing common heritage and the shared experience of colonialism and racial discrimination. Thus, it comes as no surprise that the most frequently constructed narrative of *brand-China* in Africa is one of *sameness*. Sameness speaks to a level of affinity beyond that shared by partners or friends, creating a discursive framework for establishing points of commonality between Chinese and African people, the historical and contemporary experiences of Chinese and African people, cultural propinquity, being part of a shared (or the same) community, or Chinese kinship, brotherhood, sisterhood, or family-like relations with Africa. Chinese Ambassador Tian Xuejun expressed feelings of *sameness* during his farewell luncheon when he remarked, "My wife and I regard South Africa as our second home and the people of South Africa as our brothers and sisters" (Tian, 2017).

Found in 251 of 337 artifacts, the ideology of *brotherhood*, in particular, is reinforced through promotional homily more frequently than any other theme. Throughout Chinese promotional artifacts, African people are regarded "as our *brothers* and sisters" (Wang, 2015b). When China's seat was restored in the UN, "our African *brothers* burst into tears of happiness" (K. Li, 2014), therefore, Beijing feels "the responsibility that we can by no means fail our African *brothers*" (G. Liu, 2011). For, as "a Chinese saying goes, "unity of two *brothers* gives them the strength to cut through metal" (Xi & Yang, 2016). These statements underpin sentiments that Chinese and African people are united by a sense of fictive kinship, which fortifies the Afro-Chinese relationship and presents an image of Chinese proximity to the continent and its people. Wang Yiwei (2008) explains,

> Western political discourse asks first, 'Who are you?' It is concerned with the problem of identity, with distinguishing and making friends and enemies, exploring 'us' and 'others.' It is a worldview based on splitting. In contrast, Chinese political thinking first asks, 'Who are we?' creating the concept of "the whole world as one family. (326)

Wang's reflections endorse the ingenuousness of Chinese moves toward a communion of Afro-Chinese similitude. Within the Confucian worldview as Wang describes it, China and Africa are but two brothers of the same family. In this light Chinese views of Africans (and all of humanity) are consistent with the elements of community, collective consciousness, and group solidarity manifested within the ontological expression of *Ubuntu*, which is a constitutive feature of many African societies.[8] Creating a shared astral dimensional space whereby both Chinese and (at least some) African people subscribe to similar ways of knowing strengthens the narrative of brotherhood.

3.4.1 Culture

In 1994, a rising Deputy Provincial Party Secretary in Fujian Province, Xi Jinping, proclaimed before the China Central Committee that "The stories of China should be well told, voices of China well spread, and the characteristics of China well explained" (Dynon, 2014). With those words Xi articulated the import of promoting Chinese soft power and culture abroad, with key elements of *brand-China* fashioned from an admixture of Chinese cultural components, including Confucian philosophies, historical experiences, linguistic patterns, and artistic customs. Cultural proximity and the disaffirmation of western cultural values creates an additional layer of support for Afro-Chinese similitude. Allusions to perceived connections between African and Chinese people based on their shared reverence for culture are commonplace and oft-referenced components of the Chinese nation brand in Africa. Remarks that "Chinese people cherish our own culture and tradition... (and) African people also preserve their culture very well. Some values we believe can also be found in African culture" (Zhao, 2014) illustrate this point. Although culture alone is not a determinant of individual and state perception, Wuthnow (2008) reasoned that it "lays a foundation of respect and tolerance by foreign actors, who, over time, may help to shape an international environment conducive to China's growth" (9–10).

Narratives of Afro-Chinese cultural value alignment and traditionalism are interwoven through the use of proverbs, the importance of which is instilled early in life, and which serve as daily guideposts in many African societies. Both visual and textual artifacts make obvious allusions to the shared import of proverbs within Chinese and (some) African cultural practices through pronouncements that:

> ...an African proverb which states that 'The one who asks questions doesn't lose his way', while Chinese people believe that one has to be not ashamed of to ask and learn of his inferiors to become a real master. Many similar values exist in both Chinese and African cultures. (Zhao, 2014)
>
> A Chinese saying pronounces "'When everyone paddles together, even a big ship can sail at a fast speed.' There is an African proverb, 'A single person is not strong enough to pull a boat.' I believe, as long as we join hands and redouble our efforts, China-Kenya comprehensive cooperative partnership certainly will have a (sic) even better future. (X. Liu, 2015b)
>
> In African legend, the Phoenix, a long-lived bird, dies by fire every 500 years, only to rise from the ashes to be reborn again. In Chinese culture, you can find a similar story of a mythical bird named Fenghuang that, too, cyclically regenerates itself. These two legends seem to be telling us that the great renewal of the Chinese nation and the African continent represents an unstoppable historical trend.
>
> As one Zimbabwe idiom goes, 'chikuni chimwe hachikodzi sadza', Chinese people also believe that 'when everybody adds firewood, the flames will rise high'. (Xi, 2015b)

The recurrent usage of proverbs signals attempts to establish a cultural connection between African and Chinese people, bespeaking the intentionality of a socially constructed Chinese imaginary. Repeated attempts to establish points of similitude in this manner also operate within what Mudimbe (1988) deems the intermediate space between natural and imposed definitions of an homogenous African mythic. Adopting a posture of traditionalism, resting on the postcolonial notion of extant monolithic African cultural practices, values, dialects, philosophies, and worldviews is dangerous because clings to vestiges of the past and fails to adequately account for the subtleties of individual decision-making regarding what to shift, what to discard, and what to retain for continued survival.

The oft repeated telling of these stories also convey to the audience that 'you should trust us' 'you should partner with us' and, more importantly, 'you should do so because our values are aligned.' Fennell (2013), refers to such platitudes as "false statements." Considering dissimilarities between the two regions and their cultures, she writes, "there...could (n)ever be a relationship based in...a sense of unity comparable to the relationship between the United States and England between the peoples and governments of the various African states and the people and government of the People's Republic of China" (246). In Fennell's view, the assertion that African and

Asian people are the same is unsound given obvious differences between the two regions.

3.4.2 Marginalization

The narrative of *sameness* extends to include historical reference points illustrating the experiential similarities of victimization and marginalization linking the two regions. Chinese Premier Wen Jiabao's remarks during the Opening Ceremony of the 4th Ministerial Conference of the Forum on China-Africa Cooperation (2009) illustrates a unity bolstered by the shared experience of victimization by "external aggression or colonization… [prompting Africa and China] to support each other in the fight for independence" (Wen, 2009). The Premier's comments articulate the shared experience of victimization. Building on this point, Chinese foreign minister Wang Yi noted during the 15th Lanting Forum (2015a) that

> There is a popular Chinese song named 'Hold Your Hands'. The lyrics go like this, 'Because I traveled the path you have traveled and suffered the pain you have suffered, I share your joy and pursuit.' I think it can also be borrowed to describe the relations between China and Africa. Chinese and African people have suffered from similar scourge, and both have traveled a path fraught with hardship. That is why we are able to understand each other, share weal and woe and join hands in pursuing the same goal and same dream.

Wang's remarks align with Wen's statements lowlighting the shared experience of historical oppression and domination by external (European) forces—the African Continent during the Transatlantic Slave Period and Colonialism and China following the Opium Wars—indicating a desire to analogize the experience of China's historical markers with those of Africa's to cultivate a sense of identification among the African masses.

Dr. Liu Xianfa, Chinese Ambassador to Kenya, remarked during the launch of the China-Kenya Comprehensive Cooperative Partnership, that China and Africa are united through mutual experiences of "both as victims of western colonialism and aggression" (Liu, 2015a). In a separate speech, Liu rearticulates this sentiment in his statement that in "modern times, *both as victims of western colonialism and aggression* (emphasis added), Chinese and Kenyan people have encouraged and supported each other to achieve national liberation and independence" (Liu, 2015c). Liu's sentiments reinforce denigrations that despite changes to its developmental trajectory, the PRC continues to inculcate a self-deprecating image of self, mirroring the socio-historical experiences of African people. In 2008, in response to criticism of Chinese engagement with Botswana, Ding Xiaowen, Chinese Ambassador to Botswana contributed to the Africa-China marginalization narrative thusly,

> Chinese, like the African, like Batswana (sic), suffered a lot under colonialism. China was bullied by Western colonies for almost 100 years. China was a semi-colonial, semi-feudal country from 1840 until the new China was founded in 1949. So, China as a country was bullied by Western colonies. As a people, they suffered a lot in the past. How could such a nation, such a people, become racist to bully other people? (Ding, 2008)

This imagining of the historical Chinese experience—colonized, terrorized, and disregarded—invokes equivalent claims to pain at the hands of western nations, yes; but it also obscures the neoliberal relational dynamics of modern Afro-Chinese relations by deracializing the systemic pattern of racial inequalities historically befalling Africa and her people.

African leaders, likewise, carry the mantle of Afro-Chinese similitude buttressed by shared marginalization by the West. Kenyan President Uhuru Kenyatta remarked in his *Goodwill Message on the Occasion of the Chinese New Year* (2017), that "*We fought colonialism together in the past*; today, we fight for development that serves our people and protects our planet; and for an international order that respects the equal dignity of all peoples" (Kenyatta, 2017a). Namibian President, Hage Geingob, similarly reflected in response to western claims of Chinese neo-imperialism in Africa that "It is ironic that those who warn us are the same nations who sat around the table at the Berlin Conference in 1884 and carved out colonies in Africa with the sole intent to develop their countries with our mineral resources and the blood and sweat of our forced labour" (Geingob, 2015). Jacob Zuma, former leader of South Africa, co-constructs the narrative of Afro-Chinese shared marginalization through remarks that,

> Historians record that these ancient relations were based on mutual respect and understanding, territorial integrity, similar values, solidarity and friendship. However, colonialism interrupted these mutually beneficial relations. The rise of China indicates that the world is now returning to its historical economic powers and trade patterns! Our visit is therefore a natural progression, building on relations that date back so many thousands of years ago between China and Africa. (Zuma, 2010)

China, itself, has experienced the sting of western rejection, therefore it follows that Afro-Chinese relations are rooted not only in Beijing's longstanding affiliations with many African nations but, more importantly, in a 'common south' identity of victimization by western imperialism.

3.4.3 Inclusion

The final component of *sameness* reflects new forms of social and political connections empowering African and Chinese people to conceive of themselves as part of an inclusive community, sharing the same future. In 2005, then Chinese President Hu Jintao introduced the idea of building a "harmonious world with lasting peace and common prosperity" (Hu, 2005). This world, whilst centering China, was characterized by what Hu defined as an equitable, 'harmonious coexistence' inclusive of others. Illustrating this new form of inclusivity modeled through stronger relations between African nations and China, Hu affirmed that "building strong ties between China and Africa will not only promote the development of each side but also help cement unity and cooperation among developing countries and contribute to establishing a just and equitable new international political and economic order" (Hu, 2012). This account is typical of the new world order commonly promoted within the bounds of *brand-China*, with Beijing as the sun orbited by no fewer than 54 satellites. Lu Shaye, Director-General of the African Department of China's Ministry of Foreign Affairs, activates the narrative of *inclusion* in a 2013 speech designed to encourage cooperation between the two regions. Lu observed that,

> The dream is ahead of us. The path is under our feet... China is ready to work with Africa to consolidate strategic mutual trust, safeguard and develop our relations as a community of common destinies, actively expand and deepen pragmatic cooperation for common development, and strengthen coordination and cooperation in global governance to forge a more fair, just and balanced global order that benefits all. (Lu, 2013)

While this aspect of sameness stresses the import of an international system predicated on equality amongst all members, it is important to note that in this iteration of *brand-China* Beijing remains the central focus and principal author of its vision.

3.5   China as Model (Development)

The "Chinese Dream and the African Dream are both for development" (Lu, 2013). The focus on China-led development, industry, progress, growth, capacity building, and development aid runs a close second to sameness as the second most often-cited narrative of *brand-China* in Africa. The desire to link regional destinies through the shared aspiration to the Chinese and African 'dreams' utilizing "Technological knowledge transfer," "shared opportunities," infrastructure improvement," developmental inclusiveness, and China-driven economic growth mark the foundation of Beijing's strategies for Africa's development. *Development* is distinct in its construction of an Africa-China sustained by Chinese funding, Chinese initiatives, and Chinese competencies often relegating local populations to little more than clientelist roles. In this scenario, China is the "big brother" and African states the "little brothers" who stand to benefit by association. Li Keqiang, Premier of the PRC State Council, outlined China's developmental approach to Africa in a 2014 speech before the African Union. Li remarked

> "China stands ready to exchange development experience and share development opportunities with African countries to promote inclusive development. We are willing to share with Africa those readily applicable technologies that China has developed without any reservation. We are also ready to transfer, on a priority basis, suitable labor-intensive industries to Africa to promote employment in Africa, as this is good for both sides and benefits the two peoples" (K. Li, 2014).

In this assessment, the principal source of Beijing's developmental prowess rests on the conviction that "China has gone through the development stage Africa is currently in (and) the experience and technologies it has gained over the years will dovetail with Africa's development needs" (Zhai, 2012). Li's assertions echo beliefs shared by many throughout Africa and within China that the PRC is best positioned to help the African continent as move up the developmental trajectory. The broad diversity of recent and former African leaders, such as Morocco's Head of Government,

Abdelilah Benkirane, and Namibian President Hage Geingob, have understandably praised China's developmental assistance, stating[9]:

> Above all, I should like to underscore the important role played by the People's Republic of China as well as its continued contributions to the development of our continent and its exemplary solidarity with African countries. I wish to pay tribute to this great nation, which is steeped in history, for all it has been doing for the emergence of a peaceful, multipolar world, and for its untiring action to serve the best interests of the countries of the South and support their legitimate ambitions. (Benkirane, 2015)
>
> China's investment in Africa over the past several decades has been invaluable. These include investments in transport infrastructure development and capacity building. This has enhanced Africa's capability in moving goods and services. This level of support has existed for decades and is not a new trend as some may have us believe. In Namibia, we can attest to a number of key investments by China which have made a significant impact on our economy. (Geingob, 2015)

A successful economy is an important source of attraction and China's recent developmental success and willingness to work with African leaders is a compelling inducement for African heads of state, who have yet to fully enjoy the benefits of economic development post-independence in their entirety.

3.5.1 Homegrown Development

The absence of wholesale development across the African continent has been attributed to everything from the behavior of corrupt governments and the failure of democracy to take hold (Van de Walle, 2001); small markets and a lack of market integration (Rodney, 1981); continued marginalization (Van de Walle, 2001); lack of infrastructure (Chabal, 2009); a tendency toward externalizing problems (Mills, 2011); a lack of productive capital (Sachs, 2005); and a preference for leisure time (Gilbert & Reynolds, 2011). In contrast, a small, but growing, coterie of Africanist scholars pinpoints the exact nature of underdevelopment within several African nations on the inheritance of economies with external cultural orientations (Bhengu, 2011; Okereke & Agupusi, 2015). This factor is particularly important during the current era of globalization, which like Slavery, colonialism, neocolonialism, and developmentalism before it, expands the boundaries of capital using principally Western models. Again, the orientation is external, leaving the task to African leaders to exchange the extant colonial with other nonnative systems in an effort to integrate into the global economy.

For its part, *brand-China*, though still focused on China's role as a development model, strikes a fine balance between external, Beijing-driven solutions and internally generated, homegrown development in Africa. Chinese producers co-create the narrative of *homegrown development* for Africa, insisting that African states "explore a development path suited to (each) country's conditions" (K. Li, 2014) and that the PRC can only provide developmental guidance to Africa within the limits of its capacity to do so. President Xi Jinping's speech during the Sixth Ministerial Conference of the Forum on China-Africa Cooperation (FOCAC) in 2015 underscored China's approach,

> Today's Africa is a continent of encouraging and dynamic development. Africa has actively explored a path of development suited to its conditions and adhered to the principle of solving African issues in the African way. Such a momentum of independent development is unstoppable. Africa has actively advanced industrialization and pursued sustainable self-development. Such a momentum of rapid growth is unstoppable. Africa has accelerated its integration process and speaks in one voice on the international stage. Such a momentum of pursuing strength through unity is unstoppable. (Xi, 2015a)

Chinese Ambassador to South Africa, Tian Xuejun, likewise, reinforced Beijing's commitment to Homegrown Development in Africa, sharing his thoughts thusly,

> President Xi once said 'Only the wearer of the shoes knows if they fit or not.' There is no universal development model in the world and China never exports our ideology, let alone imposes our development model on others. We believe that African people have the wisdom and capability to find paths that are suited to their national conditions. We are ready to offer help within our capacity in their endeavor. (Tian, 2015b)

Fijałkowski (2011) suggests that China's reluctance to be more prescriptive is attributable to thinking that actively promoting the Chinese developmental path would infringe upon the rights of African nations to self-determination and domestic sovereignty—each central components of the PRC's foreign policy.

3.5.2 Altruism

Western aid policies and economic conditionalities levied on the African continent have compelled its leaders to adopt neoliberal development models designed without adequate consideration for local imperatives. In this context, western developmental mandates have been likened to "re-colonization" (Edozie & Soyinka, 2010) or a "new anti-colonial imperialism" (Rist, 1997) rather than to development in Africa. The PRC adopts a vastly different strategy of dispensing developmental aid on the continent, one that is regularly reinforced within *brand-China* as a continuance of its longstanding history of altruistic acts toward African people. As a case in point, Wang Yi enumerated China's benevolence toward Africa during a speech before the 15th Lanting Forum (2015) in Beijing:

> We will never forget that, last year, when the Ebola epidemic wreaked havoc in west Africa and many international airlines stopped flying there. China rented chartered planes flying half of the globe across three continents to deliver materials urgently needed by people in the epidemic-stricken areas. When some countries were evacuating their people, China was sending in top-level experts and medical workers to join the local communities in fighting against Ebola. (Wang, 2015a)

With the emphasis on 'mutual benefit' and 'diversity of form,' very little Chinese aid to Africa follows the formula of traditional development assistance. But then again, it never has. During the Maoist-era solidarity period (1955–1976), the CCP found ways to adhere to what it felt was its internationalist duty by sending 30,000 tons of rice to Guinea, alongside blankets, "Barefoot Doctors", and infrastructural projects in Tanzania, Zambia, Mali, Rwanda, Mauritania, and Sudan during a time in which the People's Republic was reshaping its own social and political path globally. This speaks to the flexibility behind how the "self-reliance" or homegrown development was actually practiced but also underscores the multiplicity of forms Chinese aid to Africa has and continues to take across various nations and sectors, including education, health, agriculture, infrastructure development, and humanitarian assistance and peacekeeping; and profit-generating joint ventures involving Chinese State-owned enterprises (SOEs). That Chinese aid differs from the West in motivation and content has been well noted in that Beijing fails to attach particular economic or political conditionalities (save for the adherence to the 'One China Policy') to its aid packages. This narrative of China as an antithetical development partner to the West is cited throughout *brand-China,* and declarations that Chinese aid is "provided sincerely without any political conditions attached" (Xi, 2015a) are repeated in some iteration within 71 artifacts.

Journalist Howard French (2014) balks at Chinese assertions of altruism in Africa, likening Chinese infrastructure projects to a millennial version of the colonial project. French notes,

> …today one easily forgets that ports, railways, roads, and the administrative districts that became the downtowns of capitals around the world were built on an extraordinary scale all over the world by Westerners in the driven pursuit of their own interests. As manufacturing powers, they needed their goods to circulate, and they needed the raw materials from far-flung places in order to make them. Seen in this light, it scarcely seems coincidental that China, a country that has surged from near autarky to becoming the so-called factory of the world in the space of a mere generation, has quickly become the most ambitious builder of infrastructure in Africa, the world's fastest-growing region, both demographically and economically, and the source of a disproportionate share of the globe's natural resources.

Despite French's disavowal, the PRC adopts what Tuck and Yang (2012) classify as 'settler moves to innocence', deflecting the settler/colonial identity embedded in critiques of Africa-China, by sustaining narratives of patronage rather than the beneficiary. The *altruism* narrative fosters notions of China still as a developing yet selfless, a formerly colonized subject. Nevertheless, this construction of Africa-China is inconsistent with reality. Fennell (2013) sketches Chinese intervention as "part of a theoretically based international strategy" rather than one rooted in "altruism or feelings of goodwill" (253). The disconnect between the Beijing's projected image and its identity has increasingly become the subject of scholarly inquiry regarding its relationship to Africa and an important rationale for nation branding within the context of Afro-Chinese relations.

3.5.3 China Dream

Shortly upon rising to the Head of the Chinese Communist Party (CCP) in November 2012, President Xi Jinping outlined a vision for the nation's future, which he proclaimed the *Chinese Dream*. In his declaration that "the great revival of the Chinese nation is the greatest Chinese Dream" (Liu, 2013), Xi articulated the PRC's strategies for becoming a middle-income country by 2021, the 100th anniversary of the Chinese Communist Party; and for becoming a fully developed nation by about 2049, the 100th anniversary of the founding of the People's Republic. Xi's vision of the *Chinese Dream* is an oft-cited component of the *brand-China* development narrative, exemplified by statements such as,

> Chinese people are working hard to realize the 'China Dream' of achieving national prosperity and rejuvenation, as well as the people's happiness. At the same time, 2.1 million Namibian people are pursuing a "Namibia Dream" of achieving stable economic growth and national industrialization. (Xin, 2015)

Remarks by H.E. Xin Shunkang, former Chinese ambassador to Namibia, also reinforce the practice of connecting the Chinese and African *Dreams*. Xin.

> With common ideals, similar historical experiences and a shared need for development, China and Africa both pursue stability and peace in their dreams. We are both committed to safeguarding and promoting world peace. Our joint efforts to realize our dreams as peace-loving and peace-pursuing nations will greatly strengthen the force for peace and stability and add to the efforts of building a harmonious world of enduring peace and common prosperity. (Lu, 2013)

The 'Chinese Dream' for development is clearly articulated as a manifestation of the hard work and ingenuity of the Chinese people yet, rhetorically, the 'African dream' is framed as attainable through association with or to the benefit of China or other nations. According to Wang Yi, Minister of Foreign Affairs of the People's Republic of China, "Africa, once poor and backward in development, is emerging as a continent of hope and growth" thanks to Chinese support (Wang, 2015c). This is borne out by "history and reality, (which) tell us that when China develops well, Africa will get opportunities…" (K. Li, 2014). China is "willing to link the Chinese dream with the African dream and China's two centenary goals with Africa's development strategies" (Tian, 2015c). The People's Republic brings "relative advantages in development experience and production factors" to the relationship, whilst African countries, similarly to earlier eras of capital accumulation, contribute "natural and human resources and [their] huge markets" (Wang, 2015a). Industrial growth, like all modes of production, requires human resources, capital resources, and natural resources. Africa has never been short of natural or human factors, while population growth in China contributes to the declination of domestic resource stores. Surplus production, precipitated by the ongoing processes of industrialization in the PRC, makes fulfilling the Chinese Dream dependent in many ways on securing new markets outside Asia for domestically produced goods. Africa as a resource hub and new goods market is a storyline played out throughout transatlantic slavery and colonialism. The paradox within neoliberal globalization is that rather than resources and goods flowing westward, in this iteration the contraflow sends them eastward under the guise of development.

3.6 China as Friend (Friendship)

Friendship is the third most commonly communicated portrayal of *brand-China*. As a strategic narrative, artifacts in this category referred to Africa or African people (or the inverse, China or the Chinese) as friend, friends, friendly, referenced an extant friendship between the two regions, or made statements indicative of a friendship or alliance. Speakers from both regions categorized interaction between Africa and China as friendly, alternately alluding to the relationship as "long term", an "unbreakable bond" (Li, K 2014), "true friends", "deeply rooted" (Tian, 2013), "bosom friends" (Xin, 2015), and an "unwavering friend(ship)" (Sun, 2017). A 2013 speech by the Chinese Ambassador to South Africa, Tian Xuejun, celebrating the 15th anniversary of diplomatic relations between China and South Africa, epitomizes the Afro-Chinese friendship narrative:

> The first letter "F" stands for friendship, as it is the bonding tie linking China and South Africa together. Chinese has an old saying, 'Distance cannot separate true friends, even when they are thousands of miles apart'. Despite the long geographical distance, the people of our two countries enjoy a profound traditional friendship, and such a relationship is the inexhaustible driving force behind the comprehensive, rapid, and sound development of China-SA relationship. This is something that we must cherish.

Ambassador Tian reveals several key components of the *"China as friend"* narrative within his address. The first is indubitably friendship. The second is shared affinity. Despite the geographical and mental distance between the two regions, African and Chinese people are unified based on their deep regard for one another. Thirdly, Tian's statements situate Beijing's interest in Africa as fundamentally rooted in traditional or historical patterns of engagement between the two regions. Finally, Tian's remarks speak to the need to protect and cherish the relationship for the future. Whether observing a speech made by a Chinese diplomat, flipping through the pages of *ChinAfrica* magazine, or reading an editorial within *China Daily Africa Weekly*, the core message is that Africa and China are friends. It is a friendship built upon longstanding, historical, or traditional relations between the two regions, and it is this same friendship that catalyzes contemporary and future interactions between continent and country.

3.6.1 Historical Friendship

China's longstanding, historical or traditional friendship with Africa is often tethered to mentions of pre-enslavement trade relations between the regions dating back millennia. Artifacts frequently memorialize a "traditional friendship" or "historical friendship" between Chinese and African people predicated on "600 years" of cama-raderie (G. Liu, 2010). Chinese President, Hu Jintao, remarked in 2006 that "though vast oceans keep China and Africa apart, the friendship between our two peoples has a long history, and having been tested by times, is strong and vigorous" (Hu, 2006).

Remarks by the Chinese Ambassador to Namibia, Xin Shunkang, during the Evening of Nanjing Cultural Performance (2015) typify historical linkages between African and Chinese people. Xin pronounced,

> As we all know, the traditional friendship between China and Namibia came into being in the struggle of the Namibian people for national liberation and independence. Since the 1960s our two peoples support each other, help each other, and strive side by side. On 22 March 1990, the day after Namibia got independent, China established formal diplomatic relations with Namibia. Hence, no matter how the international situation changes, China and Namibia are always good friends, good brothers, and good partners.[10]

Pablo Morales' chapter in this text dedicates considerable attention to how local audiences can strengthen or diminish China's global soft power campaign. In this vein, African leaders promote the narrative of *historical friendship* using frameworks similar to the Chinese. During an address before the South Africa-China Business Forum in Beijing, Jacob Zuma, President of the Republic of South Africa (2009–2018), expressed his appreciation for Chinese friendship thusly,

> The rise of China indicates that the world is now returning to its historical economic powers and trade patterns! Our visit is, therefore, a natural progression, building on relations that date back so many thousands of years ago between China and Africa.[11]

Zuma's remarks, like those before it, challenge pernicious claims of Chinese neo-imperialism by establishing a timeline of historical interaction points between the two regions. Recapitulating tales of Africa's longstanding, traditional, and historical friendship with China, Zuma continues,

> Some of you may be surprised to hear that trade relations between China and Africa in general and South Africa in particular, dates back more than a thousand years. We know from historical records that the kingdom of Mapungubwe in Limpopo province, in the northern part of South Africa already had commercial links with China that far back. We should also recall that the famous Chinese mariner, explorer, diplomat, and fleet admiral, Zheng was sent by the Ming Emperor Yong Le, on expeditions to explore the "western oceans" in the early fifteenth century. He opened up trade routes as far south as Mozambique.[12]

Conjuring memories of Zheng He historicizes Afro-Chinese relations in a manner consistent with Chinese constructions of the relationship.[13] On the 600th anniversary of his voyage, Beijing launched a campaign in Zheng's honor, an armature connecting the navigator's contributions to China's narrative of 'longstanding', 'anti-colonial' friendship and partnership with Africa. The sentimental chronicle of Zheng He constructed within *brand-China*, though mawkishly sweet, is factually untenable. Historian Geoff Wade alleged in *The Zheng He voyages: a reassessment* (2005), that Zheng's visits were marked less by their gentility than the use of force or the threat of force to establish tributary relations with kingdoms along the East Africa Coast. In the same vein, Phillip Snow (1983) emphasized that as a representative of the Yongle Emperor, Zheng sought a clientelist relationship with African Kingdoms cemented

by a "gesture of symbolic acquiescence" (29). Acknowledging the submissive relationship desired of acephalous African states during the Ming Dynasty would indeed
reinforce the legitimacy of early Afro-Chinese relations at the expense of weakening
the narrative of ongoing, traditional friendship. Notwithstanding, Zheng He continues
to serve as a placeholder illustrating the longevity and consistency of Afro-Chinese
relations within 5% of the artifacts. A speech by Chinese Foreign Minister Wang
Yi at the 15th Lanting Forum in 2015 provides but one example of how Zheng's
memory is reactivated in contemporary Afro-Chinese relations,[14]

> This spirit is rooted in the long-standing traditional friendship and mutual support between
> China and Africa. Early in the fifteenth century, China's navigator Zheng He headed his
> fleet and arrived at the east coast of Africa four times. That was a time when China was the
> strongest in the world. What they brought to Africa were silk and porcelain, and friendship
> and goodwill. They did not grab an inch of land. Nor did they ever take back one single
> slave.[15]

Triggering Zheng's unsullied memory within *brand-China*, the PRC creates a
historical reference point and counterpoint to the European conquest of the continent. Curating an image of Afro-China established through the mutually beneficial
exchange of gifts, historical friendship, and cultural propinquity reinforces the notion
that if not for the transatlantic slave trade and colonialism, the Afro-Chinese relationship as 'friends, brothers, and partners' would have continued uninterrupted for
more than 600 *years*. Liu Guangyuan (2010), the Chinese Ambassador to Kenya,
referenced this point in an editorial to *The Nation*: "It would be appropriate, therefore, to claim that friendship between China and Kenya started almost 600 *years* ago
with a beautiful and elegant giraffe." Perhaps more importantly, the narrative also
potentially transforms how domestic and international publics view China and its
interactions with African nations, refuting claims that Beijing's interest in Africa is
tantamount to *realpolitik* foreign policy goals and thus is no different from the West.

3.6.2 Solidarity

The narrative of Afro-Chinese solidarity or 'south-south relations', creates an additional anchor point for memorializing the traditional friendship between Africa
and China. Dating from the solidarities established during the Bandung conference (1955), construction of the Tazara Railway (1970–1975) and African liberation
movements of the 1960s and 1970s (UNITA in Angola and SWAPO in Namibia,
among others), the narrative of Afro-Chinese "solidarity" establishes a timeline of
mutual support rooted in similar positioning between the two regions rather than the
pursuit of political and economic interest. President Xi Jinping asserted during the
opening to the Forum on China-Africa Cooperation in 2015 that,

> We have always supported each other in trying times. The Tazara Railway and the Convention
> Center of the African Union built with Chinese assistance are landmarks of China-Africa
> friendship. The Chinese government and people took the lead in helping Africa fight Ebola

and led the international community in its efforts to assist Africa to combat the epidemic, demonstrating the bond of brotherhood between China and Africa in time of difficulty.

The Bandung conference introduced China's official discourse of South-South cooperation and memories of the Conference are often activated as a metaphor for the might of subjugated nations united against a common adversary. Xi Jinping remarked during the Asian-African Summit that,

> Sixty years ago, leaders from 29 Asian and African countries attended the Bandung Conference, giving birth to the Bandung Spirit of solidarity, friendship, and cooperation, galvanizing the national liberation movement that swept across Asia, Africa and Latin America, and accelerating the global process of decolonization. (Xi, 2015a)

Fennell (2013) argues that before the Bandung Conference, however, "mentions of Africa in the Chinese press were virtually nonexistent, as was interaction with African people" (256), yet, Post-Bandung China claimed that it belongs "with Africans to the Third World" (Monson, 2008). Contemporary rhetoric of the conference's outcomes and Chinese and African participation within it falls short of reality. Post-Bandung, Afro-Chinese solidarities solidified in part because of a shared aversion to the Post-War Liberal World Order, which was thought to function as an appendage to the Western capitalist model underpinning colonialism. Contemporary narratives of Afro-Chinese solidarity make repeated reference to this period. Chinese Foreign Minister Wang Yi expressed during the 15th Lanting Forum in 2015 that,

> We will never forget that in the middle of the last century, the Chinese people, after winning national liberation, gave full support to African countries in their just struggle to oppose hegemonism, colonialism and to gain national independence and liberation. (Wang, 2015a)

It is here that African thoughts are expressed most resoundingly as officials across the continent regularly deploy post-Bandung solidarities between the two regions as vinculums to contemporary Afro-Chinese relations. Morocco's head of the government, Abdelilah Benkirane, expressed that "Above all, I should like to underscore the important role played by the People's Republic of China as well as its continued contributions to the development of our continent and its exemplary solidarity with African countries." South African Minister of Science and Technology, Naledi Pandor, similarly remarked: "As we look back at our struggle for liberation and our progress since 1994, we do so fully aware that the support and solidarity from China played a critical role in our success." Within South Africa, particularly, former President Jacob Zuma and his cabinet frequently cited the "Bandung Spirit" or alluded to Chinese solidarity during decolonization as symbolic of the Afro-Chinese relationship's firm foundations and Beijing's consistent loyalty to the African continent. During an Address to the South Africa-China Business Forum, Zuma intimated that "When friends were fewer, during the struggle against apartheid, China was available to assist, and we are grateful for that solidarity." South African Minister of Education, Blade Nzimande, similarly paid homage to Afro-Chinese solidarity in his speech during the launch of the Africa-China network, Gordon Institute of Business Science in 2010, when he remarked "As early as the 1950s and 1960s, China and Africa had fought side by side in the struggle against imperialism and colonialism."

3.7   China as Partner (Partnership)

In January 2006, the Chinese government released a document outlining its newly articulated 'Africa Policy'. The plan outlined a blueprint for enhancing Afro-Chinese relations beyond diplomatic and economic cooperation, into previously untapped areas such as science and technology, education, culture, and peace and security. Most distinctively, in response to public criticism, the policy detailed a blueprint for better incorporating and involving African nations in decisions regarding the direction and tenor of Chinese participation on the continent. Beijing's focus on nurturing and establishing new cooperative partnerships is the fourth most frequently cited theme within *brand-China*. Through the *partnership* narrative, the PRC stresses the equitable role of Afro-Chinese relations, unlike that of *development*, which is China-led. Repeatedly expressed through messages of 'cooperation', including references to the Afro-Chinese relationship as 'win–win', 'mutually beneficial,' 'south-south', working together to achieve a common goal, the Forum on China Africa Cooperation (FOCAC), partnership, and teamwork; construction of the Afro-Chinese relationship as one underpinned by African regard for "China as their most important and reliable partner" (Wang, 2015a) or as a relationship amongst "friends who have long supported and worked to promote China-Africa cooperation" (K. Li, 2014) is commonplace.

3.7.1   Cooperation

Similar to the rhetoric of solidarity undergirding the narrative of Afro-Chinese friendship, *cooperation* is regarded as the cornerstone of successful and ongoing partnerships between the two regions. A Speech by H. E. Li Keqiang Premier of the State Council of the People's Republic of China speaks to the potential for ongoing cooperative relations between Africa and China:

> With splendid chapters already written, China-Africa cooperation is poised to turn a brand-new page. Characterized by their unprecedented scope of common interests and a much more solid foundation, China-Africa cooperation should seize the good opportunity and focus on the future. China would like to make joint efforts with African countries to actively promote major projects in six areas to upgrade our cooperation. (K. Li, 2014)

Within the cooperation narrative, great care is taken to distinguish between the need for African nations to align their interests and practices with other states against the desire to retain national sovereignty within an increasingly interdependent world order. Chinese Vice Foreign Minister Zhai Jun at the Seventh Lanting Forum (2012) points out,

> that Africa belongs to the Africans; it is not anyone's "cheese". Any country that wishes to develop cooperation with Africa must respect the ownership of African countries. In a globalized world, countries' destinies are closely linked. China's relations with Africa are open and inclusive. It is all about cooperation rather than confrontation with any third party. (Zhai, 2012)

Leaders on the continent were also keen to point out the significance of Afro-Chinese *cooperation* as an integral component of the African development path. South African Cabinet Minister Jeff Radebe remarked on the occasion of the inaugural China-Africa Media Summit that,

> We also invite our Chinese friends to partner with us in championing development in the continent through new business ventures, infrastructure development, media capacity development, and many other areas of mutual interest. Together we can take Africa and China forward in positive ways that have never been imagined before. (Radebe, 2015)

Much of the cooperation narrative also alludes to China's benevolent desire to work with Africa and her people, such as statements by Chinese Ambassador to South Africa, Tian Xuejun, who remarked that "In light of the pressing need of Africa, China will strengthen its cooperation with Africa in areas such as infrastructure and industrialization, agricultural modernization, public health, people-to-people and cultural exchanges as well as peace and security" (Tian, 2015a).

Similar to the rhetoric of benevolence found throughout colonial constructions of Africa, in this account, Afro-Chinese *cooperation* becomes rooted in Africa's fundamentally 'pressing need' for external assistance. This narrative suggests that China works with Africa because Africa needs PRC's help. Yet, despite such needs, assistance can only paternalistically be meted out once African nations are deemed ready to receive it. African leaders, alternatively, while acknowledging the significance of collaborative partnerships to the continent's continued growth and development, collectively view *brand-China* as a vehicle through which African states can become global players no longer "entirely depend(ent) on the generosities of others for the welfare of its people" (Nzimande, 2010).

Cooperation as a constituent feature of Africa-China and, by extension, *brand-China* in Africa, works for hand in glove with the concept of Afro-Chinese relations being equal, 'win–win', and/or 'mutually beneficial' to all parties. Hage Geingob, President of the Republic of Namibia, commented during the opening of the FOCAC Summit in 2015,

> The theme of China and Africa Progressing Together in a Win-Win Cooperation for Common Development is highly appropriate and speaks respectfully towards Africa's demand for equal partnership and mutually beneficial development… In Namibia and in Africa, we value the special relations we share with China. FOCAC is the ideal platform for us to build upon those relations for the purpose of mutual benefit. (Geingob, 2015)

Geingob's reflections denote the domestic significance placed on Namibia's cooperative partnership with Beijing. Nigerian President, Mohammed Buhari, hailed the mutual benefits of Afro-Chinese cooperation during the commissioning ceremony for three Nigerian naval ships in 2016. Addressing a principally Nigerian crowd, Buhari noted, "I take this opportunity to pay tribute to … the mutually helpful military cooperation, of which the Nigerian Navy has been a major beneficiary" (Buhari, 2016). Morocco's head of the government, Abdelilah Benkirane, energized the *cooperation* narrative during the Second Forum on China-Africa Cooperation, in his remarks that "Our determination to carry out concerted action and engage in pragmatic cooperation is based on the principles of mutual benefits and shared development" (Benkirane, 2015). Collectively these statements speak to what Łukasz Fijałkowski (2011) categorizes as China's political and economic attractiveness in Africa. The PRC has dedicated tremendous resources toward "building a positive image in African states, particularly through promoting the vision of a 'win–win' strategy of mutual economic benefits" (95), which appeals the African states who have historically been divorced from the ability to direct their nations' developmental paths.

3.7.2 Common South Identity

Brand-China capitalizes on romantic depictions of Beijing's global south roots with Africa as a central component of the Africa-China partnership. Reinforcing depictions of China as a developing country and member of the 'global south' rather than a western state, this aspect of the *partnership* narrative is demonstrably most visible in artifacts produced by African leaders. Blade Nzimande, South African Minister of Higher Education and Training, as an example, remarked during the launch of the Africa-China Network (2010):

> The burgeoning relationship between South Africa and China is based on a foundation of both our countries' commitment to strengthening and deepening South-South collaboration. The new dynamic of the global political economy, especially the current global economic crisis and the threats posed by climate change, is the growing assertion of emerging powers such as South Africa and China to forge a new dispensation that seeks to challenge traditional institutions and entrenched systems and influence positive change in favour of ourselves in the developing world. (Nzimande, 2010)

Minister Nzimande's comments lend credence to *brand-China* as a foe to hegemony insisting, instead, that the partnership's utility is rooted in its longstanding affiliation and predicated upon a 'common south' identity. Proponents hold fast to the fact that relations were initiated at a time in which China could not exert its current level of diplomatic or economic power, speaking to extant equity shared between African nations and China.

Chinese President, Xi Jinping, later echoed Nzimande's remarks regarding the importance of cooperation between 'global south' partners in his declaration that,

> Second, we should expand South-South cooperation. Mr. Deng Xiaoping, the chief architect of China's reform and opening-up, once said that South-South cooperation was such a well-put term that we must give whoever invented it a big medal. Indeed, developing countries in their large numbers are all faced with the common mission of accelerating development and improving people's lives. They ought to look to one another for comfort and come to each other's aid in times of difficulty. And they should actively carry out cooperation across the board to realize their respective development blueprints. A successful Asian-African cooperation will set a good and important example for South-South cooperation in other parts of the world. (Xi, 2015a)

Xi's remarks, though not delivered before an exclusively African audience, are demonstrative of messages embedded within the 'China as partner' narrative.

3.8 Equivalent Claims to Pain

The inaugural ceremony commemorating the Madaraka Express' opening, similarly to other carefully curated presentations of the Chinese self-image, reinforced impressions of Beijing in Africa as a loyal friend, cultural traditionalist, and once- impoverished nation victimized by Western imperialism. Imagining China and its history in this light distinguishes Beijing as an antithetical construction of the West while also obscuring the neoliberal relational dynamics of Africa-China. Concomitant with the political mandate of global capital competition, nation-states intentionally create and nurture images of self that align and often realign their national imaginary in ways supportive of their neoliberal goals. This is an intentional choice, and thus, China is far from alone in doing so. The People's Republic of China, the United States, and the United Kingdom, but also Croatia, Brazil, and Nigeria among scores of other nations frequently disseminate carefully chosen images and messages reflecting the ways they want domestic and international audiences to view them. Subotic (2017) explains, that within these self-constructions "…nostalgia, origin stories, enemy construction, and others, are mobilized – through a fantastical structure of the nation that enrolls people into a particular national narrative of the imaginary." Thus, successfully constructing a narrative of China and Africa-China relations that can positively resonate with diverse African audiences requires strategically apportioning the attendant symbols of *brand-China* into easily digestible bites and then spoon-feeding African nationals with these imaginings of selfhood, Other, power, and powerlessness as extensions of an Afro-Asiatic self.

Examining official images and messages as sites of the nation's brand through which national imaginaries of self and other are produced and disseminated in societies, enables the observer to see how subtle consistent messages of "friendship," "brotherhood," "development," or "cooperation," reinforced through speeches celebrating the opening of a Confucius Center or ads depicting African women dressed as Chinese ethnic minorities, project carefully curated images of the PRC for African consumption, create an environment of imagined community with Africa. These practices are so important, according to Subovic, because "they are so routine, so prevalent, so popular, and so ubiquitous". Subovic's assertions are authenticated within the context of Africa-China relations, as *brand-China*, insightfully activates messages of *sameness,* among others, to draw upon Africa's distinct socio-historical markers. Drawing heavily upon the concept of community identity and shared ethos to inculcate a communal consciousness heightened by political and economic marginalization by the West, the Chinese State uses its brand to inculcate feelings of historical and experiential similitude with Africa. In doing so *brand-China* deracializes historical inequities by asserting equivalent claims to pain. The very formulation of *brand-China's* claims to "sameness", conflating vastly different African and Chinese experiences as equally post-colonial is problematic, however. Disingenuously adjudging the two regions' colonial and post-colonial experiences as equivalent, elides differences and overlooks the complexities of power relations between and within developing countries, between dominant and subaltern, and settler and indigenous groups. The practice overlooks internalized, racialized colonial notions of Africa and Africans embedded within the Chinese national imaginary.

By probing how Beijing utilizes nation branding to construct its image within Africa, the chapter prompts a reconsideration of the discursive power mechanisms exercised in and through national image-making. Understanding the duality of China's constructed brand image as simultaneously self-sacrificing and self-serving is important to comprehending the Chinese State's attempts to create and manage its brand in Africa and underscores the difficulty of discerning Beijing's motives. Images of both Africa and China are represented in its brand and though each is discursively constructed through Western discourse, the rhetoric imbued within *brand-China* is at once both distant from and near to Western historical notions of Africa. Beijing promotes its own long-term foreign policy goals in Africa, interrupting western influence by reviving metaphors of the solidarity movement and linking the developmentalism of the present day with Maoist discourse, thereby insinuating itself into Africa's origin, evolution, and eventual fate through the repeated telling of these stories. China adopts what Tuck and Yang (2012) classify as 'settler moves to innocence', deflecting the neocolonial identity embedded in critiques of Africa-China, by depicting itself as a member of the oppressed and never an oppressor. This is problematic considering that, within *brand-China* and through the construction of "sameness", Beijing also claims the right to enjoy the benefits of certain settler privileges, including gatekeeping admission to the 'tribe.'

Notes

1. History of Kenya Railways. Retrieved from the Kenyan Railways Website http://krc.co.ke/history/. Accessed online October 17, 2017.
2. *Kenya's Madaraka Express Launches Amid Fanfare—And Criticism.* https://allafrica.com/view/group/main/main/id/00052310.html Accessed online September 7, 2017.
3. A name concomitant with "South-South Solidarity", The Tazara or TanZam railway linked Tanzania and Zambia and was widely viewed as a solution to the stronghold southern African states held over transportation between Tanzania and Zambia post-independence. Jamie Monson (2009) writes extensively about the Tazara railway in what is widely accepted as the definite text on the subject, Africa's Freedom Railway: How a Chinese Development Project Changed Lives and Livlihood in Tanzania.
4. Zheng He was one of the great navigators of the Ming Dynasty (1368–1644) who visited Kenya during several of his western voyages (1405–1433). Although he is often referred to as the Chinese Columbus, the sobriquet is ahistorical in that Zheng voyages precipitated Columbus' by six decades; *Kenya's Madaraka Express Launches Amid Fanfare—And Criticism.* https://allafrica.com/view/group/main/main/id/00052310.html Accessed online September 7, 2017.
5. It is important to note that the practice was repeated again during the 2021 Lunar New Year show.

6. *ChinAfrica* Magazine, first launched in 1988, is an English and French language magazine designed to "further promote mutual understanding of China and African countries." The magazine, a state supported entity, targets an African audience in addition to "high-end international readers" and is designed to present "a real China to African readers." Based in Johannesburg, South Africa, the magazine was relaunched in 2012 and is distributed monthly.

7. Since the object of qualitative research is not generalizability but transferability, sampling does not need to ensure that all objects being analyzed have an equal or predictable probability of being included in the sample. Instead, sampling should be theoretical and purposive.

8. In his analysis of Ubuntu in South African society, Kamwangamalu (2014) found that the core characteristics of African ontologies: respect for human dignity and human life, group solidarity, hospitality, and collective consciousness underpin the way members of society treat one another Kamwangamalu, Nkonko M. 2013, 241.

9. It is worth noting than many such speeches were and are regularly delivered during the FOCAC Summits.

10. Ambassador's Remarks during the Evening of Nanjing Cultural Performance, April 17, 2017.

11. Address by President JG Zuma to the South Africa-China Business Forum on the occasion of the state visit to the People's Republic of China, Beijing 24 Aug 2010.

12. Ibid.

13. Zheng He was a Chinese navigator during the Ming Dynasty (1368–1644). Zheng made seven westward journeys, traveling during his fourth trip to the eastern shoreline of Kenya where he brought with him both "Chinese porcelain and friendship." Upon his departure for China, he was gifted a giraffe by the people of Malindi. Thus, according to Chinese lore, began the long-standing, traditional friendship between Bo-pa-li and Zhongguo.

14. Excerpt of speech by H.E. Wang Yi, Foreign Minister of the People's Republic of China, *Build on Past Achievements and Open up the Future of All-round Development of China-Africa Friendship and Cooperation* during the 15th Lanting Forum November 26, 2015.

15. Ibid.

Works Cited

Aaker, D. A. (2012). *2012. Building strong brands*. Simon and Schuster.

Anholt, S. (2005). *Brand new justice: How branding places and products can help the developing world*. Routledge.

Asante, M. K., Miike, Y., & Yin, J. (Eds.). (2013). *The global intercultural communication reader*. Routledge.

Atieno, W. (2017, May 31). *Kenya: It's is too early to celebrate SGR, bus owners say*. The Daily Nation. Nairobi.

Benkirane, A. (2015). *Remarks before the Second Forum on China-Africa Cooperation (FOCAC)* Johannesburg, South Africa. 2015.

Bhengu, M. J. (2011). *African economic humanism: The rise of an African economic philosophy*.

Buhari, M. (2016, December 17). *The healthy and growing diplomatic relations with China has been most beneficial to Nigeria.*. Ministry of Foreign Affairs of the people's republic of China website. http://fmprc.gov.cn.

Chabal, P. (2009). *Africa: The politics of suffering and smiling*. Zed Books.

Ding, X. (2008, March 31). *Ambassador Ding tells Botswana a real China*. Ministry of Foreign Affairs of the People's Republic of China website. http://fmprc.gov.cn.

Dynon, N. (2014, January 11). China and nation branding. *The Diplomat*. http://thediplomat.com. Accessed May 24, 2016.

Edozie, R. K., & Soyinka, P. (Eds.). (2010). *Reframing contemporary Africa: Politics, economics, and culture in the global era*. CQ Press.

Fairclough, N. (2013). *Critical discourse analysis* (Ed., Ruth Wodak). London: Sage.

Fan, Y. (2010). Branding the nation: Towards a better understanding. *Place Branding and Public Diplomacy, 6*(2), 97–103.

Fennell, V. L. (2013). Race: China's question and problem. *The Review of Black Political Economy, 40*, 3.

Fijałkowski, Ł. (2011). China's "soft power" in Africa? *Journal of Contemporary African Studies, 29*(2), 223–232.

French, H. W. (2014).*China's Second continent: How a million migrants are building a new empire in Africa*. Vintage.

Gee, J. P. (2014). *An introduction to discourse analysis: Theory and method*. Routledge.

Geingob, H. (2015, December 7). *Remarks during the opening of the FOCAC Summit*. State Website.

Gilbert, E., & Reynolds, J. T. (2011). *Africa in world history* (p. 480). Pearson Education.

Gyekye, K. (1997). *Tradition and modernity: Philosophical reflections on the African experience*. Oxford University Press.

History of Kenya Railways. Retrieved from the Kenyan Railways Website http://krc.co.ke/history/ Accessed online October 17, 2017.

Hsieh, A. T., & Li, C. K. (2008). The moderating effect of brand image on public relations perception and customer loyalty. *Marketing intelligence & planning*.

Hu, J. (2012). *Remarks during the opening ceremony of the Beijing Summit of the forum on China Africa Cooperation*. Beijing, China. Ministry of Foreign Affairs of the People's Republic of China website. http://fmprc.gov.cn.

Hu, J. (2005, September 15). *Build towards a harmonious world of lasting peace and common prosperity*. United Nations Summit. Ministry of Foreign Affairs of the People's Republic of China website. http://fmprc.gov.cn.

Hu, J. (2006, November 4). *Remarks during the opening ceremony of the Beijing summit of the forum of China-Africa cooperation*. Beijing. Accessed at http://www.focac.org on 07/07/2017.

Kamwangamalu, N. M. (2013). A sociolinguistic perspective to a Pan-African concept. *The Global Intercultural Communication Reader*, 226

Keller, K. L. (1998). *Strategic brand management*. Prentice Hall.

Keller, K. L., Parameswaran,M. G. & Jacob, I. (2011). *Strategic brand management: Building, measuring, and managing brand equity*. Pearson Education India.

Kenya's Madaraka Express Launches Amid Fanfare—And Criticism. https://allafrica.com/view/ group/main/main/id/00052310.html. Accessed online September 7, 2017.

Kenyatta, U. (2017a, January 30). *Goodwill message on the occasion of the Chinese New Year, The Nation,*.

Kenyatta, U. (2017b, June 1). *Remarks during the 54th Madaraka day celebrations at Kabiru-Ini Stadium*, Nyeri. http://president.go.ke. Accessed online October 17, 2017.

Klein, N. (2009). *No logo*. Vintage Books.

Kopinski, D., Polus, A., & Taylor, I. (Eds.). (2012). *China's rise in Africa* (p. 2012). Perspectives on a developing connection.

Krippendorff, K., & Bock, M. A. (2009). *The content analysis reader*. Sage.

Li, H. (2010). *From Chengfen to Shenjia: Branding and promotional culture in China*. In M. Aronczyk, & D. Powers (Eds.), *Blowing up the brand: Critical perspectives on promotional culture* (Vol. 21). Peter Lang.

Li, K. (2014, May 5). *Bring about a better future for China-Africa cooperation*. The AU Conference Center, Addis Ababa. Ministry of Foreign Affairs of the People's Republic of China website. http://fmprc.gov.cn.

Liu, G. (2010, October 11). *From Giraffe the diplomat to 'Peace Ark'*. The Nation, Nairobi, Kenya. Ministry of Foreign Affairs of the People's Republic of China website. http://fmprc.gov.cn.

Liu, G. (2011, March 28). *Building a better China-Africa partnership*. Ministry of Foreign Affairs of the People's Republic of China website. http://fmprc.gov.cn.

Liu, G. (2013, July 30). *The Chinese dream: How Africa can benefit from Beijing's vast experience*. Daily Nation. Ministry of Foreign Affairs of the People's Republic of China website. http://fmprc.gov.cn.

Liu, X. (2015a, June 26). *Remarks at the launching ceremony of photo exhibition commemorating the second anniversary of the establishment of China-Kenya Comprehensive cooperative partnership*. Ministry of Foreign Affairs of the People's Republic of China website. http://fmprc.gov.cn

Liu, X. (2015b, October 1). *Reception marking the 66th anniversary of the founding of the people's Republic of China*. Ministry of Foreign Affairs of the People's Republic of China website. http://fmprc.gov.cn

Liu, X. (2015c, June 7). *Rich history and shared interests define China, Kenya win-win ties*. The Standard (Nairobi).

Lu, S. (2013, July 17). *Chinese dream, African dream—Achieving common development through joint efforts*. Ministry of Foreign Affairs of the People's Republic of China website. http://fmprc.gov.cn.

Mills, G. (2011). *Why Africa is poor: And what Africans can do about it*. (Penguin Global; Reprint edition, 2011).

Monson, J. (2008). Liberating labour? Constructing anti-hegemony on the TAZARA railway in Tanzania, 1965–1976. *China returns to Africa. A rising power and a continent embrace*, 197–220.

Monson, J. (2009). *Africa's Freedom Railway: How a Chinese development project changed lives and livelihoods in Tanzania*. Indiana University Press.

Mudimbe, V. Y. (1988). *The invention of Africa: Gnosis, philosophy, and the order of knowledge*.

Nzimande, B. (2010, January 18). *Remarks at the launch of the Africa-China network*. Gordon Institute of Business Science. Accessed via the Department of International Relations and Cooperation Website. http://www.dirco.gov.za/docs/speeches/jzuma.html Accessed December 1, 2020.

Okereke, C., & Agupusi, P. (2015). *Homegrown development in Africa: Reality or illusion?* Routledge.

Radebe, J. (2015, December 1). *Remarks during the inaugural China-Africa media summit*. Cape Town. Accessed via the Department of International Relations and Cooperation Website. http://www.dirco.gov.za/docs/speeches/jzuma.html Accessed December 1, 2020.

Rist, G. (1997). *The history of development: From Western origins to global faith*. Zed Books.

Rodney, W. (1981). *How Europe underdeveloped Africa*. Howard University Press.

Rose, J. (2010). The branding of states: The uneasy marriage of marketing to politics. *Journal of Political Marketing, 9*(4), 254–275.

Roy, D., & Banerjee, S. (2007). CARE-ing strategy for integration of brand identity with brand image. *International journal of commerce and management*.

Sachs, J. (2005). *The end of poverty: Economic possibilities for our time*. Penguin Press.

Snow, P. (1988). *The star raft: China's encounter with Africa*. Weidenfeld & Nicolson.

Subotic, J. (2017, March). *Visual geopolitics and the transformation of national imaginaries: State representation in air* (Unpublished conference paper). International Studies Association. Baltimore, Maryland.

Sun, X. (2017, February 21). *Speech during the donation ceremony from the China-Lesotho People-to-People Friendship Action Fund to Maseru poverty-stricken students*. Ministry of Foreign Affairs of the People's Republic of China website. http://fmprc.gov.cn.

Szondi, G. (2007). The role and challenges of country branding in transition countries: The Central and Eastern European experience. *Place Branding and Public Diplomacy, 3*(1), 8–20.

Tian, X. (2013). *Remarks during the reception celebrating The 15th anniversary of diplomatic relations between South African and China*. Ministry of Foreign Affairs of the People's Republic of China website. http://fmprc.gov.cn.

Tian, X. (2015a, September 30). *Remarks during national day reception of the Chinese Embassy in South Africa*. Pretoria, South Africa. Ministry of Foreign Affairs of the People's Republic of China website. http://fmprc.gov.cn.

Tian, X. (2015b, September 17). *Promote exchanges and mutual learning for common development*. During the Governance of China and Africa Relations Symposium, Johannesburg, South Africa. Ministry of Foreign Affairs of the People's Republic of China website. http://fmprc.gov.cn.

Tian, X. (2015c, July 20). *Seize Development Opportunities and Achieve Win-Win Results*. Johannesburg, South Africa. Ministry of Foreign Affairs of the People's Republic of China website. http://fmprc.gov.cn.

Tian, X. (2017, March 23). *Speech by Ambassador Tian Xuejun at his farewell luncheon*. Ministry of Foreign Affairs of the People's Republic of China website. http://fmprc.gov.cn

Tuck, E., & Yang, K. W. (2012). Decolonization is not a metaphor. *Decolonization: Indigeneity, education & society, 1*(1).

Van de Walle, N. (2001). *African economies and the politics of permanent crisis, 1979–1999*. Cambridge University Press,.

Van Peter, H. (2001). The rise of the brand state: "The postmodern politics of image and reputation." *Foreign Affairs, 8*(5), 2–6.

Wang, Y. (2008). Public diplomacy and the rise of Chinese soft power. *The Annals of the American Academy of Political and Social Science, 616*, 257–273. *JSTOR*. www.jstor.org/stable/25098003.

Wang, Y. (2015a, November 26). *Build on past achievements and open up the future of all-round development of China-Africa friendship and cooperation*. During the 15th Lanting Forum. Beijing, China. Ministry of Foreign Affairs of the People's Republic of China website. http://fmprc.gov.cn.

Wang, Y. (2015b, July 23). *Remarks during the book launch of A Monument to China-Africa Friendship: First-hand Account of the Building of Tazara*. Ministry of Foreign Affairs of the People's Republic of China website. http://fmprc.gov.cn.

Wang, Y. (2015c, July 25). *A monument to China-Africa friendship: First-hand account of the building of Tazara*. Ministry of Foreign Affairs of the People's Republic of China website. http://fmprc.gov.cn

Wen, J. (2009, November 10) *Speech by premier at the opening ceremony of the 4th Ministerial conference of the forum on China-Africa Cooperation*. Ministry of Foreign Affairs of the People's Republic of China website. http://fmprc.gov.cn

Wuthnow, J. (2008, June). The concept of soft power in China's strategic discourse. *Issues and Studies, 44*(2), 1–28.

Xi, J. (2015a, April 22). *Carry forward the Bandung Spirit for win-win cooperation*. Asian-African Summit, Jakarta, Indonesia. Ministry of Foreign Affairs of the People's Republic of China website. http://fmprc.gov.cn.

Xi, J. (2015b, November, 30). *Let the flower of China-Zimbabwe friendship bloom with new Splendor*. Ministry of Foreign Affairs of the People's Republic of China website. http://fmprc.gov.cn

Xi, J. (2015c). *Open a New Era of China-Africa Win-Win Cooperation and Common Development* Johannesburg, South Africa. Ministry of Foreign Affairs of the People's Republic of China website. http://fmprc.gov.cn.

Xi, J. (2016, January 19). *Let China-Arab Friendship Surge Forward like the Nile*. Alahram, Cairo. Accessed online October 3, 2017.

Xi, J., & Yang J. (2016, August 2). *Congratulatory Message and Keynote speech to the opening ceremony of the coordinators' meeting on the implementation of the follow-up actions of the Johannesburg summit of the forum on China-Africa Cooperation.* Ministry of Foreign Affairs of the People's Republic of China website. http://fmprc.gov.cn

Xin, S. (2015, March 25). *Remarks during the reception marking the 25th anniversary of China-Namibia Diplomatic Relations.* Windhoek, Namibia. Ministry of Foreign Affairs of the People's Republic of China website. http://fmprc.gov.cn.

Zhai, J. (2012, July 19). *Broad prospects for the new type of China-Africa strategic partnership.* During the Seventh Lanting Forum. Beijing, China. Ministry of Foreign Affairs of the People's Republic of China website. http://fmprc.gov.cn.

Zhao, Y. (2014, December 19). *Speech during the Launch of the Confucius Institute at Makerere University.* Ministry of Foreign Affairs of the People's Republic of China website. http://fmprc.gov.cn

Zuma, J. G. (2010, August 24). *Address before the South Africa-China Business Forum on the occasion of the state visit to the People's Republic of China.* Beijing, China. Accessed via the Department of International Relations and Cooperation Website. http://www.dirco.gov.za/docs/speeches/jzuma.html Accessed December 1, 2020.

Tara Mock is an Assistant Professor of Africana Studies in the Honors College at the University of Alabama. Her current research and teaching interests include Afro-Chinese relations, modern Africa, diaspora, visuality, cultural identity, and community formation. She is currently working on a book combining survey research, discourse analysis and ethnography with theories of diaspora, imagined community, and visuality to situate her investigation into conceptualizations of selfhood and other between African and Chinese people within an Africana Studies framework.

Chapter 4
The Unguaranteed Hegemony of China in Global South: A Reception Analysis of China Central Television in Africa

Yu Xiang

Abstract The growing presence of China in the global arena arouses discussions on its controversial developing pattern which is heavily promoted in the Global South through financial projects such as BRI. Along with the considerable investment, China has also been exporting a series of pragmatic discourses that constitute a new hegemony proposing Global South cooperation and disintegrating Western domination. The confrontation between China and the West escalated dramatically during the global outbreak of the Covid-19 pandemic in 2020. More than ever, the consent from developing world is strongly needed for the sustainability of China's globalization. This article aims to further the discussion on the substance and the formation of the new hegemony based on the case of China Central Television in Africa. Following the critical approach of cultural studies, this research deploys the analytic framework of Stuart Hall's encoding and decoding to unfold African students' polysemic readings of CCTV-Africa and to cast light on the mechanism of how consent for hegemony is manufactured, negotiated even disrupted.

Keywords Hegemony · China in Africa · China Central Television · Reception analysis · African audience

Abbreviations

BRI   Belt and Road Initiative
BRICS   Brazil, Russia, India, China and South Africa
CCTV   China Central Television
CGTN   China Global Television Network

Y. Xiang (✉)
Shanghai University School of Journalism and Communication, Shanghai, China
e-mail: yuxlovemayo@shu.edu.cn

4.1   Introduction

During the COVID-19 outbreak in 2020, the worldwide debate about China's global rise and the implications of its turbulent relationship with the United States intensified. China is not only the largest economy in the Global South now but also developed a series of outbound global economic strategies and ideologies under Xi Jinping's governance, such as the Belt and Road Initiative (BRI) and the concept of "community of common destiny for mankind" (*renlei mingyun gongtongti*), that are designed to profoundly impact the landscape of international cooperation. However, China's somewhat aggressive investments in diverse regions of the Global South, including Africa (see Mock's chapter in this volume) and Latin America (see Morales' and van den Bos' chapters in this volume), as well as China's increasingly hostile diplomatic exchanges with the core countries of the Global North raise questions on the future of its attempts to build an egalitarian world order (Jessop, 2021). Against this backdrop, China's friction with the United States starts to resemble the residual rivalry of the Cold War (Rachman, 2020). Indeed, China makes great efforts to establish a new hegemony that endorses a seemingly divergent approach for social development and international cooperation. Some root for such divergence (Zhao & Wu, 2020) while others disapprove it (Li, 2010; Tsai, 2007).

One of the most evident strategies to promote such a hegemonic discourse is through its expanding outbound media in the Global South (see Morales's and Mock's chapters in this volume for a similar argument). This research contributes to the discussion of China's media strategy abroad by studying the African audiences' receptions of China's Africa-focused media to explore how it perceives the semantic meaning of China's new hegemony.

The first section introduces the critical framework of this article and teases out the theoretical lineage from the cultural imperialism paradigm to global media studies with a salience on Stuart Hall's reception theory of encoding and decoding. The general discussion on the alternative hegemony of the Global South is further manifested in the following section with a focus on China's outbound media and, specifically, the glocalization of China Central Television (CCTV) in Africa. This chapter shows that the hegemonic discourse produced by CCTV-Africa[1] encourages the multilateral economic activities between China and African countries by following the dominant order of global capitalism instead of resisting it. Using in-depth interviews, this chapter examines the circulation of the pragmatic discourses promoted by CCTV-Africa amongst the African audiences. The final section shows that African students studying in China decode the messages of China-Africa cooperation variously leading to the unguaranteed success of China's new hegemony.

---

[1] The international department of China Central Television became an independent institution and is renamed as China Global Television Network (CGTN) at the end of 2016. Since the field research of this study is conducted in the summer of 2016, the name used here remains CCTV instead of CGTN.

4.2 Cultural Imperialism, Polysemic Decoding, and Global Contra Flow

Herbert Schiller defines cultural imperialism as "the sum of the processes by which a society is brought into the modern world system and how its dominating stratum is attracted, pressured, forced, and sometimes bribed into shaping social institutions to correspond to, or even promote, the values and structures of the dominating center of the system" (1976: 9). Schiller's critique (1970) is based on the then-global expansion of the American media industry which retained the hegemonic position in the global information flows. Particularly, the mass media contribute significantly to spreading western culture which forms and reinforces a dominant structure centering on the developed while marginalizing the underdeveloped (Sparks, 2007: 81–103). In the late 1970s, many scholars applied these theoretical frames to examine the prevailing mediatized American lifestyle all over the world in the 1970s (Boyd-Barrett, 1977; Mattelart, 1979; Tunstall, 1977). Culture in this research is conceptualized as "a whole way of life" (Williams, 1958: 325) that "permeated the whole social fabric" (Tomlinson, 1991: 8–9). Importantly, it is reckoned that there existed a specific type of culture—one concrete formality of modernity such as capitalism that engulfs all the other possibilities. The most criticized American culture is also the victim of this homogenization as "the failure to challenge commercial culture inside the USA meant that the outside world saw only a single 'American Culture'" (Schiller, 1970: 147).

The cultural imperialism paradigm that highlights the ideological power of culture stemms from a broadly Marxist framework of cultural hegemony which unveils the mechanism of the ruling groups' dominance achieved through the manufactured consent of the subordinates (Gramsci, 1971). The Gramscian definition of ideology is to some extent equated to the concept of "organic consent" based on which hegemony is constructed. In this sense, the substance of hegemony, as Gramsci himself points out, is an "ideological unity between the bottom and the top, between the 'simple' and the 'intellectual'" (1971: 328–329). Such a unity not only works for the exploitative structure of capitalism but can be also used to facilitate the "socialist struggle to transcend the capitalist phase of historical development" (Griffin, 2006: 87–88). The formation of the dominant ideology—the superstructure of culture—covers subjective realms of human society such as language, ideas, values, beliefs, stories, discourse, and so on (McGuigan & Moran, 2014, as cited in Fuchs, 2015: 12). Hence, the semiotic output of these activities is the production of "meanings" which circulate in a complex structure of mass communication defined by the "determinate moments" of encoding and decoding (Hall, 2006: 164).

Examining the surging Thatcherism in Britain in the late 1970s, Stuart Hall develops a model of encoding and decoding that "shift[s] attention away from an exclusive focus on the ideological and institutional determinants of media texts towards including a role for a possibly active, but hitherto 'disappearing', audience" (Livingstone, 2008: 3). According to Hall (2006: 165–166), encoded messages of media content can be "transported into practice or consciousness" if they are "meaningfully decoded." The process of decoding is further divided into three segments: (1) dominant or hegemonic code, (2) negotiated code, and (3) oppositional code (Alasuutari, 1999: 4). Case studies showed that "audiences are more active and critical, their responses more complex and reflective, and their cultural values more resistant to manipulation and 'invasion' that many critical media theorists have assumed" (Tomlinson, 2002: 50). Research on narrative transparency that explores how textual apparatus "allows audiences to project their indigenous values, beliefs, and rituals into imported media" (Olson, 1999: 5) further dismantles the cultural imperialism paradigm. For instance, such studies point out that "a cross-cultural understanding of the text may take place because the audience interprets a foreign text using their own cultural beliefs and values" (Chitnis et al., 2006: 133). In sum, polysemic decoding establishes an "open horizon" of hegemony which is conditioned by concrete practices "without guaranteed closures" (Hall, 1986: 43).

Beyond deconstructing the cultural imperialism paradigm from theoretical perspectives, the "broader retreat of leftist ideas and movements during the 1980s" contributed to the ending of the ideological rivalry between East and West (Sparks, 2007: 126). Resistance against the dominant information flows as seen in the New World Information and Communication Order (NWICO) movement of the Third World countries and supported by the Soviet Union in the late 1970s and the early 1980s gradually came to naught at the end of the Cold War (Buchanan, 2015). The following global neo-liberalization wave led to the popularized idea that in the developing "world society" the state will be "less and less a significant actor at all levels" (Beck, 2000: 4). As some scholars point out, the new "global consciousness" stimulated emerging "global culture" (Thussu, 2006: 61). In the 1990s, voices of the Global South challenged the dominant media flows and enriched the global culture, refiguring the power structure (Thussu, 2007: 12). Kavoori (2007: 44) defines these media contraflows as "the semantic and imaginative referents for the institutional, cultural and political matrix of a world framed by processes of global cultural power and local negotiation." Essentially, the local negotiating processes deconstruct the one-dimensional determinacy of hegemony from top to bottom or, as in the case of the global information flow, from North to South. Nevertheless, there exists a crucial difference in the natures of resistance in the NWICO movement and current contraflows regarding providing a different imagination about modernity.

Against this backdrop, some scholars see China as an exceptional entity based on its opposite stance against norms of the Global North (Shen, 2016; Zhao, 2015). China's disputable socialist heritage becomes a symbol of the opposition to Western homogenization (Zhao & Wu, 2020). In addition to the significant economic output of the worldwide infrastructure projects under the banner of BRI (Sparks, 2018), China demonstrates ambitions to create a new world order and its outbound media support these new economic and geopolitical agendas. For example, the *Media Go Global* project initiated and funded by the government achieved enormous international attention especially in the Global South (Thussu, Shi & de Burgh, 2018) with African countries being the main destinations for the outbound media (Zhang et al., 2016). The glocalization experiences of Africa-focused state media—from journalistic practices to content production—serve as a perfect case for studying China's media strategies as they epitomize the struggle encountered by China's new hegemonic discourses.

4.3   The Struggling Glocalization of China Central Television in Africa

The boosting economic power of China has been strengthening its impact in the developing world. Along with the considerable investment, the Chinese government has exported a series of pragmatic discourses, such as win–win and multilateral cooperation. These agendas become the core element of its outbound media which is going through dramatic internationalization driven by the *Media Go Global* project. As the most eminent national TV station in China, China Central Television (CCTV) is one of the main beneficiaries of the project with its English-language news channel, CCTV-News, becoming the focus of the expansion. Established in 1958, CCTV, originally named China Beijing TV, started its internationalization journey in the late 1980*s* and produced the first English-language program, *English News* which is the foundation for the channel CCTV-9 established in 2000 and renamed as CCTV-News in 2010 (Jirik, 2008). Motivated by the *Media Go Global* project, CCTV established two media hubs in the United States and Kenya in 2012 (Farhi, 2012; McKenzie, 2012). Unlike the Washington office, it is said that the media center in Nairobi—CCTV-Africa—is popular among local audiences (Zhang & Mwangi, 2016: 73–74). However, the internationalization of CCTV in Africa encounters many challenges which are mostly caused by its nature as a state media. On the one hand, it needs to survive the international media environment in Nairobi by producing professional news following Western standards with a distinctive reporting style that tells an appealing "African story" to the local expectations of its audiences. On the other hand, behind this "African story," there was a need to create a positive "Chinese story" that satisfies the Chinese government. Such divergent, sometimes even contradictory, objectives lead to the seemingly turbid status quo of China's media in Africa.

From the perspective of journalistic practices, the friction between Chinese journalism and the westernized principles of African media in Kenya is one of the prominent difficulties faced by the local journalists working for China's media. To earn a global reputation, CCTV-Africa "made a point of recruiting prominent and highly competent African anchors and reporters" (Rønning, 2016: 71). It is equipped with a professional editorial team of nearly 100 young members and nearly half of the local African (mostly Kenyan) staff (Si, 2014: 10). As Lefkowitz's ethnographic study shows, some local staff feel that CCTV-Africa, as a state-run media outlet, is prone to censorship and its internal policies often contradict rules of journalistic professionalism (Lefkowitz, 2017). One of Lefkowitz's interviewees testifies that though the job was advertised as producing "African news for African people" the reality was different (Lefkowitz, 2017: 12). Such a situation is not exclusive in Africa. A few international journalists who worked at CCTV headquarter also confirmed that they were clearly instructed to emphasize China's interests in their reporting, use positive terms and avoid topics considered controversial by China (York, 2013). Chinese producers acknowledge such journalists' complaints, admitting that "there are subjects that generally aren't touched, such as criticism of local Chinese investments" (Rhodes, 2012). These controversial practices make many media professionals suspicious of the localization of China's media. As an Ethiopian television producer puts it, "if they don't provide these freedoms to their own citizens, why should they behave differently elsewhere" (Jacobs, 2012).

To obscure the state media bias and further highlight the international perspective in its news products, CCTV revamped its and changed its name to China Global Television Network (CGTN) at the end of 2016. The new slogan—"See the Difference"—encourages "a better understanding of international events" by "bridging continents and bringing a more balanced view to global news reporting" (Li & Wu, 2018: 42). Despite the change in its image, problems remain intact for CGTN. As a crucial part of China's new public diplomacy project, the political mission of the state media is, first and foremost, to speak for China. At the inauguration of CGTN, Xi Jinping urged journalists to "tell stories about China well and spread China's voice well" and presenting China as "a builder of world peace, a contributor to global development, and an upholder of international order" (Zhang, 2016). Yet, at the same time, in trying to effectively disseminate Xi Jinping's messages, the state media has to fully integrate into a highly saturated and Western-dominated international news market. Varral's study on the international staff of CGTN demonstrates that the production team is bogged down by the vague objective to be a global media (2020). The empty directives like "internationalization" and the emphasis on "Chinese characteristics" leave many inexperienced journalists confused as to what kind of events are newsworthy, and the self-censorship to avoid "sensitive" issues fueled by extra cautiousness to risks leads to the constrained and shallow reporting. Indeed, it seems that "despite the investment and hype, the CGTN relaunch did little to resolve the internal structural issues that undermine CGTN's ability to be a truly pro-active and agenda-setting agency" (Varral, 2020: 14). As some observers summarize, the reputation problem of CCTV that causes its low profile among international audiences cannot be solved through rebranding only (Madrid-Morales, 2016).

Yet not all observers and media professionals are cautious of Chinese media. A Kenyan observer, for example, argues that CGTN is evolving into "a powerful voice, telling Africa's story through in-depth analysis, providing values insights, and positioning itself as a trusted news source among its viewers by offering balanced views on Africa's current affairs" (Owiro, 2017). The anchor of CCTV-Africa's flagship show *Talk Africa*, Beatrice Marshal, affirms the autonomy of the local staff, claiming that they are "100 percent in control of our editorial content" (Wan, 2015). For Marshall, CCTV-Africa's journalistic philosophy coincides with the constructive journalism presented by Yanqiu Zhang: "what we want to do is say 'this is the issue, this is the challenge, and this is how it's being solved' rather than getting people to argue" (Greenslade, 2015). Wekesa's analysis of *Talk Africa* shows that it does have a preference for positive economic news, and many of which focus on the good effects of China's involvement (2014). Gorfinkel and her colleagues conclude that "African audiences are not intended" and "occasionally programming appears to target primarily Chinese audiences" (2014: 83). Vivien Marsh's findings on *Africa Live* show that the positive framing is "consistent with a 'China rising' narrative" instead of "an 'Africa rising' narrative" (2016: 67). Xiang and Zhang (2020), examining the economic news of *Global Business (Africa)*, argue that the content aims at manufacturing a consensus between Chinese and African elites to embrace Chinese investment and to promote neoliberalist economic development. Overall, China's media in Africa is less critical and tends to concentrate on the good side of the story, and "what is obviously absent is the alternative discourse that China can offer to the world" (Zhang, 2013: 28).

As Xiang's works (2018a) on media dynamics between China and Africa shows, the mechanism of the multilateral interactions between semi-peripheral and peripheral countries reproduces a sub-imperialist structure within which the dominant positions of the elite classes of both parts are maintained. Similarly, Mathias Luce (2015) demonstrates that the in-between position of semi-peripheral countries allows them to "transfer surplus values to imperialist centers," while "appropriating weaker countries' surplus value." The pragmatic principles of China-Africa cooperation, which are based on the economic development of China conditionally depending on the central countries in the past four decades, are complying with, if not accelerating, the exploitative global system. The positive reporting of CCTV-Africa demonstrates the focus of the Chinese government on celebrating urbanization and commercialization. As the previous CCTV News programming director Zhuang Dianjun says, "China has become a very strong partner in Kenya, any of the flyovers you see in Nairobi Chinese are building, any of the layings of fiber that is being done, Chinese are doing it, together with Kenyans we need to continue with these partnerships" (Zhang, 2010). The new hegemonic discourse that China's Africa-focused media attempt to establish subjects to the homogenization of global culture as an inevitable result of the end of ideology (Bell, 2000).

However, the reality of China's media struggling to glocalize and achieve popularity in Africa reserves the discussion on the unguaranteed determinacy of hegemony. Despite the institutional expansion, the lack of semiotic significance amongst the African audiences leads to the oblivion of China's media. The meaningful decoding of the audiences as the determinant moment of effective communication is essential to unveiling the semantic mechanism of the unsuccessful circulation of China's new hegemony in Africa. Therefore, a reception analysis of CCTV-Africa with empirical evidence is of great necessity.

4.4 Method: Interviewing African Students in China

Xiang and Zhang's study shows that appearances of representatives of Chinese and African elites in CCTV-Africa are more salient than other speakers (2020). China's outbound media strategically target local elites, relying on them as opinion leaders in the societies that they represent (Li, 2013: 30). Elites are widely defined as governmental dignitaries and business leaders as well as youngsters with privileged education and backgrounds who potentially become decision-makers (Allison, 2013). In 2018, more than 60,000 African students studied or were studying in China (Makundi, 2020), and the numbers are expected to grow driven by encouraging policies (King, 2020). Compared to their peers back home, international students in China are becoming more familiar with Chinese media. A 2014 study shows that nearly half of participated international students' first exposure to Chinese media was CCTV and for 80% of them it was CCTV-News (Xiang & Liao, 2017: 28). Another study indicates that African students perceive CCTV-News positively, with 72% of them having a good impression of the reporting it offers (Xiang 2018b: 151).

To further explore the reception of China's Africa-focused media, this chapter deploys in-depth interviews and examines how African students in China understand messages produced by CCTV-Africa's economic news. This chapter's findings are based on fieldwork conducted in 2016. 90 African students studying at Chinese universities participated in a pilot survey conducted before the fieldwork. Figure 4.1 shows that results corroborate findings of the 2014 study (Xiang & Liao, 2017) with the majority of respondents having a positive or relatively positive impression of CCTV-Africa. However, the generalized description of "positive impression" determined in these surveys does not correlate well with their specific understandings of CCTV-Africa's agenda. The term "positive" constitutes polysemic meanings to the interviewees. For example, some believe in the critical nature of media. Therefore, their positive impression comes from CCTV-Africa's reports on controversial topics. For others, however, the long-standing Westernized stereotype of Africa contributes to the resentment of negative news about their countries. For them, a "positive" perception of CCTV-Africa equals the positive portrayal of Africa provided in its reportings. Therefore, to explore the nature of these perceptions, we must dig deeper into the specific contexts of the interviewees.

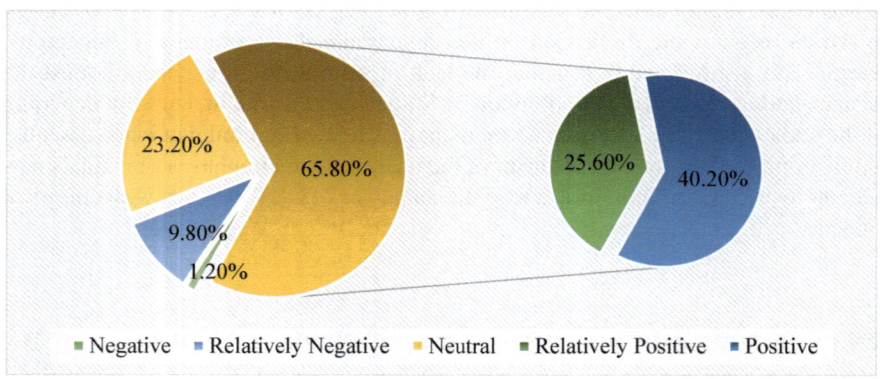

Fig. 4.1 The summary of general perceptions of 90 participants of CCTV-Africa

Table 4.1 The basic information of 90 respondents for pilot questionnaire

Gender		Diploma		Funding		Type of viewers	
Male	63.3%	Bachelor	3.3%	Chinese government	53.3%	Regular	51.1%
Female	36.7%	Master	41.1%	African government	4.4%	Non-regular	48.9%
		Doctorate	15.6%	Self-funded	42.2%		

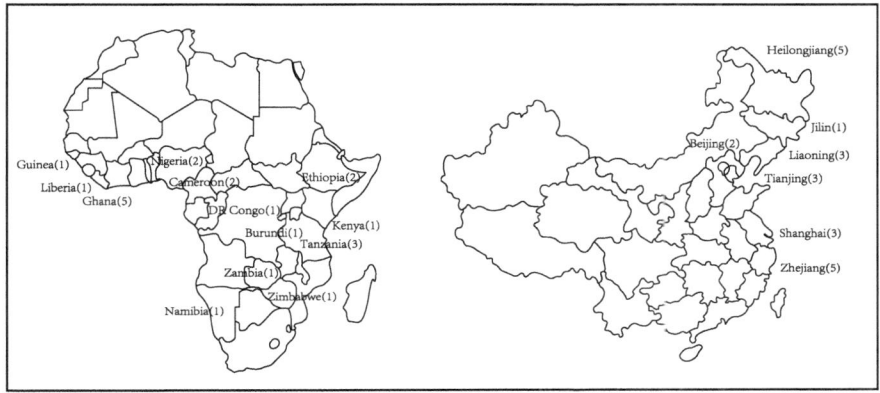

Fig. 4.2 The geographical distribution of 22 interviewees in Africa and China

The pilot survey also captures a general profile of African students, including their basic demographic information, educational backgrounds, funding sources, and watching habits (Table 4.1). Based on these profiles, we selected 37 participants[2] for in-depth interviews. This chapter only uses 22 interviews to build the argument (the reason is explained in the following paragraph). These 22 interviewees came from 13 different African countries in the Sub-Sahara region and, when the study was conducted, studied in seven different cities across China (see Fig. 4.2). As shown in Fig. 4.3, about 72.7% of the interviewees regarded themselves as either middle class or elite class in their local societies. The other specifics of these interviewees (Table 4.2) reflect the general profile of the pilot questionnaire except that none of them holding a negative impression of CCTV-Africa and the number of non-regular audiences is significantly higher than the regular. Due to the fact that the larger proportion of non-regular interviewees are less familiar with the news content, two news videos of the economic program *Global Business (Africa)* were selected to and show the interviewees during the interview (Table 4.3). The interview questions were designed to explore the audiences' reaction to the video news and their perception of China in Africa in general.

To systematically analyze the results of the interviews and unfold the African students' reception of CCTV-Africa, the researcher used the analytical framework of Hall's three decoding positions: dominant, negotiated, and oppositional. The premise

---

[2] All inteviewees consented to disclosing personal and demographic information in this study.

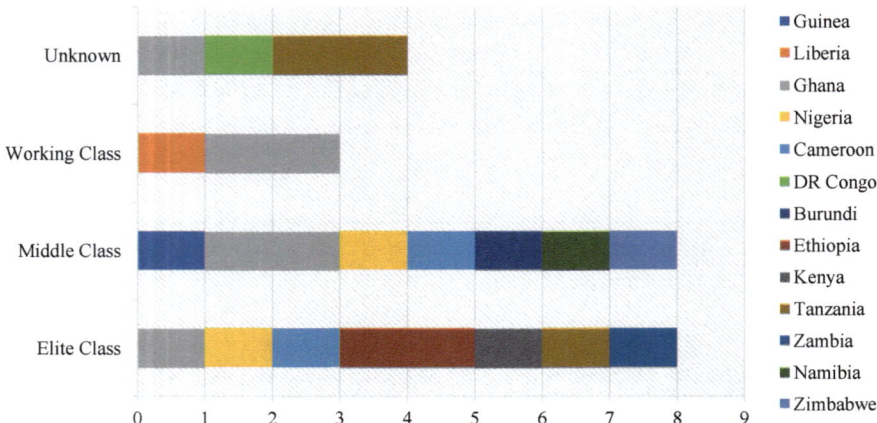

Fig. 4.3 Interviewees' self-defined class divisions

Table 4.2 The basic information of 22 interviewees

Gender		Diploma		Funding		Type of viewers		Impression of CCTV-Africa	
Male	4	Bachelor	2	Chinese government	9	Regular	9	Positive	6
								Relatively positive	9
Female	8	Master	9	African government	1	Non-Regular	3	Relatively negative	2
		Doctorate	1	Self-Funded	2			Neutral	5

of these three-fold decoding models is based on the determinant moments when encoding and decoding happen. However, the process of happening does not guarantee an absolute result. More than ever, the "connotative levels of signifiers" (Hall 2006: 169) in media content are not thoroughly interpreted by the audience. To further reveal the layered diversity of how the audience's perception is formed, this research also uses the typologies of ideologies summarized by Christian Fuchs in *Culture and Economy in the Age of Social Media* (2015: 87). The combination leads to the categories as displayed in Table 4.4. The category of being unconscious of the media's agenda points out the possibility of failed decoding, in which case the semantic significance vanishes as the audience is not consciously influenced by the media text. For this study, 15 of the 37 interviewees claimed that they had no explicit sense of the underlying purpose from the CCTV- Africa coverage. Their interviews were therefore not adopted to ensure the validity of CCTV-Africa's communication within the encoding and decoding framework. Based on the remaining 22 interviewees, the study summarizes five categories of reception, the details of which are discussed in detail in the next section.

Table 4.3 News titles of selected videos for interviewees

Country	News title		Country	News title	
Burundi	Rights Group Says Both Gov't and Opposition Involved in Killings	12 Month Crisis Causes Economic Contraction	Kenya	Athletics Agent Federico Rosa Charged for Doping	Police: Crime Drops Thanks to Tech Firms' Collaboration
Cameroon	Youth Pushing Use of Technology to Curve Opportunities	Heavy Rains Cause Flooding in Douala	Libera	First Online Platform to Order Food via the Internet	Charles Cooper—the Co-Founder of "CookShop"
DR Congo	Protesters Clash with Police: Likely Delay of November Vote	President Xi Meets Counterpart from the Republic of Congo	Namibia	Initiative Moves in to Save Dwindling Number of Cheetahs	Foreign Minister Wang Yi to Wrap Up Tour in Namibia
Ethiopia	Flash Floods Worsen Food Crisis in the Country	Global Firms Jostle for Space, 50,000 Jobs to be Created	Nigeria	Government to Use Technology to Create Jobs	Nigeria Signs Deals Worth $80 Billion With China
Ghana	Ghana Benefiting from A Joint Aviation Venture with China	Economic Concerns to Determine Vote in November Elections	Tanzania	Parliament Approves $2 bin for Railway and Roads Construction	"Rapid Buses" Introduced to Ease Traffic in Dar es Salaam
Guinea	China, Guinea to establish strategic partnership	President Welcomes Investment from China	Zambia	Copper Output: Mining Firms Set to Increase Production	Paying Respects to Chinese Relatives Who Dies in Zambia
Zimbabwe		Government Orders Disbursement of $5 min to Fired Workers		Anjin Investments Denies Smuggling Diamonds to China	

Table 4.4 Recognition and opinions of CCTV-Africa's agenda

	Agree	Partly agree/disagree	Disagree
Conscious	Dominant decoding	Negotiated decoding	Oppositional decoding
Vaguely conscious			
Unconscious	Ineffective diffusion (lack of determinant moments)		

4.5   Findings: Five Categorized Reception of CCTV-Africa

4.5.1   Conscious and Agree

Interviewees of this category are very supportive of the journalistic approach and the agenda of CCTV-Africa. They interpret the positive reporting style and the focus on Africa's modernization as the confirmation of the progress achieved by the local societies. For example, Judith from Tanzania is happy to see reports on the new infrastructure projects in his country. Similarly, Martina and Kosy are satisfied with the optimistic attitudes of CCTV-Africa as shown in the news on the emerging online shopping in Nigeria. Also, after watching the news on the innovative industry in Cameroon, Paul is glad to be informed about the social development of his country because in "most of the reports, Cameroon [is] not really showing the good side". Comparing CCTV with Western media, Henry from Liberia reckons that "for BBC, most events are political, but for CCTV they give the news on what's happening – somethings people should know or be informed about". Such diversity is understood by Boris from Burundi as the objective stance which is absent in Western media: "CCTV is good because it is not trying to take any part or any kind of position" (4th July 2016).

Interviewees acknowledge that CCTV-Africa is a state media and speaks on behalf of the Chinese government. For instance, Boris made it clear that "CCTV is Chinese" and "most of what CCTV-Africa shows is about business," which, in his opinion, reflects the strategy of the Chinese government to "encourage the Chinese investors to invest in Africa." Along a similar line, a Ghanian student, Wendy notes that "the Chinese government is trying to break into the Ghanaian market and wants to promote its cooperation with the Ghanaian government." Another student from Ghana, Yorgri, believes that the outcomes of the China-Ghana rapprochement depends on "the strings that might be attached to it" (25th May 2016). Benjamin, also from Ghana, bluntly argues that the investment from China is welcomed because his country "needs a boosted economy" (27th May 2016). Regarding the negative impact of China on African societies, interviewees tend to rationalize this controversy. Wendy, for example, argues that the cheap price is not the only characteristic of Chinese goods but rather a stereotypical prejudice. Similarly, Benjamin thinks that the environmental pollution caused by Chinese factories is the consequence that the local societies have to bear if they want to have economic development, whereas Yorgri considers that the unequal China-Africa trade is a natural phenomenon.

CCTV-Africa's positive coverage of economic development and China-Africa cooperation is perfectly in sync with interviewees' perceptions of China-Africa relations. In their opinion, China's new hegemony, as reflected in CCTV-Africa, is not a threat but rather an exemplary development model. They are convinced that Chinese investment and the China model can bring significant progress to their countries. For many, studiying in China is a manifestation of such belief. As Judith says, "the Chinese government and our country have a very good relationship in general and I support the cooperation." Further, she adds that she "learned a lot by just studying here in China," and Tanzania, her home country, "has a lot to learn from China as it is one of the developed countries in the world." The ideological power of semantic significance is therefore reinforced by the economic base of the interviewees' real-life experiences. For example, Benjamin summarizes his opinions, emphasizing that "actions speak louder than words." As he puts it, "when I was hungry, and you fed me, and this matters more than you just saying you love me." In a nutshell, interviewees of this group grip tightly on the dominant position to decode CCTV-Africa and support multilateral cooperation that underpins the new hegemony of China in Africa.

4.5.2 Conscious and Partly Agree

However, another group of interviewees who clearly comprehend CCTV-Africa's agenda does not fully accept it. African students in this category have varying understandings regarding the news style. Some, like Joe from Cameroon, are very fond of it stating that "CCTV-Africa goes deeper in the news while the western ones discuss the general matter only," or, like Mamudu from Zambia, believe that the positive reporting "can correct the false information about Africa." In contrast, a few interviewees criticize CCTV-Africa as a state media. Nmanka from Tanzania notes that "CCTV-Africa presents an ideology of giving more news about the governments' activities rather than an insight into the people's complaints to the government for the things they have done wrong." Despite the divergent opinions on the distinctiveness of CCTV-Africa's journalism, interviewees agree that its key goal is to celebrate China's growing economic involvement in Africa. As Mamudu accurately summarizes it, the message of CCTV-Africa is to encourage people to "come and invest."

Many of them believe that China-Africa cooperation is generally beneficial for Africa and, as Joe points out, gains local approval "because the changes are visible in [our] countries." However, at the same time, interviewees also acknowledge that China "has made a lot of money from that" (Mamudu) and is acting as "a businessman" who comes "to gain profit, to invest money" and is "always interested in profits." But not everyone benefits from such a profit-driven motivation. As a case in point, Mamudu claims that the scholarships provided by the Chinese government to Zambian students help to solidify the elite bond: "When your [family] is not [part of the government] you will not get the scholarship." Some interviewees did not answer questions about controversies related to China's presence in Africa but still firmly supported the promotion of the China model in their home countries. Johnny is impressed by China's pragmatic practices and considers such an approach to develop efficiency because, in his words, "everyone wants to survive." In sum, while many interviewees absorb and internalize CCTV-Africa's message on neoliberal development in Africa with the support of China's investment, others are critical of the narratives of China-Africa reciprocal partnership, pointing out the inequality prevalent in the market economy and how this inequality is reflected in China-Africa trade. In this sense, the emerging rift between media discourses and the realities of China-Africa relations leaves room for critical thinking.

4.5.3   Conscious But Disagree

Unlike the previous two groups of interviewees who follow dominant or negotiated decodings, some African students demonstrate oppositional readings of the news content. They are skeptical of the way foreign media, including CCTV-Africa, reports Africa. Instead of recognizing CCTV as an alternative to the Western news hegemony, Leroy from Zimbabwe sees it as a very westernized media and with a reporting style similar to other foreign news outlets. Mamadou from Guinea expresses his general antipathy towards media, claiming that everything media say is "just bullshit." In his opinion, media "usually focus on the negative African news and how to try to help us but not doing it." Mamadou believes that CCTV-Africa is sending the message of China proposing to help African countries, like many other news sources. According to Vanessa, the less intrusive approach of CCTV-Africa in the reports about the unrests in DR Congo does not show the full picture because "the reality is much worse than what the news reported." And, the targeted audience of such messages is the local elite who "are the only ones who have access to [the channel]" (Vanessa).

Concerns and criticism regarding China-Africa cooperation fill these interviews. The growing presence of China in Africa arouses discussions on the nature of China's financial help. Mamadou demands: "What's going to be the payback? What are they expecting from us in the future after they help us?" Vanessa points out that the profits of China's investment and the multilateral cooperation are not available to everyone: "Even if it does bring money, the population would never get to see this money, only the elite class gets it." Moreover, interviewees heavily criticize the way China does business in Africa, as some of the interviewees believe that bribery became a new language of China-Africa cooperation. As Mamadou puts it, "the Chinese officials can pay the money to get the contracts and do whatever they want to do." Consequently, China is associated not only with visible development but also with cunningness and deception. Talking about an investigation on a diamond theft involving both the Zimbabwean government and a Chinese company, Leroy and his friend insisted that the Chinese government stole two hundred million dollars worth of diamonds, rejecting CCTV-Africa's neutral tone and specifically the term "diamond trade."

All these skeptical interviewees do not watch CCTV-Africa regularly. Importantly, they are critical of China's and other international powers' presence in Africa. The legacies of the anti-colonization movement find a voice in interviewees' discussions of foreign aid. In this context, China's economic involvement is reminiscent of a new round of scramble in Africa. As Mamadou puts it, "when we talk about [Chinese aid to Africa], we usually think about the past when the French came, and they said they will help but, at the end of the day, they exploited [the country] in various ways." He further adds: "I just hope China won't do the same thing." However, despite being cautious and skeptical of CCTV-Africa's agenda, these interviewees still consider the China model exemplary for their home countries and other countries of the Global South. Mamadou articulates these ideas as follows: "Decades ago China and Africa were at the same level, [now] China's development model is a good example [to follow]." In sum, Mamadou and many other students from Africa believe that the China Model is more feasible than the alleged egalitarianism advocated in the Western media. However, China's new hegemony in Africa featured in CCTV-Africa reminds them of the unequal relations, dependency, and thorny roads to independence and, subsequently, contributes to their opposing readings.

4.5.4   Vaguely Conscious and Agree

Some interviewees of this group do not fully understand the agenda that CCTV-Africa pushes. A few had a rather vague idea about it. For example, Sidon from Ethiopia says she felt that the news videos seemed to amplify the positive side of her country, but she does not relate such a reporting style to the Chinese government's economic policies in Africa. In comparison, Issac from Ghana grasps a part of the message saying that "the media will influence to push the agenda of the Chinese government on other countries [and] mostly CCTV talks about aid to Africa." However, Issac denies that the content of CCTV-Africa has an impact on his understanding of China-Africa relations: "I see differences from my environment, it has nothing to do with whether I watched the program or not." Both Issac and Sidon tend to appreciate the vibrant images of their countries depicted by CCTV-Africa and firmly believe that it is necessary for China's investment in Africa and to spread the China model.

The changes brought by China to Ethiopia impress Sidon and she does not doubt the good nature of China-Ethiopian friendship:

> Five years ago, we did not have any trains and metros. We did not have the African Union headquarters. That was a gift from China to Ethiopia. [The Chinese] built it for us. It is helping us to develop ourselves. [And] it's good.

She also highlights the difference of China's practices in Africa in comparison with those of traditional western donors and investors:

> America helps and aids us a lot, but I think it's more with money rather than building. On the other hand, [the Chinese] train our people. They teach us and build with us. This helps more than just the money give-aways.

Similarly, Issac is very supportive of the China model with its emphasis on political stability and economic development. In his opinion, the investment from and cooperation with China are "playing a vital role in Ghanaian economy." Overall, although interviewees in this group did not identify explicitly CCTV-Africa's agenda, they all strongly agree with the positive spirit of China-Africa cooperation expressed in its reports.

4.5.5 Vaguely Conscious and Partly Agree

Besides Sidon and Issac, several other interviewees also express uncertainty of CCTV's strategy in Africa. For example, Hillary, a Kenyan student, is aware that CCTV is a state-funded media and tends to protect China's interests in Africa. He puts it as simple as this: "You have to defend yourself, so you have to talk good about yourself." Another interviewee, Alan, also agrees that CCTV presents his home country as an investment-friendly place: "Before it was negative, people died [and] had nothing, but now you see, it's a good place to live." Ephrem from Ethiopia realizes the elites-oriented agenda and admits that reports on the economic development would please the local government. Each of these interviewees focuses on a specific trait in CCTV-Africa's character while ignoring others. However, this does not hinder their appreciation of the channel's content. Hillary believes that the positive reports "bring confidence" and deliver encouraging messages such as "we are safe" and "come to invest", whereas Alan is happy that China's media shows the best side of his motherland.

Nevertheless, some of these interviewees discover the discrepancy between the news and the reality. After watching the video about the Safe City project coordinated jointly by the Kenyan government and China's Huawei, Hillary comments that "the local security isn't getting any better." Alan points out that there are some topics that CCTV-Africa will never cover in detail, such as poaching in which the Chinese are suspected. Although Alan, Hillary, and Ephrem are generally optimistic about the future of China-Africa cooperation, they also see problems related to China's rise in the continent. The changes brought by China, in the words of Hillary, were "some good, some bad." The increasing influence of China in Africa raised concerns. Acknowledging the positive changes China brought to Ethiopia, Ephrem is yet worried that the way how China supports its interests by promoting itself via globalizing media such as CCTV-Africa will contribute to a new hegemony. Ephrem admits: "it is scary, not for now but for the future when it is fully developed."

4.6 Conclusion

As scholars point out for a long time, "the press always takes on the form and coloration of the social and political structures within which it operates" (Siebert et al., 1984: 1). The Chinese government's message of reshaping the global order is well hinted at in CCTV-Africa's reporting on China-Africa cooperation. This chapter shows that many African students in China are happy to see their home countries through the lenses of CCTV-Africa's journalists. Differentiated perceptions of African students in varied contexts prove the polysemy of the media text. However, this polysemy does not suggest that the text itself is agenda-free, because the message promotes "certain meanings, even one privileged meaning, and suppress others: these are the directive closure in the message" (Morley, 2005: 20). The privileged messages of CCTV-Africa—promoting the China Model and China-Africa economic cooperation—are wrapped in its positive or constructive reporting style. As a result, these messages have been largely absorbed well by the majority of the interviewees. Even the ones of oppositional decoding expressed their approval of the China Model. The active decoding of the audience is conditioned, if not determined, by "the primary structure of subject positions" (Morley, 2005: 57). As Althusser proposes, "ideology has always-already interpellated individuals as subjects" (2004: 700). As this study shows, interviewees' identities of international students in China determine their readings of CCTV-Africa's messages, which is exactly the objective of *China's Media Go Global* project. Nevertheless, it is not the intention of this study to underline China's new hegemony achieved through ideological apparatuses, such as CCTV-Africa, but rather it focuses on the alternativeness that exists in the polysemic reading.

Although their potentials to become elites and the scholarships provided by the Chinese government appear to structurally determine African students' endorsement of the CCTV- Africa's agenda, it is demonstrated in the findings that the consent for hegemony indicated in the preferred reading of CCTV-Africa remains open for negotiation even resistance. The conflicting discourses of CCTV-Africa due to the awkward position of China's media in Africa and the less rosy reality collapsed by the hegemonic discourse but experienced by the African students create room for alternative reading. On the one hand, as a China's state media, CCTV-Africa's attributions are imprinted in the news texts it produces. For instance, as the headline of news about Namibia—*Foreign minister Wang Yi to wrap up tour in Namibia*—exemplifies the subjective perspective is on China instead of African countries. Yet, to disguise its Chineseness and to be more international, CCTV-Africa features non-Asian faces from the presenters to the field reporters, which gives it a certain ambiguity in positioning. As the interviewee, Leroy, accurately points out, "if they want to express the Chinese opinion, the Westernized style is not helping." On the other hand, the friction between Chinese actors and African society left out of the CCTV news is a lived reality for African audiences. A few interviewees, like Mamadou, complained about the environmental pollution Chinese companies brought which contributes to the rising protests in the local societies. Additionally, as Fig. 4.3 shows, the African students were not consistent in their class status. Their subject position is a fluid state rather than a defined structure. In comparison with the over-determination of Althusser on the function of ideology in interpellating subjects, Laclau points out that "interpellations are not given and absolute but conditional and provisional" (Morley, 2005: 58). There is no guarantee on the necessary correspondence between being an African student in China and supporting the hegemony of China in Africa. When watching CCTV-Africa news, they are likely to find the possibility of disrupting the encoded closure.

The disruption tends to grow significantly in the recent outbreak of the global pandemic. African students in China are faced with difficulties that challenge the proposed China-Africa cooperation. Strict border controls, for example, have caused a decline in the number of Africa students (The Economist, 2021). And more devastating than the failure to travel was the discrimination they faced in China during the epidemic (Vincent 2020). The misalignment between real-life encounters and the official discourse of reciprocity leaves African students with an alternative understanding of China in the real world outside of CCTV-Africa. The same scenario is observed in other activities of China's educational or cultural engagement with Africans (see chapter by Zhang in this volume). However, despite being chastised by the West for being responsible for the pandemic, China not only secured its hegemony but strengthened it through sophisticated diplomatic strategies (Case, 2020). China developed a vaccine and launched it in many countries of the Global South (McCarthy, 2021). Combined with the questioning of the United States over the source of Covid-19, China's international influence has grown considerably though not necessarily positive (Gill, 2020: 102–103). Backed by vaccines and financial aid, the China Model has been further diffused in the Global South (Jacob, 2020: 382). The essence of China's development model, according to the observation of Stuart Hall, is another variant of neo-liberalism (2011: 708). The global crisis of Covid-19, rather than bringing to light the coercion of China's new hegemony at the ideological and material level, exposes the precarity of the alternative imagination of the global power structure. Instead of terminating the cultural imperialism paradigm in the 1970s, the global contra flow once again brings back the previous critique of inequality with layered complexes of regional dominances. Although the findings of this research confirm the existence of alternative thoughts, the real question that how such alternativeness can be transformed into the empowerment of the subordinates that leads to a structural change remains unanswered. The China model praised by the interviewees may be problematic, but, like the Chinese vaccine, it becomes the most practical option because, as one observer puts it, "at the end of the day developing countries don't have much choice" (Santamaria 2020). Nevertheless, the discussion shall continue as the "history is never closed but remains an open horizon towards the future" (Hall, 2011: 728).

References

Alasuutari, P. (1999). Introduction: Three phases of reception studies. In P. Alasuutari (Ed.), *Rethinking the media audience* (pp. 1–21). SAGE.

Allison, S. (2013, July 5). Fixing China's image in Africa, one student at a time. *The Guardian.* https://www.theguardian.com/world/2013/jul/31/china-africa-students-scholarship-programme.

Althusser, L. (2004). Ideology and ideological state apparatuses. In J. Rivkin & M. Ryan (Eds.), *Literary theory: An anthology* (2nd ed., pp. 693–702). Blackwell Publishing.

Appadurai, A. (1990). Disjuncture and difference in the global cultural economy. *Theory, Culture and Society, 7,* 295–310.

Beck, U. (2000). *What is globalization?* Polity Press.

Bell, D. (2000). *The end of ideology: On the exhaustion of political ideas in the fifties* (2nd ed.). Harvard University Press.

Boyd-Barrett, O. (1977). Media imperialism: Towards an international framework for the analysis of media systems. In J. Curran, M. Gurevitch, & J. Woollacott (Eds.), *Mass communication and society* (pp. 116–135). Edward Arnold.

Buchanan, C. (2015). Revisiting the UNESCO debate on a new world information and communication order: Has the NWICO been achieved by other means? *Telematics and Informatics, 32*(2), 391–399.

Case, J. (2020, December 16). China's Covid-19 propaganda campaign. *CNA*. https://www.cna.org/news/InDepth/article?ID=68.

Chitnis, K., Thombre, A., Rogers, E., Singhal, A., & Sengupta, A. (2006). (Dis)similar readings: Indian and American audiences' interpretation of friends. *International Communication Gazette, 68*(2), 131–145.

Farhi, P. (2012, January 16). In D.C., China builds a news hub to help polish its global image. *The Washington Post*. https://www.washingtonpost.com/lifestyle/style/china-building-news-hub-in-dc/2012/01/12/gIQAh2Ps3P_story.html.

Fuchs, C. (2015). *Culture and economy in the age of social media*. Routledge.

Gill, B. (2020). China's global influence: Post-Covid prospects for soft power. *The Washington Quarterly, 43*(2), 97–115.

Gorfinkel, L., Joffe, S., Van Staden, C., & Wu, Y. (2014). CCTV's global outreach: Examining the audiences of China's 'new voice' on Africa. *Media International Australia, 151*, 81–88.

Gramsci, A. (1971). *Selections from the prison notebooks of Antonio Gramsci* (Q. Hoare and G. N. Smith, Trans. and Eds.). New York: International Publishers.

Greenslade, R. (2015, August 20). Chinese media in Africa illustrate difference from western media. *The Guardian*. https://www.theguardian.com/media/greenslade/2015/aug/20/chinese-media-in-africa-illustrate-difference-from-western-media.

Griffin, R. (2006). Ideology and culture. *Journal of Political Ideologies, 11*(1), 77–99.

Hall, S. (1986). The problem of ideology—Marxism without guarantees. *Journal of Communication Inquiry, 10*(2), 28–44.

Hall, S. (2006). Encoding/decoding. In M. Durham & D. Kellner (Eds.), *Media and cultural studies: Keyworks* (Revised, pp. 163–173). Blackwell.

Hall, S. (2011). The neo-liberal revolution. *Cultural Studies, 25*(6), 705–728.

Jacobs, A. (2012, August 16). Pursuing Soft Power, China puts stamp on Africa's News. *The New York Times*. https://www.nytimes.com/2012/08/17/world/africa/chinas-news-media-make-inroads-in-africa.html.

Jacob, J. T. (2020). "To Tell China's Story Well": China's international messaging during the Covid-19 pandemic. *China Report, 56*(3), 374–392.

Jessop, D. (2021, January 29). China, the US and a new world order. *Dominican Today*. https://dominicantoday.com/dr/opinion/2021/01/29/china-the-us-and-a-new-world-order/.

Jirik, J. C. (2008). *Making News in the People's Republic of China: The case of CCTV-9* (Ph.D. Dissertation, University of Texas at Austin).

Kavoori, A. P. (2007). Thinking through contra-flows: Perspectives from post-colonial and transitional cultural studies. In D. K. Thussu (Ed.), *Media on the move: Global flow and contra-flow* (pp. 49–64). Routledge.

King, K. (2020). China-Africa education cooperation: From FOCAC to Belt and Road. *ECNU Review of Education, 3*(2), 221–234.

Lefkowitz, M. (2017). *Chinese media, Kenya lives: An ethnographic inquiry into CCTV Africa's head offices* (Working Paper No. 2017/9). China-Africa Initiative, School of Advanced International Studies, John Hopkins University, Washington, DC.

Li, A., & Wu, M. (2018). "See the difference": What difference? The new missions of Chinese International Communication. *Westminster Papers in Communication and Culture, 13*(1), 41–47.

Li, X. (2010). *The rise of China and the capitalist world order* (Ed.). London and New York: Routledge.

Li, Z. (2013). *Duiwai Chuanbo zhong de "Erji Chuanbo" Celue – Yi Zhongyang Dianshitai Weili* (The two-step flow strategy of outward communication—A case study on China Centre Television). *International Communication, 2*, 30–33 (In Chinese).

Livingstone, S. (2008). *Relationships between media and audiences: Prospects for audience reception studies.* LSE Research Online. Retrieved April 15, 2021, from http://eprints.lse.as. uk/1005/.

Luce, M. (2015). Sub-imperialism, the highest stage of dependent capitalism. In P. Bond & A. Garcia (Eds.), *BRICS: An anti-capitalist critique* (pp. 27–44). Pluto Press.

Madrid-Morales, D. (2016, December 31). *China Global Television Network (CGTN): Old wine in new bottles?* Retrieved May 20, 2021, from http://danimadrid.net/blog/china_global_televi sion_network_cgtn_old_wine_new_bottles.html.

Makundi, H. (2020, January 23). I asked Tanzanians about studying in China: Here's what they said. *The Conversation.* https://theconversation.com/i-asked-tanzanians-about-studying-in-china-heres-what-they-said-129358.

Marsh, V. (2016). Mixed messages, partial pictures? Discourses under construction in CCTV's Africa Live compared with the BBC. *Chinese Journal of Communication, 9*(1), 56–70.

Mattelart, A. (1979). *Multinational corporations and the control of culture: The ideological apparatuses of imperialism.* The Harvest Press.

McCarthy, S. (2021, April 9). How China took an unlikely lead in the global supply of Covid-19 vaccines. *South China Morning Post.* https://www.scmp.com/news/china/science/article/312 8831/how-china-took-unlikely-lead-global-supply-covid-19-vaccines.

McGuigan, J., & Moran, M. (2014). Raymond Williams and sociology. *The Sociological Review, 62*(1), 167–188.

McKenzie, D. (2012, September 25). Chinese media make inroads into Africa. *CNN.* https://www. cnn.com/2012/09/05/business/china-africa-cctv-media/index.html.

Morley, D. (2005). *Television, audiences and cultural studies.* Routledge.

Nordenstreng, K., & Thussu, D. (2015). *Mapping BRICS media (Eds.).* London: Routledge.

Olson, S. R. (1999). *Hollywood planet: Global media and the comparative advantages of narrative transparency.* Lawrence Erlbaum.

Owiro, D. (2017, December 27). CGTN/CCTV's growth and influence in Africa. *People's Daily.* http://en.people.cn/n3/2017/1227/c90000-9309157.html.

Rachman, G. (2020, December 4). A new cold war: Trump, Xi and the escalating US-China confrontation. *Financial Times.* https://www.ft.com/content/7b809c6a-f733-46f5-a312-9152ae d28172.

Rhodes, T. (2012, May 7). China's media footprint in Kenya. *Committee to Protect Journalists.* https://cpj.org/2012/05/chinas-media-footprint-in-kenya/.

Rønning, H. (2016). How much Soft Power does China have in Africa? In X. Zhang, H. Wasserman, & W. Mano (Eds.), *China's media and soft power in Africa* (pp. 65–78). Palgrave Macmillan.

Santamaria, C. (2020, December 14). Vaccine diplomacy: China in the global South. *GZERO.* https://www.gzeromedia.com/vaccine-diplomacy-china-in-the-global-south.

Schiller, H. (1970). *Mass communication and American empire.* Augustus M. Kelly.

Schiller, H. (1976). *Communication and cultural domination.* M.E. Sharpe.

Shen, H. (2016). China and global internet governance: Toward an alternative analytical framework. *Chinese Journal of Communication, 9*(3), 304–324.

Si, S. (2014). *Expansion of international broadcasting: The growing global reach of China Central Television* (Working Paper). Reuters Institute for the Study of Journalism. University of Oxford.

Siebert, F., Peterson, T., & Schramm, W. (1984). *Four theories of the press.* University of Illinois Press.

Sparks, C. (2007). *Globalization, development and the mass media.* Sage.

Sparks, C. (2018). China's soft power from the BRICS to the BRI. *Global Media and China, 3*(2), 92–99.

Thussu, D. (2006). *International communication: Continuity and change.* Bloomsbury.

Thussu, D. (Ed.). (2007). *Media on the move: Global flow and contra-flow*. London and New York: Routledge.

Thussu, D. (2018). *A new global communication order for a multipolar world*. Online Publication. https://doi.org/10.1080/22041451.2018.1432988

Thussu, D., Shi, A., & De Burgh, H. (Eds.). (2018). *China's media go global*. New York: Routledge.

The Economist. (2021, January 30). *Covid-19 disrupts China's rise as a destination for foreign students*. https://www.economist.com/china/2021/01/30/covid-19-disrupts-chinas-rise-as-a-destination-for-foreign-students.

Tomlinson, J. (1991). *Cultural imperialism: A critical introduction* (J. S. Feng, Trans.). Shanghai: Shanghai People's Publishing House (In Chinese).

Tomlinson, J. (2002). *Cultural imperialism*. Continuum.

Tsai, K. S. (2007). *Capitalism without democracy: The private sector in contemporary China*. Cornell University Press.

Tunstall, J. (1977). *The media are American*. Constable.

Varral, M. (2020). *Behind the news: Inside China Global Television Network*. Lowy Institute.

Vincent, D. (2020, April 17). Africans in China: We face coronavirus discrimination. *BBC*. https://www.bbc.com/news/world-africa-52309414.

Wan, J. (2015, August 18). Propaganda or proper journalism? China's media expansion in Africa. *African Arguments*. https://africanarguments.org/2015/08/18/propaganda-or-proper-journalism-chinas-media-expansion-in-africa/.

Wasserman, H., & Madrid-Morales, D. (2018). How influential are Chinese media in Africa? An audience analysis in Kenya and South Africa. *International Journal of Communication, 12*, 2212–2231.

Wekesa, B. (2014). *An analysis of China Central Television's Talk Africa debate shows*. Paper presented at the international conference "China and Africa Media, Communications and Public Diplomacy," Beijing, 10–11 September.

Williams, R. (1958). *Culture and society, 1780–1950*. Columbia University Press.

Xiang, Y. (2018). China in Africa: Refiguring centre-periphery media dynamics. In D. K. Thussu, A. Shi, & H. de Burgh (Eds.), *China's media go global* (pp. 213–229). Routledge.

Xiang, Y. (2018). African students watching CCTV-Africa: A structural reception analysis of oppositional decoding. *Westminster Papers in Communication and Culture, 13*(1), 123–142.

Xiang, Y., & Liao, D. (2017). *Fazhan zhong Guojia Waixuan Meiti de Quanqiu Chuanbo Tanjiu* (Global communication of developing countries). *TV Research, 1*(326), 27–30 (In Chinese).

Xiang, Y., & Zhang, X. (2020). CCTV in Africa: Constructive approach to manufacturing consent. *Journal of African Media Studies, 12*(12), 171–188.

York, G. (2013, September 11). Why China is making a big play to control Africa's media. *The Globe and Mail*. https://www.theglobeandmail.com/news/world/media-agenda-china-buys-new srooms-influence-in-africa/article14269323/.

Zhang, J. (2016, December 31). President Xi urges new media outlet to "tell China stories well." *CCTV*. http://english.cctv.com/2016/12/31/ARTIdbvXHYpQnQ35nWBGttZg161231.shtml.

Zhang, N. (2010, undated). CCTV opens Africa office in Kenya. *CCTV*. http://english.cntv.cn/pro gram/newsupdate/20101126/103373.shtml (In Chinese).

Zhang, X. (2013). *How ready is China for a China-style world order? China's state media discourse under construction* (Working Paper Series). China Policy Institute. The University of Nottingham.

Zhang, X., Wasserman, H., & Mano, W. (Eds.). (2016). *China's media and soft power in Africa: Promotion and perceptions*. Palgrave Macmillan.

Zhang, Y., & Mwangi, J. M. (2016). A perception study on China's media engagement in Kenya: From media presence to power influence? *Chinese Journal of Communication, 9*(1), 71–80.

Zhao, Y. (2015). The BRICS formation in reshaping global communication: Possibilities and challenges. In K. Nordenstreng & D. K. Thussu (Eds.), *Mapping BRICS media* (pp. 66–86). Routledge.

Zhao, Y., & Wu, J. (2020). Understanding China's developmental path: Towards socialist rejuvenation? *Javnost—The Public, 27*(2), 97–111.

Yu Xiang is an assistant professor of media and communication at Shanghai University in Shanghai, China. She received her master's and doctoral degrees from the University of Westminster in London, UK. Her major research interests lie in the areas of international communication, audience research and critical media studies. Her publications include but are not limited to China in Africa: Refiguring Centre-Periphery Media Dynamics (In D. K. Thussu, A. Shi and H. de Burgh, eds., China's Media Go Global), African Students Watching CCTV-Africa: A Structural Reception Analysis of Oppositional Decoding (Westminster Paper in Communication and Culture) and CCTV in Africa: Constructive Approach to Manufacturing Consent (co-written with Xiaoxing Zhang, Journal of African Media Studies).

Chapter 5
China's Global Media in Latin America: Exploring the Impact and Perception in Mexico and Argentina

Pablo Sebastian Morales

Abstract This chapter explores the presence of China's global media in Latin America and its perceptions by local populations. It first discusses the phenomenon as part of a comprehensive public diplomacy strategy that seeks to improve its international image, shape perceptions around the globe, and ultimately create positive public sentiment to its advantage (soft power). It then describes how this strategy has been deployed in Latin America, paying particular attention to Spanish-speaking countries. As the success of this strategy depends on the perceptions of local audiences, the core of the chapter is dedicated to exploring the perceptions of Mexicans and Argentinians. The analysis is based on a series of focus groups conducted in September–October 2016 and discusses how, beyond any association to the Chinese government, cultural distance and differences in journalistic style are also important factors that may be hindering acceptance by audiences. The chapter finishes by arguing that the impact is and will be minimal in Latin America unless broadcasters address cultural and journalistic differences. It will also briefly discuss some of the other avenues that China seems to be taking, such as encouraging collaborations with local broadcasters and production companies.

Keywords Public diplomacy · Soft power · CGTN · China · Latin America

Abbreviations

CCP   Chinese Communist Party
CCTV   China Central Television
CGTN   China Global Television Network
CNC   China Xinhua News Network Corporation
CRI   China Radio International
PRC   People's Republic of China

P. S. Morales (✉)
London School of Economics and Political Science, London, UK
e-mail: P.S.Morales@lse.ac.uk

© The Author(s), under exclusive license to Springer Nature Singapore Pte Ltd. 2022
T. Tudoroiu and A. Kuteleva (eds.), *China in the Global South*,
https://doi.org/10.1007/978-981-19-1344-0_5

5.1 Introduction

For more than a decade, China has been strengthening its public diplomacy intending to improve its international image and create a soft power advantage. Originally coined to explain the attractiveness of the United States and the willingness of other countries to follow Washington's leadership, Joseph Nye (2004) defines soft power as the ability to persuade others to act in ways that are aligned to one's interests. The concept soon became popular among Chinese scholars and policymakers who recognised its utility in their efforts to improve China's international image. On the 17th National Congress of the CCP in 2007, even the then President of the PRC Hu Jintao stressed the need to enhance China's "cultural soft power" (CNS, 2007), which soon became the focus of Beijing's international communication strategy to counter the negative portrayal of the country by the foreign media—especially by the press and broadcasters from Europe and North America. Scholars from the mainland had long been analysing the "demonisation" of China (Li & Liu, 1996) in the foreign press as part of an effort seeking to undermine its rise by either vilifying the country as a military and economic threat both to its neighbours and the entire world (Wu, 2009) or even foretelling China's inevitable internal collapse (Duan, 2007). China's response was to accelerate its public diplomacy efforts and set up its own international media. In line with Nicholas Cull's (2008) view on international broadcasting as one of the main components of public diplomacy, Cheng and Wang (2011) recognised a direct correlation between international broadcasting, national image shaping, and strengthening China's soft power. For over a decade, scholars around the world have been discussing the scope of China's pursuit of soft power through public diplomacy (J. Wang, 2011), how its media are developing (Thussu et al., 2018), and how China struggles to convert the country's rich soft power resources into genuine international affection (Edney et al., 2020).

Since the early 2000s, China has been investing in a comprehensive global media strategy that is both multiplatform and multilingual. Traditional media such as newspapers (*People's Daily*, *Global Times*, *China Today*, etc.), television (CCTV, now rebranded as CGTN for its international channels), radio (CRI), and even news agencies (Xinhua, CNC) have expanded and strengthened its presence online. In recent years, their presence on social media platforms has increased not only on Chinese domestic platforms such as Weibo or WeChat but also on internationally popular social media networks such as Facebook, Twitter, and Instagram. By publishing and broadcasting in the most widely spoken languages across the world, the *multilingual* aspect reflects China's interest to reach audiences both in developed countries in the Global North as well as diverse regions of the Global South across Asia, Africa (see the chapters by Mock and Xiang in this volume), and Latin America.

In the case of Latin America, China's image has largely been influenced by reporting from mainstream Western media (Guo, 2016). Ospina Estupinan (2017) identifies EFE, Agence France Presse, and Associated Press as the main sources used by newspapers in five Latin American countries for China-related stories. To influence the way the country is perceived, Beijing first targeted the region with its own international media, from newspapers and news websites to radio stations and a television channel. In the last few years, China has diversified its strategy in multiple ways by organising China-Latin America media summits since 2016 (Xinhua, 2016), as well as inviting Latin American journalists to attend training courses in China (An, 2018) and signing cooperation agreements between Chinese and Latin American media companies (Empresa Brasil de Comunicação, 2019). Between 2019 and 2020, China has also strengthened its digital diplomacy in the region by increasing the interactions of its diplomatic network in the continent on social media platforms such as Twitter (Micolta, 2020).

Compared to other regions in the world, studies on China's soft power push in Latin America are scant (see Ellis, 2020; Peña González, 2015; Rodríguez & Leiva, 2013). While a few researchers have focused on how this strategy has been articulated through Spanish-language media (Madrid-Morales, 2015; Ye & Albornoz, 2018), the reception by audiences is still an underexplored area (see Morales, 2018). This study considers soft power as the ability to influence a foreign country's policies to one's advantage by non-coercive means. By examining China's own media presence in Latin America and the perceptions by audiences in Mexico and Argentina, this chapter argues that international media can hardly contribute to creating a soft power advantage without addressing issues of reception such as negative associations with governments, cultural distance, and differences in journalistic styles.

5.2   China's Global Media and Latin America

China's news outlets have targeted Latin America by broadcasting in Spanish and Portuguese for decades. Spanish is ranking only second to Chinese in the number of native speakers worldwide, thus it is no wonder that China's global media have prioritised the use of Spanish over Portuguese. This choice is justified by the fact that out of more than 483 million native speakers worldwide, almost 396 million live in Latin American countries (82%). Furthermore, with more than 41 million native speakers of Spanish, the United States has also become increasingly important venue in this strategy.

China's international media in Spanish includes both traditional and new media. Among the traditional print platforms, the magazine *China Today* is one of the most notable propaganda efforts and one of the earliest publications to target Spanish-speakers. Conceived as a window to China and its history, culture, traditions, economy, social progress, and problems, it was founded in 1952 by Soong Ching-Ling, one of the most powerful stateswomen of the Mao era who served then as the Vice-chairwoman of the Standing Committee of the National People's Congress and the chairwoman of the Chinese People's Relief Administration. *China Today* was first published in Spanish in January 1960 with the name of *China Reconstruye* (*China rebuilds*), which in 1990 was changed to *China Hoy* (*China Today*). The Mexican branch of the Latin American Subsidiary opened in 2004 as a distribution centre covering Mexico, Central and South America ('China Hoy México' n.d.).

The popularisation of the internet at the turn of the century opened up a new frontier for China's external communication in Latin America. As new dedicated platforms started to emerge such as the China Internet Information Centre (china.org.cn), the major traditional media platforms also started to migrate online. China's most prominent newspaper, *People's Daily*, launched its Spanish-language website as early as 2000—and in Portuguese in 2014. China Radio International and CCTV's Spanish channel also started to broadcast online.

5.2.1 China Radio International

Founded in 1941 as Radio Peking, it was renamed in 1983 as Radio Beijing and as China Radio International (CRI) ten years later. In more than 70 years, CRI's production has expanded to 61 languages, either by broadcasting on shortwave, FM or online. The Spanish service started broadcasting on shortwave in 1956 and in 1998 it opened its website, which arguably receives 150 thousand visits per month, primarily from Spain, Mexico, Argentina and the USA, among other countries (CRI, 2010). Besides having correspondent offices in Mexico City and Buenos Aires, in 2010 CRI started broadcasting live on Uniradio AM1470 from Tijuana, on the border between Mexico and California, to also target Spanish-speaking audiences in the USA.

CRI's target audience is composed of people from the "middle-higher group, young, diplomats and businesspeople from Spanish-speaking countries living in China" (ibid.). Despite the access restrictions to social media sites such as Facebook, Twitter, or YouTube within mainland China, CRI has put considerable effort into strengthening its presence on those platforms as a means to promoting its programmes and website (ibid.). Acknowledging the changing habits of its audiences, CRI has been undergoing a process of transformation into a multilingual and multifunctional broadcasting organisation by the name of China International Broadcasting Network (CIBN), which was formally established in 2011 (CRI, 2017). The goal is to maximise its global reach by expanding beyond radio broadcasts and strengthening its online presence with audio-visual material. Besides Spanish, CRI also broadcasts in Portuguese both via shortwave and re-broadcasts by local FM radios in Brazil. In fact, CRI's General Bureau in Latin America was established in 2011 in Rio de Janeiro.

5.2.2 CCTV/CGTN

China's Central Television started broadcasting in Spanish in 2004 first via a joint French-Spanish channel (Zhu, 2012). In 2007 CCTV-E was launched as a Spanish-only channel (CCTV, 2007). On the 31 December 2016, its name was changed to CGTN (China Global Television Network) following CCTV's rebranding of its international channels (M. Wang, 2016). The channel is currently known as CGTN Español, despite an announcement in 2018 that CCTV, CRI and CNR would merge and form a new international media organisation known as the Voice of China (Xinhua, 2018). Its Latin American regional offices are located in São Paulo, Brazil (Stenberg, 2015).

Besides news bulletins, CGTN Español also broadcasts a wide range of shows that often feature Spanish speakers living in China, including documentaries (*Así es China*), interviews (*Diálogo, Enfoque*), cultural magazine (Café de CGTN, Prisma), current affairs (*América Ahora*), cooking shows (*De China a tu Cocina*), travelling shows (*Diarios de viaje*), entertainment (*Brillando en Escena*), and a show about foreigners (*Extranjeros en China*). The popularity of telenovelas in Latin America has prompted CCTV/CGTN to include drama series (Silva-Ferrer, 2012). While in previous years, drama series were broadcast in Chinese with subtitles, recently it has opted to dub them in Latin American Spanish, following a similar trend of popular Korean and Turkish productions.

To expand its online presence, former CCTV Español opened accounts on mainstream social networks, albeit with little traction. After the rebranding as CTGN, it opened new accounts on the most popular social media platforms. By 17 December 2020, it has over 16.8 million followers on Facebook (@cgtnenespanol) and almost 600 thousand followers on Twitter since opening its new account (@cgtnenespanol) in August 2016. CGTN *en Español* broadcasts live on YouTube and its official account has more than 236 thousand subscribers and over 80 million views. On Instagram, it has over 91 thousand followers. While initially the content published on social media tended to be replicated across platforms, in the last few years there is evidence of a greater effort to adapt messages to the different platforms and their unique style, thus increasing audience attention and interaction.

In 2015, CCTV *en Español* included an online survey on its website. By 7 April 2017, it was still possible to participate, but only 132 people had taken part. Although the quality of the survey is dubious due to numerous mistakes, it is possible to point out some key facts (CCTV, n.d.): When asked about how participants heard about CCTV, 22.64% said it was "by chance", followed by "rebroadcasts by other channels" (13.21%). Most respondents (51.55%) had accessed the channel through its website, followed by cable TV (16.77%). An 85.47% said watching CCTV-E had improved the image they had about China. When asked about CCTV-E's presence on social media, 43.66% knew CCTV's Facebook account, followed by 30.99% that knew its YouTube channel. The two largest groups of viewers describe themselves as "professionals (physician, lawyer, teacher)" (33.88%) and "students" (13.22%). Besides the low number of respondents, the main issue with this survey is that it is not clear whether the respondents would classify as *sinophiles* or not, and to what extent their opinions would be biased positively towards China due to a previous interest in the country and its culture.

5.3 Methodology

To test the likelihood of CCTV being accepted by audiences in Latin America and having an impact in the region, a series of focus groups were conducted in Mexico and Argentina between September and November 2016, with participants being recruited from a total of seven universities in both countries: Colegio de México (Colmex), Universidad Nacional Autónoma de México (UNAM), Universidad Autónoma Metropolitana (UAM), Universidad de Congreso (UC), Universidad Torcuato di Tella (UTdT), Universidad de Belgrano (UB), and Universidad Nacional de Buenos Aires (UBA). The sessions started with a discussion about the participants' news consumption habits and their knowledge of international news organisations. In the second part, they were shown a total of eight excerpts selected from different programmes broadcast by CCTV-E in 2016, from which six were shown to all groups and two were country-specific. The participants were encouraged to make notes about their impressions regarding three aspects: presenters, style and content.

The compilation started with a video about a report published by the Chinese government about human rights issues in the United States. Because China itself is often targeted by the media due to human rights violations (Ruz, 2015), this excerpt was considered appropriate to test the participants' reaction. Two videos (i.e., second and fifth) were selected because, besides covering news from Latin America, they featured newsreaders from the region. One (published 10 April 2016) is led by the Mexican Jorge Octavio Fernández Montes and the other (published 17 April 2016) by the Peruvian Lourdes Fernández Esquivel. The third excerpt focuses on Africa and was selected to show how China's attention is not solely directed to news from the industrialised countries, but also to the Global South. The video (published 10 April 2016) reports on the Angolan Nadir Tati and her successful career as a fashion designer, thus portraying Africa in a positive light through what has been called a "Constructive Journalism" approach (Greenslade, 2015; Wekesa & Yangqiu, 2014). Two excerpts relate to China itself (the fourth and sixth): one (published 19 April 2016) is a report on reading habits in China and the other one (published 18 April 2016) was extracted from the programme *Puntos de Vista* (Points of view) and features a female host and two female guests—a Chinese and a Venezuelan- discussing the issue of demography and gender imbalance in China, and the concern over the so-called "leftover women". The country specific videos (seventh and eighth) were selected from the magazine-format programme *América Ahora*, which showcases reports from the American continent. Therefore, the videos selected were related to Mexico and Argentina respectively.

The video clips were followed by a discussion prompted by questions from the moderator. The analysis of emerging themes shows that an association with the Chinese government and other cultural differences are some of the main factors hindering acceptance by audiences.

5.4 Association to the Government

Compared to other international broadcasters, CCTV was perceived as being distinctively focused on China and Chinese news. Described by some participants as "auto-referential", this practice was also related to the use of Chinese sources even when reporting about other countries. Furthermore, the association with the Chinese government appeared as the detrimental factor that undermined the channel's credibility and weakened its efforts to attract viewers. In Mexico, Cristian (M3) expressed his dislike of CCTV since "all the information they quoted were studies inside China", which instilled mistrust about their reliability. He suggested he would rather trust reports using a variety of both Chinese and non-Chinese sources. Although this would help balance out any bias, Cristian was also dubious about information provided by government agencies in general. Similar opinions were echoed in other focus groups in Argentina, where Jimena and Javier (A2) expressed their mistrust of China's statistics agency. In Marcelo's (A4) opinion, the sources quoted by CCTV were unknown to viewers in Argentina, which would hardly inspire trust.

Participants in both Mexico and Argentina expressed mistrust towards news channels' objectivity regarding the country they were based in. For example, if a channel was reporting about the G20 Summit in Hangzhou (China) on 2–5 September 2016, some participants said they would rather trust an Argentinian correspondent than a TV channel with links to the Chinese government:

Nadia (A5)   […] the Chinese State does not instil a lot of confidence, in general. And regarding their policies, especially issues such as Human Rights and that, I would not trust a channel from the government […]. The Argentinian correspondent would report information that will be interesting to me. I am not interested in anything that has to do with South Africa, but it would be interesting for me [to know] what the Argentinians think, or about Brazil, or maybe the USA.

Similarly, some participants in Mexico expressed their trust in Mexican journalists, because arguably they would have no vested interests that could influence their reporting. Such was the opinion of Fernanda (M6), who elaborated on this opinion saying they probably "would not have any interest in presenting the news in a biased way, because they are not from the country, and it does not match either private or public interests of the Mexican foreign policy".

The assumption that correspondents from local media would pay more attention to how international news affects the country added an extra layer of complexity to this apparent preference. Martín (A4) suggested that he would trust more an Argentinian correspondent reporting from China because they would focus more on matters related to Argentina than maybe a journalist from another country would deem insignificant. In contrast, Mauricio (A4) argued that journalists from CCTV may be better prepared to cover international affairs and elaborated on his argument by saying:

Mauricio   [...] I think the Chinese channel would look at it from a different angle than an Argentinian one that is not used to reporting that kind of news. The news bulletins in Argentina, for instance TN (Todo Noticias), they have five or ten minutes of international news, and I am not exaggerating. And that news... are not meaningless, but they are not really that relevant. [They present international news in a segment such as] "Round around the world in 80 seconds", which is nonsense. [...]

María (A4)   When I mentioned that I watch international news on other channels is exactly because I see what you are talking about. There is a lack of...

Mauricio   ...of training, of interest [in international news] ...

María   ...[lack] of space for international news because they are not seen as important and therefore, I would go to foreign sources. [...]

Consequently, María's opinion was that even a Chinese channel would report news about China with a too strong focus on a local outlook; therefore, she would rather look for other sources than relying on either CCTV or an Argentinian correspondent. Some participants in Mexico expressed a similar concern regarding the lack of interest in international news by the local media. For example, Alejandro (M1) said that he would not trust Mexican media reporting on international news, "because they do not even have a section of their team that is dedicated to international issues; in other words, they actually copy reports from other [news] agencies".

Respondents also negatively related the association with the Chinese government to perceived tight control over the news media. Pre-conceived images of China and its censorship system appeared to influence the participants' first impressions of CCTV by undermining its credibility. Fernanda (M6) described China as a country where the information published by the media is highly biased, due to tight control by the government. In her understanding, this control extends to the internet by blocking access to foreign websites and search engines such as Google. She believed all these limitations, in turn, would weaken Chinese people's awareness of current affairs. Fátima (M6) added that even access to Western social media platforms such as Facebook was blocked. María (A4) also pointed out the censorship as the reason for her negative impression of China.

A final association with the Chinese government was related to the country's human rights record. Manuel (A4) considered that there were many important issues that CCTV should address such as "the violation of human rights or the situation that China is going through in the conflicts it may have with its neighbours than a cultural exhibition in Cuba". Regarding a report compiled by China about the human rights situation in the USA, Martín (A4) thought it was hypocritical of China to talk about this topic. Manuel did not question CCTV's right to talk about anything but criticised the fact of not addressing the same issue within China. In his opinion, this rendered CCTV unqualified to discuss Human Rights violations in other countries. The discussion concluded with most of the participants agreeing that reflecting on China's issues would help CCTV gain authority and make it more trustworthy in the eyes of viewers. This seems to demonstrate Joseph Nye's (2004: 107) view that "information that appears to be propaganda may not only be scorned but also may turn out to be counterproductive if it undermines a country's reputation for credibility."

5.5   Cultural Differences and Journalistic Style

The first cultural difference noticed by the participants was the presence of news-readers, presenters and reporters from China. As non-native speakers of Spanish, the fluency of the Chinese presenters was a matter of discussion among participants, with some describing their command of Spanish as "very bad" (Esteban, M5) or even "terrible" (Enrique, M5). Others pointed out that the problem was elocution or a lack of clarity when speaking, marked by the pronunciation and articulation (Germán, M7). The opinion of the participants ranged from "some words were difficult [to understand]" (Esteban, M5) to "[I] did not understand anything of what one of the girls that were there said" (Juan, A2). While university students would make the effort to grasp the essence of the discussion, Esteban pointed out that the general public would easily get distracted by the superficiality of a foreign accent and not pay attention to the content itself. This entailed the risk of losing their patience and deciding to watch a different channel. For example, while Manuel (A4) felt their way of talking was very boring, María (A4) admitted she would not hesitate to switch it over to another channel. To avoid this problem, some participants suggested Chinese presenters could speak Chinese and the translation could be provided with subtitles (Fátima, M6; María, A4). However, this led to another discussion about viewers being less inclined to read subtitles, particularly while watching news programmes. Another suggestion was to include more presenters that were native speakers (Josefina, A2).

CCTV-E's style failed to attract the attention of the participants. The word "boring" was first uttered by Antonio (M1) during the first focus group and echoed at later sessions both in Mexico and Argentina. Carlos (M3) linked this to CCTV's use of the traditional news bulletin format featuring an anchor reading the news, which was less appealing to younger audiences such as the focus group participants. In Damián's (M4) opinion, reading from a teleprompter proved that newsreaders strictly followed a predefined script, alluding to tight state control over the content. In contrast, other participants seemed to like the formality of both the presenters' outfits as well as the studio, which according to Luis and Leticia (A3), resembled a "spaceship".

CCTV-E's choice of the colour red and the design of its logo prompted some participants to draw comparisons with CNN. Estefanía (M5) bluntly described CCTV-E as a Chinese CNN, and Fernanda (M6) argued it was a visual strategy to borrow legitimacy by association, i.e., viewers may believe CNN's journalistic values and other features also apply to CCTV. Fernanda also noticed the similarity between the colours used for the visual design of the studio and those of the Chinese flag: red and yellow. However, after CCTV-E was rebranded as CGTN Español, the visual design also changed, with the red being abandoned in favour of different shades of blue.

5.6   CGTN's Future in Latin America

The future of CGTN in Latin America greatly depends on the degree of acceptance by audiences in the region. The most compelling finding that shows the level of difficulty faced by CGTN is that, despite it has been broadcasting for more than a decade, none of the participants had watched the Spanish-language channel and most were unaware of its existence. This is even more troubling when considering the participants' profile as university students of international relations and politics. Nevertheless, these findings are not unique and bear a certain degree of similarity to other regions. In her study in Kenya, Jacinta Mwende Maweu (2016) observed that most respondents were either not aware of the existence of CCTV or, if they were, they seemed not to be watching it. Wasserman and Madrid-Morales (2018) suggested that despite limited effect, "some students, both in Kenya and South Africa, were receptive toward some of the news values and journalistic norms that characterize Chinese news reporting in Africa" (2226). As such, the first key challenge for CGTN will be to increase its visibility, by expanding its distribution channels and making it accessible to more viewers across the region (Morales, 2018).

Although the brief exposure to CCTV's programmes during the focus groups seemed to generate some curiosity among participants, very few expressed positive opinions about its chances of success in the region. Andrés (M1) believed China was increasingly more present in Latin America and therefore CCTV could win viewers interested in China. Nancy (A5), a Peruvian student in Argentina, thought that CCTV's positive news approach with a "frivolous and uncontroversial way of looking at things" could attract some viewers dissatisfied with the constant flow of negative news on the local media. Similarly, Estefanía (M5) believed the topics could be attractive to certain audiences such as housewives but stressed the need to solve the language barrier issue. Esteban (M5), however, dismissed completely the idea that CCTV could become a source of news, saying "the way they read the news or speak the language" would make viewers find it too funny to take it seriously. His pessimistic opinion was shared by many participants across different groups. Daniel (M4) doubted CCTV could succeed in being accepted by audiences in Latin America even if modifications were put in place because the channel would be unable to remove influence from the government. He mentioned racism against Asians as being another barrier to its acceptance. In a similar vein, Héctor viewers would hardly accept being lectured by Chinese people. Other participants stressed the cultural and geographical distance would be major obstacles, saying the "news was not interesting" (Nadia, A5) and "everything was very schematic and kind of far" (Natalia, A5).

Being perceived as controlled by the government together with a rather negative pre-conceived image of China among participants, proved to be undermining the effort of making the country attractive to the eyes of viewers. This finding is in line with the idea that "being perceived as a government mouthpiece does not resonate with a global audience" (Geniets, 2013: 145), which seems to apply even more so when governments are perceived as authoritarian. Similarly, disregarding other factors such as cultural differences may undermine its acceptance by audiences. Beyond the packaging of the product, cultural proximity has other dimensions, and it also affects the viewer's perceptions at other levels, e.g., the way certain stories are framed and the way characters in those stories are portrayed may not correspond to what is standard practice in the culture where audiences are based. Thus, understanding how stories are read or de-codified by audiences in different cultural and developmental contexts can help these broadcasters tailor their productions in a way that preserves the original message, but that is relatable to viewers and their socio-economic context. Deciphering cultural differences can help fine-tune international broadcasting strategies in a way that the messages can be easily de-codified by the audiences. The challenge will be then to make global messages resonate with local audiences (Geniets, 2013). This does not equal feeding audiences ideologically easy-to-digest information, nor it means feeding audiences what they are supposed to like. It means navigating cultural differences, acknowledging them, and re-codifying messages to ensure a successful de-codification by the audiences. The ultimate goal of exerting soft power is to have an effect that is persuasive enough to shape policy in the long term. This depends on how messages are received and processed by audiences. Joseph Nye (2004: 111) warns about the risks of not paying attention to how messages are received:

> Preaching at foreigners is not the best way to convert them. Too often political leaders think that the problem is simply that others lack information, and that if they simply knew what we know, they would see things our way. But all information goes through cultural filters, and declaratory statements are rarely heard as intended. Telling is far less influential than actions and symbols that show as well as tell.

The latest developments in China's communication strategy in Latin America reveal a gradual movement towards an approach that is mindful of audiences by learning from local media. Besides organising media-summits and training local journalists, China Media Group (merger of CCTV, CNR and CRI) has signed cooperation agreements with broadcasters in Venezuela, Argentina and Brazil. In some cases, this has led to the co-production of TV programmes with local broadcasters. For example, CCTV/CGTN and the Venezuela-based international broadcaster Telesur collaborated in the production of *Prisma*, a monthly programme first broadcast in August 2016 and focused on cultural news and reports from both China and Latin America. In Argentina, China Media Group (CMG) and Argentina's public broadcaster TPA co-produced the series of documentaries *Sorprendente Argentina/Meili Agenting* (surprising Argentina) and *Sorprendente China/Meili Zhongguo* (Surprising China) and other TV programmes such as *China en una mano* (China in the palm of a hand) and *Sorprendente ArgenChina* (Xinhua, 2019). In Brazil, Grupo Bandeirantes signed an agreement with CCTV, later extended to CMG (Camoça & Araújo, 2021). Since 2019, BandNews has been broadcasting *Mundo China* (China World), a five to ten minute-long daily segment on China produced by CCTV and anchored by presenters from both broadcasters (de Sá, 2019). This novel approach has the potential of assisting Chinese broadcasters bridge the cultural gap with viewers in Latin America.

5.7 Discussion and Conclusion

China's global media strategy has created several channels of communication with audiences around the world. Aiming to counter narratives from both dominating western international news organisations and local media, China's determination to establish alternative flows of information contributes to the much-discussed shift towards a new cartography of global communication, i.e., "media flows and contra-flows form part of the wider struggle over information flows which define power relations in the global information economy" (Thussu, 2007: 27). As increasingly active actors in the global *mediascapes* (see Appadurai, 1996: 35), Chinese media offer image-centred, narrative-based, and ideologically charged accounts of China and the world that inevitably reproduce state interests and expand the latitude of global *ideoscapes*. Furthermore, even news production practices reflect the hegemonic ideology of the political apparatus. Even so, the findings show that the impact in Latin America remains limited due to major challenges at the level of access, in terms of both accessibility to the platform as well as a disjuncture between the encoding practices of the broadcaster and the decoding processes of audiences. As discussed in this chapter, perhaps the most important challenge is that many participants were unaware of the existence of CCTV/CGTN's Spanish-language channel. A short exposure to it proved helpful to identify a series of issues that may undermine CGTN's future in Latin America. It was perceived as autoreferential, i.e., not merely a news channel *from* China, but fundamentally *about* China. The participants' average impression was that CCTV-E's main task was to disseminate a particular vision of the country in line with PR activities of self-promotion, rather than striving to adhere to shared journalistic values. Newsreaders were seen as formal and constrained by a predefined script, which made viewers associate the channel with the Chinese government and subsequently doubt its credibility. Were it to go ahead, the channel's planned name-change to the Voice of China would further consolidate this image.

CGTN's future in Latin America depends on how effectively it adapts its approach to align its content and style to the audiences' preferences. A perceived cultural distance and the failure of some presenters to convey their message further demonstrated a disjuncture between the encoding processes of the broadcaster and the decoding processes of audiences, which constitutes an additional barrier to attract viewers. The place of CCTV/CGTN in the Latin American mediascape is largely dependent on its capacity to adapt to a distinct cultural environment. Even though technology and broadcasting practices may appear to be similar around the world, audio-visual products are shaped by the cultural context where they have been produced. For a message to have an 'effect', "it must first be appropriated as a meaningful discourse and be meaningfully decoded" (Hall, 2005: 109). Originally a product of the Chinese media system, CCTV/CGTN needs to understand its role at a transcultural level and how it fits within the media systems in Latin America and their regional and/or national variations. This is because, once messages are encoded, CCTV/CGTN is unable to prescribe how these will be decoded by viewers. In line with Stuart Hall's (2005) encoding–decoding theory, the data shows that audiences in Latin America decode messages and produce culturally sensitive readings, which can reproduce dominant-hegemonic, negotiated, or oppositional positions (as also seen with regards to African audiences in the previous chapter by Xiang). Thus, to reduce any degree of incompatibility at the level of media systems, transcultural media ought to adjust their output according to the political and societal structures that determine audiences' expectations of the role of the mass media in society. This can be an arduous process, especially when considering the complexities of the media systems in Latin America, which "are not static structures of power, but organic and dynamic bodies that change, integrate and mutate, both internally and externally, especially in relation to global phenomena as a whole" (Lugo-Ocando, 2008: 10). While some countries lean towards liberal models and are close to what Daniel Hallin and Paolo Mancini (2004) call *internal* or *external pluralism*—i.e., the plurality of voices and opinions at the level of media outlets or the level of the media system—, in others the media are still subject to greater control by the government (e.g., Cuba and Venezuela). Censorship and tight control are still prevalent in many countries, even when freedom of speech is enshrined in the Constitution (Lugo-Ocando, 2008: 3). Additionally, at an international level, "the USA still exercises a quasi-hegemonic presence in Latin America's media systems, although with different degrees of influence and power" (Lugo-Ocando, 2008: 10). Consequently, for any other international news channels seeking to enter the region, CCTV/CGTN needs to evaluate the media ecosystem within national borders, as well as assess regional and international flows of information.

China has successfully created multiple channels of communication that potentially can help Beijing re-frame issues of interest to it and respond to hegemonic narratives of Western media. However, this is no guarantee of soft power gains. Joseph Nye (2004) reminds us that the countries more likely to gain soft power are those "…whose dominant culture and ideas are closer to prevailing global norms (which now emphasize liberalism, pluralism, and autonomy); and whose credibility is enhanced by their domestic and international values and policies" (31). Thus, China's global media may become a resource of soft power only when viewers perceive their values reflected on the screen of CGTN. While the continent's cultural diversity may pose a challenge to effectively identify values that are shared both across Latin America and with China, the signature of cooperation agreements with local media organisations, together with the organisation of media summits and the invitation of local journalists to participate in training courses in China constitute a clear attempt to increase mutual understanding and narrow down the cultural gap between China and the region. In any case, since "soft-power resources often work indirectly by shaping the environment for policy and sometimes take years to produce the desired outcomes" (Nye, 2004: 99), future research is needed to assess the success of this new approach, which would ultimately also contribute to further test the effectiveness of government-led public diplomacy efforts seeking to create soft power.

References

An, X. (2018, May 22). *Zhong guoo guoji xinwen jiaoliu zhongxin Lamei fenzhongxin 2018 nian xiangmu zai Jing kaiban. China Today.* http://www.chinatoday.com.cn/zw2018/zgysj/201805/t20 180522_800130433.html

Appadurai, A. (1996). *Modernity at large: Cultural dimensions of globalization.* University of Minnesota Press.

Camoça, A., & Araújo, M. (2021). Desocidentalizando a imagem sobre a China: um olhar sobre o contra-fluxo midiático chinês no Brasil. *Intuslegere: historia, 15*(1), 186–204.

CCTV. (n.d.). *Encuesta 2015 CCTV en Español - Resultados.* http://app1.vote.cntv.cn/viewResult. jsp?voteId=14720.

CCTV. (2007, September 27). *Zhongyang dianshitai Xiyu, Fayu guoji pindao jiang yu shi yue yi ri kaibo.* http://news.cctv.com/science/20070927/105325.shtml

Cheng, M., & Wang, W. (2011). *Duiwai chuanbo ji qi xiaoguo yanjiu.* Peking University Press.

China Hoy México. (n.d.). https://www.chinahoy.mx/

CNS. (2007, October 15). Hu Jintao: Tuidong wenhua da fazhan da fanrong tigao ruanshili. *China News Service.* http://www.chinanews.com/cul/news/2007/10-15/1049126.shtml

CRI. (2010, March 10). *CRI en español.* http://espanol.cri.cn/742/2009/03/10/1s174183.htm

CRI. (2017, February 16). *History.* http://chinaplus.cri.cn/aboutus/aboutcri/62/20170216/391.html

Cull, N. J. (2008). Public diplomacy: Taxonomies and histories. *Annals of the American Academy of Political and Social Science, 616*(1), 31–54. https://doi.org/10.1177/0002716207311952

de Sá, N. (2019, November 12). O que imprensa mostra de Hong Kong está longe da verdade, diz executivo chinês. *Folha de São Paulo.* https://www1.folha.uol.com.br/mundo/2019/11/o-que-imp rensa-mostra-esta-longe-da-verdade-diz-executivo-chines.shtml

Duan, P. (2007). *Guojia xingxiang jiangou zhong de chuanbo celüe.* Communication University of China Press.

Empresa Brasil Comunicação. (2019, November 13). *EBC e China Media Group firmam acordo para troca de conteúdos Institucional - EBC.* https://www.ebc.com.br/institucional/sala-de-imp rensa/noticias/2019/11/ebc-e-china-media-group-firmam-acordo-para-troca-de-conteudos

Edney, K., Rosen, S., & Zhu, Y. (2020). Soft power with Chinese characteristics: China's campaign for hearts and minds. *Routledge.* https://doi.org/10.4324/9781315208671

Ellis, R. E. (2020). The evolution of Chinese soft power in the Americas. In K. Edney, S. Rosen, & Y. Zhu (Eds.), *Soft power with Chinese characteristics: China's campaign for hearts and minds* (pp. 171–187).

Geniets, A. (2013). The global news challenge: Market strategies of international broadcasting organizations in developing countries. *Routledge.* https://doi.org/10.4324/9780203082607

Greenslade, R. (2015, August 20). Chinese media in Africa illustrate difference from western media. *The Guardian.* https://www.theguardian.com/media/greenslade/2015/aug/20/chinese-media-in-africa-illustrate-difference-from-western-media

Guo, C. (2016). Zhongguo de guojia xingxiang goujian: Lamei de shijiao. *Lading Meizhou Yanjiu, 38*(5), 43–58. https://doi.org/10.20805/micromechatronics.42.1_93

Hall, S. (2005). Encoding/decoding. In *Culture, media, language: Working papers in cultural studies, 1972–79* (2nd ed., pp. 107–116). Routledge.

Hallin, D. C., & Mancini: (2004). *Comparing media systems three models of media and politics.* Cambridge University Press.

Li, X., & Liu, K. (1996). *Yaomohua Zhongguo de bei hou.* China Social Science Press.

Lugo-Ocando, J. (2008). An introduction to the maquilas of power: Media and political transition in Latin América. In J. Lugo-Ocando (Ed.), *The Media in Latin America* (pp. 16–27). Open University Press.

Madrid-Morales, D. (2015). China's international broadcasting and the Spanish speaking world. In Q. Luo (Ed.), *Global media worlds and China* (pp. 187–203). Communication University of China Press.

Maweu, J. M. (2016). Journalists' and public perceptions of the politics of China's soft power in Kenya under the "look east" foreign policy. In X. Zhang, H. Wasserman, & W. Mano (Eds.), *China's media and soft power in Africa: Promotion and perceptions* (pp. 123–134). Palgrave.

Micolta, M. C. (2020). *La comunicación de China con el público extranjero.* https://fundacionandresbello.org/es/la-comunicacion-de-china-con-el-publico-extranjero/

Morales, S. (2018). Could Chinese News Channels Have a Future in Latin America? *Wesminster Papers in Communication and Culture, 13*(1), 60–80. https://doi.org/10.16997/wpcc.276

Nye, J. (2004). *Soft power: The means to success in world politics.* Public Affairs.

Ospina Estupinan, J. D. (2017). The coverage of China in the Latin American Press: Media framing study. *Cogent Arts & Humanities, 4*(1), 1287319. https://doi.org/10.1080/23311983.2017.1287319

Peña González, M. A. (2015). El poder blando de China y sus expresiones en América Latina. *Jiexi Zhonguo. Análisis y Pensamiento Iberoamericano sobre China, 17*(3), 44–53. www.politica-china.org

Rodríguez, I., & Leiva, D. (2013). El soft power en la política exterior de China: consecuencias para América Latina. *Polis, 35.*

Ruz, C. (2015, October 21). Human rights: What is China accused of? *BBC News Magazine.* http://www.bbc.co.uk/news/magazine-34592336

Silva-Ferrer, M. (2012). Para verte mejor, América Latina. *Nueva Sociedad, 240,* 41–52. http://nuso.org/articulo/para-verte-mejor-america-latina-las-mutaciones-en-la-geopolitica-del-poder-y-el-escenario-comunicacional-globalizado-de-habla-hispana/

Stenberg, J. (2015). An Overseas Orthodoxy? Shifting towards Pro-PRC media in Chinese-speaking Brazil. In W. Sun & J. Sinclair (Eds.), *Media and communication in the Chinese diaspora: Rethinking transnationalism* (pp. 48–68). Routledge.

Thussu, D. K. (2007). *Media on the move: Global flow and contra-flow.* Routledge.

Thussu, D. K., de Burgh, H., & Shi, A. (2018). *China's media go global.* Routledge.

Wang, J. (2011). *Soft power in China: Public diplomacy through communication.* Palgrave.

Wang, M. (2016, December 30). CCTV to launch CGTN. *CGTN.* http://news.cgtn.com/news/3d4d6a4e3555544d/share_p.html

Wasserman, H., & Madrid-Morales, D. (2018). How influential are Chinese Media in Africa? An audience analysis in Kenya and South Africa. *International Journal of Communication, 12,* 2212–2231. https://ijoc.org/index.php/ijoc/article/view/7809/2355

Wekesa, B., & Yangqiu, Z. (2014). *Live, talk, faces: an analysis of CCTV's adaptation to the African media market.* Stellenbosch.

Wu, Y. (2009). *Zhongguo guojia xingxiang suzao he chuanbo.* Fudan University Press.

Xinhua. (2016, November 23). China, LatAm media should increase cooperation, says Cuban leading newspaper chief. *Global Times.* https://www.globaltimes.cn/content/1019718.shtml

Xinhua. (2018, March 21). *Zhonggong zhongyang yinfa 'shenhua dang he guojia jigou gaige fang'an'.* http://www.xinhuanet.com/2018-03/21/c_1122570517_3.htm

Xinhua. (2019, October 18). *Documentary looks at lives of Chinese in Argentina.* http://www.xinhuanet.com/english/2019-10/18/c_138482729.htm

Ye, P. & Albornoz, L. A. (2018). Chinese media 'going out' in Spanish speaking countries: The case of CGTN-Español. *Westminster Papers in Communication and Culture, 13*(1), 81–97. https://doi.org/10.16997/wpcc.277

Zhu, Y. (2012). *Two billion eyes: The story of China central television.* New Press.

Pablo Sebastian Morales is a Fellow in the Department of Media and Communications at LSE. After obtaining a master's degree at Zhejiang University, he worked as a journalist and translator for China Radio International and People's Daily Online in Beijing. He holds a PhD degree from the University of Westminster, UK. His research interests lie in the impact of globalisation on international media flows and journalistic cultures in the global South, with a particular focus on China and Latin America. His research has featured in Media, Culture and Society and Global Media and China, among other international journals.

Chapter 6
Kung Fu vs. Radio Calisthenics: The Confucius Institute and Chinese Culture Education in Madagascar

Mingyuan Zhang

Abstract The Confucius Institute (CI)—a worldwide educational project sponsored by the Chinese government aiming to promote Chinese language and culture—has established its regional headquarters in Madagascar since 2008. The spread of China's educational projects represents China's intensive engagement in Africa in the past two decades, as it is usually considered as a form of 'soft power.' This paper aims to bring anthropological insights into discourses related to 'soft power' where the concept of 'culture' is often used but rarely analyzed. Based on long-term ethnographic fieldwork, this paper critically examines the practices of teaching and learning Chinese language and culture on the ground. In Madagascar, CI classrooms provide much desired yet unsatisfying opportunities for Malagasy students. CI represents 'Chinese culture' as a timeless, bounded, and homogeneous entity by only emphasizing its 'traditional' elements. As a result, CI instructors often find their individual understandings of 'Chinese culture' incommensurable with the hegemonic concept promoted by CI. Such disjuncture benefits actors of knowledge production but disadvantages those of knowledge application. Malagasy students often find the knowledge they have gained from CI inadequate. As such, CI educational projects share with many other development projects the features of disconnectedness and discontinuity that characterize Africa's participation in the postcolonial world.

Keywords Culture · Incommensurability · The Confucius Institute · China-Africa · Madagascar

Abbreviations

CI   The Confucius Institute

M. Zhang (✉)
University of Oslo, Oslo, Norway
e-mail: mingyuan.zhang@medisin.uio.no

6.1 Introduction

Many Malagasy people are bilingual in Malagasy and French and many are also fluent in other languages such as English, Arabic, Comorian, and Italian, just to name a few. The multilingualism in Madagascar is partly due to the island's long history of encountering outsiders and hosting foreign powers. Various language interest clubs at universities are thriving and many students believe learning a new language is like opening a window to a new world, as one slogan on a poster says: *bâtissez votre avenir en apprenant des langues étrangères*—build your future by learning foreign languages. Like elsewhere, in Madagascar, understanding foreign languages is often perceived as a personal asset leading to more opportunities, broader visions, and, potentially, brighter futures. With China's growing engagement with Africa and the western Indian Ocean in the past two decades, Mandarin Chinese has started to attract more enthused Malagasy students and they are not shy to test out their Chinese vocabularies when encountering a Chinese person. Walking on the streets in Madagascar, I always hear strangers greeting me by *nihao*—'hello' in Mandarin Chinese. Although I have met many self-taught language prodigies during my fieldwork, it is hard to find people who can communicate in Chinese proficiently to provide translation services or to offer high-quality language classes. An obvious explanation is that Mandarin Chinese is very difficult to learn as a second language. Recognizing the tremendous enthusiasm from Malagasy learners, the Confucius Institute (CI) started to offer language classes in 2008. Within ten years, CI has established branches in almost all major cities in Madagascar. However, the outcomes of Chinese-language education hardly seem fruitful to the eyes of local communities and the Chinese educational institution itself. The enthusiasm of many Malagasy students has proven short-lived. Their improvement journey is usually blocked by an array of administrative and pedagogical problems that have rendered Chinese language education fragmented and, sometimes, incomprehensible.

The Confucius Institute (CI) is a worldwide educational project sponsored by the Chinese government agency named 'The Office of the Chinese Language Council International' (also known as, and hereafter referred to as, *Hanban*) under the supervision of the Ministry of Education of China. It aims to promote Chinese language and culture on the global stage. The promotion of Confucianism as a symbolic pillar of Chinese culture within and outside of China has contributed to "a new cultural nationalism" in China's accelerated march towards the embrace of "a new global economic order dependent upon cheap goods, cheap labor and new markets" (Jensen, 2012, 277). Following Mock's argument in this volume, Confucianism, as how it is used indiscriminately by CI, plays a central role in China's nation-branding processes in global competition. In China-Africa encounters, China's global educational ambitions "[aim] at matching the country's growing economic influence in Africa with greater ideological appeal" (Haugen, 2013, 316). This paper focuses on CI classes and cultural events to shed light on the educational context of Chinese-Malagasy encounters in northern Madagascar. On the one hand, activities carried out in the name of CI offer Malagasy students with opportunities to glimpse into Chinese society and culture. The classrooms of CI provide much-desired opportunities for students to engage with the world through China as a global actor. On the other hand, however, these opportunities are often unsatisfying because many instructors lack proper training in local languages, pedagogical methods, and cultural awareness to provide effective teaching in Madagascar. Further, CI represents 'Chinese culture' as a timeless, bounded, and homogeneous entity by only emphasizing its 'traditional' elements such as Kung Fu in cultural events. As a result, the CI instructors responsible for disseminating knowledge of 'Chinese culture' found their personal understandings of the concept incommensurable with the hegemonic production of CI. Such disjuncture benefits actors of hegemonic knowledge production but disadvantages those of knowledge application. As such, Malagasy students often find the knowledge they have gained from CI inadequate in understanding China and their everyday interactions with Chinese people. In this sense, CI projects represent the features of "discontinuity," "disconnectedness" and "exclusiveness" that characterize Africa's participation in the postcolonial world (Ferguson, 2006). By focusing on the experiences of CI instructors on the ground, this paper also highlights the heterogeneous composition of the Chinese communities working in Africa (Guccini & Zhang, 2021), and challenges the assumption that all Chinese workers affiliated with state-promoted programs are agents of the Chinese state pursuing a political agenda.

The research for this article is based on ethnographic fieldwork conducted in Madagascar over 16 months from 2015 to 2019. I applied anthropological research methods including participant observation that took many forms, both in improvisatory opportunities and in everyday life, such as living on the campus of a local university, working as a colleague of CI instructors teaching Chinese language, helping facilitate Chinese cultural gala shows, singing competitions, and dance rehearsals, as well as grocery shopping and cooking together with CI instructors and Malagasy students. I also conducted structured and semi-structured interviews with CI instructors, Malagasy students who had experiences learning Chinese, and school instructors and administrators. During these conversations, I mainly used Mandarin Chinese and Malagasy with my research participants. To maintain the anonymity of all the interlocutors and to minimize all possible identifying information, I do not provide the exact date when the conversation took place when I quote them in this paper. All people and university names are pseudonyms. For the same purpose, I have also slightly altered information related to the job responsibilities and personal background of my interlocutors when needed. In the following sections, I will first provide a theoretical review on how the concept of cultural hegemony and incommensurability can shed new lights on the global production, circulation, and application of Chinese culture in the context of the Confucius Institute. Then I will analyze the revival of Confucianism as the 'authentic' Chinese culture and discuss the influence of such revival over China's overseas educational projects exemplified by the Confucius Institute. Then I proceed to provide ethnographic details featuring the experiences of teaching and learning Chinese language and culture recounted by Chinese instructors and Malagasy students. In the conclusion, I will also briefly touch on the aftermath effects of the termination of collaboration between the Confucius Institute and the local university.

6.2 Culture, Incommensurability, and Confucianism

Many scholars have recognized the expansion of China's educational projects parallel to its economic engagement in Africa as an indication of the country's instrumental strategy to "win hearts and minds" by exerting 'soft power' on the continent (Jensen, 2012; Haugen, 2013, see also Xiang's analysis on the influence of Chinese media in Africa and Morales on the same topic in Latin America in this volume). Since Joseph Nye (1990) coined the term 'soft power' and defined it as the power to achieve a state's goal through the attractiveness of culture, political ideals, and policies rather than through coercion or payment, the concept has been widely used by international relation practitioners and scholars and 'culture' has become a default concept without being further analyzed. However, for anthropologists, 'culture' itself is a loaded concept, partly because the notions of "social units as neatly bounded, culturally homogeneous entities" (Handler, 2009, 631) have long been abandoned. Abu-Lughod (1991) warns against the incautious use of 'culture' since it is an essential tool for perpetuating differences and distinguishing 'self' and 'other.' As such, anthropologists pay special attention to how 'culture' is represented, circulated, and applied in global–local encounters by highlighting the fluidity, disjuncture, and power that the concept entails in such processes. Refusing to take the concept of 'culture' for granted, anthropologists can contribute to the macro-level analysis of international relations by further dissecting what 'culture' *means*, and more importantly, what 'culture' *does*, to different actors involved in global–local encounters, and thereafter, shed new lights on international relations manifested on the ground.

In the West, 'Chinese culture' is often associated with an essentialized, homogeneous, and univocal ethnic identity (Chow, 1998). Meanwhile, discussions on contemporary Chinese culture are often equated with Chinese political culture, or rather, its critics. As many anthropologists have cogently argued, the understanding of 'other' cultures is always constructed in tandem with an active yet implicit focus on one's own culture. In his influential work, Said defined Orientalism as the style of thought and the mode of discourse based upon "an ontological and epistemological distinction" made between the East and the West (Said, 1978, 2). By authorizing views about the East, the West "gained in strength and identity by setting itself off against the Orient as a sort of surrogate and… underground self." (Said, 1978, 3, cited in Zhang, 2021). For instance, as Handler argues, Benedict's work (1946) on Japanese culture is fundamentally an American interpretation of Japanese culture rather than a kind of objective truth (2009, 637). Similarly, in observing the operation of CI in the U.S., Hubbert (2019) points out that American students' expectations of Chinese culture greatly influence their learning experiences insofar as participating in 'authentic' experiential learning opportunities in China does not necessarily lead to a clear understanding of what 'Chinese culture' really entails. As this paper will further demonstrate, the 'real' essence of 'Chinese culture' remains elusive to not only American students but Chinese people alike.

Further, Lambek (1997, 2013) expands the scope of incommensurability beyond cross-cultural comparison by cogently arguing that incommensurability is not only a feature of the relationship *between* cultures but also *internal to* one particular 'culture,' particularly salient in analyzing the production, circulation, and application (or consumption) of knowledge in human societies. Studying the three disciplines— Islam, cosmology, and spirit possession—among Malagasy populations in Mayotte, Lambek argues that culture is inevitably composed of incommensurables and its vibrancy, complexity, and thickness is often a consequence of such incommensurability (1997, 143). Since incommensurables cannot be "conclusively mediated or fully absorbed into one another" (Lambek, 1997, 144), rather than taking culture as an umbrella concept for any element vaguely included in the 'complex whole' of meanings and practices, it is more important to pay attention to how cultural ideas and practices contribute to "rendering knowledge real, objective, particulate, authoritative and valuable" (Lambek, 1997, 134). In other words, it is important to understand not only what 'culture' *means*, but also what 'culture' *does*. Incommensurability internal to a culture is often observed in the discrepancies among hegemonic production of culture and pluralized notions of the same concept due to differences of subjectivity and power. In Gramsci's analysis, educational institutions play significant roles in the apparatus of the political and cultural hegemony of the ruling class to internalize domination (Bocock, 1986). For instance, in Thailand, the establishment of the Ministry of Culture and its promotion of 'Thai-ness' since the 1980s made it a site of contestation between conservative nationalist and progressive international perspectives on Thai national identity (Conners, 2005). Perhaps such incommensurability cannot be more saliently manifested in the ambiguous cultural boundaries amidst the adoption of multiculturalism as the core of 'Canadian culture' since the 1980s (see, for example, Thobani, 2007).

As such, not only must the meaning of 'Chinese culture' be carefully contextualized in cross-cultural comparisons; but the status of Confucianism within 'Chinese culture' must also be put into historical contexts. The revival of Confucianism in and outside of China is closely related to the hegemonic representation and the strategic use of 'culture' in China's state agenda. Confucianism permeated almost every aspect of life before it was greatly diminished during the Cultural Revolution (1966–1976) when radical Maoists considered it to be one of the feudal 'Four Olds' (*sijiu*) that needed to be eliminated (Billioud, 2007; Lam, 2008).[1] Since the 1980s, many observers of China have noted a return of Confucianism in the political and cultural domains. The subsequent economic reform signaled the start of a "long process of re-evaluating Confucianism," leading eventually to its reification as the "crystallization of Chinese national culture" (Billioud, 2007: 52–53). During the reform era, Chinese President Deng Xiaoping's regime aimed to "increase reliance on market mechanisms for the distribution of capital, resources and goods," and to open the country to "broader cultural and economic exchanges with the capitalist world" (Osburg, 2013: 4). Confucianism served several functions for Chinese

---

[1] The 'Four Olds' or *sijiu*, refer to "Old Customs, Old Culture, Old Habits, and Old Ideas"—a political propaganda discourse used during the Cultural Revolution, to include elements of Chinese culture that the Chinese Communist Party felt needed to be eradicated for the sake of modernity and development.

authorities in implementing reform policies: its "authoritarian" aspects supported the construction of a "socialist spiritual civilization;" its essentialization as the core of "traditional Chinese culture" contributed to the state promotion of social cohesion against the threat of "Westernization" (Meissner, 2006, cited in Billioud, 2007: 53); it was employed as "an instrumental rationality of futurist modernism and as a moral force to domesticate capitalism to contribute to the official constructions of Chinese modernity" (Ong, 1996: 70); and it replaced extreme nationalism and Marxist Leninism, filling an "ideology vacuum" of the country (Bell, 2006). Despite the hegemonic promotion of Confucianism, different regions of China construct their unique identities by claiming their own ties to 'authentic' and 'traditional' Chinese culture perceived to have been lost in China's rush toward Western-oriented modernization (Oakes, 2000). In this way, the Chinese society maintains its internal diversity while adhering to a national cultural ethos encapsulated by Confucianism.

Since 2000, as the study of 'Chinese classics' or Sinology (*guoxue*) gained popularity in public culture, Chinese 'traditional culture' (*chuantong wenhua*), exemplified by Confucianism, has been endowed with new meanings. The first decade of the twenty-first century saw the 're-entering' of Confucianism into China's public space. The ceremony to celebrate the birthday of Confucius was broadcast on the national television channel, and more Confucian Classics have been included in the syllabi of elementary and post-secondary classes (Lam, 2008). However, disputes on what is considered 'core Confucianism' widely exist. To what extent Confucianism can still represent the fast-evolving contemporary 'Chinese culture' is also contested. According to research conducted among Chinese youth in Shanghai on their understandings of Confucianism, college students' interpretations of classic Confucianism are filtered through their own experiences based on their diverse social-economic backgrounds. Key Confucian values, such as filial piety and the emphasis on extended family networks, are considered differently among students from urban and rural backgrounds (Xing, 2017). In 2018, China's national television channel CCTV advertised and broadcast a 'cultural program' featuring celebrities singing ancient Chinese poetry and classic texts. A well-known American-Taiwanese songwriter performed a rap based on 'Three Character Classic' (*san zi jing*)—a Confucian canon aiming to advocate the principle and philosophy of children's education. The combination of Confucianism canon with pop culture was considered creative by some but profane by others. Hence, the rise of Confucianism in the twenty-first century can only be described as a *revival* instead of a *return* because the knowledge that people have gained about Confucianism through the channels mentioned above is sometimes considered superficial and fragmented (Xing, 2017). As I will further elaborate in this article, the CI instructors working in Madagascar rarely refer to Confucianism in their teaching. Besides, they also have their criticism against equating traditional cultural elements with the totalizing concept of 'Chinese culture.'

6.3 Becoming a Confucius Institute Instructor

The iconic figure of Confucius and his teachings have become symbols of 'authentic' Chinese tradition both within and outside of China, especially in the field of education. Since 2004, private Confucius-style schools have attracted many elite Chinese parents to enroll their children (Lam, 2008). At the same time, the Confucius Institute—officially announced as a non-profit public educational organization affiliated with the Ministry of Education of the People's Republic of China—was founded in 2004. According to the official website of *Hanban*, as of 2020, 545 Confucius Institutes and 1170 Confucius Classes have been established in 162 countries/regions around the world (39 countries in Asia, 61 in Africa, 187 in Europe, 142 in North and South America, and 20 in Oceania. A brief introduction to the Institute's history and mission found on its website emphasizes the non-profit educational nature of the organization and demonstrates that its goals are:

> …to suit the language-studying needs of people in different countries, to improve understandings of Chinese languages and culture, to develop amicable relationships and strengthen cooperation between China and other foreign countries, to promote the development of multiculturalism, and to construct a harmonious world.

China, among many other countries, supports the international spread of its official language and culture by sponsoring educational institutions and programs. CI is often compared with Germany's Goethe Institute and Spain's Cervantes Institute, for example, as all three educational institutions are named after iconic cultural figures of the countries they represent. It might also be considered alongside *Alliance Française*, British Council and the American Peace Corps, all of which share the Confucius Institute's goals of promoting language education and cross-cultural communication. However, CI is often harshly criticized by Western scholars (see, for example, Sahlins, 2015). Based on research in North American and European contexts, scholars have problematized the Chinese government's political and ideological engineering of the educational institute, drawing attention to issues related to academic freedom. CI is particularly criticized for its selective use of teaching materials and deliberate avoidance of politically controversial topics (Hubbert, 2014; Sahlins, 2015). In the CI programs in Madagascar, however, conversations in and outside of the classes rarely touch on controversial political topics. In fact, communications between Chinese language instructors and Malagasy communities are limited due to an array of factors related to living and transportation arrangements, language barriers, institutional regulations, and personal lifestyle choices, a point I will return to in the following sections. Another critique levelled against CI is that, unlike its European counterparts, it usually seeks to graft its programs with a local educational institution (e.g. primary school, high school, vocational school, community college, or university), offering generous funding packages as an incentive. Since 2008, all CI programs and activities in Madagascar have been carried out by two Chinese universities and almost all instructors were selected from newly graduated students from these two universities. Both two Chinese universities work in collaboration with several Malagasy educational institutions, and they recruit instructors and develop programs independently from one another. In principle, only when there are not enough candidates from the two designated universities, can applicants from other Chinese universities be considered to work in Madagascar.

The personal journeys of CI instructors from China to Madagascar had not been easy. Among the nine Confucius Institute instructors with whom I interacted during my fieldwork, there were eight women and one man, all of whom were in their early to mid-twenties. They had all recently graduated from university with a bachelor's or master's degree. Their undergraduate and graduate majors varied from Human Resource Management to Russian Literature. They had all learned English as a second language throughout their studies in China, but none of them were fluent in French or Malagasy. Their working terms with CI varied from one to three years, mainly depending on personal preferences. Two were working at a primary school; four were teaching at a vocational school in a regional capital and living off-campus in a house arranged by the school administration; and the other three were living and working on the campus of a reginal university. Unlike American Peace Corps volunteers who in principle are encouraged to mingle with local communities where they are sent to practice the "optimism, can-do spirit, and selfless nature of the United States" (Strauss, 2008), CI instructors usually stay together with one another due to both personal preferences and institutional regulations. During their tenure, their main duty was to teach Mandarin Chinese to students under the teaching schedules of their local partnership institutions. Besides teaching, the instructors were also responsible for organizing Chinese cultural events, singing competitions, and preparing students for the Chinese Proficiency Test (HSK) if required by their regional headquarters or the Chinese embassy.

Instructor Ma was 22 years old and in her third year of working in Madagascar when I met her. I first encountered her when she was searching for Wi-Fi signals in her office while waiting for a school-designated driver to take her home. She and another instructor, Tang, were living in a three-bedroom house fenced by high walls of concrete bricks assigned to them by the local educational institution with which they were working. Her experience of becoming a CI instructor is largely shared by other instructors I met, including document application, 'psychological' evaluation, in-person interview, and intensive training. Applicants who demonstrate knowledge of Chinese folk dance, traditional Chinese painting, martial arts, Tai Ji, and paper-cutting art are usually given priority. In principle, all applicants should demonstrate knowledge in a foreign language such as English or French. However, due to the low number of applicants for positions located in Africa, the selection criteria are not always strictly followed. Ma described her recruitment experiences as follows:

> I first introduced myself to the examiners then they asked me to write some Chinese idiomatic expressions and to identify and correct grammar mistakes on the blackboard. Then I did a short mock-teaching session as the examiners pretended to be my foreign students. Then I sang a Chinese song at the talent show section. I remember that there were so many applicants choosing to sing or to practice Tai Ji. So, unless you are superb in singing, it will not give you much advantage. The young woman waiting in front of me brought a box of Chinese dumplings for the examiners to taste. Then I was asked to answer a question in English.

> The question I got was to describe the historical origin of a traditional Chinese festival — the Dragon Boat Festival (*duanwu jie*). They also asked about my personal motivations to teach Chinese in Madagascar, although I did not know much about the country at that time. (Personal Conversation with Ma)

Compared to the emphasis on knowledge of traditional Chinese culture defined by the Confucius Institute, instructors' knowledge about the culture and language of destination countries is not considered as important. Cai was a 23-year-old woman from northern China and she remembered her recruitment and training as follows:

> I did not know the French language at all before coming to Madagascar. I vaguely remember that there was a student from Cameroon who taught us a little bit of French, probably one session per week during a period of seven weeks. There was also someone from Madagascar who briefly talked about the baobab trees, lemurs, and Malagasy food. I do not think there were enough applicants interested in working in Africa, particularly in Madagascar, and that was why I was selected in the end. Had *Hanban* made knowledge of French a prerequisite for this job, they would have ended up finding few people for this position. By the end of the training process, we were only asked to submit a short essay to demonstrate our knowledge about Madagascar. (Personal conversation with Cai)

Instructors were usually motivated to work with CI by the desire to explore the world, expand their horizons, and take steps towards future education or career goals. All strongly believed that overseas experiences offered by CI would work to their advantage in their respective envisioned futures. As described in detail by Ma and Cai, to gain this opportunity for global travel, personal and professional development, CI instructors had to work through the selection process. They were aware of their affiliation with a Chinese government agency and they generally did not transgress CI regulations. Some instructors adopted a housebound, inactive lifestyle due to regulations prohibiting them from going out to discos and karaoke bars or developing romantic relationship with local people. They spent much of their spare time preparing for their graduate school applications or looking for future jobs. As a result, interactions with Malagasy students outside of the class were uncommon. For individual instructors, CI works as a double-edged sword in their lives: on the one hand, it offers hard-earned opportunities for young university graduates to learn about the world outside of China; on the other hand, the institution restricts what they can do and learn while being abroad. In this sense, the relationship between CI instructors and the institution for which they work is at times conflicted. Although CI as a state-sponsored educational institution is often considered as an agent of 'soft power' serving China's grand global strategies, it is clear that individuals affiliated with CI rarely see their jobs as opportunities to fulfill a state agenda. Instead, when CI instructors recounted their personal journeys to Madagascar, they highlighted their individual experiences and efforts in getting the employment opportunities motivated by individual goals for the future. However, the individual agency that CI instructors have is a kind of "encompassed agency" (Wardlow, 2006) because they are positioned as encompassed by the more powerful projects of others.

6.4 Teaching and Learning Chinese in Madagascar

The selection and training process of the institution directly influences the teaching practice and learning outcome of CI classrooms. As mentioned in the previous section, successful applicants of the Confucius Institute receive training prior to their postings outside of China. However, very little emphasis has been put on local languages and country-specific cultural awareness. While those most fluent in English or French are assigned to positions in Western countries, others go to work in less developed countries like Madagascar. The ability to communicate effectively can have significant impact on the relationship between CI instructors and Malagasy students. Having limited ability in English and virtually no knowledge of Malagasy or French, almost all CI instructors struggle to get their message across. Recognizing their limits, they sometimes seek help by hiring a French language tutor. Some attend *Alliance Française* during their stay. No instructors show much interest in learning the local dialect of the Malagasy language, as they feel that learning French would be more helpful for their future study or career.

Not surprisingly, the inadequate language competence of the instructors usually becomes the greatest hurdle in providing effective teaching. As a result, pedagogical methods used in CI language classes are somewhat monotonous, reminding people of the much-criticized rote-learning style pervasive in China. Class content often consists of little more than the teacher writing Chinese vocabulary on the blackboard with English or French translations, and students writing down notes and reading the words out loud after the instructor. Effective conversations between Chinese instructors and Malagasy students are mostly realized in English—the third or fourth language of many Malagasy students. One Chinese instructor had to bring a Malagasy graduate student who understood English and French along with her to help translate lessons in her class over several months. Not surprisingly too, then, many Malagasy students felt that they could not learn much Chinese language from the CI instructors and decided to skip or drop classes. During my fieldwork, only ten percent of registered students showed up for a final exam. One university student told me:

> We would definitely like to learn Chinese, but we do not understand anything in the classes. It is hard for us to follow the teachers. Also, their classes are boring. We spend most of the time taking notes and repeating after the instructors. There are no class activities like our English or French language classes. There is no 'atmosphere' (*ambiance*) in the class. It is hard to personally connect with our Chinese instructors too. So, after several classes, many of us do not want to continue anymore. (Conversation with Malagasy student A)

Besides communicative and pedagogical inadequacy, most Chinese instructors are young, inexperienced and have never lived outside of China alone. Their lack of cultural awareness about local social etiquette often leaves them unconscious of their behavior deemed rude in the eyes of local people. It is almost ironic that some Chinese instructors frequently talked about China as 'a country of courtesy' (*liyi zhibang*) according to textbook materials while behaving rudely themselves according to local standards. Some of them internalize the imagined hierarchy of the global world where

Madagascar is allegedly ranked far behind China in cultural and social advancement, feeling that they have been sent to the country to 'develop' its education from a superior vantage. What is more, instead of reflecting on their own imperfections in teaching, some CI instructors tend to blame the Malagasy institutions and students for their poor teaching outcomes. When I asked instructors what they thought of as the biggest challenge in their teaching, two instructors provided contradictory yet thought-provoking answers. Ma, who taught at an urban vocational school, argued that the mandatory nature of the classes she taught was the main cause of poor teaching outcomes:

> At my school, I think the biggest problem is the design of their general curriculum. All Chinese language classes are mandatory for students and many are forced to be in my class to learn Chinese. If students do not choose to learn Chinese voluntarily, they have no motivation. The classes on the university level are different because they are elective, which means students choose the Chinese classes because they are actually interested in learning the language, so they will be more motivated and more willing to put effort into memorizing and reviewing class content. Another problem is that there is no continuity in curriculum design. Students are changing every year, so are the instructors. There is just no cumulative effect. (Conversation with Ma)

Contradicting Ma's assumptions, Cai argued that elective classes at the university do not, in fact, adequately motivate Malagasy students to learn:

> I believe that the main problem at the university is that Chinese language classes are all scheduled as elective classes. There are no mandatory Chinese classes. That is why students do not take our classes seriously and always drop off during the term. Students take their French or English classes a lot more seriously because they are mandatory for their degree. I always feel that students do not really want to learn Chinese. They register and come to the classes in the beginning because they think 'Chinese is cool,' but they do not know how hard it is to learn it. It feels like we are providing Malagasy students 'educational aid' here. I personally do not mind helping the students, but it is frustrating for us if the students are not willing to learn. (Conversation with Cai)

When instructor Guo negotiated class schedules with the university administrators, there were many misunderstandings and he found the result unsatisfactory. He noted:

> I do not really care about learning the [Malagasy] culture and language here, and I do not want to communicate much outside of my classroom. I have already read a lot about the geography of this country and it should be enough. The curriculum at this school is always poorly organized because the university administrators never do their job properly. If we cannot reach an agreement with the university, the worst-case scenario would be to cease the cooperation and find another local institution to be affiliated with. It is not a big deal because there are so many institutions that want to work with CI. Anyhow, learning Chinese is already an irresistible trend in the world. Chinese is such a beautiful, musical, and sophisticated language! (Conversation with Guo)

There is indeed a lack of competent bilingual speakers of Malagasy and Mandarin Chinese in northern Madagascar, and many Chinese state-owned and private companies have difficulty finding interpreters. The communication barriers are usually mitigated by two strategies: some Chinese workers start picking up Malagasy after working in Madagascar for several months; or the Chinese companies hire Mandarin-French translators from China. When new Chinese companies set up their business projects in Madagascar, they often contact local CI instructors for recommendations of good interpreters. However, the language ability of the recommended candidates is rarely satisfactory for the companies. From this perspective, improving the teaching outcomes of the CI instructors will benefit both the Malagasy students who are eager to learn and the various Chinese companies working in the country in the long term.

Since CI mainly collaborates with local educational institutions, resources for learning the Chinese language are restricted to registered full-time students but not available to the public, especially adult learners who may be motivated to learn Mandarin Chinese for business purposes. A Malagasy employee of a Chinese company once complained to me that "Chinese people are 'selfish' because they do not want to teach us the Chinese language." After I told him that there were instructors at local schools to teach Mandarin, he questioned me: "yes, I know that. But only children at school can learn your language. What about us — older people who are not in school but want to learn the language to work with Chinese companies?" For many Malagasy people, the ability to speak a foreign language is one of the few ways for them to stay connected to the global world: being able to talk to Chinese people is the first step to getting involved in Chinese-led projects, to studying in China, or to making personal connections with Chinese people. In northern Madagascar—a region that has long seen a variety of foreign influences—many people take pride in being able to connect with foreigners. As China's influence in Madagascar grows, many Malagasy people are seeking to improve the ability to speak Chinese because they see it as a great potential for advancing their careers and for leading to a better life. Since CI regulations forbid instructors from offering private classes outside of their designated collaborating institutions, opportunities for adult learners to study Chinese are scarce.

6.5   Incommensurable Understanding of 'Chinese Culture'

It is not only in the classroom that CI instructors engage with Malagasy students. As noted earlier, they are also expected to organize public events such as festivals or singing competitions. What is included in and excluded from 'Chinese culture' manifested in these events reflects how the Chinese state constitutes hegemonic definition of the concept. In such situations, the hegemonic production and representation of 'Chinese culture' is at times incommensurable with the personal understandings and practices of the same concept by individual instructors. As I have described in previous sections of this paper, applicants to CI teaching positions need to demonstrate their individual 'talents' related to what is loosely categorized as 'traditional Chinese culture' such as Kung Fu, Tai Ji, paper-cutting, dumpling making, singing, and dancing. Such selecting criteria have created an effect that Chinese people who possess such 'traditional talents' are deemed more 'authentic' cultural subjects than those who do not. In this section, I offer an ethnographic account of how these 'talents' of the CI instructors were applied through the organization of a Chinese cultural festival in the regional capital and its implications on incommensurability as an internal feature of culture.

After almost one month of preparation, three instructors—Guo, Ma, and Tang—organized a 'Chinese Cultural Festival' in the name of CI. During the rehearsal period, Ma and Tang spent half of their class time teaching students to memorize the pronunciation of the lyrics of a few Chinese pop songs that they had chosen. They also selected two small groups of female students who were willing to learn traditional Chinese dance from videos saved on the instructors' laptops. Guo, meanwhile, gathered a group of male students and taught them Tai Ji according to a video that he randomly found from the Internet. Some Malagasy students participated in both dancing and singing performances. The event took the form of a gala show with seven performances: three Chinese songs, one Kung Fu performance, and two Chinese traditional dances, as well as one *erhu* (a traditional Chinese musical instrument) solo performed by instructor Guo. CI invited some Chinese state-owned corporation workers, private business owners, and Malagasy school representatives to attend this event, but most of the audience was made up of students from the local university and vocational schools. A journalist from a local newspaper attended and reported the event. The regional CI headquarters sent beforehand stage costumes such as Tai Ji clothes, long dresses with patterns found on blue and white porcelain, and traditional *Han* Chinese clothing. Organizers also provided litchi and bottled mineral water for the Chinese and Malagasy VIP guests sitting in the front rows.

While I do not want to diminish the efforts that the instructors and their students put into preparing for this event, it is clear that the performances were prepared with no long-term goal to further improve students' language ability. The Malagasy students who participated in the event enjoyed fitting into Chinese-style stage costumes; however, they did not learn much about the meaning of the choreography they were performing. In a similar fashion, students who sang Chinese songs on the stage remembered the tune, rhythm, and pronunciation of the lyrics but had no idea what the songs were about. For their part, students in the audience were more amazed by seeing their friends comically pronouncing Chinese lyrics in shiny costumes than by their progress in learning the Chinese language. However, when covered by local Malagasy media and reported to the CI headquarters, the event was reported by CI instructors as an affirmation of their teaching effectiveness in the field.

In such events, CI tends to represent 'Chinese culture' as a bounded and timeless entity only composed of 'traditional' activities like those featured in the performances described above. According to the current guiding spirit of CI, 'culture' is equated with 'tradition'—both unsettling concepts that are frequently contested in the discipline of anthropology—resulting in a "systematic reduction of the diverse cultures of Chinese tradition to a uniform, quaint commodity" (Jensen, 2012: 295). In northern Madagascar, by showcasing 'traditional Chinese culture' through staged performances in cultural events and festivals, CI has been contributing to the self-construction of a concept of culture "shadowed by coherence, timelessness, and discreteness" that is often used to "freeze difference" (Abu-Lughod, 1991: 144–147). Some CI instructors found the representation of Chinese culture problematic and incommensurable with their personal understandings of the concept. For example,

Tang, a young woman in her early 20s working on a one-year contract, criticized the representation of Chinese culture based on her experience:

> My understanding of 'Chinese culture' is very different from the understanding of the institution that I am working for. I keep asking myself what Chinese culture really is! I do not think that the Confucius Institute is teaching the *real* Chinese culture by any means. What they want us to teach is only *ancient* Chinese culture. I can see a huge gap between the real contemporary Chinese culture that my generation experiences and the ancient Chinese culture that I have to teach but do not fully understand. For example, they want us to teach ancient Chinese royal court dances or Kung Fu to Malagasy students. But we do not know this stuff either! We learned Kung Fu and the dance from movies and videos too. However, we have to teach our students as if it is more authentic when taught by Chinese faces. *We never learned Kung Fu in our entire life, and we do not all graduate from the Shaolin Temple; however, we grew up learning and practising radio calisthenics at school!* In my interactions with my students, I tried to teach them the China that I understand, for example, the real benefits of development in our everyday life such as the rise of online shopping and overnight delivery; as well as the actual problems faced by my generation, like skyrocketing property prices and environmental degradation. I also think that if foreign students really want to understand Chinese people and our culture, they need to learn how social networks influence relationships in China, and the pragmatics of the language. But we never have any opportunity to teach these deeper issues. I cannot stress enough that even in ancient China, Chinese culture was not entirely about Kung Fu or dancing either! The Confucius Institute just wants to use these elements to represent Chinese culture because they are so distinctive, iconic, and catchy, but nothing authentic. Sometimes we want to teach the dining culture of China and to provide students opportunities to try authentic Chinese cuisine. However, it is not feasible to cook for our students due to our living and financial conditions. Since we do not have extra funding at hand to take our students to Chinese restaurants, it is too expensive for us to treat them out of our own pocket. Our words are mostly empty cheques for our students. When they ask us, "teacher, how does authentic Chinese food taste?" we can only say, "it is delicious" but cannot provide them anything to try. (Conversation with Tang)

What is striking from Tang's comment is her sharp insider's critique of how the Confucius Institute represents Chinese culture by contrasting Kung Fu with radio calisthenics—the latter being a popular sporting activity in China that offers an interesting glimpse into changes in the country's social contexts. Radio calisthenics were first introduced to China in 1951, following the example of a similar program in the Soviet Union, to promote fitness activities nationwide and thereby to strengthen Chinese people's physical health. The tradition of practising radio calisthenics in China was established during Mao's socialist regime. For decades, since the introduction of radio calisthenics into China, it is the most accessible fitness activity nationwide. Even now, students from Grade one to twelve in China's public schools are still required to participate in daily goosestep and radio calisthenics routines to develop a collective sense of honour and respect for discipline and conformity (Liu & Tobin, 2017). Although Chinese Kung Fu has a long history of being portrayed as the essence of Chinese culture, especially in Chinese movies, most Chinese people in the same generation as the CI instructors who went through China's mandatory nine-year education system have never practised Kung Fu; Tai Ji, meanwhile, enjoys greater popularity among Chinese seniors than among young adults in their 20s. To expect CI language instructors to teach Kung Fu that they have seldom practiced reflects the incommensurability between 'Chinese culture' in its discursive everyday form and the hegemonic image that CI wants to represent to the world. The thickness and vibrancy of the 'complex whole' that 'Chinese culture' entails is wiped out by CI's tendency to treat 'culture' as a static and bounded entity. Working under such a scheme, some instructors obediently accept the identity of 'cultural ambassadors' given to them by the Confucius Institute, but others have pinpointed the incommensurability between their own cultural experiences as native Chinese and the representation of Chinese culture promoted by CI in Madagascar. As we can see from the ethnographic examples from Madagascar, in the production, circulation, and consumption of knowledge in global–local encounters, what truly matters is not what 'culture' *means*, but what 'culture' *does* by defining boundaries, including, and excluding due to the very boundaries it establishes. The meaning of 'Chinese culture' varies among actors from different positionalities, but hegemonic understandings of 'Chinese culture' promoted by CI set an artificial boundary demarcating what cultural elements and which cultural subjects are considered more 'authentic' than others.

6.6   Conclusion

In Madagascar, the challenge of Chinese language and culture education is the inadequacy and inaccuracy of knowledge itself. The global flow of 'Chinese culture' to Africa and the western Indian Ocean serves the strategic agenda of the Chinese state, benefits the institutional and individual goals of instructors circulating knowledge, while disadvantages African students and institutions with inadequate capability in knowledge application. For young instructors, the job opportunities provided by CI both broaden their horizons and limit how and what they can learn about the world. For Malagasy students, CI classes and events provided opportunities to glimpse into 'Chinese culture,' but no practical knowledge addressing the urgent needs of African students. CI representations of 'Chinese culture' are flawed as they ignore the incommensurability internal to the culture. The incommensurable understandings of 'Chinese culture' among different actors should be analysed within the broader social and historical contexts. While CI is promoting a unifying image of 'Chinese culture,' the concept itself is contested, both internally and externally. Just as how Chinese youth experiencing a revival of Confucianism are often developing a superficial, simplified, and fragmented understanding of the concept, Malagasy students are also learning a superficial, simplified, and fragmented version of 'Chinese culture,' which often creates counter effects against the goals and missions of CI.

Not only is the knowledge provided to Malagasy students about Chinese language and culture inadequate, China's global educational projects in Africa also disadvantage African students by lacking continuity and consistency. Very soon after I finished my fieldwork, some students at the university sent me a message with crying emojis. They told me that there would not be any Chinese instructors coming to teach them next term. The CI instructors that I had befriended confirmed the news later. Only one instructor decided to extend her stay in Madagascar for another year, but she had been transferred to a different location. Two other instructors decided to develop their careers back in China, and another had received an offer from a European university to pursue a graduate degree. When I asked why CI had decided to cease their collaboration with the university, a former instructor told me:

> The teaching outcomes of the university are frustrating for us. The Confucius Institute has worked hard to continue providing Chinese language instructors to the university, but the university has not done a good job in incorporating the Chinese language classes in the curriculum. The university is poorly organized, and students are not motivated to learn. Although the Confucius Institute receives funding from the Chinese government and the institute is under the mission to 'help,' we still have to calculate our input-output ratio somehow like a business. What is the point of sending teachers to a place where there are hardly any students? That is why the headquarters finally made the call to cease the cooperation. I feel sorry about it too because I lived and worked on the campus and I became attached to my job. But there is nothing I can do to change the final decision. (Conversation with a former instructor)

The decision was sudden but not without warning. The Confucius Institute does not risk losing much by ceasing cooperation with one university in Madagascar. With the generous funding package associated with cooperating with the Confucius Institute, it does not experience much difficulty finding willing educational institutions in the region. The instructors are fully aware of the backlash that CI has been experiencing in North America and Europe since 2010. However, they are also aware that the CI will continue to expand by establishing more branches and classes. Indeed, in Africa alone, CI classrooms have expanded from 39 countries in 2018 to 46 in 2020. However, it is crucial to ask the question of who the CI benefits most, and whether the educational agency is operating in a development model where discontinuity and inconsistency characterize Africa's participation in the global world (Ferguson, 2006). As Ferguson's (2006) cogently argues, Africa's global connections are often made in tandem with economic declines and crises, disconnection, marginalization, and exclusion. Although Ferguson's argument focuses primarily on Africa's position in the global economy, it is certainly also pertinent to the realm of global education and 'soft power' projects such as those undertaken by the Confucius Institute.

Acknowledgements I wish to thank my interlocuters during my fieldwork who generously shared their knowledge and thoughts with me. I am grateful to the editors of this volume for their insightful comments and feedback. This work could not have been possible without the support of Dr. Andrew Walsh and the Department of Anthropology at the University of Western Ontario. The writing process of this article was also supported by the Fellowship in Ethnographic Writing offered by the Centre for Ethnography at the Department of Anthropology, University of Toronto Scarborough.

References

Abu-Lughod, L. (1991). Writing against culture. In R. G. Fox (Ed.), *Recapturing Anthropology: Working in the present* (pp. 137–162). School of American Research Press.

Bell, D. A. (2006). *China's leaders rediscover Confucianism*. Editorials and Commentary—International Herald Tribune. *New York Times*. https://www.nytimes.com/2006/09/14/opinion/14ihtedbell.2807200.html. Accessed 2 January 2021.

Benedict, R. (1946). *The Chrysanthemum and the Sword: Patterns of Japanese culture*. Hough-ton Mifflin.

Billioud, S. (2007). Confucianism, "Cultural Tradition", and official discourse in China at the start of the new century. *China Perspectives, 3*, 50–65.

Bocock, R. (1986). The Concept of Hegemony. *Hegemony* (pp. 21–39). Ellis Horwood Ltd.

Chow, R. (1998). Introduction: On Chineseness as a theoretical problem. *Boundary 2, 25*(3), 1–24.

Conners, M. K. (2005). Ministering culture: Hegemony and the politics of culture and identity in Thailand. *Critical Asian Studies, 37*(4), 523–551.

Ferguson, J. (2006). *Global shadows: Africa in the Neoliberal world Ooder* Duke University Press.

Guccini, F. & Zhang, M. (2021). 'Being Chinese' in Mauritius and Madagascar: Comparing Chinese diasporic communities in the Western Indian Ocean. *Journal of Indian Ocean World Studies, 4*(2), 91–117. https://doi.org/10.26443/jiows.v4i2.79

Handler, R. (2009). The uses of incommensurability in Anthropology. *New Literary History, 40*(3), 627–647.

Haugen, H. Ø. (2013). China's recruitment of African University students: Policy efficacy and unintended outcomes. *Globalization, Societies and Education, 11*(3), 315–334.

Hubbert, J. (2014) Ambiguous states: Confucius institutes and Chinese soft power in the U.S. classroom. *Political and Legal Anthropology Review, 37*(2), 329–349.

Hubbert, J. (2019). *China in the world: An Anthropology of Confucius institutes, soft power, and globalization*. University of Hawai'i Press.

Jensen, L. (2012). Culture industry, power, and the spectacle of China's "Confucius Institutes." In T. B. Weston & L. M. Jensen (Eds.), *China in and beyond headlines* (pp. 271–299). Rowman & Littlefield Publishers Inc.

Lam, J. (2008). *China's revival of Confucianism*. USC US-China Institute. https://china.usc.edu/chinas-revival-confucianism. Accessed 2 February 2021.

Lambek, M. (1997). Knowledge and practice in Mayotte: An overview. *Cultural Dynamics, 9*(2), 131–148.

Lambek, M. (2013). The value of (performative) acts. *Journal of Ethnographic Theory, 3*(2), 141–160.

Liu, C., & Tobin, J. (2017). Group exercise in Chinese preschools in an Era of child-centered pedagogy. *Comparative Education Review, 62*(1), 5–30.

Meissner, W. (2006). China's search for cultural and national identity from the nineteenth century to the present. *China Perspectives, 68*, 41–54.

Nye, J. (1990). Soft power. *Foreign Policy, 80*, 153–171.

Oakes, T. (2000). China's provincial identities: Reviving regionalism and reinventing "Chineseness." *The Journal of Asian Studies, 59*(3), 667–692. https://doi.org/10.2307/2658947

Ong, A. (1996). Anthropology, China and modernities: The geopolitics of cultural knowledge. In H. L. Moore (Ed.), *The future of Anthropological knowledge* (pp. 60–92). Routledge.

Osburg, J. (2013). *Anxious wealth: Money and morality among China's New Rich*. Stanford University Press.

Sahlins, M. (2015). *Confucius institutes: Academic malware*. Prickly Paradigm Press.

Said, E. (1978). *Orientalism*. Vintage Books.

Strauss, R. (2008). Think again: The peace corps. *Foreign Policy*. https://foreignpolicy.com/2008/04/22/think-again-the-peace-corps/. Accessed 19 March 2022.

Thobani, S. (2007). *Exalted subjects: Studies in the making of race and Nation in Canada*. University of Toronto Press.

Wardlow, H. (2006). *Wayward women: Sexuality and agency in a New Guinea society*. University of California Press.

Xing, T. (2017). How Chinese Youth enable the revival of Confucian culture. *Sixth Tone*. http://
www.sixthtone.com/news/1001151/how-chinese-youth-enable-the-revival-of-confucian-cul
ture. Accessed 2 February 2021.
Zhang, M. (2021). *Writing against "Mask Culture": Orientalism and COVID-19 responses in the
West. Anthropologica* 63(1). DOI: https://doi.org/10.18357/anthropologica6312021327

Mingyuan Zhang is a postdoctoral research fellow at the Department of Community Medicine
and Global Health, University of Oslo (Norway). She holds a PhD in Sociocultural Anthropology from the University of Western Ontario (Canada). She was a writing fellow at the Centre
for Ethnography and a lecturer at the Department of Anthropology and the Centre for Critical
Development Studies at the University of Toronto Scarborough (Canada).

Part II
China as a Dividing Factor Within Countries of the Global South

Chapter 7
Melanesian Self-Reliance Discourses and Chinese Investment: The Ramu Nickel Mine in Papua New Guinea

Henryk Szadziewski ⓘ

Abstract This work analyzes how Papuan/Melanesian narratives of self-reliance in an era of decolonization in Oceania rationalize and contest Chinese investments in the state and civil society domains. The case study shows that both supporters and opponents of Chinese investment at the Ramu Nickel Mine in Papua New Guinea build their claims around self-reliance. The state actors present Chinese investment as an alternative to and autonomy from Papua New Guinea's traditional donor, Australia. In contrast, the civil society demonstrates agency by rejecting China's "neo-colonial" attitude towards local natural resources. These self-reliance discourses translate into different practical outcomes. For example, Chinese financing enables the state to demonstrate new assertiveness regionally and on the global stage, especially regarding critical issues, such as the climate crisis. On the other hand, civil society makes modest gains from Chinese companies, which indicates that in the future Chinese interventions will be forced to consider local interests more carefully and negotiate with sub-state actors. Tensions in responses to Chinese investment from the civil society and the state not only reveal different visions of the future for Papua New Guinea but also translate into conceivable patterns across the Oceania region as China increases its aid and investment presence.

Keywords Papua New Guinea · Chinese investment · Natural resources · Self-reliance · Sub-state actors

Abbreviations

BRG   Bismark Ramu Group
MCC   Metallurgical Corporation of China Limited
PNG   Papua New Guinea

H. Szadziewski (✉)
University of Hawai'i at Mānoa, Honolulu 96822, Hawai'i, USA
e-mail: henryksz@hawaii.edu

© The Author(s), under exclusive license to Springer Nature Singapore Pte Ltd. 2022   115
T. Tudoroiu and A. Kuteleva (eds.), *China in the Global South*,
https://doi.org/10.1007/978-981-19-1344-0_7

7.1 Introduction

In 2001, I was teaching at the British Cultural Institute in Lima, Peru. When a fellow teacher heard that I graduated in modern Chinese and invited me to act as an interpreter for a friend who did business with a company from mainland China. I jumped at the chance to supplement my income. My colleague's friend was attempting to broker a deal supplying machinery to the Chinese company, which engaged in a major mineral extraction project in the interior of Peru. Woefully out of my depth in terms of Chinese language mining vocabulary, I did the best I could, and the deal went ahead; however, the incident brought to light the growing interest of Chinese corporations in natural resources investment since the inception of the reform period in the late 1970s and the "going out" policy in the early 2000s. This interest now encompasses minerals, fisheries, and timber in all parts of the globe, and the Pacific Islands region is no less impacted than elsewhere with the heaviest investment targeted at the mining sector. As disparate as the highlands of Peru and the island states of the Pacific may seem, the ties between them of Chinese investment are now clearly visible. While Chinese presence in these spaces may not make headlines, they are no less important in our understanding of Beijing's global imprint.

The imprint of a global China on local economies and societies offers new directions for research, particularly in how local peoples interpret large-scale intervention coming from a non-Western power. This chapter examines the intersection between grounded impacts and perceptions of Chinese mining interests in Papua New Guinea (PNG), as expressed discursively by the host state and non-state actors within it. The chapter analyzes how these discourses shape Papua New Guinean narratives of self-reliance in an era of decolonization in Oceania. Furthermore, it offers perspectives on how government and civil society in decolonizing states rationalize and contest Chinese engagements while disentangling former colonizers.

Specifically, the chapter focuses on the case study of the influence of the mainland Chinese presence at the Ramu nickel mine in PNG on Melanesian narratives of self-reliance. A mainland Chinese entity Ramu NiCo Limited owns an 85% interest in the Ramu mine and controls the largest China-led investment project in Oceania so far. This chapter explores how a member of diverse local communities discusses this formidable intervention from China into the national economy. The author examines texts originating from PNG regarding Chinese investment at Ramu. Texts were gathered from the media and civil society, with the views of the private sector and the government frequently represented in the media coverage of the Ramu nickel project. Media reports, particularly those reflecting government views, remained positive about Chinese investment at Ramu citing a non-Western donor offers more opportunities than traditional ones, such as Australia and the United States. Civil society, in contrast, focused on more negative aspects of Chinese presence at Ramu. Consequently, similarly to Herlijanto's and Tudoroiu and Ramlogan's contributions in this volume, PNG's case shows that non-state actors tend toward critical views of China over their state counterparts. Specifically, contributions of PNG civil society to the debates over China expressed concerns over environmental and labor rights issues, as well as problems of adequate compensations to local landowners. Neverthe-less, this chapter asserts that these perspectives—positive and negative alike—reflect a broader societal discourse regarding self-reliance. Positive discourses focused on how Chinese investment supported PNG's self-reliance by decreasing dependence on former colonial powers, while critical voices engaged with the concept of self-reliance by asserting PNG citizens' rights in response to China's alleged violations of environmental or labor standards. In all cases, self-reliance is not just about "doing things for ourselves" but also includes the power-knowledge nexus. In this context, who gets to speak about the land and the people of PNG influences the local responses to Chinese mining interests.

This chapter opens with a discussion of the PNG/Melanesian self-reliance discourse, exploring the contributions of regional scholars through the lens of power-knowledge. It then discusses the history of mining in PNG with a focus on external interests and how these interests have been instrumental in the development of contrasting expressions of self-reliance discourses. Following the analysis of rele-vant texts from 2005 to 2017, the chapter discusses the impact of the 2019 toxic spill at Ramu and the COVID-19 pandemic on self-reliance narratives. In sum, this chapter argues that civil society and sub-national actors meaningfully exert agency on PNG's interactions with China. These actors belie a popular metropolitan discourse that perceives the Global South as passive in the face of Beijing's economic expan-sion. Thus, PNG civil society and sub-state entities find the increasing visibility of China presents an opportunity to reflexively promote self-reliance to further local interests.

7.2   Self-Reliance Discourses in Papua New Guinea

Natural resources are frequently contested. Conflict over ownership, adequate compensation, and environmental impacts are common public conversations. In Oceania, as in many other places in the world, sovereignty and natural resources are one of the key topics in natural resource extraction discourse. Specifically, the discussion is vital in this region given its histories of colonialism, the spread of market globalism, and ongoing struggles with decolonization. The role of overseas corporations in the expensive process of mineral extraction is therefore informed by sovereignty over land and resources. This work explores the power-knowledge nexus in Melanesian discourses of self-reliance, which highlight indigeneity as a means of emancipation from colonizers. In more pragmatic terms, the achievement of this goal often enlists third parties as an enabling factor. In many Oceanic states, this third party is China. Given China's predilection to conduct overseas work with other state entities, Oceanic governments often discuss relations with China in a posi-tive light to promote self-reliance from former colonizers. However, the leveraging of Chinese presence in Oceania to promote self-reliance frequently experiences a negative reflexive response in civil society towards China and national governments giving rise to contested versions of the decolonization process.

Contrasting and often contradictory narratives of natural resource extraction and self-reliance within the field of power-knowledge are pertinent to this research on PNG perspectives on Chinese investment at the Ramu Nickel Mine. The ideas proposed here about Melanesian and PNG forms of discourse as articulated by regional and national discourse-makers are cautiously applied due to the sheer diversity of peoples and interests in PNG. However, as Keating (2015) asserts, the place is a key factor in determining forms of discourse, and it is further shaped by interactions with the discourses of other places. This fluidity between space and narrative formation opens the possibility to analyze locally situated discourses through a Foucauldian lens.

Diamond and Quinby (1988: 185) describe a Foucauldian understanding of discourse as "a form of power that circulates in the social field and can attach to strategies of domination as well as those of resistance." Consequently, discourse production simultaneously creates hegemonic and counter-hegemonic responses within the same context. Weedon (1987: 108) considers a Foucauldian reading of discourse with more profound consequences, arguing that it has a propensity to create an ontological change: "Discourses are more than ways of thinking and producing meaning. They constitute the 'nature' of the body, unconscious and conscious mind and emotional life of the subjects they seek to govern." In this framework, discursive production and reproduction is an act of power assertion, as it seeks to embed "the truth" in others.

In *Re-Presenting Melanesia: Ignoble Savages and Melanesian Alter-Natives*, Kabutaulaka (2015) discusses forms of "Melanesianisms" proposed by various scholars that demonstrate the relationship between ontological shifts and discourse. Kabutaulaka (2015: 125) adds that while he is sympathetic to Epeli Hau'ofa's "proposal to strengthen our trans-Oceanic connections and identities, it must be noted that national and subregional boundaries persist and have become 'realities' for most Pacific Islanders." Furthermore, he notes that "there is relatively less discussion about how the terms 'Polynesia,' 'Micronesia,' and 'Melanesia' have taken on lives of their own, appropriated by Pacific Islanders and used to frame their identities and influence relationships among themselves *and with others* [my italics]" (Kabutaulaka, 2015: 125–126). Kabutaulaka cites the work of Bernard Narokobi in exemplifying the development of "Melanesianisms." Narokobi proposes the "Melanesian Way" that casts off the bondage of colonialism and the dominance of external "expertise." This Melanesian Way is positive and free of categories that tie Melanesians to the conditioning of dominant external narratives. Narokobi (1983: 4–5) asserts the Melanesian Way offers a choice that is grounded in intrinsically-held values: "More than any people in the world, we can choose. We can choose to ape the West and the East or we can choose to be ourselves in our philosophy, our life-styles and our whole beings." An indigenous form of self-reliance is another important characteristic of the Melanesian Way. Narokobi (1983: 14) states: "We often talk of self-reliance as if it was some great political ideology we have to learn from China or Tanzania. But in fact, the spirit of self-reliance has always been in Melanesia."

The discourse of self-reliance is also prominent in Utulua Samana's work. In *Papua New Guinea: Which Way?*, he makes a similar claim to Narokobi, arguing that Papua New Guineans face a choice between "self-reliance or mutual destruction" (Samana, 1988: 3). Samana links "mutual destruction" to the industrial extraction of natural resources and, in particular, to mining and government cooperation with foreign investors. In Samana's (1988: 7) worldview, self-reliance comes from rebuffing these associations:

> What has been the experience in the past when PNG governments have pressed the idea of a partnership between government and foreign investors for large-scale mines and large-scale development? The experience has been that the people have actually rejected the government's proposals.

Both Narokobi's and Samana's writings *reclaim* the right of Papua New Guineans to represent PNG and its people. These notions build a discourse of self-reliance and resist colonial discursive constructions of PNG created through military and political dominance of the Global North. As Regis Tove Stella (2007: 2) writes,

> While Papua New Guineans have always had indigenous forms of representation, including cultural expressions and political institutions, these were subsumed, subjugated, and at worst erased at the interface with European representational modes, to be replaced by new images constructed by the dominant group.

Further, metropolitan post-colonial representation of PNG dismissed forms of resistance to colonial narratives tending to focus on the "fatal impact" of encounters with Europe. The colonial disruption fits into a longer arc of history within PNG and Oceania and indigenous dissemination of knowledge often conveyed counter-messaging. A scholar and a poet, Steven Winduo (2011: 1) offers insights into how such a discourse is transmitted in Oceania. He writes: "Indigenous communities in Oceania have always used folktales to explain their social, psychological, political, and cultural environment." Winduo (2011) adds that Oceanic peoples tell folktales to challenge power and tradition. Furthermore, referring to the run-up toward sovereignty and independence, Papua New Guineans told folktales to promote nationalism. The folktale as a form of discursive contestation projected assertiveness in the face of retreating colonial powers. The form also facilitated the communication of the internal realm into the external. Kabutaulaka (2015: 127) expands on his concept of "Melanesianisms" through a discussion of *tok stori*, which he describes as "a discourse that creates an 'imagined community' and invokes shared values—both imagined and real—that are fluid, dynamic, and constantly reinvented through ongoing *tok stori* (conversations) and shared experiences." Therefore, "Melanesianisms" is made real through iterative communication between the peoples of Melanesia. With the creation of multilateral entities, such as the Melanesian Spearhead Group, *tok stori* has constructed enduring political, economic, and cultural structures.

Orality is one of many forms of representational expression within PNG's power-knowledge field. Writers in PNG "saw literature as a weapon to combat western imperialism, denounce colonialism and agitate for independence" (Regis Tove Stella, 1999: 222). Stella (1999: 222) writes that this spoken and written production "has risen from the interface of orature with Western cultural practices." He further adds that "although these orientations are seemingly antithetical, in fact they inform each other and form a literary seedbed from which writers produce their works and construct social and national identities" (Regis Tove Stella, 1999: 222). This chapter extends the understanding of these texts of contestation to the online domain, especially when disseminating knowledge on self-reliance. A report from the Pacific Institute on Public Policy (2012: 2) on Internet usage in Oceania claims that "the dynamics of social networks are strikingly similar to the age-old family and community based social dynamics found in all Pacific societies." This dynamic is a strident assertion, and this work views online interaction with a more cautious approach, as online conversations differ from spoken interactions in three key ways. Firstly, accessibility of mobile and computer technologies vary, and secondly, the nature of oral communications is contemporaneous, whereas online conversations can occur across varying lengths of time. Although Internet interactions differ from oral conversations, they nevertheless become an important means to assert political claims of self-reliance and resist dominant narratives. While we must keep in mind Steven Winduo's (2000: 599) caution of overwriting indigenous "self-representations and cultural expressions," it is arguable that *tok stori* simultaneously occupies physical spaces through conversation and in cyberspace through text. In sum, the Internet has become another forum in which to externalize the internal world:

> Greater access to mobile media technologies and expanding communications infrastructure are fundamentally altering the ways Papua New Guineans participate in personal and mass communications. A new social media culture is emerging, one characterized by assertive, highly critical Papua New Guineans who are increasingly discontented with a political environment that is often complicit in the exploitation of PNG's natural resources. (Capey, 2013: 8)

Logan (2012) asserts that information communication technologies have fundamentally changed the political scene in PNG with discernible changes in the nature and activities of civil society, calls for transparency, and the emergence of a new political agency. However, we must acknowledge the limits of Internet penetration in PNG and the boundaries of this shift. In 2011, mobile phone penetration reached 35% of the population up from 1% in 2005, and the International Telecommunications Union estimated Internet access from mobile technology in PNG would reach approximately 50% by 2017 (Logan, 2012). In an indication of the unreliability of such estimates, in 2016, the Real Time Statistics Project's Internet Live Stats webpage records only 906,695 internet users in PNG, or 11.7% of the total population (Internet Live Stats, 2016). Furthermore, the activists leveraging the Internet to influence political discourse are more likely to come from the young and educated from PNG's urban elites and be connected to the networks of the global justice movement (Capey, 2013; Logan, 2012). The subsequent sections trace historical legacies of mining in PNG and the emergence of contrasting resource extraction discourses and examines how these are disseminated online.

7.3 Mining in Papua New Guinea

The industrialized exploitation of PNG's mineral resources dates to the nineteenth century; however, the indigenous peoples of PNG have mined and traded stone and ocher for over 40,000 years (Mineral Resources Authority, 2009). Beginning in the 1850s, non-native peoples began to report the presence of gold deposits to the west of Port Moresby and by the end of the century presence of the precious metal had set in motion several overseas-led expeditions (Neale, 2005). In addition to gold, Luigi d'Albertis recorded sighting copper specimens in the Fly River in 1876. Because of these activities, the mineral wealth of PNG became known to the wider world.

The beginning of colonial administration and the onset of systematic mineral resource extraction in PNG intersect. Colonialism and capitalism, in a pattern familiar elsewhere, consolidated territory and increased revenues for colonial enterprises. The individual stories of everyday Papuan engagement with colonial mining projects are largely lost and histories skew toward Eurocentric interpretations of events. Germany's annexation of the northern part of PNG in 1884 was quickly followed by Great Britain's annexation of the southern portion with the border between the two new colonies settled in 1885. Twenty years later, Britain transferred the administration of New Guinea to Australia. During the early colonial period, overseas prospectors discovered gold at sites across the PNG mainland and on the islands off the southeast, including locations in Milne Bay and the lower Ramu River. Most of the mining activity focused on the British/Australian territory and by 1896 underground mining had commenced at "Mt. Adelaide" with investment from the British New Guinea Gold Pty Ltd. Signs of a maturing industry were in evidence during the first two decades of the twentieth century with the development of large-scale infrastructure objects, such as the railroad built by the Pacific Island Mines company in 1917 (Neale, 2005).

After World War I, the League of Nations granted Australia trusteeship of the German colony effectively granting Canberra control of what is now PNG. In 1949, Australia merged the two colonies to become the Territory of Papua and New Guinea. Mining centered on continuing gold extraction, which comprised a significant proportion of the colonial income. A centralized administration permitted the colonial authorities and private sector to work closely on accelerating mineral exploitation in PNG. The government improved supporting infrastructure, such as a road from Wau to Lae to facilitate mining at the Morobe Goldfield, and mining companies provided the financial, human, and physical capital for mineral extraction (Mineral Resources Authority, 2009).

The 1960s oversaw a variety of new mineral reserves projects with the discovery of copper and nickel across PNG. Prospectors, aided by new technologies, found nickel at Ramu in 1962 and copper at Panguna in 1964. In 1968, Australian state-funded geologists uncovered copper and gold at Ok Tedi. Diversification of known reserves came at an auspicious time given the decline in global gold prices and by 1972 the Panguna mine was in production. With the formal independence of PNG in 1975 an "air of uncertainty" pervaded the public discussions of foreign investment in the mining sector, particularly after the Utah-based Kennecott Copper Corporation withdrew from the new state as it failed to come to terms the first post-colonial administration (Neale, 2005).

Periods of prosperity and depression in the mining sector characterized the three decades following independence. The recovery of gold prices in the 1980s initiated a mining revival culminating in a rapid decline as the decade ended. From the 1990s to the early 2000s, despite a stock market crash, nascent mining projects came to the fore as earlier prospects entered production (Neale, 2005). By 2017, the PNG government reported active mines at Ok Tedi, Lihir, Porgera (95% owned by the Canadian Barrick Gold Corporation and Chinese Zijin Mining Group), Hidden Valley, Ramu, Simberi (owned by Australian firm St. Barbara Limited), Sinivit and Woodlark (Papua New Guinea Chamber of Mines and Petroleum (2017).

7.4   Ramu Nickel Mine

The history of mining in PNG is punctuated with the involvement of and exploitation by entities external to PNG. Given the colonial context, European and Australian interests dominated the mining landscape in PNG. A historical overview permits an understanding of the kinds of discursive settings all overseas investors enter when working in PNG. Mineral resources, as with other kinds of natural resources, and sovereign control are closely linked. The long history of overseas ownership of mining projects can be connected to the development of self-reliance discourses in PNG. The *Constitution of the Independent State of Papua New Guinea* explicitly declares:

> We declare our third goal to be for Papua New Guinea to be politically and economically independent, and our economy basically self-reliant. We accordingly call for– …the State to take effective measures to control and actively participate in the national economy, and *in particular* to control major enterprises engaged in the exploitation of natural resources (National Parliament of Papua New Guinea, undated: 3).

As such, external investment, as well as the vulnerability PNG experiences in the global fluctuations of commodity prices, is a test of these self-reliance assertions.

The Ramu mine is situated in Madang Province in the northeast of mainland PNG. It consists of the Kurumbukari open-pit mine, Basamuk refinery, and a 135-km slurry pipeline (Ramu Nico Management, 2019). In 1992, Highlands Gold, a Queensland-based company, undertook the management of the Ramu joint venture. After a period of feasibility studies, the Ramu project received a Special Mining License from the government in 2000. Construction began in 2008 with completion four years later and the total estimated cost of the project is placed at US$2.1 billion. In May 2019, Toronto-based Nickel 28 acquired Highlands Gold (Nickel 28, undated). The mine is expected to have a life of twenty to thirty years and nickel output is projected at 32,800 tonnes per year.

The incorporation of Chinese interests into the Ramu Nickel Mine opened a new element into the discourse on overseas mining interests in PNG. In 2005, the Metallurgical Corporation of China Limited (MCC) became a member of the Ramu joint venture with responsibilities covering financing and construction. MCC undertook an 85% interest in the mining project with the remaining 15% spread across Highlands Gold, the Mineral Resource Development Company (an entity wholly owned by the PNG government), and landowners (Neale, 2005). MCC has its origins in the mesh of state and private sector interests prevalent in China. According to the MCC website, the corporation was established in 1982 after the official approval of the State Council and is affiliated with the Ministry of the Metallurgical Industry. Further, the website specifies that in December 2008, MCC set up the Metallurgical Corporation of China Ltd. MCC Ramu NiCo Limited, owned by MCC-JJJ Mining, manages the Ramu Nickel Mine interests of MCC and three partners including, the Jinchuan Group, Jinlin Jien Nickel Industry Corporation, and Jiuquan Iron and Steel Group (Ramu Nico Management, 2019). The involvement of MCC-JJJ Mining at Ramu "is the largest single ODI project undertaken by a Chinese company in the Pacific" (Smith, 2013: 180).

Chinese aid and investment in the mining sector have become an increasing feature in Pacific Island countries and territories. For example, Chinese investors have interests or potential interests in the extraction of bauxite in Fiji and nickel in Kanaky/New Caledonia. However, infusions of Chinese capital in the mining sector have been most prominent in Papua New Guinea (PNG), where the Ramu nickel and Porgera gold mines have attracted significant investment. In keeping with the strong connection between the Chinese state and the private sector, the Ramu project characterizes an "infrastructure for resources" pattern used by Chinese investment in other overseas contexts. The pattern, "whereby large Chinese companies effectively bring the state with them," involves loan packages from the China Development Bank and the construction of roads and other infrastructure (Smith, 2013: 182). For example, projects include significant upgrading of the road systems on the mainland, in New Britain and New Ireland, constructing an industrial park in Sandaun Province worth US $4 billion, and improving water supply in Eastern Highlands Province. Another expensive (US $3.5 billion) road project was penned with China Railway Group, a private entity whose major shareholder is the state-owned, and stock exchange-listed, China Railway Engineering Corporation. The Sandaun deal was agreed with China Metallurgical Group, the majority investor in the Ramu Nickel mine. In sum, Chinese commercial entities and infrastructure projects grew in visibility after MCC's 2005 investment in Ramu, adding new external interests in the PNG economy.

7.5 Text Analysis

The research for this chapter included an analysis of texts to understand PNG perspectives of Chinese investment at Ramu Nickel Mine. The author entered the term "Chinese investment + Ramu" into Google's main search engine and then filtered results by webpages published in PNG through the Advanced Search feature. The author collected ninety-one meaningful articles into *Zotero*, which the author read and categorized by sector of origin (media, government, private, and civil society). During a second critical reading of the articles, the author determined the core claim in each piece, as well as the general tone (positive, negative, and neutral). Overall, the author cataloged three aspects of determining agency over the message:

- Who was speaking;
- What was communicated;
- And the tone of the message.

The analysis covers the period between 2005 and 2017, just before PNG signed the Memorandum of Understanding for cooperation on the Belt and Road Initiative with China. This agreement changed subsequent messaging of Chinese economic engagement in PNG, as trade, aid, and investment fell increasingly under the branding of the Belt and Road Initiative. The next section of the chapter covers the analysis of the post-2017 period.

In total, the text analysis yielded 70 articles from PNG-based media organizations and 21 from other non-state and state sources. As some of the media and other non-state articles cited government (PNG and Chinese) or Ramu NiCo officials this was also recorded. Out of 91 articles collected 28 cited a government official and 20 cited a Ramu NiCo official. Overall, 48 had a positive tone towards Chinese investment at Ramu nickel mine, while 30 gave a negative portrayal of Chinese ownership. The remaining 13 articles were neutral in tone often referring to uncontested informational elements to the mining project. The claims made in the articles were wide-ranging with pieces dedicated to the good corporate citizenship of the Chinese investors to the damaging effects of importing labor from China. Table 7.1 specifies broad coding categories, breaking down claims made in the articles:

Media articles predominately came from sources such as *The National, Post-Courier, Loop PNG*, and PNG's television broadcaster EMTV. Of the 70 articles from a media source, 48 were positive (i.e., all positive stories). From other non-state and state sources, 19 of the 21 articles (including blogs such as *actnowpng, ramumine,* and

Table 7.1 Core claims identified in PNG articles concerning Chinese investment at Ramu nickel mine

Core claim	Frequency
Conflicts with locals	20
Investment opportunities	20
Bilateral relations	17
Environmental issues	9
Corporate achievement	8
Informational	7
Community development	6
Corruption	4
Total	**91**

pngexposed) were categorized as negative. Media articles were almost exclusively the source of citations from government officials from China and PNG, as well as representatives of the Ramu NiCo project.

The results of the text analysis demonstrate a vigorous public debate over the merits of Chinese investment at the Ramu Nickel mine. In the exchange of information and claims, PNG asserts agency over external investment and articles also discuss the wider implications of Chinese interventions in the Oceania region. The existence of a predominance of negative stories among civil society actors and the prevalence of positive media stories, often reported through quotations from state and company officials, demonstrate a clear difference in discursive approach. It is interesting to note in the articles, particularly from *The National*, that there is a scant presentation of counter-perspectives of Chinese investment at Ramu Nickel mine. However, it would not be accurate to suggest these media outlets are mere surrogates, as some negative reporting is observable. Nevertheless, the analysis establishes which narratives on Chinese investment are offered and where they are available. The broad range of perspectives on display highlight an environment rich in discourse. In other words, a PNG-led discussion on the merits of Chinese investments.

The claims with the highest frequency (investment opportunities and conflicts with locals) show the dominance of opposing narratives; however, this work claims that this contradiction demonstrates two aspects of the self-reliance narrative. On one side, investment opportunities from China open PNG to new possibilities aside from traditional donors, such as Australia, the United Kingdom, and the United States. In other words, Chinese investment lessens dependency on former colonial powers. The following quote is typical of investment opportunity claims: "[Minister for Mining Byron] Chan updated his Chinese counterpart on the operations of the Ramu nickel project and the opportunity to develop additional impact projects such as infrastructure to service both the mine and the Madang province" (*The National*, 2012). Elsewhere, media quotes of PNG government officials suggest China's involvement in the Ramu Nickel mine will lead to more investment (*The National*, 2009). One commentator writing in *The National* extended the presence of Chinese investors at Ramu to a broader discussion of China's role in PNG as compared to the United States. "China's presence is felt in here more than the US. China is providing loan after loan to PNG. As if that is not enough, China has personally undertaken to develop certain impact projects in PNG such as our proposed International Convention Centre and building of new classrooms" (*The National*, 2011, April 14).

In contrast, the claims made in articles on conflict with investors and government officials likewise show a form of self-reliance, in that Papua New Guineans openly contest problems of inadequate compensation to landowners, poor working conditions, and restricted employment opportunities. A typical excerpt reads: "He [Chairman of the Kurumbukari Landowners Association Mathew Dengu] said the landowners' company was only receiving a pittance of business spin-offs while the Chinese were enjoying a 10-year tax-free holiday bringing in all materials from China and working out the profit margins when giving out small contracts (Safihao, 2013). Another noted: "Chinese miners have not always enjoyed a warm welcome in PNG. There have, for example, been clashes between locals and employees of the

Metallurgical Corporation of China, which operates the Ramu nickel–cobalt project via its subsidiary Ramu NiCo (Oxford Business Group, 2015). Negative articles also extended Chinese presence at Ramu into the wider geopolitics of Oceania with one writer explaining: "I previously thought that Chinese investment trade and aid was generally a good thing for the Pacific, but Chinese behaviour I believe has altered over the last year (*The National*, 2011, January 20).

Another dominant claim evident in the text analysis was Ramu's contribution to cordial and productive PNG-China relations. From the articles, PNG and Chinese governments generally perceive bilateral relations as economically "mutually beneficial," under the framework of South-South cooperation, and the close involvement of Port Moresby and Beijing in Ramu is clear. From the PNG perspective, the following is illustrative: "…the direct support from the Papua New Guinea Government and succeeding governments since PNG and China agreed to see Ramu NiCo project as a flagship project…will contribute greatly to PNG's GDP" (*The National*, 2015). While a quote from the Chinese Ambassador demonstrates Beijing's view: "Li Ruiyou has commended Ramu NiCo Management's operation, hoping it will become a model in economic cooperation and friendship between China and Papua New Guinea" (*The National*, 2017, February 23). Community development initiatives led by Ramu NiCo scale this claim of "good relations" to the local through stories on good corporate citizenship with opportunities afforded to PNG nationals, such as internships and safety campaigns (*The National*, 2017, February 1; 2014). The point here is that ongoing economic cooperation between PNG and China, while mutually beneficial in the language of officials, also presents the government of PNG with enduring alternatives to traditional donors.

Environmental groups outside PNG have raised concerns about the Ramu project alleging irreversible damage to human habitat and marine ecosystems due to toxic waste dumping (Cultural Survival, 2010). In one of the articles analyzed, the civil society organization, Act Now for a Better Papua New Guinea links to a Mineral Policy Institute report detailing the economic, social, and environmental hazards of the Ramu project (Act Now!, 2010). However, after winning a two-year long case attempting to prevent deep-sea waste dumping, Ramu NiCo pledged to "continue to work closely with the government and other stakeholders to meet the environmental obligations and international best practices" (*The National*, 2011, December 23). Despite the legal decision, the company made at least a verbal acknowledgement of a non-state actor's environmental concerns.

Nevertheless, critical discourse surrounding environmental problems at Ramu was not only aimed at Chinese investors, but also the PNG government. With regard to Chinese presence, one article collected from the *ramumine* blog raises resident's concerns about the safety of the mining process. Chinese companies are linked to the exploitative commercial approaches of former colonizers, especially in regard to the safe disposal of tailings:

Neville, Bustin, Joe, Mina, Awan – their names have been changed – live within sight of the refinery operated by China Metallurgical Group Corporation (MCC). Their hatred for former colonial masters – Papua New Guinea was under Australian control until 1975 – has faded and they now have a new target. 'Australians, Americans, Europeans – they were all welcome, but the Chinese are unscrupulous,' one of them says. The inhabitants of Mindere are engaged fighting against the mine, the metals extraction plant and a pipeline for dumping the slurry offshore at a depth of 150 metres. That kind of sea disposal of tailings is hazardous, as studies have shown, but other methods are more expensive. 'They are coming here with their 1960s technology. They are raping our country'. (Oelrich, 2011)

Such excerpts illustrate the depths of sensitivities over external investment and the fears of Chinese neo-colonialism. While the villagers make "the Chinese" 'their target others reserved contempt for the political leadership in PNG perceived as exchanging self-reliance for economic gain: "Peter O'Neill is selling PNG to China. Like Michael Somare, when he brought in the Chinese Ramu Nickel mining operation to Madang Province told the Chinese that 'this land is yours now', Peter O'Neill will take things one step further. The trade agreements that Peter O'Neill is forging are all in China's favour because PNG as the negotiator shows itself easily to be the most desperate of the 2 negotiating parties" (Ponowi Siwi Remo, 2016).

In addition to the materials available through the text analysis, other publications, such as Ramu NiCo bulletins, PNG Mineral Resources Authority publications and activist writings support the conclusions of the research; namely, there is a wide-ranging debate about the effect external investment in PNG has on self-reliance. The Bismark Ramu Group (BRG) are a civil society organization opposed to the environmental and livelihood impacts of the Ramu Nickel mine. One of BRG's representatives, Steven Sukot, writes in an activist publication, *Aid Watch*, on how globalization and neo-colonialism are threatening Papua New Guinean lives. The author offers a vision of PNG under pressure from external interests, which are listed as multinational corporations: "Our people depend on their land for food, hunting, fishing, cultural practices, medicine, and housing amongst other needs. There are also spiritual and cultural connections between land and our people. Our people's culture and traditions are neatly interwoven with their land, often times it is very difficult to untangle. This connection is not easily noticeable as well as relatively and poorly understood by non-indigenous people. Land is one's identity; it is one's existence; it is our birth right" (Sukot, 2008).

In concluding the article, Sukot refers to the founding principles of an independent PNG. These principles caution against exchanging economic progress for happiness and "spiritual poverty" (Sukot, 2008). The author then aligns this approach to the Melanesia region and prioritizes PNG interests over those of multinational corporations: "We also share this dream with our Melanesian brothers in the Pacific. Let's put our people before other interests. And as much as we the people of PNG appreciate the assistance from Australia through AusAID and various other arrangements, our country's development should be in line with this dream" (Sukot, 2008; Tavurvur, 2010).

Publications from the Mineral Resources Authority, such as the annual/biannual *Mining & Exploration Bulletin* offer straightforward appraisals of the Ramu project focusing on information regarding production, operations and export and sales (PNG Mineral Resources Authority undated). The section on the "Environment" of the bulletin from 2016 is typical of the output regarding this contested issue. The document merely describes the process of waste dumping in a neutral tone (PNG Mineral

Resources Authority, 2016). The Ramu NiCo publication, *Ramu Garamut*, dissemi-
nates positive information on the project with sections on "Corporate and Community
Relations" and "Community Development" that speak to the good citizenship initiatives of the company (Nickel 28, undated). Both publications reinforce the idea that
maintaining positive relations with China is good for investment into other parts of
PNG. All of the cited examples in this section demonstrate that conflicting opinions
across the range of stakeholders on the Ramu project should be read as articulations
on a broader and contrasting PNG-led discourse on what self-reliance means in the
context of Chinese investment.

7.6   Ramu Nickel Mine After 2018

In May 2019, James Marape replaced Peter O'Neill as Prime Minister with the
promise to seek greater benefits over oil, gas, and mineral resources for the people
of PNG by renegoting extraction licenses. This recommitment to putting natural
resources towards the service of the country became the latest iteration of the self-
reliance discourse. In the period between 2018 and 2020, the mining sector in PNG
went through several convulsions, including a major toxic spill and the COVID-
19 pandemic that have added new layers of complexity to interactions between the
state, civil society, and Chinese investors in PNG. Nevertheless, at the beginning
of these two years, reports in the PNG media led to increases in income at the
mine, plans for an expansion in operations, and how Ramu exemplified friendly
bilateral relations. On October 1, 2019, the *Post Courier* announced that the K4.8
billion (US $1.4 billion) expansion would result in 1,000 new jobs for PNG nationals
adding the growth that came on the back of record production and strong profits
(*Post-Courier*, 2018, October 1). The positive messaging went beyond the discussion
of bilateral relations with the leadership of the landowner association highlighting
burgeoning infrastructure development in the area surrounding the mine, including
roads and bridges (*Post-Courier*, 2019). This tone came amidst the Madang provincial
government's interest in the mine. Towards the end of 2018, Madang governor Peter
Yama discussed environmental concerns and complaints from local people about the
lack of infrastructure. Yama added the 2004 deal made with MCC was "rubbish,"
and that the provincial authorities needed to be at the table to represent the Madang
people at talks to renegotiate the agreement which expired in November 2018.

However, it was the August 2019 spill that hardened attitudes towards operations
at Ramu. Approximately 200,000 L of toxic slurry entered the ocean in Madang
province changing water to bright red and staining the coast (Fox, 2019). Yama
called it "the worst environmental disaster in PNG history" (Burton & Daly, 2019)
and appealed for the mine to be shut down following the publication of a commissioned report on the incident. The lead researcher of the report shared that toxic
dumping into the sea from the mine extended further back than 2019 by the mine
management expected the waste to "disappear" (*Radio New Zealand*, 2019, October
11). Ramu rejected the report stating the investigators had no official standing and the

company would only abide by decisions made by the state entity the Conservation and Environmental Protection Authority.

On October 23, 2019, PNG media reported the mine had been temporarily closed by the PNG national authorities and Marape had commissioned a new report to investigate the spill. The PNG government allowed the mine to reopen less than a week after it shut down. Despite assurances, local people were unhappy with conditions, one of the locals told Radio New Zealand:

> Our main source of protein we getting from the sea but they stopped it. People are all suffering especially those ones who live on the coast who mainly live on fish," while another one added: "Kids went down to the sea to have their washing. They were touched by this acid or poison from the sea and they developed a skin itchiness. Now we told all the kids not to go and wash in the sea. (*Radio New Zealand*, 2019, October 30)

By the end of 2019, the Ramu mine reported a drop in production (*Reuters*, 2020).

2020 proved as challenging as 2019. In February, Ramu management suspended travel from China to prevent the spread of COVID-19, and the Madang provincial government along with 13 landowners sued the company for K18 billion (US $5.1 billion) for breaches in the rights of local people to use customary land and water because of dumping of tailings and slurry spills. In an indication that opinions on the mine between Port Moresby and Madang were not in lockstep, positive articles began to appear in the PNG media. These included pieces on the benefit to local fisherpersons of having a ready market at the mine (*Post-Courier*, 2020, August 12), as well as the generous company donations towards coronavirus mitigation in Madang province (*Post-Courier*, 2020, February 26). The goodwill was nevertheless squandered when Chinese mineworkers, given special permission to enter PNG after the closure of the border, were refused entry because they had been administered an experimental version of a COVID-19 vaccine. The company belatedly warned PNG authorities that some of the 48 workers could test positive upon entry to PNG; however, Port Moresby stopped the flights from landing as the National Department of Health moved to stem an outbreak in the country.

The conflicts over Ramu came as a second part Chinese-owned mineral resource enterprise in PNG experienced a change in its relations with the PNG state. In April 2020, Port Moresby withheld the renewal of the gold mining lease at Porgera held jointly by Zijin and Canada's Barrick Gold. The Marape administration stated the mine would shift to state ownership. In an illustration of the close links between bilateral relations and natural resource extraction, Zijin Chairman Chen Jinghe warned if the Chinese company's investment was not properly safeguarded, there would be negative implications for PNG's relations with China (*Week in China*, 2020). On social media, Chen's statement prompted anti-Chinese sentiment, as well as admiration for the Marape government's position. However, rumors the mine might be sold to a different Chinese group elicited more anti-Chinese reactions in addition to criticism of Marape" (Kemish, 2020).

As noted, social media reaction to Chinese ownership of PNG's natural resource extraction enterprises can be viscerally negative. In a brief survey of two of the most active Facebook pages devoted to politics, society, and economy in PNG, "Sharp

Talk" and "The PNG News Page," this appears to also be the case for commentary on Ramu. Many posts voiced opinions on the toxic spill in August 2019, particularly on how the PNG state was culpable for not protecting national interests. The writer of the following comment alleges the corruption of state officials not only as an exacerbating factor in environmental damage but also as traitorous:

> The Ramu nickel mine should have been closed and ceased operation the day the spill occurred damaging the environment. The Mining Minister was so silent on this environmental damaging issue. Hon. Tuke, come out straight and say you got bribe money from the Chinese company operating the Mine…When and how much longer will it take for you to be a true PNG patriot… When will we change our attitude of benefiting and living luxuriously at the expense and suffering of the people and the country?

Posts on The PNG News Page voiced a range of grievances over the Ramu's tax-exempt status and export of profits. Comment writers frame their concern as patriotism and anti-colonial. Further, the promise of Chinese investment as an employment windfall is harshly condemned. For example, one user wrote:

> It is time now to wake up and see what these multinational companies are doing to us Papua New Guineans… I don't hold any personal grudges with any company- I speak as a concerned and disgusted patriotic Papua New Guinean.

A second added:

> When is somebody going to stand up and say – Enough is enough???? Since when did we become a colony of China so that they can push us to bypass our set processes? Forget the promised 1000 plus job – its rubbish, breadcrumbs, bullshit – as the majority of the workforce will be Chinese again – people whole don't speak a word of English.

Among the commentary, solutions to endemic corruption and self-interest are proposed through a call for a revolutionary overhaul of the ruling class in PNG:

> Chinese/Mafia Syndicates are protected by Government/Corporate Syndicates including our law, law makers and enforcers. Its systematic. This country needs a group of likeminded radical intelligent politicians and educated elites who are concerned about the future of this country to bring all these giants down.

In sum, after 2018, the impact of a toxic spill and the COVID-19 pandemic brought into sharper focus critical discourses that were in circulation up to 2017. That is, the purported benefits of Chinese presence at Ramu are unconvincing to many civil society actors. Further, Chinese operations at Ramu exist within a space of grounded disempowerment felt by grassroots Papua New Guineans. Under such conditions, frustration at Chinese companies is easily converted into anger with the PNG government.

7.7 Analysis and Conclusion

This chapter examines state and civil society approaches towards self-reliance in the context of decolonization, particularly in the ways this concept is interpreted as China becomes a global presence. Within Papua New Guinea, there are forms of power/knowledge in the process of defining self-reliance, as well as emerging counter-hegemonic interpretations. The PNG state has linked Chinese economic presence, exemplified through mining in this chapter, to a form of political and economic freedom from former colonizers or traditional partners, such as Australia and the United States. As the range of "non-traditional" partners expands, the "freer" PNG is from the interests of external states. Self-reliance is therefore exercised within sovereignty and independence of decision-making on the geopolitical stage. In other words, PNG makes decisions based on its interests and not on those of external powers. The narrative of self-reliance as "strategic independence" is aligned with the People's Republic of China's diplomatic messaging to prioritize the sovereignty of other states and to not interfere in their internal affairs (Rodd, 2020: 14). On the other hand, in shaping Papua New Guinean civil society discourses regarding China, the freedom to be critical, either of the PNG, Chinese, or any other states, emerges as the principal expression of self-reliance. This is not only a response borne from skepticism, but also from an assertion of national identity and political representation. In offering their views on Chinese presence, Papua New Guineans reclaim the right to PNG representation. While the state has placed agency within the Sino-PNG relationship, civil society exercises agency in resistance.

These patterns have implications on power-knowledge in PNG. The state's attempt to naturalize Chinese presence by making it consistent with PNG interests is incomplete. The following quote from Narokobi, cited earlier in this work, is essential in understanding why this is the state of affairs. He states that "the Melanesian Way is positive and free of categories that tie Melanesians to the conditioning of dominant external narratives." In this framework, critical commentary on Chinese presence in the mining sector informs us that in an ontological sense resistance to externalities, regardless of where they come from, is self-reliance. These criticisms are expressed in defending grounded interests, such as environmental conditions, and not just an absorption of overseas narratives outlining a vague "China threat." Transmission of contrasting self-reliance narratives occurs across all kinds of discursive spaces, including cyberspace. The state through media and government websites and civil society through its public forums, such as Facebook groups. A further point bears repeating, self-reliance is not just about "doing things for ourselves" but also about the field of power-knowledge in which who gets to speak about the land and people of PNG influences local responses to Chinese mining interests.

Overall, this chapter explores how the self-reliance discourse in PNG is enlisted by different domestic actors in conversation with Chinese investors in the natural resources industry. In particular, state, sub-state, and non-state actors attempt to construct the tone of Chinese interventions toward their interests. While there has been much discussion over Chinese messaging to the Global South, images of China created by host societies have been explored less. This work reveals the range of discourses surrounding Chinese presence at Ramu at various scales. I argue that holding positive, negative, or neutral views alike on Chinese investment at Ramu, PNG actors, ranging from civil society to the local and national government to the media, believe their claims stem from Melanesian post-colonial self-reliance narratives. Hence, the assertion of self-reliance informs relations with external entities.

A key element of self-reliance discourse is how it translates into policy. As such, the PNG national government is actively pursuing alternative sources of donor funding, provincial governments are advocating for more local benefits, and civil society is making modest gains regarding adequate compensation over impact. While all claims cannot be met in such a high-stakes environment, these processes indicate degrees of agency in relations with Chinese investors that should factor into regional geopolitical analyses of Chinese influence in Oceania. What the text analysis conducted in this work also tells us about Chinese investments in the PNG economy is that the government and civil society are vigilant regarding external interventions whether it is over public health, the environment, or financial benefits. Chinese investment has focused aspects of PNG society toward the dangers of neocolonialism through natural resource extraction whether it is from China or other countries.

An additional implication of this research concerns discourse and natural resources in general. Discourses of self-reliance are not limited by the kind of resources exploited for development. The discussion surrounding the mining industry in PNG could be equally applied to fisheries and logging in the country. Therefore, the kinds of discourse outlined in this research form part of greater conversations about development in PNG and Oceania, particularly as China becomes increasingly entangled in the domestic economy. The tensions outlined between civil society and the state regarding Chinese investment in state-building not only reveal different visions of the future for PNG but also translate to conceivable patterns across the Oceania region as China increases its aid and investment presence. In sum, the social context, subjective messaging, and identities of a variety of actors matter in any assessment of China's imprint on the Global South.

References

Act Now! (2010). *A brief history of the Ramu nickel mine and the submarine tailings disposal issue.* Retrieved June 3, 2021, from https://actnowpng.org/sites/default/files/A%20brief%20history%20of%20the%20Ramu%20nickel%20mine.pdf

Burton, M., & Daly, T. (2019, August 28). Chinese-owned nickel plant spills waste into Papua New Guinea bay. *Reuters.* Retrieved June 6, 2021, from https://news.yahoo.com/chinese-owned-nickel-plant-spills-085158980.html

Capey, D. (2013). *Blogging for social change in Papua New Guinea: A case study investigation of The Namorong Report.* PhD dissertation, Auckland University of Technology.

China Metallurgical Group Corporation. (undated). *About us.* Retrieved June 3, 2021, from http://www.mcc.com.cn/mccen/about_mcc/about_mcc60/index.html

Cultural Survival. (2010, March). *Papua New Guinea campaign.* Retrieved June 3, 2021, from https://www.culturalsurvival.org/publications/cultural-survival-quarterly/what-we-are-doing-your-money-papua-new-guinea-campaign

Diamond, I., & Quinby, L. (1988). *Feminism and Foucault: Reflections on resistance.* Northeastern University Press.

Fox, L. (2019, August 30). *Chinese-owned Ramu Nickel plant spills 200,000 litres of 'toxic' slurry into the sea.* Australian Broadcasting Corporation. Retrieved June 6, 2012, from https://www.abc.net.au/news/2019-08-30/chinese-owned-mine-in-png-spills-200 000-litres-of-toxic-slurry/11464108

Internet Live Stats. (2016). *Papua New Guinea internet users.* Real Time Statistics Project. Retrieved June 3, 2021, from https://www.internetlivestats.com/internet-users/papua-new-guinea/

Kabutaulaka, T. (2015). Re-presenting Melanesia: Ignoble savages and Melanesian alter-natives. *The Contemporary Pacific, 27*(1), 110–145.

Keating, E. (2015). Discourse, space, and place. In D. Tannen, H. E. Hamilton, & D. Schiffrin (Eds.), *The handbook of discourse analysis* (Vol. 1., pp. 244–261). John Wiley & Sons.

Kemish, I. (2020, July 3). *China's push into PNG has been surprisingly slow and ineffective: Why has Beijing found the going so tough?* The Conversation. Retrieved June 6, 2021, from https://theconversation.com/chinas-push-into-png-has-been-surprisingly-slow-and-ineffective-why-has-beijing-found-the-going-so-tough-140073

Logan, S. (2012). *Rausim! Digital politics in Papua New Guinea.* SSGM Discussion Paper 2012/9. Australian National University. Retrieved June 2, 2021, from http://dpabellschool.anu.edu.au/sites/default/files/publications/attachments/2015–12/2012_9_0.pdf

Mineral Resources Authority. (2009). *Mining history in PNG.* Retrieved June 3, 2021, from http://www.mra.gov.pg/Portals/2/Publications/mining%20history%20in%20png%20final.pdf

Narokobi, B. (1983). *The Melanesian Way.* Institute of Papua New Guinea Studies.

National Parliament of Papua New Guinea. (undated). *Constitution of the independent state of Papua New Guinea.* Retrieved June 3, 2021, from http://www.parliament.gov.pg/images/misc/PNG-CONSTITUTION.pdf

Neale T. (2005). *Historical overview of mining in PNG.* Melanesian Resources. Retrieved June 3, 2021, from http://infomine.com/

Nickel 28. (undated). *Ramu Nickel Cobalt operation: Overview.* Retrieved June 3, 2021, from https://www.nickel28.com/our-assets/ramu-nickel-cobalt-operation/overview/

Oelrich, C. (2011). *Ethnic conflict flares over Chinese nickel mine pollution.* Papua New Guinea Mine Watch. Retrieved June 3, 2021, from https://ramumine.wordpress.com/2011/12/27/ethnic-conflict-flares-over-chinese-nickel-mine-pollution/

Oxford Business Group. (2015, July 1). *China looks to mine Papua New Guinea assets.* Papua New Guinea Mine Watch. Retrieved June 3, 2021, from https://ramumine.wordpress.com/2015/07/01/china-looks-to-mine-papua-new-guinea-assets/

Pacific Institute of Public Policy. (2012, April). *Net benefits. Upgrading the coconut wireless: Internet uptake in the Pacific.* Retrieved June 2, 2021, from http://pacificpolicy.org/wp-content/blogs.dir/2/files/2012/04/DP20.pdf

Papua New Guinea Chamber of Mines and Petroleum. (2017). *Papua New Guinea Mineral Sector.* Retrieved June 3, 2021, from https://www.pngchamberminpet.com.pg/images/misc/17–117c_Overview_of_the_PNG_Minerals_Sector,July2017_Small.pdf

PNG Mineral Resources Authority. (undated). *Regular MRA publications.* Retrieved June 3, 2021, from http://www.mra.gov.pg/Publications.aspx

PNG Mineral Resources Authority. (2016). *Mining and exploration bulletin 2016.* Retrieved June 3, 2021. http://mra.gov.pg/Portals/0/Publications/Mining%20&%20Exploration%20Bulletin%202016.pdf

Ponowi Siwi Remo. (2016, July 13). *Future Papua New Guineans will pay for O'Neill reckless borrowing.* PNGBLOGS. https://web.archive.org/web/20200804140532/, https://www.png blogs.com/2016/07/future-papua-new-guineans-will-pay-for.html

Post-Courier. (2018, October 1). *Ramu NiCo announces K4.8b mine expansion.* Retrieved June 3, 2021, from https://postcourier.com.pg/ramu-nico-announces-k4-8b-mine-expansion/

Post-Courier. (2018, November 28). Probe into Ramu Nico. Retrieved June 3, 2021, from https://postcourier.com.pg/probe-into-ramu-nico/

Post-Courier. (2019, April 18). *Ramu NiCo has brought positive changes, says LO.* Retrieved June 3, 2021, from https://postcourier.com.pg/ramu-nico-brought-positive-changes-says-lo/

Post-Courier. (2020, February 26). Miner donates K10,000 for Madang coronavirus surveillance. Retrieved June 6, 2021, from https://postcourier.com.pg/miner-donates-k10000-for-madang-cor onavirus-surveillance/

Post-Courier. (2020, August 12). Mines provide ready market for fishermen. Retrieved June 6, 2012, from https://postcourier.com.pg/mine-provides-ready-market-for-fisherman/

Reuters. (2020, April 1). China-owned PNG nickel plant output down in 2019 after spill. Retrieved June 6, 2021, from https://www.reuters.com/article/mcc-nickel-papuanewguinea/china-owned-png-nickel-plant-output-down-in-2019-after-spill-idUSL4N2BP1ND

Safihao, J. (2013, May 17). *Ramu Mine landowners want more benefits and workers strike.* Papua New Guinea Mine Watch. Retrieved June 3, 2021, from https://ramumine.wordpress.com/2013/05/17/ramu-mine-landowners-want-more-benefits-and-workers-strike/

Sukot, S. (2008, June 1). *People's perspectives: Understanding the relationship between people and land in PNG and the struggle to maintain these important relationships.* Melanesian Indigenous Land Defence Alliance. Retrieved June 3, 2021, from http://milda.aidwatch.org.au/resources/documents/people%E2%80%99s-perspectives-und erstanding-relationship-between-people-and-land-png-and

Radio New Zealand. (2019, October 11). PNG's Ramu nickel mine mismanaged waste—Probe. Retrieved June 6, 2021, from https://www.rnz.co.nz/international/pacific-news/400752/png-s-ramu-nickel-mine-mismanaged-waste-probe

Radio New Zealand. (2019, October 30). Controversial PNG mine reopens but locals unhappy. Retrieved June 6, 2021, from https://www.rnz.co.nz/international/pacific-news/402018/controver sial-png-mine-reopens-but-locals-unhappy

Ramu Nico Management. (2019, July 20). *The project: Introduction.* Retrieved June 3, 2021, from http://www.ramunico.com/introduction/

Regis Tove Stella. (1999). Reluctant Voyages into Otherness: Practice and Appraisal in Papua New Guinean Literature. In V. Hereniko & R. Wilson (Eds.), *Inside out: Literature, cultural politics, and identity in the new Pacific* (pp. 221–230). Rowman & Littlefield.

Regis Tove Stella. (2007). *Imagining the other: The representation of the Papua New Guinean subject.* University of Hawai'i Press.

Rodd, A. (2020). A road to Island Sovereignty and empowerment? Fiji's aims within the Belt and Road initiative. *Island Studies Journal, 15*(2), 93–118.

Samana, U. (1988). *Papua New Guinea: Which way?* Arena Publications.

Smith, G. (2013). Nupela Masta? Local and expatriate labour in a Chinese-Run Nickel Mine in Papua New Guinea. *Asian Studies Review, 37*(2), 178–195.

Tavurvur. (2010, June 11). *Ramu Nickel Mine—Arguments against uprooting our people.* The Garamut. Retrieved June 3, 2021, from https://garamut.wordpress.com/2010/06/11/ramu-nickel-mine-arguments-against-uprooting-our-people/

The National. (2009, November 5). Nickel project entry to offset OTML exit. Retrieved June 3, 2012, from http://www.thenational.com.pg/nickel-project-entry-to-offset-otml-exit/

The National. (2011, January 20). China's role more negative in Pacific, says think-tank. Retrieved June 3, 2021, from http://www.thenational.com.pg/china%E2%80%99s-role-more-negative-in-pacific-says-think-tank/

The National. (2011, April 14). Who Is genuine investor—The US or China? Retrieved June 3, 2021, from http://www.thenational.com.pg/who-is-genuine-investor-%E2%80%93-the-us-or-china/

The National. (2011, December 23). Ramu NiCo wins deep-sea waste case. Retrieved June 3, 2021, from http://www.thenational.com.pg/ramu-nico-wins-deep-sea-waste-case/

The National. (2012, November 6). Chan: Mining driving PNG economy. Retrieved June 3, 2021, from http://www.thenational.com.pg/chan-mining-driving-png-economy/

The National. (2014, March 26). Ramu NiCo: Safety at mining site. Retrieved June 3, 2021, from http://www.thenational.com.pg/ramu-nico-safety-at-mining-site/

The National. (2015, November 16). Mine progressing well, firm says. Retrieved June 3, 2021, from http://www.thenational.com.pg/mine-progressing-well-firm-says/

The National. (2017, February 1). Students on internship training with Ramu NiCo. Retrieved June 3, 2021, from http://www.thenational.com.pg/students-internship-training-ramu-nico/

The National. (2017, February 23). Envoy commends mine. Retrieved June 3, 2021, from http://www.thenational.com.pg/envoy-commends-mine/

Weedon, C. (1987). *Feminist practice and poststructuralist theory*. Wiley-Blackwell.

Week in China. (2020, May 8). *Digging a deep hole*. Retrieved June 6, 2021, from https://www.weekinchina.com/2020/05/digging-a-deep-hole/

Winduo, S. E. (2000). Unwriting Oceania: The repositioning of the Pacific writer scholars within a folk narrative space. *New Literary History, 31*(3), 599–613.

Winduo, S. E. (2011) *Reconstituting Indigenous Oceanic Folktales*. Folktales and Fairy Tales: Translation, Colonialism, and Cinema, University of Hawai'i at Mānoa International Symposium. Conference Presentation.

Henryk Szadziewski earned his PhD at the Department of Geography and Environment at the University of Hawai'i at Mānoa. He holds a bachelor's (hons) in modern Chinese and Mongolian studies from the University of Leeds and a master's (econ.) in development management from the University of Wales. His research focuses on the local impacts of Chinese state economic interventions in Xinjiang and Oceania.

Chapter 8
China's Tied Aid to Trinidad and Tobago: Impact and Perceptions

Theodor Tudoroiu and Amanda Reshma Ramlogan

Abstract This chapter engages the theoretical literature on development assistance and tied aid in order to assess, on the basis of interviews conducted in Trinidad, the local perception and consequences of China's development assistance. Trinidad and Tobago has the highest connectivity with China in the Commonwealth Caribbean and is a major recipient of Chinese foreign aid. As elsewhere in the region, the latter mainly takes the form of large infrastructure projects loan-financed by Beijing. Critically, this is tied aid: all contractors, materials, and workers have to come from China. Trinidad's political leaders welcome the projects, which they use to increase their political legitimacy and electoral support. But the tied aid has important negative socio-economic consequences that have triggered contractors and labor large-scale frustration and protests. Moreover, the secret negotiation of projects is damaging good governance. All this leads to a rather dark picture of what is officially presented as a Sino-Caribbean solidarity-based, win-win cooperative relationship. A gap has emerged between Trinidadian political elites and the society at large. The former fully accept the harmonious image of China-the-benefactor. But common citizens reject this image and perceive the pro-Beijing actions of the political elites as detrimental to the interests of their own country.

Keywords Trinidad and Tobago · China · Development assistance · Tied aid · Infrastructure projects

Abbreviations

DAC   Development Assistance Committee
OECD   The Organization for Economic Cooperation and Development
IDB   Inter-American Development Bank
CAF   Development Bank of Latin America

T. Tudoroiu (✉) · A. R. Ramlogan
The University of the West Indies, St. Augustine, Trinidad and Tobago
e-mail: theodor.tudoroiu@sta.uwi.edu

8.1 Introduction

This chapter explores an aspect of China's seldom scrutinized presence in the Caribbean. As the region is better known for its beaches than for relevant international interactions, its relations with the rising global power have been much less studied than those of neighboring Latin America. In addition to filling this relative gap, the case study of Trinidad and Tobago presented in the following pages is illustrative of a very interesting situation characterized by the totally different perceptions of and attitudes toward China's aid of political elites and the society at large, respectively. The choice of Trinidad is due to the fact that it represents the largest economy and one of the most developed countries in the Caribbean; moreover, it has "the highest connectivity with China in the region" (Khan, 2017). Yet, both investment and trade are limited and by far inferior to those between Trinidad and the United States. Beijing's main presence consists in massive development assistance that takes the form of large loan-financed infrastructure projects similar to those constructed in many other Global South countries (see the chapters by Herlijanto and Mock in this volume). Critically, this is tied aid—*i.e.* all contractors, materials, and workers have to come from China—and the consequences of this aspect greatly impact Trinidad's economy and society. In order to analyze this topic, this chapter engages the theoretical literature on development assistance and tied aid. Special attention is paid to the conceptual apparatus, debates, and collaborative efforts developed in the framework of the Development Assistance Committee (DAC) of the Organization for Economic Cooperation and Development (OECD), which are contrasted with Beijing's very different approach. The Trinidadians' perception of China's tied aid is assessed through 30 interviews conducted in 2017–2018 with public servants, journalists, businessmen, members of the public, and scholars with an interest in Chinese-related topics. Given the sensitivity of certain questions, special attention was given to ensuring the anonymity of respondents. The 40- to 90-minute interviews were based on a structured questionnaire containing 35 multiple choice closed-ended questions and 5 open-ended ones. The respondents were also asked to make extensive written and oral comments; these were extremely useful in revealing beliefs and attitudes absent from the scholarly literature. In a number of cases, the analytical depth of responses was remarkable.

The chapter is structured as follows: the next section constructs the appropriate theoretical framework. Section 8.3 scrutinizes the general features of China's development assistance. Section 8.4 presents the bilateral relationship between China and Trinidad and Tobago. Sections 8.5 and 8.6 analyze Beijing's tied aid to Trinidad and its economic, social, and governance effects. Their diverging perception by political elites and citizens as well as ensuing issues for both Trinidad and China are further discussed in the concluding section.

8.2 Development Assistance and Tied Aid

8.2.1 Defining Development Assistance

Between the end of the Cold War and the recent rise of "new" donors that include China, undisputed Western hegemony in the field of foreign aid resulted in the creation of a "thin" institutional framework that still provides the largest amount of development assistance: the international aid regime centered on the Development Assistance Committee (DAC) of the Organization for Economic Cooperation and Development (see Bräutigam, 2011; Strange et al., 2017: 936). Importantly for this section, the DAC has used its know-how and influence to define key concepts and to impose them in the theory and practice of "official development assistance", which it defines as flows to countries and territories on its list of recipients and to multilateral institutions that are provided by official agencies, including state and local governments, or by their executive agencies, and whose transactions (a) are administered with the promotion of the economic development and welfare of developing countries as its main objective, and (b) are concessional in character and convey a grant element of at least 25% (calculated at a rate of discount of 10%) (OECD, 2018). Starting with 2018 data, conditions under point b) have become more complex. The size of the grant element and the rate of discount now vary significantly based on the level of development of the recipient country. The development of the DAC's conceptual apparatus was accompanied by a number of debates and collaborative efforts intended to increase the effectiveness of development assistance; the relevant case of tied aid is detailed later in this section. However, the rise of China as a massive donor is increasingly challenging the DAC-centered system. Beijing is not an OECD member and completely ignores DAC criteria; tends to be non-transparent in its interactions with developing countries; and its very philosophy of development and development assistance diverges greatly from that shared by DAC members. Unsurprisingly, these differences have led to a conceptual clash that accompanies the more general Sino-Western rivalry in the developing world.

As explained in more detail in Sect. 8.3, an important aspect of this clash is represented by the Western conditionality-based approach to development assistance as opposed to China's win–win, South–South cooperative discourse. Beijing's key claim is that, unlike the exploitative West, China is a developing country that disinterestedly provides development assistance as a form of international solidarity with fellow Global South peoples. However, the literature is explicit on the fact that "the aid relationship between donor and recipient is an extremely asymmetric power relationship" (Stokke, 1995/2006: 33) that places the recipient state in a clear position of inferiority while giving obvious advantages to the donor. Two aspects need to be mentioned. On the one hand, "foreign aid, by definition, represents an intervention in the recipient country": the way it is channeled, its form, and especially its target groups create within the recipient state beneficiaries and losers that see their resources and power position significantly influenced by the donor. Section 8.6

will show how this general statement actually applies to the case of China's development assistance to Trinidad and Tobago. Political elites represent the main target and beneficiary of Beijing's aid; and this has resulted in Chinese-friendly policies that ignore public frustration with tied aid. A major perception gap has emerged, with citizens questioning the legitimacy of their elites' aid-related actions. On the other hand, despite frequent altruistic statements, development assistance is always "an instrument to pursue foreign policy objectives" (Ibid., 2, 34). In fact, it represents—in addition to trade and investment—an important component of economic diplomacy. As such, it is used to achieve both the political goals and the commercial objectives of foreign policy. The former, (geo)political dimension is illustrated by Trinidad's alignment with Beijing in terms of voting at the UN General Assembly and its strong support for China's Caribbean and global policies and interests in exchange for generous Chinese development assistance (see Sect. 8.4). The latter, "business end" dimension (Trinidad, 2013: 22) is directly concerned by the use of tied aid.

8.2.2   Tied Aid

Tied aid is defined as aid granted to countries that, in most cases, belong to the developing world, "on the condition that the goods or services acquired with the aid funds are purchased from the donor (…) or a limited group of other countries" (La Chimia & Arrowsmith, 2009: 707). It represents a perfect illustration of the idea once expressed by President Nixon: "remember that the main purpose of American aid is not to help other nations but to help ourselves" (Opeskin quoted by Brakman & van Marrewijk, 1998: 133). Accordingly, tied aid "has been called 'devalued aid' as the recipient may have to purchase goods higher in price and lower in quality than are available on international markets" (Rutherford, 2013). There are three types of tying. Formally tied aid imposes that goods be purchased from the donor country only. Partially tied aid limits procurement to goods originating in specific countries or regions, usually including the donor and recipient. Informally tied aid "is untied in principle but tied in practice" (La Chimia & Arrowsmith, 2009: 708): donors may fund projects in sectors where their own companies have a competitive advantage; impose bidding procedures that favor their companies; link present aid donations to larger future purchases; or require that only companies with good access to credit markets be selected (Carbone, 2014: 104). It should be mentioned that empirical evidence clearly indicates that donors concentrate tied aid on specialized areas where their firms hold comparative advantages (Jepma, 1991: 12). As shown in the following sections, this explains why China's development assistance to the Caribbean consists mainly in infrastructure projects. Various scholars have argued convincingly that tying does not bring significant advantages to the donor country as a whole (Brakman & van Marrewijk, 1998: 135; Carbone, 2014: 105; Jepma, 1991: 14; Morrissey & White, 1996: 209; Pincin, 2013: 375). However, benefits can be "very substantial indeed" for concerned individual business firms and sectors

(Jepma, 1991: 13–14; Tajoli quoted by Pincin, 2013: 375). For example, given the fact that, as explained in Sect. 8.5, Trinidad has well-entrenched and competent local construction firms as well as a capital market able to support them, Chinese companies would have never entered its construction market in the absence of Beijing's tied aid.

Unfortunately, benefits on the donor side are accompanied by considerable negative consequences for the recipients of tied aid. They are denied the best-value goods and services available in the global market (La Chimia & Arrowsmith, 2009: 707). Competition for tied aid contracts being usually limited to a few donor firms, procurement prices tend to be higher. Tying limits the choice open to recipients to products and technology supplied by the donor, which are not necessarily the most appropriate (Morrissey & White, 1996: 209). It was also noted that tied aid tends to lead to the funding of projects requiring imports of capital-intensive goods such as telecommunications and—as shown by the Sino-Trinidadian example—infrastructure instead of smaller and more poverty-focused projects such as rural development (Carbone, 2014: 104). In addition, patterns of trade are distorted in favor of the donor country: it is highly unlikely that, in the absence of tied aid, anyone in the Caribbean would import construction materials from remote China. This might limit opportunities for industrial development in the recipient country, whose industry is deprived of the opportunity to provide goods and services. It might also frustrate the development of trade between developing countries (La Chimia & Arrowsmith, 2009: 708, 711), thus hampering their economic development. Ultimately, the tying of aid reduces its very concessionality (Morrissey & White, 1996: 208), which represents the *raison d'être* of development assistance. It should be added that, in addition to these negative economic consequences, tied aid can undermine local institutional capacity and generate a "lack of ownership" attitude toward aid in the recipient country (Pincin, 2013: 376). This is precisely the case of Trinidad and Tobago, where various governments have repeatedly stated that the Chinese side has the right to take key decisions such as choosing contractors because it finances the infrastructure projects (see Sect. 8.5). The financing, however, is represented by Chinese loans; accordingly, Trinidadian tax-payers are denied control of projects they ultimately pay for. It can therefore be argued that tied aid undermines developing countries' ownership of their own development process, preventing them from taking full responsibility of actions that impact directly on the welfare of their citizens (Kim & Kim, 2016: 290).

The actual cost of tying aid depends on the flexibility of substitution (*i.e.* on recipient's access to more than one source of aid); on the extent to which substitution is permitted by donors; and on the recipient's willingness and ability to exploit substitution possibilities by promoting competition among donors (Jepma, 1991: 15). Various authors have assessed the average direct cost to aid recipients at 20–25% (Bhagwati quoted by Carbone, 2014: 104), 10–30% (Jepma, 1991: 16), and 15–30% (Pincin, 2013: 375). It should be mentioned that it was impossible to make such an assessment in the case of China's tied aid to Trinidad. But because Beijing does not allow for any flexibility of substitution with respect to the infrastructure projects that represent most of its development assistance, the direct cost is likely to be closer to the upper limits mentioned in the literature.

The high cost to recipient countries and the donor's limited benefits lead to the obvious conclusion that the tying of aid is detrimental and should be brought to an end. It is the OECD Development Assistance Committee that, for some decades, has taken the lead in the effort to untie aid. The first major step was the 1991 adoption of the OECD Helsinki Arrangement on Officially Supported Export Credits and Ex Ante Guidance Gained for Tied Aid (La Chimia & Arrowsmith, 2009: 721). Negotiations initiated in the late 1990s resulted in the May 2001 OECD Recommendation to Untie Official Development Assistance to the Least Developed Countries. This was the key document that "marked the acceptance of the principle that aid tying represents a bad practice in international development" (Carbone, 2014: 108). However, it was not legally binding (Ibid., 103, 107–108; Engelbert, 2014: 270; La Chimia, 2013; La Chimia & Arrowsmith, 2009: 712). Continued DAC efforts to untie aid were marked by declarations, forums, and conferences held in 2002, 2005, 2008, and 2011. But progress was limited; it was even claimed that after 2011 "the issue of aid untying has disappeared from the radar of donors" (Carbone, 2014: 110, 103). Still, DAC-related international pressure has led to the significant reduction of tied aid levels during the last four decades. The share of tied aid was 15% in 2011 as compared to 48% in 1987 (Kim & Kim, 2016: 289). Formally untied aid reached 76% in 2010 from 40% in 2000. The problem is that the distribution of contract awards suggests that informal tying practices continue to exist (Carbone, 2014: 105). The literature shows that a "prisoner's dilemma" is at work, as donors that initiate the process of untying damage their own interests if other do not follow (Jepma, 1991: 14; La Chimia & Arrowsmith, 2009: 711).

However, the most important challenge to the untying of aid is of a different nature. Despite their reluctance, DAC members have accepted the principle that tied aid represents a bad practice and have progressively diminished its level. This, however, is limited to OECD members, a category that does not include the emerging donors (Engelbert, 2014: 271). These increasingly visible providers of development assistance do not share negative views of tied aid and, through their practices, endanger the decades-long efforts of the DAC. The largest and most representative member of this category is China.

8.3   China's Development Assistance

Recent decades have witnessed what is generally called "the rise of new donors", even if some of them—such as China—had in fact started to provide development assistance back in the 1950s. What is indeed new is the sharp increase in the amount of foreign aid provided by these non-OECD states both in absolute terms and as a share of global development finance. The category is large and its members range from major donors such as China, Russia, India, and—for a time—Venezuela (Strange et al., 2017: 936) to less expected ones such as Liechtenstein, Cyprus, Malta, Latvia, Lithuania, Romania, and Thailand. The latter tend to officially report their development assistance flows to the OECD; but their impact is much smaller than that of states in the first group, which are not interested in joining the DAC regime or in respecting its principles (Ibid.; OECD, 2012: 258).

As already mentioned, China is in fact an old donor whose first aid programs were launched after the 1955 Bandung Conference. Since then they have changed, diversified, and "continuously adapted to the shifting international landscape, the domestic situation, and national objectives" (Trinidad, 2013: 19). The literature has identified four main stages (for a recent detailed presentation see Kilby, 2017: 11–30). The first was strongly influenced by political and ideological motives related to Maoist China's anti-Western, anti-Soviet, and non-aligned foreign policy choices. In particular, Prime Minister Zhou Enlai's 1963–1964 visit to ten African countries led to the rapid expansion of Chinese development assistance to that continent, which culminated in 1972 at US $450 million and included the iconic TAZARA railway. Starting with the late 1970s, Deng Xiaoping's economic reforms marked a visible turn toward profit-oriented relations with Third World states that resulted in a considerable decrease in China's foreign aid. This changed once more after the 1989 Tiananmen massacre, when leaders of developing countries were the only ones to support the actions of the communist government and to condemn Western criticism and sanctions. This convinced the leadership in Beijing of the need to stimulate such support through the provision of aid. Finally, spectacular economic development since the 1990s turned China into a huge consumer of Global South raw materials; impressive amounts of development assistance have been used by Beijing to consolidate a mutually beneficial relationship (Zhang, 2015: 52, 57–59; Freeman, 2015: 1–2, 6; Kilby, 2017: 11–30).

While interesting and representing a topic worth being studied in its own right, the Chinese actors and mechanisms involved in the complex and complicated dynamic of foreign aid-related decision making in Beijing (see Zhang & Smith, 2017: 2330; Varrall, 2016: 21) fall outside the scope of this chapter. Another important aspect cannot be appropriately examined due to the generally acknowledged scarcity of reliable information: China is famous for its lack of transparency on development assistance-related statistical data. Moreover, the limited available information does not follow the same reporting criteria as DAC donors, which makes comparisons difficult (Stahl, 2018: 12–13; Bernal, 2016: 4105–4106; Brautigam, 2009: 20; for more details, see below). Fortunately, the exact value of China's overall foreign aid is not an issue of particular importance for this chapter. Accordingly, it will suffice to say that, in many regions of the Global South that include the Caribbean, China's massive aid is actively and effectively challenging the West's post-Cold War hegemony in the field of development assistance. A third, better-known aspect is represented by the instruments used by the Chinese government to finance its foreign aid. They are represented by China Development Bank, which "offers mostly commercial interest rates that are fairly analogous to the World Bank, IDB, and the CAF, and sometimes slightly higher" (Gallagher, 2016: 78); and China ExIm-Bank, which receives subsidies directly from the Ministry of Finance and uses them to subsidizes its smaller loans to low-income countries. The interest rates of these loans are somewhat lower than those of the US Ex-Im Bank, but only a fraction of total Chinese lending—1.2% in the case of Latin America—is concerned. No less than

82% of the China ExIm-Bank loans to Latin American recipients carry commercial interest rates. The formula preferred is that of "blending export promotion with development aid to offer lower-cost options to countries in need" (Ibid., 79–80), which is very different from the DAC approach.

So are the principles of China's development assistance. The 1963 "Eight Principles" of foreign aid stem from the famous 1954 "Five Principles of Peaceful Co-existence"; all were articulated by Prime Minister Zhou Enlai. They "have been the bedrock of Chinese foreign aid over the past 50 years" and are used to contrast China's and Western development assistance policies (Kilby, 2017: 19). The Eight Principles are

> equality and mutual benefit in providing aid to other countries; respect for the sovereignty of recipient countries (…); provision of interest-free or low-interest loans often with extended time limits; empowerment of aid recipient countries to embark on the road to self-reliance and independent economic development; a focus on affordable projects that produce quick wins; provision of the best quality equipment and materials manufactured by China at international market prices; provision of technical assistance that ensures that the personnel of the recipient country fully masters the technology; and the provision of amenities to Chinese experts despatched to help in construction in recipient countries consistent with local living standards. (Varrall, 2016: 21)

They allow Beijing to present itself as a disinterested member of the Global South that engages other developing countries in a win-win, solidarity-based form of mutually profitable South-South relationship. This is detailed in the two white papers on China's foreign aid made public in 2011 and 2014. The first one enumerates five principles—unremittingly helping recipient countries build up their self-development capacity; imposing no political conditions; adhering to equality, mutual benefit and common development; remaining realistic while striving for the best; and keeping pace with the times and paying attention to reform and innovation—and eight forms of foreign aid: complete projects, goods and materials, technical cooperation, human resource development cooperation, Chinese medical teams working abroad, emergency humanitarian aid, overseas volunteer programs, and debt relief (Information Office of the State Council of the People's Republic of China, 2011; see Kitano, 2014: 308–309; Trinidad, 2013: 35–36). The second white paper of 2014 also mentions three types of financial foreign assistance (grants, interest-free loans, and concessional loans) and notes that complete projects and goods and materials had been the main forms of China's foreign assistance (Information Office of the State Council of the People's Republic of China, 2014). This reflects Beijing's special interest in infrastructure projects that is highly relevant to this chapter.

The "distinctiveness" of Chinese foreign aid from the DAC one is equally important. Studies of China's socialization into the international norms and practices of the Western development assistance regime show that, while such a trend has been noted by some scholars, overall results remain irrelevant (Reilly, 2012: 71–72). Differences start with Beijing's self-presentation as a development partner instead of a donor (Trinidad, 2013: 38). They continue with the content of what China defines as foreign aid: unlike the DAC, it includes military aid, construction of sports facilities, export credits, non-concessional state loans, and aid used to foster Chinese investment, but—surprisingly—not flows through multilateral institutions, scholarships for Global South students studying in China, or assistance to newly arrived refugees inside the host country (Bräutigam, 2011: 752, 756; Kitano, 2014: 302; Zhang & Smith, 2017: 2332). Furthermore, the Chinese frequently use original financial instruments such as natural resource-backed loans. Their "package financing" mixes aid, investment, as well as concessional and non-concessional financing (Grimm *et al.* quoted by Strange et al., 2017: 939). Accordingly, "China's cooperation may be developmental, but it is not primarily based on official development aid" (Bräutigam, 2011: 752).

In addition, China's aid modality is state-centered. As non-governmental organizations portray an image of altruism and flexibility while their activity is related to the promotion of transparency and good governance, many DAC donors channel a considerable amount of development assistance to civil society. Mirroring their domestic policies, Chinese policymakers "see important roles for the state in helping an economy to develop" and completely exclude NGOs from their foreign aid activities (Trinidad, 2013: 38–39). This is related to the more general development purpose of aid. The DAC "emphasizes the social and institutional underpinnings of development and focuses on a more comprehensive notion of development that embraces all dimensions of poverty" (Goldin *et al.* quoted by Trinidad, 2013: 36); importantly, democracy and good governance are considered to be conducive to growth. For its part, the Chinese aid disproportionately focuses on infrastructure development, which "indicates that China puts more premium on the physical capital requirement of economic growth" (Trinidad, 2013: 36). In the process, it does not pay attention to the domestic situation of recipient states and does not see a problem in cooperating with brutal dictatorial regimes. Section 8.6 shows that even in a consolidated democracy such as Trinidad and Tobago specific features of Beijing's aid endanger existing policies and practices of public transparency and accountability, thus negatively affecting the Caribbean country's good governance. Accordingly, China's development assistance has "weakened the leverage of the West in the broader liberal regime around social justice, gender justice, human rights, environmental norms, and other hard-won global agreements" (Kilby, 2017: 34). This has led many scholars and journalists speak about Chinese "rogue aid", which is "toxic" as it is in the process of "underwriting a world that is more corrupt, chaotic, and authoritarian" (Naím, 2007: 95; see Trinidad, 2013: 19). The opposing view notes that China's development assistance offers a new source of financing that introduces competitive pressure, thus allowing Global South governments to engage in more aggressive bargaining and implicitly decreasing the power of traditional donors (Swedlund, 2017: 391). In fact, this is part of the wider "China good vs. China bad" debate that represents one of the most heated contemporary IR disputes. It is important to remind that, historically, the activity of the DAC—and especially the fact that this committee does not provide an official voice for developing countries—has in no way been free of similar if not harsher criticism (see Ashoff, 2000; Carbonnier, 2010; Hynes & Scott, 2013). The analysis of these two vast debates, however, falls outside the scope of this chapter. Therefore, we will only note that (1) Beijing's massive development assistance is in many regards very different from that provided by DAC donors; and (2) some of these differences have been subject to heavy criticism. Despite its contribution to the development of the Global South, China's foreign aid is by no means unanimously perceived as a positive phenomenon.

While this is hardly the most important difference between China's and the DAC's development assistance principles, Beijing does not share the view that tied aid is detrimental and should be brought to an end. Accordingly, China's Ministry of Commerce offers only grants and preferential loans that are tied to Chinese firms, labor, and materials. The Chinese prepare a list with companies eligible to bid on foreign aid project tenders. The concessional aid guidelines of China ExIm-Bank officially tie the aid at a level of 50%, but in many cases the actual figure is much higher. The contractor or exporter needs to be Chinese; likewise, inputs for concessional aid projects have to come from China (Brautigam, 2009: 152; Lahtinen, 2018: 42). Up to a certain level, local or international sub-contractors, labor, and supplies can also be used, at least in principle; but this depends on the bargaining power of the recipient government, which is seldom significant (Ellis, 2014: 2, 49). Accordingly, as shown in Sect. 8.5, almost all of the Chinese aid to Trinidad and Tobago has been tied at a level of 100%.

8.4   China's Relations with Trinidad and Tobago

8.4.1   China in the Caribbean

China's interest in the Caribbean is due to the following factors: (1) the "diplomatic duel" between Beijing and Taipei, which was the initial cause of China's involvement in one of the two main regions that still recognize Taiwan (the other being the South Pacific); (2) the assertive global agenda of the new generation of Chinese leaders; (3) the associated growing rivalry between China and the United States; (4) marginally, the perception of the Caribbean as a market for Chinese goods; and (5) in the case of certain countries that include Trinidad and Tobago, the view of the region as a source of raw materials. For their part, Caribbean states—except the few that still recognize Taiwan—are interested in China due to (1) Beijing's development assistance; (2) hopes for tourism-, investment-, and export-led growth, many of which are rather unrealistic; (3) the idea of South-South cooperation as an alternative to American and Western dominance; (4) Caribbean political elites' self-interested political and electoral instrumentalization of actual and potential China-related economic benefits; (5) the preference of these elites for the Chinese approach of development assistance as opposed to the Western conditionality related to human rights, the rule of law, and good governance; and (6) citizens' positive overall perception of China (see Ellis, 2009: 9–32; Montoute, 2013: 112, 122–123; Bernal, 2016: 5676–5807).

The initial Taiwan-related Chinese presence in the Caribbean was considerably upgraded in 2013, when President Xi Jinping visited Trinidad and Tobago and met the leaders of eight Caribbean nations only some month after taking power. He expressed the "firm commitment to building comprehensive partnerships of cooperation", which involved US $1.5 billion of concessional loans and US $1.5 billion of special loans for infrastructure development (Ministry of Foreign Affairs of the People's Republic of China, 2018). The Chinese leader also made clear that, in addition to trade and investment opportunities, China also sought "strategic partnerships" in the region (Southerland, 2017). Accordingly, bilateral relations with all Caribbean states that recognize Beijing were dramatically expanded. China has also engaged the region in the framework of Latin American-Caribbean organizations such as the Organization of American States, the UN Economic Commission for Latin America and the Caribbean, the Inter-American Development Bank, the Inter-American Investment Corporation, and the China-CELAC (the Community of Latin American and Caribbean States) Forum; and in that of exclusively Caribbean ones, such as the biennial China-Caribbean Consultations, the Caribbean Development Bank, the China-Caribbean Joint Business Council, and the China-Caribbean Economic and Trade Cooperation Forum. Moreover, in 2018 the Caribbean states were invited to join the Belt and Road Initiative (Barrios 2018; Bernal, 2016: 4185–4200; Oosterveld et al., 2018: 24, 34; Roett & Paz, 2015: 499). It is important to note that much of this was done during the 2008–2016 "diplomatic truce" between Beijing and Taipei and therefore has nothing to do with the issue of Taiwan (Tudoroiu, 2017: 206). Observers have explained it as a consequence of the increasingly visible Sino-American rivalry and, more specifically, as a response to Washington's anti-Chinese actions in the South China Sea. The resulting strategy is based on a multidimensional and multitask Chinese policy that builds new trade, aid, and diplomacy cooperation mechanisms as well as ad hoc institutions. The goal is to integrate China into the Caribbean framework of economic and diplomatic governance while simultaneously transforming the parameters of engagement. By constructing its own institutional architecture and by projecting political and legal power, "Beijing has set about achieving nothing less than the genesis of a new regional order, built on functioning institutions and rules (...): *its* regional order" (Haro Navejas, 2013: 147, 203, 209–210; emphasis in the original).

8.4.2 The China–Trinidad Relationship

Due to its gas and oil reserves, Trinidad and Tobago (1.4 million inhabitants) represents the Caribbean's largest economy (Braveboy-Wagner, 2010: 424) and, from a socio-economic point of view, one of the most developed countries of the region. Unlike many of its neighbors, it possesses an industry and natural resources that already are—be it on a small scale—exported to China. In particular, Trinidad's production of liquefied natural gas is one of the largest in the world. As demand in the United States—its traditional market—is expected to diminish due to the shale gas revolution, it was believed that the expansion of the Panama Canal would allow for the reorientation of Trinidadian exports to China (Mander, 2013). Moreover, from a political point of view the government in Port of Spain is an influent regional actor that cannot be ignored by any external power with an interest in the Caribbean.

Accordingly, Trinidad and Tobago "has the highest connectivity with China in the region" as noted by two 2017 reports of the International Labor Organization and the Caribbean Development Bank, respectively (Khan, 2017). It is China's largest trade partner in the English Caribbean (Yue, 2018), the largest recipient of Chinese loans in the region, which reached US $2.5bn in 2015 (Eduardo Pastrana Buelvas and Hubert Gehring quoted by Oosterveld et al., 2018: 67), and the first Caribbean state to have joined the Belt and Road Initiative (Office of the Prime Minister Republic of Trinidad and Tobago, 2018; Shiwei, 2018). It was Port of Spain that President Xi Jinping chose to visit in 2013 to meet Caribbean leaders. On that occasion, he agreed to "actively advance" bilateral cooperation in the fields of energy, minerals, infrastructure development, telecommunications, and agriculture. In particular, he offered a US $250 million loan for the Chinese-built Couva Children's Hospital and attended the launching ceremony of the project (*BBC*, June 1, 2013; Ministry of Foreign Affairs of the People's Republic of China, 2018). It should be noted that the massive Chinese development assistance to Trinidad consists mainly in loan-financed infrastructure projects; the largest three ones built between 2005 and 2016 were worth US $2 billion (Khan, 2017). The 2013 visit was followed by a flurry of bilateral interactions that included then Prime Minister Kamla Persad-Bissessar's February 2014 visit to Beijing, where she opened the embassy of the Republic of Trinidad and Tobago. She also secured an agreement to purchase a long-range patrol vessel, which represented a major breakthrough for China's arms sales to the region (Badri-Maharaj, 2016; Southerland, 2017) and sought assistance on five key issues that included the construction of six new economic zones, the development of a trans-shipment port and dry dock, two new hospitals, and loan agreements to finance these projects (*Power102fm News*, February 25, 2014). Cooperation in many other fields was initiated or expanded. The second Confucius Institute in the Caribbean had been inaugurated in Trinidad in October 2013; that same year, a partnership was launched between the China Agricultural University and the St. Augustine Campus of the University of the West Indies that led to the 2015 creation of an Agricultural Innovation Park at Orange Grove (*UWI Campus News*, October 23, 2015). Overall, more than 65 China–Trinidad agreements had been concluded by November 2019 in fields ranging from cultural to military cooperation (*Loop News*, August 10, 2017; Rampersad, 2019). The cooperative trend continued under the government led by Prime Minister Dr. Keith Rowley, who visited China in May 2018 to successfully negotiate projects that included the construction by the Beijing Construction and Engineering Group of a US $104 million industrial park in Point Lisas, financed through a loan from Exim Bank of China (Waithe, 2018). In September 2018 he signed with China Harbor Engineering Company a cooperation agreement for the development of a large dry dock facility in La Brea (Webb, 2018). Also in 2018, five Chinese banks were invited to operate in Trinidad and Tobago in order to turn the country into "a clearing house for the Chinese currency", to quote Communication

Minister Stuart Young (Kowlessar, 2018). The most important 2018 development, however, was the signing of the memorandum that turned Trinidad and Tobago into the first Caribbean state to join the Belt and Road Initiative (Office of the Prime Minister Republic of Trinidad and Tobago, 2018; Shiwei, 2018). Trinidad has indeed "the highest connectivity with China in the region" (Khan, 2017). Of course, there is a price to pay: the government in Port of Spain has closely been aligned with Beijing in terms of voting at the UN General Assembly (Oosterveld et al., 2018: 34, 70) and is strongly supportive of its regional and global policies and interests. At the same time, China has profited economically from the bilateral relationship mainly due to its use of tied aid.

8.5 China's Tied Aid to Trinidad

8.5.1 Elites' Interests and Public Perception

As elsewhere in the Caribbean, China's aid to Trinidad and Tobago is mainly represented by large infrastructure projects. Until very recently, all of it was tied at a level of 100%. Typically, one specific Chinese contractor was chosen for each project through non-transparent government-to-government negotiations resulting in undisclosed agreements. As shown below, this has created a high degree of frustration and discontent among local contractors, laborers, and the society at large. Yet, Trinidad's political elites have constantly considered this price worth paying in exchange for their own political and electoral benefits. In principle, Chinese development assistance is welcomed because geopolitical reasons and the financial crisis have made the United States and the European Union neglect the Caribbean. At the same time, China's "prime target remains the top elites" (Shen, 2015: 114). The associated "flattering diplomatic demarche" allows leaders of tiny islands "for a fleeting moment to live the illusion of respect" (Bernal, 2016: 3222–3223, 3230–3241). Instead of Western "lessons" and criticism of bad governance and corruption, they have their real or imaginary merits praised in eulogistic speeches that present their states as peers of the Middle Kingdom. More pragmatically, they are offered prestige infrastructure projects carefully calculated to increase their political legitimacy and electoral support. Prime Minister Patrick Manning opened the impressive Chinese loan-financed and built National Academy for the Performing Arts in November 2009, some months before the early general election of May 2010 (Webb, 2018). The following Prime Minister, Kamla Persad-Bissessar, negotiated in 2013 the purchase of a Chinese patrol vessel because it was deliverable prior to the 2015 election (Oosterveld et al., 2018: 66). Furthermore, she officially opened the Chinese loan-financed and built Couva Children's Hospital less than one month before that election despite the fact that it was not complete (Rogers, 2016). Things do not work differently between elections. The present Prime Minister, Dr. Keith Rowley, insisted on the fact that the La Brea project he negotiated with the Chinese would transform one of the most depressed communities in the country into "a place of excellence that the world is looking to" (Webb, 2018). Opposition politicians do criticize some of the China-related actions of the government; but, as illustrated by the case of Dr. Rowley, once in power they become champions of Beijing's infrastructure projects and instrumentalize them for their own political and electoral purposes. To quote a Trinidadian respondent, the Chinese "are willing to give [money] and politicians that really just are looking for getting headlines, they may be tempted to say OK, sign too quickly" (Respondent 30).

Indeed, they do sign too quickly. In a small Caribbean island, a huge infrastructure project represents a considerable part of the local construction market. The exclusion of national contractors and laborers affects severely the business sector as well as the level of employment of some of the underprivileged social groups. Contrary to initial local expectations, the Chinese development assistance results in lucrative activities whose profit goes back to China instead of benefiting the weakened local economy. The general public is fully aware of this situation. Beijing might represent an alternative to Western donors, but there are "conditionalities that come with Chinese money" (Respondent 1): "you don't get something for nothing" (Respondent 28). China's South-South cooperative discourse is regarded with skepticism: "even in South-South cooperation there are big players and bullies". "Chinese contractors are used, Chinese materials are used and [this] (…) is no different from the initiatives used by the US and some countries" (Respondent 28). Because "we have no bargaining power" (Respondent 3), the Chinese "tie you into using Chinese construction companies, Chinese workers etc. etc. So basically the money flows in and then out right back to China" (Respondent 20). This is an opinion shared by 60% of the respondents. The relationship is "very very beneficial essentially to China" because it "creates a substantial amount of monopoly" (Respondent 28).

8.5.2 Chinese Contractors

Trinidadian construction firms are well-entrenched, competent, and have access to a relatively well-developed capital market that does not need Chinese money to fund construction projects (Ellis, 2014: 79–80). This is why both local contractors and relevant professional associations such as the Trinidad and Tobago Institute of Architects have protested vocally against the non-transparent government-to-government negotiations associated with China's tied aid that result in all contracts being given to specific Chinese firms with no public tender (Bernal, 2016: 6702–6710). The president of the Local Content Chamber, Lennox Sirjusingh, stated that he was "deeply disturbed" by this practice (Sookraj, 2013). A local contractor, Emile Elias, described it as "a disaster for national development, for the local construction sector and for local labour" (*The Economist*, March 10, 2012). Such sectoral protests have found a considerable audience due to the outrageously poor quality of Chinese-built projects. Due to this aspect, it is in Trinidad that "Chinese-constructed projects have stirred more controversy than perhaps anywhere else in the region" (Oosterveld et al., 2018: 67).

The best example is the National Academy for the Performing Arts (NAPA), "an iconic space", "the jewel of the Caribbean" (*Trinidad Express*, November 22, 2016), that was opened in 2009 by then Minister Patrick Manning "with much fanfare" (*The Trinidad and Tobago Guardian*, August 21, 2016). The contract had been given without competitive tender to the Shanghai Construction Group as decided in an undisclosed China–Trinidad government-to-government agreement. NAPA was supposed to show how Chinese development assistance contributes to Trinidad's social and cultural advancement. In 2014, however, the building had to be closed as tiles were falling off, the foundation began failing, the moving stage showed major defects, and the support stands for the stage were crumbling (Ibid.). Repairs took two years and cost US $2.9 million (*TTWhistleBlower*, August 31, 2016). Moreover, the associated outstanding debt to China amounts to US $64 million (*CNC3*, March 3, 2018). A less spectacular but similar situation was that of the Southern Academy for the Performing Arts (SAPA), built by the same Shanghai Construction Group. Approximately 300 issues had to be corrected at the same cost of US $2.9 million (Bernal, 2016: 4814–4826). The SAPA outstanding debt to China amounts to US $26 million (*CNC3*, March 3, 2018).

The Couva children's hospital is a more complex example that reveals how the Chinese-built prestige infrastructure projects are instrumentalized by the leadership in Beijing to serve political interests, by Chinese firms for profit, and by local political elites for political legitimacy and electoral support. Then Prime Minister Kamla Persad-Bissessar launched the project in March 2012 to prove that "we are about being people centred" (Office of the Prime Minister, 2013). The money was found in China, which in December 2012 signed a government-to-government agreement for a US $150 million loan (*Caribbean Journal*, June 3, 2013; Office of the Prime Minister, 2013). In May–June 2013, President Xi Jinping visited Trinidad and showcased the project as "an example of the type of benefits provided by the P.R.C. to nations of the Caribbean" (Ellis, 2014: 51). The government in Port of Spain stated that the Chinese would choose the contractor, and it was once more the Shanghai Construction Group which was given preference. The project was to be completed in March 2015 (Gang, 2015). Then Prime Minister Kamla Persad-Bissessar officially opened the hospital in August 2015, less than one month before the general elections that, despite the electoral instrumentalization of the project, she eventually lost. Once in opposition, her party started to criticize the new government for not allocating money for the hospital's completion. The new finance minister, Colm Imbert, ironically noted that the hospital had already been opened and reminded that China was supposed to provide all funding (Rogers, 2016). It was only in April 2018 that Prime Minister Dr. Keith Rowley decided to complete the facility as an offshore medical school under the form of a public-private partnership (Hunte, 2018; Williams, 2018). However, the first actual use of the hospital was as a 230-bed Covid-19 quarantine facility, as decided by the Government in Port of Spain on February 27, 2020 (Douglas, 2020). It should be added that, only two years after their construction, a part of the roadway leading up to the hospital and the hospital's cooling tower collapsed (Rogers, 2016; Sookraj, 2018). Needless to say, many associated these failures with the NAPA and

SATA ones. Moreover, Trinidad's outstanding debt to China for the hospital amounts to US $135 million (*CNC3*, March 3, 2018).

Other smaller but similar examples could be given (see Oosterveld et al., 2018: 67–69). The conclusion is that, in Trinidad, general tied aid issues detrimental to local contractors and workers are supplemented by serious failures of the Chinese-built infrastructure projects that involve costly repairs and prevent the use of the completed buildings for long periods of time. Not all Chinese companies do such poor work, and the seriousness of failures varies widely. However, China frequently imposes contractors of dubious repute. China Railway Construction Caribbean Company, which was given the contract for the Chinese loan-financed US $233 million Arima Hospital without tender, was under investigation in China for shoddy work in the construction of railway projects. Chinese regulatory authorities ordered it and other four firms to fix structural problems on 12 rail lines, including a high-speed one where a deadly train crash occurred in July 2012 (Sookraj, 2013). The contractor imposed by the Chinese for the large dry dock facility in La Brea (see Sect. 8.4) is China Harbor Engineering Company, which illicitly funded the 2015 failed re-election campaign of the Sri Lankan President, was blacklisted for some years by the World Bank for fraud and corruption related to construction projects in the Cayman Islands (Kakaire, 2014), and was involved in corruption in a road construction project in the Philippines (Douglas, 2018b). The most visible Chinese contractor is Shanghai Construction Group, which besides NAPA, SAPA, and the Couva Children's Hospital built a terminal of the Piarco International Airport, the Cycling Velodrome and Aquatic Centre in Couva, the Ministry of Education Tower, Prime Minister's Residence and Diplomatic Centre, the Chaguanas administrative complex, and several police stations (Bagoo, 2010; Bernal, 2015: 1421; Fraser, 2014a). It is alleged that its controversial history in Trinidad was launched by a special relationship with Calder Hart, then chairman of the Urban Development Corporation of Trinidad and Tobago (UDeCOTT), the state-owned real estate development agency, and a close associate of then Prime Minister Patrick Manning. Shanghai Construction Group was awarded almost US $292 million in UDeCOTT contracts during Hart's tenure; in response to harsh criticism, the latter was praised and defended by the Prime Minister 45 times over two years, but proof of massive embezzlement finally made him flee the country with his Shanghai-born wife in March 2010 (Bagoo, 2010; *The Trinidad and Tobago Guardian*, February 20, 2012; Oosterveld et al., 2018: 67). Such events could hardly be beneficial to the image of Chinese contractors:

> Ask the average Trinidadian about the Shanghai Construction Group (SCG), and you will likely get an earful about it being former prime minister Patrick Manning's hand-picked contractor, an invasion of Chinese labourers, something about those funny looking multi-million dollar buildings, and of course, that National Academy for the Performing Arts (NAPA) in Port of Spain and its problems. (Fraser, 2014a)

Accordingly, the huge majority of Trinidadian respondents associated China's firms with unfair competition, poor business ethics, the fact that "in constructions, they use inferior materials" (Respondent 8), and a "quality of the work" that "in many ways it is very very substandard" (Respondent 20). As summarized by one respondent,

"I think they have lost the battle in terms of the public opinion. There is generally extraordinarily negative viewpoint of Chinese firms" (Respondent 1).

It is clear that, much more than the protests of directly concerned local firms and professional associations, the image problem due to project failures has been the main cause of the public awareness and rejection of Chinese contractors imposed by Beijing as a precondition for its development assistance. The existence of this subjective dimension related to public perception, however, does not mean that criticism targeting the tying of Chinese aid with respect to contractors has no objective reasons. In similar situations elsewhere in the Global South, Beijing prepares a short list of potential firms, all of which are Chinese. In Trinidad, this list typically contains one company; furthermore, its credentials might be quite suspicious and project failure frequently ensues. This obviously means that the recipient country is denied the best-value construction services and materials available in the global market (La Chimia & Arrowsmith, 2009: 707). It is also likely that, due to total lack of competition, project prices are higher (Morrissey & White, 1996: 209). At the same time, the very patterns of trade are distorted in favor of China. Both opportunities for local industrial development and the possible use of contractors from other developing countries are greatly affected (La Chimia & Arrowsmith, 2009 708, 711). Overall, it is difficult to deny that the imposition of Chinese firms has been detrimental to Trinidad's economic development even if, at least in a certain measure, the infrastructure projects they construct do contribute to the country's social and cultural advancement.

The negative consequences of Beijing's tied aid do not stop here. If the contractors have become their most visible illustration, an almost invisible one concerns materials used in infrastructure projects. There is the unanimous opinion that they are brought from China; yet, few Trinidadians are aware of details. At times, project failures are associated with the use of "inferior materials" (Respondent 8), but there is little hard data for an in-depth analysis. It can only be speculated that, as it generally happens in the case of tied aid, prices are likely to be significantly higher than those on the global market (Baffour quoted by Pincin, 2013: 376). Full visibility becomes once more the norm, however, when imported Chinese labor is considered.

8.5.3 Chinese Laborers

China has constantly insisted on using large numbers of Chinese laborers on construction projects (Campbell, 2014). Their presence is always associated with Beijing's tied aid. Chinese firms appreciate their skills, hard work, and willingness to accept low wages and poor working conditions, which typically compare favorably with those in the target country. China's government sees them as an opportunity to diminish unemployment back home and to repatriate much of the wages paid as part of its foreign aid. But workers in receiving countries feel unjustly deprived of employment, and this has led to various forms of protests from trade unions and professional associations all over the Caribbean. Targets have included Hutchinson Port Holdings and the China State Construction Engineering Corporation in the Bahamas, Shanghai Construction Group in Guyana, China Harbor Engineering Company in Jamaica, and China Jiangsu in Trinidad (Bernal, 2015: 1420, 4784–4798). In the latter country, trade unions and professional organizations have been highly critical of the use of Chinese labor in general (Wilkinson, 2007). Data is scarce, but in 2005–2016 three large Chinese infrastructure projects in Trinidad directly employed 4,700 persons; 12,700 associated jobs were also created. Most were taken by Chinese nationals (Khan, 2017). Work permits granted to them amounted to 1,071 in 2007, to 1,756 in 2008 (*The Trinidad and Tobago Guardian*, July 5, 2009), and to 2,996 in 2008–2011; out of the latter, 2,731 concerned the construction sector (Montoute, 2013: 121). These figures might seem modest, but in such a small country the impact on the construction labor market was considerable. Predictably, it led to a high degree of frustration: "Chinese nationals were coming in, they were living in squalid conditions, they wouldn't contribute to the national economy, they took jobs away from us" (Respondent 12). The "national economy" part refers to the fact that most of the Chinese workers' wages were sent back home. As a consequence, after 2013 Trinidad ceased to represent a net receiver of remittances for the first time in its history (Khan, 2017). Accordingly, the use of Chinese labor in infrastructure projects was criticized by two-thirds of the respondents.

Trinidadian political elites, however, have had a very different perception of this issue. Former Prime Minister Kamla Persad-Bissessar did acknowledge "concerns from the national community" about foreign workers "boxing bread out of the mouths of the citizens of Trinidad and Tobago". Yet, she rejected them: the Chinese are needed in order to deal with "serious shortages of skilled labour" (Fraser, 2014b). In response to such needs and to suggestions made by Chinese officials she had met while visiting Beijing, the then Prime Minister launched a process leading to the complete removal of visa requirements for Chinese nationals. Its first stage was represented by the visa exemption of Chinese citizens who already had a US or Canadian visa, which was finally approved in May 2018 by the following government. Incidentally, acting Prime Minister Colm Imbert announced this measure in a speech that expressed his gratitude for China's participation in the Point Lisas project (Douglas, 2018a).

Chinese labor is imposed by Beijing as part of its tied aid to Trinidad; local political elites accept it as they want to benefit politically and electorally from this aid. Still, a serious contradiction has emerged between the increase in political legitimacy and electoral support expected to result from the Chinese-built infrastructure projects and the loss incurred in the same regards due to the public rejection of foreign workers. Aware of the danger represented by the second trend, successive Trinidadian governments have sometimes initiated measures intended to diminish tensions. In June 2012 Errol McLeod, Labor Minister in the Persad-Bissessar government, mentioned plans to create a foreign migrant policy that would ensure the protection of Trinidadian workers. The "social cost of keeping people inactive while we engage Chinese labour" was to be analyzed in a position paper (Dickson, 2012). However, no such paper has ever been made public. On the contrary, President Xi Jinping's 2013 visit to Trinidad was followed by a major upgrade of the bilateral relationship that was not affected by the 2015 government change and was obviously incompatible with the imposition of any restriction on Chinese labor. It was only in 2018 that, one month after his visit to China, Prime Minister Dr. Keith Rowley announced that the contractor for the construction of the Phoenix Park Industrial Estate, Beijing Construction Engineering Group, would use 60% local labor (*Trinidad and Tobago Daily Express*, June 20, 2018). While a similar development had been noted a couple of years earlier in the case of two Chinese companies operating in Jamaica (Bernal, 2016: 6710–6726), it remains to be seen if China has indeed decided to change its approach. The scarcity of such examples in the Caribbean might indicate that they represent one-time, tactical concessions intended to appease the local public opinion and to increase the room for maneuver of Beijing-friendly governments. For the time being, in Trinidad and elsewhere in the region, China's incomplete tying of aid in terms of labor remains the exception. Overall, Trinidadians' widespread dissatisfaction with Chinese contractors and laborers has considerably tarnished the image of China-the-benevolent-donor despite political elites' claims that Chinese-built infrastructure projects greatly contribute to the advancement of the country. The situation has been aggravated by Beijing's actions that damage Trinidad and Tobago's good governance.

8.6 Negotiating Poor Governance

While Trinidad-specific details might be less known to readers from outside the region, China's tying of its aid to developing states is hardly a secret and, especially in the case of Africa, it has been studied extensively (see Brautigam, 2009: 152; Lahtinen, 2018: 42). Yet, such studies normally focus on tied aid's main components examined in the previous section: contractors, materials, and labor. In the case of the Caribbean in general and of Trinidad and Tobago in particular a further aspect is prominent. The prestige infrastructure projects financed (through loans) and built by the Chinese as part of their development assistance represent the outcome of non-transparent negotiations that result in secretive government-to-government agreements. The general public as well as a surprisingly large number of government experts in the recipient country are unaware of their exact content (Oosterveld et al., 2018: 16–24). It is widely believed that NAPA-type failures are at least in part due to the fact that these agreements allegedly stipulate lax conditions and lack appropriate control measures with respect to the contractors. A number of causes can be identified that explain Beijing's insistence for this atypical style of negotiations. Some authors mention the Chinese business culture based on opaque state-business relations (Hess & Aidoo, 2015: 14, 130). Others point to the fact that, in Latin America, Chinese companies fared poorly in competitive bidding due to the inferior detail and technical quality of their proposals and to lack of familiarity with the bidding process. But there was no problem when the ideologically-motivated friendlier environment of Venezuela and Ecuador or the development assistance provided to Caribbean states allowed for the replacement of formal competition with government-to-government negotiations. Accordingly, Beijing prefers to start by setting up high-level relationships; agreements are eventually concluded between the two governments that circumvent bidding by choosing a specific Chinese contractor (Ellis, 2012: 3, 32). The questionable quality of some of these contractors, as well as the exclusive use of Chinese labor could well lead to public protests that would place the recipient government in a difficult position; this is why secrecy has become the permanent ingredient of China's tied aid to Trinidad and other similar states in the Caribbean.

This approach might be beneficial to Chinese economic interests, but is very detrimental to good governance in Trinidad as it endangers existing policies and practices of public transparency and accountability. Like the rest of the Caribbean, the country is significantly affected by high-level corruption; in such a context, secretiveness is hardly the most fortunate feature of negotiations that involve hundreds of millions of dollars. The aforementioned relationship between Calder Hart, former Prime Minister Patrick Manning's protégé, and Shanghai Construction Group provides a good illustration of the resulting ambiguity. To quote Trevor Munroe, a Jamaican clean government activist, "shadowy deals between governments and China will fuel even more graft" in the Caribbean. Even when explicit corruption is not concerned, "hunger for Chinese investment" will lead to "far too many compromises" hidden from the public opinion (Wigglesworth, 2013). Indeed, the very *raison d'être* of China's prestige infrastructure projects in the Caribbean seems to be related mainly to gaining the sympathy and support of political elites that use them for political and electoral purposes. This raises obvious ethical questions; moreover, one might wonder in what measure projects constructed for such purposes do actually qualify as genuine development assistance.

It is interesting to note that China's official discourse on cooperation with Caribbean states does mention governance. The second Policy Paper on Latin America and the Caribbean of 2016 repeatedly claims the goal of strengthening "exchanges in governance experience"; but the attributes of what is generally understood by good governance—law-based, accountable, transparent, and participatory government—are never mentioned. Instead, the goal of "promot[ing] the modernization of governance system and governance capacity" in the region is directly related to China's authoritarian interpretation of the concept: it is meant to "ensure social stability and order" (Ministry of Foreign Affairs of the Republic of China, 2016: III, IV.1.2, IV.3.1). This can indeed be done by increasing the legitimacy of local political elites; hence the use of prestige infrastructure projects. But this is hardly what good governance means to people outside the Politbureau in Beijing.

As already mentioned, many critics have accused China of jeopardizing local and Western good governance efforts in the Global South and especially in Africa (Wissenbach, 2011: 21; Ziso, 2018: 8). In the Caribbean, scholars have noted that Chinese economic activities give preference to states with the lowest scores for governance and rule of law indicators, which include Trinidad (Oosterveld et al., 2018: 35, 43, 44). The lack of transparency imposed as part of China's tied aid further worsens governance in such states. This vicious circle has been vocally criticized by civil society activists who try to "provide pushback against unbridled ambitions shared between Chinese firms and local elites" (Ibid., 44) and by many citizens:

> In terms of contracts [the Chinese] get from Trinidad and Tobago, I think that any document that is executed on behalf of the people of Trinidad and Tobago by any government, there should be full transparency, accountability, responsibility and full disclosure. (Respondent 15)

The negative perception of governance-related aspects of China's aid to Trinidad and Tobago is widely shared by the general public. The political elites, on the contrary, have never given the impression of being disturbed by or even aware of China-induced governance issues despite the fact that in the past Trinidad, like other Caribbean states, used to have an "interest in developing a reputation for good governance and social consciousness" (Braveboy-Wagner, 2010: 423). At present, Beijing's persuasive efforts and material incentives seem to be more attractive.

8.7 Analysis and Conclusion

As China uses the same pattern all over the Caribbean, the very benefit of its development assistance to the region has been described at times as "very questionable" (Badri-Maharaj, 2016). In Trinidad, contractors and labor frustration, infrastructure project structural flaws, and governance issues contribute to a rather dark picture of what was supposed to be a solidarity-based, win-win cooperative relationship: "I think the citizens will suffer" (Respondent 30). "Let's quantify how much money China has put in Trinidad and has resulted in what, at the end of the day? Decaying infrastructure" (Respondent 23). A respondent from the civil society bluntly stated that, under such conditions, Trinidad doesn't need Chinese aid (Respondent 28).

An interesting aspect of this criticism concerns Trinidad's domestic dimension and, more precisely, the public perception of political elites' pro-Beijing actions that are viewed as detrimental to the interests of their own country. One respondent claimed that "the general Trinidadian population is extraordinarily weary of whether the Trinidad and Tobago government is selling out the country to the Chinese" (Respondent 1). But in their overall assessment of the relationship between Trinidad and China, many respondents did not blame the latter for pursuing—be it cynically—its national interest. Rather, they believed that the problem lies with the official policies of Caribbean states "for not being strategic or protective" (Respondent 17). In turn, this is "the fault of Trinidadians who were involved in the exercise" (Respondent 24), i.e. of political leaders. And, taking one step further, this is due to "the political system that gives these leaders too much room to act against the national interest": the constitutional system lacks "robust checks and balances" (Respondent 30). The ultimate cause, therefore, is "the immaturity of the state" (Respondent 15). Similar opinions have been noted elsewhere in the Caribbean (Green & Liu, 2017: 28) as well as in Africa (Mohan et al., 2014: 123, 134; see also the chapter by Szadziewski in this volume). While not all Trinidadian respondents fully share such views, 80% of them do believe that their government should be more conscious in its dealings with the Chinese; a further 13% share this opinion to an extent. This criticism is illustrative of a serious perception gap between society and political elites; more importantly, it questions the very legitimacy of the governing class with respect to China's tied aid. Ironically, Beijing's infrastructure projects at the origin of this questioning have been welcomed by Trinidad's leaders precisely because they were supposed to help them increase their political legitimacy.

These findings confirm Olav Stokke's claim that foreign aid represents an intervention in the recipient country that significantly influences the resources and power position of various social groups, which are turned into beneficiaries or losers based on the donor's choice (Stokke, 1995/2006: 34; see Sect. 8.2). This is an important but seldom addressed aspect of development assistance. In both Latin America and the Caribbean, "top elites" represent China's preferred targets (Shen, 2015: 114; see Sect. 8.5). Beijing's generous aid to Trinidad serves to build impressive (if faulty) NAPAs or to buy unneeded long-range patrol vessels. It is not clear in what measure such projects actually improve citizens' standard of living; but they are typically calculated to be opened or delivered "with much fanfare" (*The Trinidad and Tobago Guardian*, August 21, 2016) one month before elections. This is to say that they turn the political elites into beneficiaries while the negative socio-economic impact of China's tied aid places a part of the society on the losing side. This obviously contradicts Beijing's win-win discourse but is fully in line with the rationalist International Relations literature that analyzes the mechanisms used by great powers to influence the behavior of weaker states. Their goal is to use material incentives in order to alter the behavior of leaders in the target state. If such a change takes root only "among the populace", it remains irrelevant; it is the elite level alone that has important effects on state behavior (Ikenberry & Kupchan, 1990: 284–285). While Constructivist scholars might have a different opinion, this is exactly the line of reasoning followed by China with respect to Trinidad; and the Beijing-friendly attitude of successive governments in Port of Spain suggests that, from their point of view, the Chinese have been highly successful in their well calculated use of foreign aid.

As shown earlier in this chapter, China's philosophy of development assistance is very different from that shared by DAC members. Yet, despite the beautifully worded win-win discourse about disinterested South-South cooperation, it hardly represents an exception from the general rule stating that "aid giving clearly has political purposes and indeed may be regarded in large measure as a political act" (Copper, 2016: 1). On the one hand, geopolitical objectives are pursued that include expelling Taiwan's embassies from the Caribbean, responding to American anti-Chinese actions in the South China Sea, and, in the long run, constructing a new regional order based on functioning institutions and rules (see Sect. 8.4). On the other hand, there is the "business end" dimension (Trinidad, 2013: 22) well illustrated by China's tying of its development assistance. It was noted that states that tie a larger proportion of their aid—Australia, Canada, France, and the US—also promote more visibly their own objectives. On the contrary, a smaller proportion of aid is tied by donors such as the Scandinavian states, which are more altruistic and less focused on geostrategic objectives (Pincin, 2013: 376). For its part, China ties all its aid to the Caribbean and, in most cases, the level of tying reaches 100%. This is clearly not a Scandinavian approach.

The reasons for tying are obvious. An important part of the development assistance financial outflow to Trinidad returns to China, improving the latter's balance of payments. Chinese workers take advantage of job opportunities abroad, which diminishes unemployment. Importantly, at present China is facing a surplus of capital and considerable overcapacity in construction-related heavy industries (Lairson, 2018: 41; Summers, 2018: 24). In general, donors concentrate tied aid on specialized areas where their firms hold comparative advantages (Jepma, 1991: 12); the tying of aid also shapes the nature of funded projects, which are selected based on their requirements of capital-intensive goods (this is why telecommunications and infrastructure are preferred to poverty-focused projects such as rural development) (Carbone, 2014: 104; see Sect. 8.2). All this explains why the tied aid offered by China to Trinidad takes the form of infrastructure projects. The benefit might be very small if compared to the Chinese GDP, but it certainly is substantial for concerned Chinese firms. Moreover, if the numerous similar projects all over the developing world are taken into consideration, the consolidated profit is in no way negligible even with respect to the size of the Chinese economy. It should be added that Beijing loan-financed infrastructure projects have allowed Chinese firms to enter Trinidad's construction market, on which they are now very active. Incidentally, this goes against the very first principle proudly heralded in China's first white paper on foreign aid of 2011: "unremittingly helping recipient countries build up their self-development capacity" (Information Office of the State Council of the People's Republic of China, 2011). Before the arrival of the Chinese, sufficient capital, contractors, and labor ensured Trinidad's self-development potential in the construction industry. Today, a large part of the market is controlled by Chinese competitors that repatriate profits to their country of origin. President Nixon's already mentioned statement—"remember that the main purpose of American aid is not to help other nations but to help ourselves" (Opeskin quoted by Brakman & van Marrewijk, 1998: 133)—certainly applies to China's development assistance to Trinidad and Tobago.

Two types of problems ensue. In Trinidad, Chinese tied aid is not conducive to socio-economic development. Instead, it has led to losses for contractors and workers, frustration within the society, and public discontent with the political elites. For its part, China uses aid for geopolitical objectives and ties it for economic gain. The tying, however, damages its image; in the long run, this will endanger the bilateral relationship and its geopolitical significance. As already noted in the literature on China's development assistance to the Global South, the "twin forces" of economics and politics are pursued by Beijing in competition to each other. This "diplomatic schizophrenia" is "untenable" (Varrall, 2016: 39–40) as it has highly detrimental consequences for both China and its development partners. Ultimately, it would be much wiser for the Chinese leaders to adopt the DAC principle that aid tying represents a bad practice in international development (Carbone, 2014: 108). However, present trends do not suggest that such a change might take place in the predictable future.

Acknowledgements The authors of this chapter are grateful to the Campus Research and Publication Fund Committee of the University of the West Indies, St. Augustine campus, for its financial support under Grant CRP.3.NOV16.10.

References

Ashoff, G. (2000). *The OECD's development assistance committee and German development cooperation: A relationship under scrutiny* (Briefing Paper 1). Bonn: German Development Institute/Deutsches Institut für Entwicklungspolitik (DIE). Retrieved May 28, 2021 from https://www.die-gdi.de/en/briefing-paper/article/the-oecds-development-assistance-committee-and-german-development-cooperation-a-relationship-under-scrutiny/

Badri-Maharaj, S. (2016, August 3). *China's growing influence in the Caribbean.* The Institute for Defence Studies and Analyses, New Delhi. Retrieved May 28, 2021 from https://idsa.in/idsacomments/china-growing-influence-in-the-caribbean_sbmaharaj_030816

Bagoo, A. (2010, December 19). Zhang's $5mn house. *Trinidad and Tobago Newsday.* Retrieved May 28, 2021 from http://archives.newsday.co.tt/2010/12/19/zhangs-5m-house/

BBC. (2013, June 1). China leader Xi Jinping in Trinidad and Tobago. Retrieved May 28, 2021 from http://www.bbc.com/news/world-latin-america-22744040

Barrios, R. (2018, July 11). *China's Belt and Road lands in Latin America.* China Dialogue, London. Retrieved May 28, 2021 from https://www.chinadialogue.net/article/show/single/en/10728-China-s-Belt-and-Road-lands-in-Latin-America

Bernal, R. L. (2015). The growing economic presence of China in the Caribbean. *The World Economy, 38*(9), 1409–1437.

Bernal, R. L. (2016). *Dragon in the Caribbean: China's global re-dimensioning—Challenges and opportunities for the Caribbean* (Rev. and Updated ed.). Kindle Edition, Ian Randle Publishers.

Brakman, S., & van Marrewijk, C. (1998). *The economics of international transfers.* Cambridge University Press.

Brautigam, D. (2009). *The Dragon's gift: The real story of China in Africa.* Oxford University Press.

Bräutigam, D. (2011). Aid "with Chinese characteristics": Chinese foreign aid and development finance meet the OECD-DAC aid regime. *Journal of International Development, 23*(5), 752–764.

Braveboy-Wagner, J. (2010). Opportunities and limitations of the exercise of foreign policy power by a very small state: The case of Trinidad and Tobago. *Cambridge Review of International Affairs, 23*(3), 407–427.

Campbell, C. (2014, May 16). *China's expanding and evolving engagement with the Caribbean.* U.S.-China Economic and Security Review Commission Staff Report. Retrieved May 28, 2021 from http://origin.www.uscc.gov/sites/default/files/Research/Staff%20Report_China-Caribbean%20Relations.pdf

Carbone, M. (2014). Much ado about nothing? The European Union and the global politics of untying aid. *Contemporary Politics, 20*(1), 103–117.

Carbonnier, G. (2010). Official development assistance once more under fire from critics. *International Development Policy/Revue internationale de politique de développement, 1*(1), 137–142.

Caribbean Journal. (2013, June 3). China to fund $150 million children's hospital project in Trinidad. Retrieved May 28, 2021 from https://www.caribjournal.com/2013/06/03/china-to-fund-150-million-childrens-hospital-project-in-trinidad/#

CNC3. (2018, March 3). TT owes China $2.229 billion in loan debts. Retrieved May 28, 2021 from http://www.cnc3.co.tt/press-release/tt-owes-china-2229-billion-loan-debts

Copper, J. F. (2016). *China's foreign aid and investment diplomacy, Volume I. Nature, scope, and origins.* Palgrave Macmillan

Dickson, D.-A. (2012). At what cost, Chinese labour? *Trinidad & Tobago Guardian*, June 7. Retrieved May 28, 2021 from http://www.guardian.co.tt/business-guardian/2012-06-06/what-cost-chinese-labour

Douglas, S. (2018a, May 24). Imbert: US$104m Chinese complex for Pt Lisas. *Trinidad and Tobago Newsday*. Retrieved May 28, 2021 from https://newsday.co.tt/2018/05/24/imbert-us104m-chinese-complex-for-pt-lisas/

Douglas, S. (2018b, September 12). Moonilal: Review China Harbour deal. *Trinidad and Tobago Newsday*. Retrieved May 28, 2021 from https://newsday.co.tt/2018/09/12/moonilal-review-china-harbour-deal/

Douglas, S. (2020, February 28). Deyalsingh: Couva Hospital can quarantine patients. *Trinidad and Tobago Newsday*. Retrieved May 28, 2021 from https://newsday.co.tt/2020/02/28/deyalsingh-couva-hospital-can-quarantine-patients/

Ellis, R. E. (2009). *China in Latin America: The whats and wherefores*. Lynne Rienner.

Ellis, R. E. (2012). Learning the ropes. *Americas Quarterly, 6*(4), 28–33.

Ellis, R. E. (2014). *China on the ground in Latin America*. Palgrave Macmillan.

Engelbert, A. (2014). Annamaria La Chimia, Tied aid and development aid procurement in the framework of EU and WTO law, Book review. *VRÜ Verfassung und Recht in Übersee, 47*(2), 270–272.

Fraser, M. (2014a, September 15). From Shanghai to Trinidad. *Daily Express*. Retrieved May 28, 2021 from https://www.trinidadexpress.com/news/local/from-shanghai-to-trinidad/article_d4507526-0182-55f7-89d1-cfde43c8bf74.html

Fraser, M. (2014b, June 16). PM to consider removing visas for Chinese. *Trinidad Express*. Retrieved May 28, 2021 from http://www.trinidadexpress.com/news/PM-to-consider-removing-visas-for-Chinese-263377741.html

Freeman, C. P. (ed.). (2015). *Handbook on China and developing countries*. Edward Elgar.

Gallagher, K. P. (2016). *The China triangle*. Oxford University Press.

Gang, D. (2015, July 16). Win-win hospital plan in US backyard. *Global Times*. Retrieved May 28, 2021 from http://www.globaltimes.cn/content/932337.shtml

Green, C. A., & Liu, Y. (2017). A "transnational middleman minority" in the Eastern Caribbean? Constructing a historical and contemporary framework of analysis. *Social and Economic Studies, 66*(3–4), 1–31.

Haro Navejas, F. J. (2013). China in the Central American and Caribbean Zone. *Latin American Policy, 4*(1), 144–156.

Hess, S., & Aidoo, R. (2015). *Charting the roots of anti-Chinese populism in Africa*. Springer.

Hynes, W., & Scott, S. (2013). *The evolution of official development assistance: Achievements, criticisms and a way forward* (OECD Development Co-operation Working Papers, No. 12). OECD Publishing. Retrieved May 28, 2021 from https://www.oecd.org/dac/financing-sustainable-development/development-finance-standards/Evolution%20of%20ODA.pdf

Hunte, C. (2018, April 26). Rowley reveals plan for Couva Children's Hospital. *Daily Express*. Retrieved May 28, 2021 from https://www.trinidadexpress.com/news/local/rowley-reveals-plan-for-couva-children-s-hospital/article_5edd2e04-4995-11e8-b86b-73098f0d9c6c.html

Ikenberry, G. J., & Kupchan, C. A. (1990). Socialization and hegemonic power. *International Organization, 44*(3), 283–315.

Information Office of the State Council of the People's Republic of China. (2011). China's foreign aid. Retrieved May 28, 2021 from http://english.gov.cn/archive/white_paper/2014/09/09/content_281474986284620.htm

Information Office of the State Council of the People's Republic of China (2014). China's foreign aid. Retrieved May 28, 2021 from http://english.gov.cn/archive/white_paper/2014/08/23/content_281474982986592.htm

Jepma, C. J. (1991). *The tying of aid*. Development Centre of the OECD. Retrieved May 28, 2021 from http://www.oecd.org/development/pgd/29412505.pdf

Kakaire, S. (2014, September 2). Uganda: Railway deal winner banned by World Bank over graft. *The Observer* (Kampala). Retrieved May 28, 2021 from https://allafrica.com/stories/201409030 522.html

Khan, A. (2017, September 20). China infrastructure projects in T&T employed 12,700 over last decade. *Daily Express*. Retrieved May 28, 2021 from https://www.trinidadexpress.com/news/ local/china-infrastructure-projects-in-t-t-employed-over-last-decade/article_5e685fd1-7812- 51d0-b873-c394b17c6328.html

Kilby, P. (2017). China and the United States as aid donors: Past and future trajectories. *Policy Studies*, 77. East-West Center, Honolulu, Hawai'i.

Kim, S.-K., & Kim, Y.-H. (2016). Is tied aid bad for the recipient countries? *Economic Modelling*, 53(C), 289–301.

Kitano, N. (2014). China's foreign aid at a transitional stage. *Asian Economic Policy Review, 9*(2), 301–317.

Kowlessar, G. (2018, June 19). MoU signed for US$104m industrial park. *Trinidad & Tobago Guardian*. Retrieved May 28, 2021 from http://www.guardian.co.tt/business/2018-06-19/mou- signed-us104m-industrial-park

La Chimia, A. (2013). *Tied aid and development aid procurement in the framework of EU and WTO law*. Hart Publishing.

La Chimia, A., & Arrowsmith, S. (2009). Addressing tied aid: Towards a more development-oriented WTO? *Journal of International Economic Law, 12*(3), 707–747.

Lahtinen, A. (2018). *China's diplomacy and economic activities in Africa*. Palgrave Macmillan.

Lairson, T. D. (2018). The global strategic environment of the BRI: deep interdependence and structural power. In W. Zhang, I. Alon, & C. Lattemann (Eds.), *China's belt and road initiative* (pp. 35–53). Palgrave Macmillan.

Loop News. (2017, August 10). T&T, China sign framework agreement for patrol vessel. Retrieved May 28, 2021 from http://www.looptt.com/content/tt-china-sign-framework-agreement-patrol- vessel

Mander, B. (2013, June 14). China-Trinidad and Tobago: A closer embrace. *Financial Times*. Retrieved May 28, 2021 from https://www.ft.com/content/41991098-5703-3dce-b452-877f54 1c73eb

Ministry of Foreign Affairs of the People's Republic of China. (2018). *China and Trinidad & Tobago*. Retrieved May 28, 2021 from http://www.fmprc.gov.cn/mfa_eng/wjb_663304/zzjg_6 63340/ldmzs_664952/gjlb_664956/3528_665138/

Ministry of Foreign Affairs of the Republic of China. (2016, November 24). *China's policy paper on Latin America and the Caribbean*. Retrieved May 28, 2021 from http://www.fmprc.gov.cn/ mfa_eng/zxxx_662805/t1418254.shtml

Mohan, G., Lampert, B., Tan-Mullins, M., & Chang, D. (2014). *Chinese migrants and Africa's development: New Imperialists or agents of change?* Zed Books.

Montoute, A. (2013). Caribbean-China economic relations: What are the implications? *Caribbean Journal of International Relations & Diplomacy, 1*(1), 110–126.

Morrissey, O., & White, H. (1996). Evaluating the concessionality of tied aid. *The Manchester School, 64*(2), 208–226.

Naím, M. (2007, March/April). Rogue aid. *Foreign Policy, 159*, 95–96.

OECD. (2012). Notes on non-OECD providers of development co-operation. In *Development Co-Operation Report 2012. Lessons in Linking Sustainability and Development*, 257–263.

OECD. (2018). *Official development assistance—Definition and coverage*. Retrieved May 28, 2021 from http://www.oecd.org/dac/stats/officialdevelopmentassistancedefinitionandcoverage.htm

Office of the Prime Minister. (2013, June 1). *Couva Children's Hospital expected to be complete by March 2015*. Retrieved May 28, 2021 from http://www.news.gov.tt/content/couva-childrens- hospital-expected-be-complete-march-2015#.XAXESGhKi1s

Office of the Prime Minister Republic of Trinidad and Tobago. (2018, May 18). *Chinese fact finding delegation to visit Trinidad and Tobago to explore investment opportunities*. Retrieved May 28,

2021 from https://www.opm.gov.tt/chinese-fact-finding-delegation-to-visit-trinidad-and-tobago-to-explore-investment-opportunities/

Oosterveld, W., Wilms, E., & Kertysova, K (2018). The belt and road initiative looks east: Political implications of China's economic forays in the Caribbean and the South Pacific. *The Hague Centre for Strategic Studies*. Retrieved May 28, 2021 from https://hcss.nl/report/belt-and-road-initiative-looks-east

Pincin, J. A. (2013). Political power and aid-tying practices in the development assistance committee countries. *Oxford Development Studies, 41*(3), 372–390, previously published in 2012 as part of the IDEAS Working Paper Series.

Power102fm News. (2014, February 25). China sending ships to Trinidad and Tobago. Retrieved May 28, 2021 from http://news.power102fm.com/china-sending-ships-to-trinidad-and-tobago-16727

Rampersad, J. (2019, November 14). Govt, China sign loan for US$104m. *Trinidad and Tobago Newsday*. https://newsday.co.tt/2019/11/14/govt-china-sign-loan-for-us104m/

Reilly, J. (2012). A norm-taker or a norm-maker? Chinese aid in Southeast Asia. *Journal of Contemporary China, 21*(73), 71–91.

Roett, R., & Paz, G. (2015). China's expanding ties with Latin America. In C. P. Freeman (Ed.), *Handbook on China and developing countries* (pp. 496–517). Edward Elgar.

Rogers, A. (2016, February 7). Broken is the road of political promises in Trinidad & Tobago. *Global Voices*. Retrieved May 28, 2021 from https://globalvoices.org/2016/02/07/broken-is-the-road-of-political-promises-in-trinidad-tobago/

Rutherford, D. (2013). Tied aid. In *Routledge Dictionary of Economics* (3rd ed.). Routledge. Retrieved May 28, 2021 from https://search.credoreference.com/content/entry/routsobk/tied_aid/0?institutionId=1795

Shen, S. (2015). Another angle on a new intimacy: Chinese perceptions of Africa and Latin America. In C. P. Freeman (Ed.), *Handbook on China and developing countries* (pp. 109–132). Edward Elgar.

Shiwei, S. (2018, May 16). Opinion: China and Trinidad and Tobago strengthen ties on BRI cooperation. *China Global Television Network*. Retrieved May 28, 2021 from https://news.cgtn.com/news/3d3d414d3145544e77457a6333566d54/share_p.html

Sookraj, R. (2013, October 6). Chinese firm picked for T&T project faces corruption probe. *The Trinidad and Tobago Guardian*. Retrieved May 28, 2021 from https://www.guardian.co.tt/news/chinese-firm-picked-tt-project-faces-corruption-probe-6.2.408820.600f15629e

Sookraj, R. (2018, January 9). Couva Children's Hospital tower collapses. *Trinidad & Tobago Guardian Online*. Retrieved May 28, 2021 from http://www.tobagotoday.co.tt/news/2018-01-08/couva-children%E2%80%99s-hospital-tower-collapses

Southerland, D. (2017, August 30). China makes inroads in Caribbean nations through aid, trade. *Radio Free Asia*. Retrieved May 28, 2021 from https://www.rfa.org/english/commentaries/caribbean-china-08302017165130.html

Stahl, A. K. (2018). *EU-China-Africa trilateral relations in a multipolar world: hic sunt dracones*. Palgrave Macmillan.

Stokke, O. (1995/2006). Aid and political conditionality: core issues and state of the art. In O. Stokke (Ed.), *Aid and Political Conditionality* (pp. 1–87). Frank Cass.

Strange, A. M., Dreher, A., Fuchs, A., Parks, B., & Tierney, M. J. (2017). Tracking underreported financial flows: China's development finance and the aid-conflict nexus revisited. *Journal of Conflict Resolution, 61*(5), 935–963.

Summers, T. (2018). Rocking the boat? China's "Belt and Road" and global order. In A. Ehteshami & N. Horesh (Eds.), *China's presence in the Middle East* (pp. 24–37). Routledge.

Swedlund, H. J. (2017). Is China eroding the bargaining power of traditional donors in Africa? *International Affairs, 93*(2), 389–408.

The Economist. (2012, March 10). A Chinese beachhead? https://www.economist.com/node/21549971

The Trinidad and Tobago Guardian. (2016, August 21). Millions needed to repair Napa defects. Retrieved May 28, 2021 from http://www.guardian.co.tt/news/2016-08-20/millions-needed-rep air-napa-defects

The Trinidad and Tobago Guardian. (2012, February 20). The saga of Udecott and Calder Hart. Retrieved May 28, 2021 from http://www.guardian.co.tt/business-guardian/saga-udecott-and-cal der-hart-6.2.416593.b663e934c5

The Trinidad and Tobago Guardian. (2009, July 5). 12,212 Non-Caricom nationals get work permits. Retrieved May 28, 2021 from http://m.guardian.co.tt/archives/news/general/2009/07/04/foreign-invasion

Trinidad, D. D. (2013). The foreign aid philosophy of a rising Asian power: A Southeast Asian view. In Y. Shimomura & H. Ohashi (Eds.), *A study of China's foreign aid* (pp. 19–45). Palgrave Macmillan.

Trinidad and Tobago Daily Express. (2018, June 20). China to fund Phoenix Park industrial estate. Retrieved May 28, 2021 from https://www.trinidadexpress.com/business/local/china-to-fund-pho enix-park-industrial-estate/article_31be9880-7498-11e8-aa35-134f694d9978.html

Trinidad Express. (2016, November 22). NAPA reopens. Retrieved May 28, 2021 from http://web. trinidadexpress.com/20161122/features/napa-reopens

TTWhistleBlower. (2016, August 31). $20M spent to repair NAPA. Retrieved May 28, 2021 from http://ttwhistleblower.com/20m-spent-to-repair-napa/

Tudoroiu, T. (2017). Taiwan in the Caribbean: A case study in state de-recognition. *Asian Journal of Political Science, 25*(2), 194–211.

UWI Campus News. (2015, October 23). UWI fosters agricultural innovation with new park at Orange Grove. Retrieved May 28, 2021 from http://sta.uwi.edu/news/releases/release.asp?id= 1499

Varrall, M. (2016). Domestic actors and agendas in Chinese aid policy. *The Pacific Review, 29*(1), 21–44.

Waithe, M. (2018, June 21). China belts TT. *Trinidad and Tobago Newsday.* Retrieved May 28, 2021 from https://newsday.co.tt/2018/06/21/china-belts-tt/

Webb, Y. (2018, September 13). US$500m windfall. China Harbour promises returns on La Brea Dry dock project. *Trinidad and Tobago Newsday.* Retrieved May 28, 2021 from https://newsday. co.tt/2018/09/13/us500m-windfall/

Wigglesworth, R. (2013, December 17). Caribbean in crisis: Chequebook diplomacy. *Financial Times.* Retrieved May 28, 2021 from https://www.ft.com/content/7f7b0d8e-5ea8-11e3-8621-001 44feabdc0

Wilkinson, B. (2007, July 27). Caribbean: Influx of Chinese workers irks local unions. *Inter Press Service News Agency.* Retrieved May 28, 2021 from http://www.ipsnews.net/2007/07/caribbean-influx-of-chinese-workers-irks-local-unions/

Williams, L. (2018, May 14). Govt talks Couva children's hospital. *Trinidad and Tobago Newsday.* https://newsday.co.tt/2018/05/14/govt-talk-couva-childrens-hospital/

Wissenbach, U. (2011). China-Africa relations and the European Union ideology, conditionality, realpolitik and what is new in South-South co-operation. In C. M. Dent (Ed.), *China and Africa development relations* (pp. 21–41). Routledge.

Yue, Z. (2018, May 15). Belt, road will assist in country's development. *China Daily.* Retrieved May 28, 2021 from http://usa.chinadaily.com.cn/a/201805/15/WS5afa124da3103f6866ee851c. html

Zhang, Q. (2015). China's relations with developing countries: patterns, principles, characteristics, and future challenges. In C. P. Freeman (Ed.), *Handbook on China and developing countries* (pp. 51–70). Edward Elgar.

Zhang, D., & Smith, G. (2017). China's foreign aid system: Structure, agencies, and identities. *Third World Quarterly, 38*(10), 2330–2346.

Ziso, E. (2018). *A post state-centric analysis of China-Africa relations: Internationalisation of Chinese capital and state-society relations in Ethiopia.* Palgrave Macmillan.

Theodor Tudoroiu is a Senior Lecturer at the Department of Political Science of the University of the West Indies, St. Augustine campus. He earned his Ph.D. in Political Science from the Université de Montréal and an M.A. from the College of Europe in Bruges, Belgium. His China-related publications include *The Myth of China's No Strings Attached Development Assistance: A Caribbean Case Study* (Lexington Books, 2020), *China's International Socialization of Political Elites in the Belt and Road Initiative* (Routledge, 2021), and *China's Globalization from Below: Chinese Entrepreneurial Migrants and the Belt and Road Initiative* (Routledge, 2022).

Amanda Reshma Ramlogan is a Ph.D. student at the Institute of International Relations of the University of the West Indies, St. Augustine campus. She works on a thesis on the China–Trinidad political, economic, and social relationship. She co-authored the article 'China's International Socialization of Caribbean State-Society Complexes: Trinidad and Tobago as a Case Study' (*Asian Journal of Political Science*, 2019) and contributed to the books *The Myth of China's No Strings Attached Development Assistance: A Caribbean Case Study* (Lexington Books, 2020) and *China's International Socialization of Political Elites in the Belt and Road Initiative* (Routledge, 2021).

Chapter 9
Indonesian Elite Perception of China During the Presidency of Joko (Jokowi) Widodo

Johanes Herlijanto

Abstract The chapter explores how various groups of Indonesian elites during the presidency of Joko (Jokowi) Widodo perceive China. It examines how these elites use their old and new knowledge about China to project their perception of China today. The old perception of China, which portrays China as an expansionist power with an intention to intervene in Indonesian internal politics is combined with a new knowledge regarding China's capability and its recent international behaviors, which are regarded by some groups of Indonesian elites as assertive. The result of the above combination is the prevalence of negative perceptions of China, which are especially held particularly by the non-governing elites who are critical toward Jokowi and his administration. Meanwhile, positive views of China are present amongst the governing elites and the non-governing elites who are sympathetic with President Jokowi. However, these latter groups of elites also hold certain concerns and caution toward China. Particularly for some members of the governing elites, the presence of these concerns, cautions, as well as a negative perception of China, both amongst the elites and in the society at large, should be taken into consideration by the government as they are making policies about Indonesian relations with China.

Keywords Sino—Indonesian relations · Elite perception of China · Post-Suharto Indonesia · Chinese investments in Indonesia · Indonesian politics

Abbreviations

DPR   Dewan Perwakilan Rakyat (People's Representative Council)
EEZ   Exclusive Economic Zone
NGO   Non-Governmental Organization
PKI   Partai Komunis Indonesia (Indonesian Communist Party)
PCA   Permanent Court Arbitration

J. Herlijanto (✉)
Department of Communication, Pelita Harapan University, Jakarta, Indonesia
e-mail: johanes.herlijanto@uph.edu

© The Author(s), under exclusive license to Springer Nature Singapore Pte Ltd. 2022   167
T. Tudoroiu and A. Kuteleva (eds.), *China in the Global South*,
https://doi.org/10.1007/978-981-19-1344-0_9

U.S.   The United States

9.1   Introduction

Most residents of Surabaya, the capital city of East Java province and the second-largest city in Indonesia, have at least heard of the Surabaya-Madura (Suramadu) Bridge. Stretching across the Madura Strait, the bridge connects the city of Surabaya with Madura island, located on its eastern side. Operating since 2009, the Suramadu bridge is one of the longest inter-island bridges in Southeast Asia. More than that, it also symbolizes a successful model of collaboration between two large countries in the Eastern part of Asia: Indonesia and China. Through its financial and technical assistance, China was involved in the project of constructing the bridge (Suryadinata, 2017: 4). The locals warmly welcomed this cooperation. The Chinese workers who participated in the project were often subjects of the media reports, while the way they did their work (and even the way they stopped working on time) was perceived by members of the local community as a model of work ethic that the Indonesians needed to emulate. As an example, in June 2009, *Koran Tempo*, a leading newspaper in Indonesia, interviewed a group of Indonesian students who did an internship in the bridge construction project and reported how they praised the work ethic performed by the Chinese engineers participating in the project (*Koran Tempo*, 12 June 2009). Similarly, in an interview with me in March 2009, an Indonesian engineer admitted that his Chinese counterparts had a good work ethic and were so disciplined (Herlijanto, 2013: 221–224).

Today, over half a decade after the Chinese president Xi Jinping announced the 21st Century Maritime Silk Road project in Jakarta, the incoming flows of investments from China to Indonesia have significantly increased. In 2019, China even overtook Singapore as Indonesia's biggest foreign investor. Nevertheless, unlike a decade ago, public enthusiasm for cooperation with China has diminished. In contrast, public outcry over the arrival of Chinese migrant workers looms large in the Indonesian media. As happening in countries located in other regions, such as Trinidad and Tobago in the Caribbean (see Tudoroiu's chapter in this volume), the coming of Chinese migrant workers to work in quite a few China-funded infrastructure projects in Indonesia are also seen by the Indonesian public as unjustly depriving the local workers of employment. Likewise, resentments about the massive influx of China's investments circulate widely on various social media platforms in this Southeast Asian country. Indeed, as in the case of Papua New Guinea (Szadziewski's chapter in this volume), social media in Indonesia have become an important vehicle for the public to communicate their negative views of China too. Meanwhile, China's international behavior, particularly in the South China Sea, is often considered concerning by the Indonesian public. Chinese coast guard's vessels encroached into Indonesia's Exclusive Economic Zone (EEZ) in the northeast of Natuna islands several times over the last few years, evoking a growing discontent among many Indonesians.[1] In which way are these negative public narratives about China reflected in the views held by the Indonesian elites? How do various elite groups in Indonesia perceive China's rise? How do we explain the presence of such perceptions? How do these elite perceptions of China affect Sino-Indonesian relations? This chapter answers the above questions by focusing on the perception held by members of the pribumi (indigenous Indonesian) elites, which presumably constitute the largest part of the Indonesian elite.

The data used for this chapter was mainly collected between January and June 2016 in Jakarta amongst members of various elite groups in Indonesia, when the author researched the Indonesian "pribumi" elites' perception of China and the ethnic Chinese in Indonesia. The elites in this study are broadly defined so that this concept includes both government and non-government elites. Representatives of government elites in this research include individuals who hold mid-ranking and high-ranking positions in the government, whereas non-government elites comprise former senior officials, retired high-ranking military officers, senior politicians, senior scholars and researchers, religious leaders, non-government organization (NGO) activists, as well as high profile professionals. The author interviewed roughly 30 of these elites during the 2016 research. Some other interviews, conversations, and text-based communications with fewer members of these two elites groups were also conducted between 2016 and 2019. All of these interviews were carried out in Indonesian.

The first section of this chapter sketches out a short historical account of Indonesian relations with China. Next, the chapter discusses the importance of research on perceptions and reviews how China had been perceived by various groups that might be regarded as the Indonesian elites in the past. The third section portrays various ways of perceiving China amongst the Indonesian elite groups today. Finally, an analysis of the persistence of certain views of China will be provided. Concluding remarks summarize the key argument: while the Indonesian elites do not have uniform views of China, a negative image of China is dominantly present among these elites. This negative image is projected through the reproduction of the old perceptions which influence how some of these elites interpret Indonesian relations with China today.

9.2 A Historical Overview of Indonesian Relations with China

The diplomatic ties between Indonesia and China have been established as early as 1950. It was the Indonesian prime minister (and vice president) Mohammad Hatta

---

[1] Natuna Islands are located in the northernmost point of the Indonesian archipelagic state, and in between Peninsula Malaysia to the west and Kalimantan (Borneo) to the east (Suryadinata & Izzuddin, 2017). Indonesia does not only have sovereignty over the islands, but also has sovereign rights over the waters north of the islands, which are part of the Indonesia's 200 nautical miles Exclusive Economic Zone.

who indicated Indonesia's willingness to establish diplomatic relations with China (Sukma, 1999: 20). But the early phase of the relationship between the two countries was marked with suspicion on the side of Indonesia's government and political elite toward China's intention, particularly in securing the loyalty of ethnic Chinese minority to Beijing, instead of to the Chinese Nationalist Republic in Taiwan (Sukma, 1999: 24). The relationship between the two-country remained unstable for the next seventeen years. A better relationship began to take place in 1959 and reached its peak in August 1965 when Sukarno announced the establishment of the "Jakarta - Beijing Axis." But even the period was marred with a diplomatic hassle resulting from the regulation that banned aliens from operating retail shops in the rural areas in 1959.

A further deterioration of the two countries' relationship occurred in the aftermath of the coup attempt masterminded by the Indonesian Communist Party (PKI) in 1965—an event that preceded the establishment of a new regime that named itself the New Order. Involving some military units allegedly under the influence of the PKI, the coup targeted several senior generals who held key positions in the Indonesian Army. Six of the generals and one junior officer of the Indonesian Army were kidnapped and killed in Jakarta in the early morning of the first of October that year, while two other senior officers who commanded an army battalion faced a similar fate in Yogyakarta on the next day. The coup was thwarted by General Suharto, who a year later rose to power and established the New Order anti-communist regime, with himself as the president. Before the establishment of the new regime, the Indonesian Army and its allies launched a series of anti-communist purges in which a few hundred thousand people allegedly associated with the PKI perished (Brown, 2003: 199; Vickers, 2005: 54–160).

Indonesia's New Order government alleged China has been involved in the 1965 coup attempt and provided some help to the PKI. While there is no sufficient evidence to prove these allegations (Mozingo, 1976; Suryadinata, 1990; Zhou, 2019), their effect on Indonesia-China relations has been detrimental. Prolonged tensions following the communist coup had led to the suspension of the diplomatic ties of the two countries in 1967. The allegations also provided the basis for the development of the "China threat" discourse prominent throughout the New Order period (1966–1998). Suharto and his allies believed that communist China posed both ideological and security threats to Indonesia. They worried that China might help resurrect the PKI, which they banned during the post-coup anti-communist campaign. Indonesia's ethnic Chinese (Chinese Indonesians hereafter) has been subjected to suspicions too. The New Order elites believed that this group potentially can act as a "fifth pillar" that furthered China's ideological interests in the country (Sukma, 1999: 47). Such negative perception of China was not only confined to the elite groups but circulated widely among the Indonesian society at large.

The resumption of diplomatic ties in 1990 has opened the way for an improved relation between Indonesia and China. Enhanced diplomatic and people-to-people exchanges between the two countries emerged as a result of what Rizal Sukma calls "the policy of seeking active re-engagement with China" adopted by the post-Suharto Indonesian governments (Sukma, 2009: 145–149). President Abdurrahman

Wahid emphasized this policy shift by making China the first country that he officially visited. Indonesia's relationship with China remained cordial during the presidency of Megawati Sukarnoputri (2001–2004) and her successor Susilo Bambang Yudhoyono (2004–2014). Under Yudhoyono's leadership in 2005, Indonesia signed a "strategic partnership" with China. It was also in this period that China began to provide its development assistance to Indonesia. The construction of the Suramadu Bridge mentioned at the beginning of this chapter is a case in point. In 2013, the two countries expanded their "strategic partnership" agreement into a "comprehensive strategic partnership." At the end of Yudhoyono's presidency, Xi Jinping chose Jakarta to announce plans to launch the 21st Century Maritime Silk Road.

During the presidency of Joko Widodo (Jokowi), Indonesia's warm relationship with China developed further and, as a prominent Indonesian political scientist put it, has "come full circle" (Anwar, 2019). Soon after entering the presidential office in 2014, Jokowi declared his vision of making Indonesia the Global Maritime Fulcrum. His first presidential term (2014–2019) was focused on improving connectivity between many different regions of Indonesia through the accelerated transportation infrastructure development, such as ports, airports, and highways. Jokowi's administration regards China as one of the potential funding sources for infrastructure projects that it planned (Suryadinata, 2017: 18). For example, Indonesia's government used the loan from China to complete the Jakarta-Bandung high-speed railway project, which was contracted to China in August 2015. China's investments in other sectors, including power plant projects and the mining industry, have also increased significantly. China has even become the third-largest investor in Indonesia between 2016 and 2018, replacing Singapore as the largest investor in 2019.

Yet, Indonesia-China relations are by no means perfect. Issues that only began to emerge recently as well as the reproduction of the issues that were already present in the past might equally pose challenges to the two countries' relationship. Incidents between the Indonesian authorities and Chinese coast guard vessels in what Indonesia calls the North Natuna waters provide an example of the recently emerging challenges. The root of the problem could be traced back to the late 1990s when the currently famous nine dash-line began to appear in maps published in China. However, it only began to become public scrutiny in 2013, when an incident involving an Indonesian patrol team affiliated with the Ministry of Maritime and Fishery, the Chinese illegal fishing boats, and China's coast guard vessel broke and was reported in Indonesian media. During the incident, an Indonesian law enforcement vessel, the Hiu Macan 001, was arresting Chinese fishing boats that operated in Indonesian EEZ in the waters off Natuna Islands. But two Chinese coast guard vessels intercepted and ordered Hiu Macan to release the Chinese fishing boats. Similarly, the public's negative attitude toward Chinese migrant workers is also a relatively new phenomenon, which emerges as late as 2015, when the Indonesian government gave the contract to construct the Jakarta-Bandung high-speed railway project to China. Meanwhile, issues pertinent to Chinese Indonesians and their alleged relations with China have always been persistent since many decades ago. The issues have often reemerged, albeit in different forms, in each period of Indonesian post-Independence history. It is against this background that this chapter wishes to analyze how various groups of Indonesian elites today perceive the phenomenon of the rise of China and evaluate the current state of Sino-Indonesia relations.

9.3   Image Theory and the Study of Indonesian Elite Perception of China

The study of how people project the mental picture of countries other than their own has attracted many international relations scholars since over a half-century ago. These scholars consider such projection worth studying because it has a significant influence on the relationship between a country and another country or a group of other countries. This is particularly the case in the projection of the other country's image among the elite groups, who play a significant role in the decision-making process in their country. But the image that is widely popular in society, in general, is by no means less important. As the American scholar Kenneth Boulding argues, the image of the ruling elites cannot diverge critically from the image of the society, whose support is of significant importance for the ruling elites to retain their power (Boulding, 1959: 122).

Thus, whether among the elites or in the mind of the ordinary people, the image of a foreign country is believed to determine the behavior toward that country. This belief is based on the assumption that people's behavior is significantly influenced by their perception of the surrounding world. Boulding presented this assumption when he wrote that, "it is what we think the world is like, not what it is really like, that determines our behavior" (Boulding, 1959: 120). The assumption is also reflected clearly in Boulding's argument that members of the elite groups "do not respond to the 'objective' facts of the situation, whatever that may mean, but to their 'image' of the situation" (Boulding, 1959: 120). The image, thus, serves as a guide for both members of the elites as well as the ordinary people to perceive and interpret the current actions of a certain foreign country (Oppermann, 2011: 306).

The image of a certain foreign country contains various information which, according to Martha L. Cottam (1994), concerns that country's military and economic strength, its domestic polity, its goals relative to the goals of own country, and its cultural sophistication (p. 190). Cottam (1994) explains further that, "this information contributes to summary perceptions of the type of state's intentions toward our own country (threatening, benign, positive, and friendly), its power, its cultural sophistication, its expected behavior, and our responses" (p. 190). Thus, the perceptions of the other country's intentions, its power, as well as its culture are seen as the most important aspects of a person's or a group of people's image of that other country. Similarly, Herrmann, Voss, Schooler, and Ciarrochi also regard the perceived relative capability of the other actor, threat and/or opportunity that another actor represents, and the perceived culture of the other actor, as the three important judgments that guide basic foreign policy choices (Herrmann et al., 1997: 408). The analysis of the ways of perceiving other countries as discussed above has enabled scholars to find out certain types of images of those other countries. Cottam discussed the importance of another country's images as a dependent, enemy, or neutral, while Herrmann with colleagues focused their experiment on four types of image, that is, enemy, ally, colony, and degenerate, despite imagining 27 possible perceived relationships based on their model (Herrmann et al., 1997: 409).

The approach that emphasizes the importance of the image has also been adopted by scholars focused on Indonesian relations with China. Among the works that take such an approach are those published by Carl Taylor (1963), Liu Hong (2011), Rizal Sukma (1999), and Daniel Novotny (2010). Taylor's article, which was published in 1963, is perhaps among the earliest works focused on how China has been viewed by Indonesians. Both the article and Liu's 2011 book are important sources to understand how Indonesian people, including members of certain groups of the Indonesian elites, perceived China before the establishment of the New Order government. Meanwhile, the latter two books are also very important because they provide a detailed discussion of how the image of China was constructed during and after the New Order period. In particular, these books offer a complete picture of the New Order and post-New Order elite perception of China, the picture that takes into account the historical construction of China's image and its transmission from one generation to another.

Taylor's work informs us that despite a close relationship between Indonesia and China in the early 1960s, Indonesians had both negative and positive perceptions of China. The depiction of historical China as an imperialist, expansionist, and colonialist power was present in those years, while the view that regarded Mao's China as equally expansionist and colonialist was observable at least in a publication analyzed in the article (Taylor, 1963: 166–169). Indonesians consider Chinese culture, particularly achievements of the Tang and Ming Dynasties, as a superior culture, yet the Chinese—the carriers of this culture—are often associated with superstitious beliefs such as the ancestor worship tradition, and characterized as industrious but arrogant at the same time (Taylor, 1963: 169–171).

In contrast, Liu's book exposes the more positive representations of China among those whom he identifies as Indonesia's "political intellectuals" and "cultural intellectuals" between 1949 and 1965. Liu conceptualizes "political intellectuals" are "individuals who, despite assuming administrative or political responsibilities in the government and other political bodies, still maintained certain broad intellectual concerns for the nations' social and political development" (Liu, 2011: 18–19). For "cultural intellectuals," he adopts Max Weber's definition, that is "a group of men who by virtue of their peculiarity have special access to certain achievements considered to be 'cultural values,' and who, therefore usurp the leadership of a cultural community" (Liu, 2011: 19). Liu's analysis of how these two groups perceived China reveals three sets of master narratives about China among Indonesian intellectuals (Liu, 2011: 268). One of the narratives depicted China as a purposeful and harmonious society experiencing rapid economic progress, whereas the other one presented China as a nationalistic and populist regime profoundly different from the Soviet Union. Finally, intellectuals also regarded China as a nation living through a vibrant cultural and intellectual renaissance. The simultaneous presence of these three master narratives allowed Liu to argue that for Indonesian intellectuals between 1949 and 1965 "China served as an important and viable alternative to Western-dominant notions of the modernity project in Indonesia" (Liu, 2011: 271).

While the Taylor and Liu focus their study on the image of China in the Sukarno era that ended in 1966, Sukma explores the period between the establishment of the New Order government and the resumption of the Indonesia-China diplomatic ties in 1990. The image of China in Indonesia throughout this period was predominantly negative, and Sukma provides a detailed analysis of how such a negative view had emerged and persisted. In his analysis, Sukma explains how the portrayal of China as a potential threat to Indonesia served a certain function for the New Order regime. Faced with the worsening economic crisis that it inherited from the previous government, the New Order set for itself the task of rebuilding the country's economy. To achieve the goal of developing Indonesia, the government designed a long-term economic development plan, which was divided into several five-year development plans (*Rencana Pembangunan Lima Tahun* or *Repelita*). The New Order government believed that the maintenance of national stability was a very crucial factor for the successful implementation of its development strategy. As such, the government made economic development and the maintenance of national stability its two significant policy priorities (Sukma, 1999: 46). Sukma argues that the popularity of the "China threat" discourse should be understood in the context of these two policy priorities. Specifically, he maintains that the legitimacy of the New Order's development agenda was "reinforced by its threat perception, and such a threat was found in the form of communist subversion" (Sukma, 1999: 46). Suharto and his allies believed that China continues to interfere in Indonesia's internal affairs via the Chinese Indonesian community to revive the PKI in the country (Sukma, 1999: 51) and, as a result, they viewed the remnant of the PKI, China, and the Chinese Indonesians as the three different but intertwined sources of national insecurities. Sukma argues that this triad constituted "the logic of New Order's threat perception" (Sukma, 1999: 46).

However, it is worth noting that the aforementioned logic was not a newly manufactured one. Instead, as Sukma elucidates, it was built on some pre-existing perceptions which were already present before the New Order came into being. The portrayal of historical China as an aggressive and expansionist power, a portrayal discussed in Taylor's aforementioned work, constituted one of these perceptions. Interestingly, the Yuan Dynasty's invasion of Java was seen as a historical example of the aggressiveness and expansionist nature of China, although China was ruled by the Mongols during that era. Similarly noteworthy is the negative take of the expedition conducted by Zheng He, a Ming Dynasty Muslim Eunuch, to Southeast Asia in the early fourteenth century. While in the early twenty-first century the expedition was regarded as friendly, in the early 1970s it was seen as another example of China's aggressive and expansionist nature. The text quoted in Sukma's book wrote that during the expedition Zheng He captured many Southeast Asian kings, including the King of Palembang. In Sukma's opinion, these views suggest implicitly that Indonesia itself had been the victim of Chinese expansionist policy (Sukma, 1999: 53). Further-more, the Indonesian leaders at the beginning of the New Order period also believed that today's China still perceived itself as the 'center of the world' (Zhongguo) and regarded such self-perception as indicating "the arrogance of the big power" (Sukma, 1999: 54). While the perception of China as an aggressive and expansionist power constituted the external dimension of the New Order's 'China threat perception', the stereotypes about Chinese Indonesians formed its internal dimension. Sukma analyzes five major stereotypes that had already been widespread even before the New Order government was founded. These include the perception of the Chinese Indonesians as a separate nation (referred to as *Bangsa* in Indonesian), as an econom-ically dominant group, and as a privileged group in the colonial era (Sukma, 1999: 54–55). There is also the belief that the Chinese people were changeless, and the view of the Chinese Indonesians as an ethnic group whose concern rested only with their safety and economic well-being (Sukma, 1999: 54–55).

Novotny's book, which was based on research conducted between 2003 and 2006, becomes another important work that contains a detailed analysis of the Indonesian elite views of China. The period in which the research was conducted is in itself significant not only because it is within the first decade after Indonesia entered its post-New Order period, but also because it was carried out at the time Sino—Indonesian relation was already much closer and China's economic rise began to be felt in Indonesia. Hence the book provides invaluable insights into how China was perceived by the Indonesian elites in that period. However, unlike the other authors whose works discussed above, Novotny does not only focus on the Indonesian elites' views of China but also compares their views of China with their perception of the United States of America (U.S.). In regards to the perception of China, Novotny (2010) points out that Indonesian leaders still harbored some aspects of the perception that was held by the Indonesian elites during the New Order period. As he explains, the concern about China's expansionist tendencies as well as the deep-rooted stereotypes toward the Chinese Indonesians continues to shape the Indonesian leaders' perception of China (Novotny, 2010: 228–29).

Yet Novotny regards the Indonesian elite as having a pragmatic attitude toward China. He describes that "the Indonesian foreign policy elite consider China as an ambiguous threat that is, however, increasingly displaying its positive side" (Novotny, 2010: 228). Their attitudes toward China's rapid economic growth were ambivalent, and the elite in that period viewed China as a threat, and concurrently, as an economic opportunity (Novotny, 2010: 228–229). However, their view of the growing Chinese military power was described as characterized by uncertainty. While some believed that Indonesia should not have a concern about China's conventional military threat, there was uncertainty about whether China would not use the military power it had acquired to "put pressure on regional countries pursuing their national interest" (Novotny, 2010: 222). This uncertainty about how China will use its power in the future made the Indonesian elites conclude that "it is absolutely vital for Indonesia to hedge its relations with China" (Novotny, 2010: 347). It is in this context that despite high-profile hostile anti-American sentiments that emerged as a result of the U.S. policy in Iraq and Afghanistan in that period, "the U.S. is in the long run seen as benevolent and friendly power without any territorial design. [...] and its security role as the indirect psychological insurance for the stability of the region" (Novotny, 2010: 347).

As a summary, this section describes how studies focusing on how Indonesian elites saw China had been conducted by some scholars in the last period. As revealed by some of these studies, both negative, as well as positive perceptions of China, were concomitantly present, before the establishment of the New Order government. Those who had an appreciative view of China regarded the newly born communist country as an alternative to the western version of modernity. However, since Indonesia entered the New Order period, the perception that saw China as a threat was dominant amongst the government elites. Interestingly, such a view persisted during Yudhoyono's presidency, even though the relationship between Indonesia and China in this period was cordial, and a view that regarded the rise of China as providing an economic opportunity to Indonesia was present.

The discussions in the above works have also shown how Indonesian elites' perception of China's intentions, power, and culture have played an important role in the construction of China's image among these elites. For example, as Sukma (1999) has shown, New Order Indonesia's elites' perception of China as an aggressive and expansionist power, and their suspicion toward China's intention to interfere in Indonesia's internal affairs had influenced how they saw China. As discussed by the image theory scholars cited above, the perception of another country's intention, power, and culture are the most important aspects of a person or a group's image of that other country (Cottam, 1994) and may function as "the three important judgments that guide basic foreign policy choices" (Hermmann et al., 1997: 409). How do Indonesian elites' perceptions of China's intention, power, and culture shape these elites' image of China in present-day Indonesia? Which views become dominant amongst the Indonesian elites in the Jokowi era? The next section is devoted to providing an answer to these questions.

9.4   Indonesian Elites Perception of China in the Jokowi Era

In its effort to provide an answer to the question regarding how Indonesian elites today perceive China, this chapter uses the statements and comments articulated by members of data based on interviews and conversations with members of the government and the non-government elite groups that have been mentioned earlier in the introduction to this chapter While the non-government elites group included in this chapter consist of people with many different backgrounds, for the analysis purpose, they may be simplistically distinguished into the non-government elites who take an oppositional stance against President Jokowi's administration, and those who either maintain a neutral position or explicitly show their support to the government. Observation of these elites reveals that their perceptions of China are divided. Negative views of China are dominant among the non-government elites who are critical of the government but are also observable among those who take a neutral stance. As will be discussed further in this section, these people mostly harbor a suspicion that China may have a negative intention to Indonesia. Some of them resent China's assertive behavior, while at least a few of them worry that in the future China may use its military power to solve its issues with some other countries in the East and Southeast Asian region. Meanwhile, positive views are usually found among those who are sympathetic with Jokowi as well as among the government elites. But even among the latter, ambivalent attitude as reported in Novotny's work is also observable. Some of the non-government pro-Jokowi elites also have critical views of China although only regarding certain issues. Concerns regarding China have also been articulated even by members of the government elites. However, the appreciation of China, combined with a positive attitude toward it, is still observable both amongst the non-government elites who support Jokowi, as well as amongst the government elites.

9.4.1 Resentments Against China Amongst the Non-government Elites

Critical views of China are rampant among the non-government elites, particularly among those who take an oppositional stance against Jokowi. Their perception in many instances reflects the critical views of China which dominate the Indonesian public during the president Jokowi era, which is in stark contrast to the public discourse regarding China during a decade of Yudhoyono's presidency. During Yudhoyono's presidency, despite the persistence of the view of China as a threat amongst some sections of the Indonesian elites, China was mostly narrated positively in the Indonesian public. For example, Indonesian academics often saw how the Chinese leaders manage their country—which results in rapid economic development and a relatively increased power of the state vis à vis foreign powers—as worth emulating. The discourse of "learning from China" became relatively popular among the Indonesian public. In contrast, negative views of China spread widely in the Indonesian public within a year after Jokowi became the president of Indonesia (See Suryadinata, 2017: 18–20). In mid-2015, less than a year after the presidential inauguration, concerns about possible mass migration from China went viral in Indonesian media. The concern was initially a response to China's vice premier's speech during her visit to Jakarta in May 2015. The vice-premier encouraged a more intensive exchange between Chinese and Indonesian students. However, in the news that circulated in social media and non-mainstream media, her statement was interpreted as a signal that China planned to persuade millions of its people to migrate to Indonesia (Suryadinata, 2017: 18). The fear of possible mass migration from China grew larger alongside the massive arrival of Chinese migrant workers to work with Chinese construction and mining companies. The number of these Chinese workers, together with other 'new Chinese migrants' (referred to in many publications as Xinyimin) who have come to Indonesia for many different purposes, is estimated between 30.000 and 50.000 people. Nevertheless, criticism of these workers' arrival spreads widely in Indonesian media and social media. The media also scrutinize violations of EEZ by China's fishing boats and coastal guard vessels every time such an incident takes place. The last widely publicized incidents involving the Indonesian authorities and Chinese coastal guard representatives occurred in June 2016 and late December 2019. The latest event which raises public concern is the discovery of a foreign autonomous underwater vehicle in Selayar Island, South Sulawesi in December 2020. The fact that the vehicle reportedly resembles the model produced by China sparks an allegation, which is spread in the media, that the vehicle belongs to China and might be used for intelligence gathering.

Some of the above pictures of China are reflected in the views held by members of the non-government elite group. However, some of these elites offer different insights regarding China and its relations with Indonesia. In general, the non-government elites' perceptions of China may be classified into several themes. Concerns regarding the increased influx of Chinese migrant workers constitute one of these themes. Many among the non-government elites point to the negative impacts that these migrant workers might have on the local people. As many Chinese migrant workers are low-skilled, they are seen as potentially taking job opportunities from the Indonesian workers. The practice among Chinese companies to import blue-collar workers from China to Indonesia evokes criticism even among Jokowi's supporters. As an example, a top Indonesian lawyer who supports President Jokowi considers such a practice unacceptable. In an interview with the author, the lawyer expressed his wish that the Indonesian government took the necessary measure to ensure that all positions that could be filled by Indonesians were not filled by foreigners (Interview with a senior lawyer, Jakarta 14 May 2017). Another concern came from a pro-Jokowi NGO activist, who questioned the government's decision to eliminate the Bahasa Indonesia (Indonesian Language) requirement for foreigners who applied for a work permit in the country. For the activist, the abolishment of such a requirement puts Indonesia's national pride at stake.

Criticism against the practice of importing Chinese workers was also expressed by a labor union leader. Comparing the practice applied by the Chinese companies and their European, Korean, and Japanese counterparts, the leader emphasized the contribution given by the latter to the Indonesian society. In her view, the European, Korean, and Japanese investors only imported from their countries the skilled workers who might transfer their knowledge to Indonesian workers. In contrast to the European, Korean, and Japanese professionals, "the skill possessed by the Chinese workers is of the same level as those possessed by the Indonesian workers" (Interview with a labor union leader, Jakarta 9 May 2016). In the opinion of the labor union leader, the coming of these unskilled Chinese migrant workers potentially deprive the local people of employment opportunities. Thus, "conflicts between the migrants and the local people are potential to occur" (Interview with a labor union leader, Jakarta 9 May 2016).

In addition to their impact on the Indonesian workers, the coming of the Chinese workers also raises national security concerns amongst the non-government elites.

The suspicion that these migrants are either undercover intelligence agents or military personnel infiltrating Indonesia might be found amongst members of the non-government elites. For example, a businessman and political activist affiliated with an Islamic organization critical towards the government stated in an interview that, "we are suspicious [...] that the workers that they (China) export are the criminals who are meant to be banished, or even members of the Chinese Red Army" (Interview with a political activist, Jakarta 12 May 2016). Similarly, the labor union leader mentioned earlier disclosed that many of the union activists were worried if the Chinese migrant workers were agents of the Chinese intelligence services. A highly respected political scientist also expressed a similar concern when he posed the following rhetorical question in an interview: "How could you be sure that they (the Chinese migrant workers) are not military personnel? We have so many unemployed laborers, why do they have to use laborers from China?".

Some other members of the non-government elites even relate the coming of these migrant workers to the "Chinese migration strategy" that China is allegedly adopting. In their view, China adopts such a strategy to solve the population issue that it has been facing. Such a view was articulated, for example, by a retired major general of the Indonesian Army. In a personal communication, the retired general explained his opinion that China needed a place to relocate its people, and as a result, designed such a strategy. He believes that China's investment in infrastructure projects in Indonesia should be seen in the above context. He saw the Jakarta-Bandung high-speed railway project as a clear example of this. Regarding the project, the retired general commented as follow,

> It is a long-term project. The concession agreement grants China the right to manage the operation of the railway for 50 years. In that period, they will have children and grow into a sizable community. China must have designed it. For me, it is a demographic movement strategy. (Personal communication with a retired major general of the Indonesian Army, 23 June 2019)

Hence in the view of the above-retired general, infrastructure projects like the Jakarta-Bandung high-speed railway projects, allow China to implement its strategy to solve the population issue that this country is facing at home, that is, by encouraging its people to work in the projects and stay in the host country as long as possible.

As observable in the view expressed by the retired general cited above, China's investment in infrastructure projects in Indonesia is another theme that is often present in the discussions regarding China amongst the Indonesian elites. Quite a few non-government elites, particularly those with an opposition stance against President Jokowi criticized the government for welcoming massive investment from China. These elites were concerned over China's possible hidden objective behind the influx of its investments in various infrastructure projects in many different regions in Indonesia. A researcher who heads an independent research center was suspicious that China wished to control some strategic location in Indonesia, such as the Sunda Strait, a strait that separates Java Island from Sumatra. In the view of the researcher, China might be interested in controlling the strait because it is "the second shortest route from the Indian Ocean to the Pacific Ocean after the Malacca Strait" (Interview with a researcher, Jakarta 16 January 2016). The researcher also opined that China might also be interested in Bitung, a city on the north end of Sulawesi Island, because its strategic location enabled China to balance the U.S. presence in the Philippines and Pacific Ocean (Interview with a researcher, Jakarta 16 January 2016).

However, it is the increased reliance on Chinese investments in Indonesian infrastructure projects that are considered as most worrisome by the aforementioned groups of elites. In their view, it might give a reason for China to take ownership over some Indonesian assets. An example of such concern was voiced by a senior Indonesian leader who in the past served as the speaker of the Indonesian House of Representatives (DPR). While the senior leader praised the economic side of the rise of China and showed his hope that Indonesia could get some benefits from it, he still could not stop being suspicious of the intention behind China's investment in other developing countries' infrastructure projects. "I worry if China has the ambition to colonize other countries," he mentioned. But he believes that the model of colonization that China may adopt is not the one practiced by the European colonizers in the past. Instead, it is "a modern form of colonization which, unlike in the past, is characterized by political, rather than by physical domination" (Interview with a senior politician, Jakarta 25 May 2016).

In the view of the above senior politician, Jakarta-Bandung high-speed railway project is one of the projects that Indonesians should pay attention to. He views that the project is not economically feasible. But on the other hand, he worries that after the project is completed, the management of the Jakarta Bandung high-speed train service will be given to China. Furthermore, in the case China experiences financial loss due to the unprofitability of the project, the politician worries that China may demand compensation for its loss in the form of its acquisition of a large area of land surrounding the railway network. As he specifies, if such a scenario takes place, "our [Indonesian] economy will be completely under their [China's] control." As a result of the above concern, the above senior leader wishes that the government reviews the investment plan from China carefully. "Will it burden Indonesia in the future? It won't be good if it increases the debt of the Indonesian state and gives a reason to them [China] to take over our assets," he maintained.

A third theme encountered during the discussions with the above group of elites is China's behavior in the South China Sea. The South China Sea geographic location is, "between the southern coasts of China and Taiwan to the north, the mainland coast of Southeast Asia to the west, and the archipelagic island groups of the Philippines, Borneo, and Indonesia to the east and south" (Schofield, 2016: 22). The sea is disputed by seven claimant states including China, Taiwan, the Philippines, Vietnam, Malaysia, and Brunei. Indonesia consistently declares that it is a non-claimant state although, as Clive Schofield explains,

Indonesia's maritime claims in the Southwest South China Sea overlap with those of other littoral states, notably Malaysia and Vietnam, and are, more also likely to overlap with the claims of whichever state or states is ultimately determined to hold sovereignty over the disputed Spratly Islands. (Schofield, 2016: 22)

The disputes in the South China Sea have caused tensions that began to rise in the 1990s when China became more assertive in trying to uphold its claims (Storey & Lin, 2016: 8). The tensions eased in the first half of the 2000s but have been rising again since 2007 and 2008 because of China's renewed assertiveness (Storey & Lin, 2016: 8). Such an assertive behavior persisted in the aftermath of the arbitration award published by the Permanent Court Arbitration (PCA) in The Haque in 2016, which ruled against China's claim of historic rights in the South China Sea (See, for example, Fitriani, 2018: 396, 398).

China's assertiveness, which led to rising tensions in the South China Sea, has evoked negative responses from many representatives of Indonesian opinion leaders. Rene Pattiradjawane, a senior journalist and a China expert, called China's behavior in the South China Sea "maritime colonialism with Chinese characteristics" (Pattirad-jawane, 2016). A top leader of Muhammadiyah, one of the largest Muslim organiza-tions in the country, disclosed how some *pribumi* elites worried that the dispute in the South China Sea might turn into an immense problem for the countries in the region (Interview with a top Muhammadiyah leader, Jakarta 11 April 2016). In a similar tone, a highly respected political scientist mentioned earlier in this chapter regards that, "Indonesia should treat the aforementioned dispute as a challenge, which poten-tially threatens Indonesian interest in the future" (Interview with a senior political scientist, Jakarta 29 February 2016). In the view of the political scientist, Indonesia must be prepared, and should not think that the South China Sea issue only affects Malaysia, Brunei, Vietnam, and the Philippines. "What if China one day claims a part of our territory? Are we ready? China's military is incredible. We should be prepared," claimed this senior scholar.

A fourth theme that often appears in the views of China expressed by the non-government elites is the incidents involving Indonesian authority and Chinese coast-guards in the waters near Natuna Islands. The area where the incidents took place is within EEZ but overlaps with China's so-called "nine-dash line" territorial claim, which Indonesia does not recognize. On 20 March 2016, a patrol team from the Indonesian Ministry of Marine Affairs and Fisheries seized a Chinese fishing boat operating illegally within EEZ. But when the team was towing the boat to the Indone-sian port, a Chinese coastguard ship intervened and freed the boat, which according to China was within their "traditional fishing ground." The incident alarmed quite a few elite Indonesians, especially because this was neither the first time nor the last time for such incidents to take place. As mentioned earlier, a similar incident took place in late 2019 and sparked public outcry. A number of the non-government elites express their disappointments concerning this issue too. For example, the top Muhammadah leader whose view discussed earlier, recounted how quite a few people complained about the fact that "even though we [Indonesia] have shown our kindness to China, they [China] still claim the waters off Natuna as their territory […], and they still don't want to admit that they already encroached into Indonesia's EEZ" (Interview with a top Muhammadiyah leader, Jakarta 11 April 2016). In the view of the Muslim leader, the escalating tension in the South China Sea, as well as the incidents occur-ring in Natuna, have provided evidence that the rise of China potentially threatens the political stability in the region. Meanwhile, a former ambassador expressed his suspicion that China intended to alter Indonesia's current border by encouraging its fishing boats to repeatedly encroached into the Indonesian EEZ near Natuna.

In addition to the above four themes, a suspicion that China may still maintain a relationship with the Chinese Indonesians and use the latter for their interest is another theme that becomes visible during the discussions with the above group of elites. The portrayal of the Chinese Indonesians as people "whose Indonesian nationality was at best dubious" (Coppel, 1983) has already been popular since the country gained its independence. Today, the perception that Chinese Indonesians still harbor a certain level of loyalty toward China is still popular in Indonesian society in general. A survey conducted by ISEAS Yusof Ishak Institute in 2017 reveals that 47.6% of the respondents of the survey agree with the statement that says that Chinese Indonesians may still harbor loyalty toward China, compared to 17.9% who disagrees with that statement (Fossati et al., 2017: 26).

Such a suspicion might also be found amongst the non-government Indonesian elites today. For example, a businessman and political activist mentioned earlier in this chapter expressed his suspicion that the Chinese migrant workers were Chinese military personnel who came to smuggle weapons from the sea. In his view, the Chinese migrants might smuggle weapons into the north coast of Java because its residents were predominantly Chinese Indonesians. Such a view indicates an assumption that the Chinese Indonesians will help the Chinese from China in their effort to infiltrate Indonesia. Similarly, a retired high-ranking military officer uttered his suspicion that the political success of Basuki Tjahaja Purnama (Ahok), a Chinese Indonesian politician who served as the governor of Jakarta between 2014 and 2017, was a part of China's strategy to dominate Indonesia. The military officer mentioned that there was an allegation that he received financial support from China for his political campaign. A concern regarding the possibility of China making use of the Chinese Indonesians was also expressed by a former senior diplomat. The retired ambassador believed that the *ius sanguinis* nationality law adopted by China enabled the country to co-opt the so-called "overseas Chinese." As such, the senior diplomat emphasized the need to remind the Chinese Indonesians that they should not have double loyalty, a reminder that has been expressed frequently by members of the *pribumi* elites in the past.

But the view voiced by a *pribumi* Indonesian businessman who comes from an elite business family informs us how the resentment against a relationship between China and the Chinese Indonesians may have a business motif. The businessman uttered concern regarding China's tendency to build business relations with ethnic Chinese business entrepreneurs in Indonesia, which he saw as a big mistake. "It is a time bomb that would one day explode," he stated (Interview with an Indonesian businessman). The businessmen pointed to the fact that negative attitudes toward the Chinese Indonesian business tycoons were popular in Indonesia. However, in his view, the popularity of such a negative attitude would not greatly affect China if the businessmen from that country build business alliances with *pribumi* entrepreneurs, instead of with their Chinese Indonesian counterparts.

9.4.2 Concerns Among the Government Elites

The views of China amongst the Indonesian government elites are varied and divided. Nonetheless, the themes that have alarmed certain segments of the Indonesian non-government elites have also become a source of concern for some members of the government elites as well. The arrival of Chinese migrant workers constitutes one of these concerns. Professor Dewi Fortuna Anwar, a senior political scientist at the Indonesian Institute of Science, maintains that the Indonesian government should pay attention to the above issue. According to her, concerns about the coming of the Chinese workers could be traced back to more than a decade ago, when they came to participate in the Suramadu construction project. However, resentments about the issues have recently increased alongside the increased flow of these people. As Anwar explains,

> For example, they create their enclave in Southeast Sulawesi Province, where they participate in a project. Even the low-skilled workers (who work in that project) came from China. They do not interact with local people. I was informed that a district leader in that region complained because his district residents could not have the opportunity to work on the project. Conflicts with the local community have begun to take place as well. (Interview with Anwar, Jakarta, 24 May 2016)

The professor also highlights several cases that have sparked the Indonesian public suspicion toward the Chinese workers. One of these is the case that took place in a military base in Halim, East Jakarta, in which a few Chinese workers who work for the Bandung-Jakarta high-speed railway project were found digging illegally in the area close to the military compound, which is restricted to civilians. In the view of Professor Anwar,

> This case has two dimensions. First of all, many people are caught by surprise with the fact that the contractors have again brought the workers from China to participate in the Bandung-Jakarta high-speed project. But more than that, they also question what these workers did, 'how dare they dig without permission?' This sparks speculative concerns among the Indonesians, 'are they members of the intelligence agency?', 'is there any security issue related to the case?' I think, such an issue, if not handled with care, can trigger a backlash. (Interview with Anwar, Jakarta, 24 May 2016)

In line with Anwar, a senior diplomat admits that the arrival of the Chinese workers creates a big problem, even though the diplomat regards the issue in terms of violation of the immigration regulation in general, and not as a problem uniquely related to the relationship between Indonesia and China. As such, in his view, "what we (Indonesia) should improve is our law enforcement. We can reduce the emergence of this issue if we are stringent" (interview with a senior diplomat, 3 June 2016). In the same vein, a senior officer of the Indonesian Navy mentioned in an interview that Indonesia should channel its suspicion against the coming of Chinese migrant workers in a positive way. The suspicion should drive the Indonesian government to apply a set of rules that regulate the influx of the workers, such as by permitting only the skilled workers or higher-level staff and managers to enter Indonesia and work in this country (Interview with a high-ranking military officer, Jakarta 7 March

2016). Similarly, China's increased flow of investments to Indonesia is also seen with caution by some government elites. A high-ranking government official, for example, commented that the government needed to be very careful in responding to China's proposal to provide loans to Indonesia under the Belt and Road Initiative scheme (Personal communication with a high-ranking government official, 6 May 2019).

As discussed in the last section, China's behavior in the South China Sea and the water near Natuna Islands are among the issues that have become a source of concern for a group of non-government elites. Likewise, certain members of the government elites also consider the issue alarming. For example, a senior diplomat regards the recent development in the South China Sea as worrisome due to the increasing tension between China and the US. Meanwhile, regarding the incidents that have repeatedly occurred in the water near Natuna Islands, the senior Navy officer mentioned earlier opined that Indonesia should be suspicious toward China's behavior in that area. The military officer particularly pointed out the presence of the nine-dash line, which in his view worried Indonesia as it was not clear if the line covered EEZ or not. The military officer understands that China's Foreign Ministry in Jiang Zemin Era already made a statement that China did not have any territorial problem with Indonesia and that the Indonesian Foreign Ministry has decided not to question China's above statement. Nevertheless, he also mentioned that to his knowledge, the statement did not stop some government elites from becoming worried about the issue.

As observable in the above discussion, the fear that China might have insincere motives behind the economic and cultural ties that it establishes with Indonesia is still dominant among the non-government elites, as well as among several government officials. Indeed, suspicion toward China is still present even among the officials who are supposed to implement President Jokowi's China policy. Officials in the Ministry of Foreign Affairs are not the exception. As explained by a high-ranking official in this ministry, Indonesian diplomats often observe suspiciously each time China is making a move, particularly the move that potentially affects Indonesia (Interview with a high-ranking official in the Ministry of Foreign Affairs, Jakarta 1 March 2016). In the view of the senior Navy officer quoted earlier, "such suspicious attitudes made it difficult for the bureaucrats to stay in line with President Jokowi's wish to build a close relationship with China" (Interview with a high-ranking military officer, Jakarta 7 March 2016). As a result, lower-level government elites might pass to their Chinese counterparts a signal different from the message that the president wants to deliver. The military officer admitted that even he still retained a certain extent of suspicion, although he always tries to manage the suspicion and use it only for a positive purpose.

Finally, some of the governing elites are also unhappy with the alleged relationship between China and the Chinese Indonesians. The view expressed by a high-ranking official shows how the concern regarding such a relationship persists at least amongst a few members of the government elites. In an interview, the official articulated his concern regarding "the tendency of delegations from China and of the people from the Chinese embassy in Indonesia to visit and establish a relationship with the Chinese Indonesian community" (Interview with a high-ranking official, Jakarta 22 June

2019). In another discussion, the high-ranking official also questioned the national loyalty of certain Chinese Indonesian businessmen toward Indonesia. In his view, there were a group of Chinese Indonesians who became China oriented for business purpose. According to him,

> These people even defend (talk on behalf of) China. For example, I once had a text conversation with a Chinese Indonesian leader in which I mentioned my concern about China claiming Natuna Islands. My interlocutor denied such a possibility, defending China. (Interview with a high-ranking official, Jakarta 12 January 2016)

In another conversation, the official once again disclosed his worries that if these Chinese Indonesian leaders attend a meeting with China's representatives, they would take China's side rather than defend Indonesia's interests (Conversation with a high-ranking official, Jakarta 28 March 2016).

9.4.3 Positive Views of China

The persistence of critical views of China, and the cautious attitudes demonstrated by some high-ranking government officials should not lead us to downplay the presence of optimistic views of China among Indonesian elites. The view that sees China positively is still present among the Indonesian elites. But unlike the negative perceptions of China, which exist among both Jokowi's political opponents and supporters, the positive views of China may be observed mostly among members of the government elites and pro-Jokowi non-government elites. For example, despite his concern regarding the arrival of Chinese workers, a pro-Jokowi activist mentioned earlier in this article argued that China had neither a colonizing mentality nor a history of colonialism in Indonesia (Interview with pro-Jokowi activist, Jakarta 5 March 2016). The activist stated that many members of the Indonesian elites knew this fact. While such a claim may be an exaggeration, the presence of a similar view is evident in my interview with a Muslim Javanese public intellectual and politician affiliated with the National Democrat Party (Nasdem). The politician viewed that China had never supported any separatist movement operating outside the country, been involved in any espionage action against Indonesia, or conduct any political operation to install someone as an Indonesian president, or to topple him/her (Interview with a politician affiliated with Partai Nasdem, Jakarta 24 March 2016). Thus this politician does not see the rise of China as a real military threat.

A positive perception of China was also expressed by another pro-Jokowi activist who joined the 'national secretariat of Jokowi' (Seknas Jokowi), an organization founded to encourage Jokowi to contest in the 2014 presidential election. The activist who is also an academic has a positive view of Chinese state-owned oil and gas company, PetroChina, because, according to him, it has made some positive contributions to the wellbeing of locals. He praised how PetroChina had financed a project to improve nutrition for the local families in Jambi, an Indonesian province located in Sumatra (Interview with a pro-Jokowi activist, Jakarta 4 May 2016). He also told the story of how PetroChina finances projects that improve the quality of life at Brojonegoro regency in East Java where it operates. The activist disagreed with those who resented against Chinese workers. He questioned the resentment because, in his view, other foreign investors are no different from China. Citing Japan as an example, he pointed out that Japanese companies that participated in a project funded with loans from the Japanese government also imported lower-skill workers, including bulldozers drivers, and kitchen staff, from Japan. "But we never problematized that," he summarized.

Positive perceptions are also found among the government elites, including high-ranking military officers. Some of these people see the rise of China as a natural phenomenon. "All countries might one day rise," said a senior military officer who holds a position in the National Defense Council (*Wantanas*) (Interview with a senior military officer, Jakarta 8 March 2016). "The rise of China might trigger Asian economic and improve our bargaining position against the West," he commented further. He also thought that the phenomenon might become a source of learning for Indonesia: "If China can rise, why can't we?".

Meanwhile, Anwar explained how the closeness between the two countries has begun since the Yudhoyono era and is becoming much closer today. "Mrs. Rini (Rini Mariani Soemarno – the minister of state-owned enterprises) is given a special task by President Jokowi to manage the investment from China, and the trade with China," she asserted. In addition to infrastructure, cooperation between Indonesia and China is also taking place in the defense industry, such as, in the production of radars and small arms. According to the professor, "this is part of our strategy to avoid being dependent only on one supplier, like in the previous time" (Interview with Anwar, Jakarta, 24 May 2016).

9.5 Historical Legacy, China's International Behavior, and Indonesian Internal Politics: Factors of the Persistent Negative View of China

As discussed in the previous sections, Indonesian elites' perceptions of China are varied. The negative perception of China might be found amongst non-government elites, particularly—but not only—those who have an oppositional stance against President Jokowi. Concerns regarding China are also observable amongst the governing elites. Meanwhile, the positive take of China is still discernable among some members of the government elites as well as amongst the non-government elites who support President Jokowi. While the presence of the positive perception may be explained in the context of benefits that China's investments give to Indonesia, how do we explain the persistence of negative perceptions against the backdrop of the increasingly close relationship between the two countries? This section is devoted to discussing this issue.

Several factors may have contributed to the dominance of the negative perception of China amongst the Indonesian elites today. One of these is the tenacity of the historical view of China in the mind of quite a few members of elites. A close look at the negative perception that the Indonesian elites have regarding China reveals how these elites see China today is to a certain extent similar to the perception held by the Indonesian elites in the past. The 'China Threat Perception' that was rooted in the Indonesian society particularly during the New Order period, is reproduced in the views held by today's elite. The suspicion that China may have hidden intentions behind the coming of Chinese migrant workers as well as the increased influx of Chinese investments attest to the presence of the above "China Threat Perception." At the same time, the view of China as an expansionist power, a view that already existed in the 1960s, is also observable amongst some groups of the Indonesian elites today. As mentioned earlier, when discussing China's alleged strategy to relocate its people through migration, some members of the elites associate China's behavior with the behaviors of the European colonizers. Finally, concerns regarding China's relationship with the Chinese Indonesians may be seen as an indication that the question regarding the loyalty of this ethnic group, a question that has frequently appeared since the independence of the Republic of Indonesia, continues to be asked by some amongst the elites today.

But several events related to China that have emerged in different parts of the world have fueled the re-emergence of the negative perception of China that had existed in history. Some of the elites interviewed mentioned the fate experienced by Srilanka, which leased its Hambantota Port to China for 99 years. Some even talked about Darwin Port, which is leased to China's Shandong Landbridge Group, also for 99 years. But the most significant is the recent development in the South China Sea as well as the incidents taking place in Natuna Waters. In particular, the Natuna incidents have a potential to be seen by some members of the Indonesian elites as China's demonstration of power, despite the fact that China's vessels involved in the incidents are civilian (Coast Guard) vessels. This may in turn further validate the perception of China as a threat among some groups of the Indonesian elites.

Finally, the Indonesian internal political atmosphere has also become a significant factor. Despite his success in consolidating majority support in parliament a few years after his inauguration, President Jokowi still encountered resilient opposition from his political opponents. Among these political opponents were the political parties that remained outside of the 'pro-government coalition' in the Indonesian House of Representatives. Facing difficulty to gain enough support for their opposition against the president in the parliament, Jokowi's political opponents, "shifted their focus from intra-institutional opposition in the legislature to extra-parliamentary mobilization in the streets" (Mietzner, 2017: 168). The government's close relations with China became one of the issues that might be raised in their criticism against Jokowi's administration. Some of the anti-China campaigns had targeted the president later before the 2019 presidential election. As observed by Anwar, "Jokowi has become the target of a massive black campaign on social media that accuses him of being a handmaiden of both China's and local Tionghoa's interests" (Anwar, 2019: 158). For Anwar and some other Indonesian scholars who are critical of Indonesian politics, such a practice is worrisome because "in the increasingly charged political climate the rise in anti-Chinese sentiment could again be manipulated for political purposes."

Furthermore, opposition against Jokowi was combined with the resistance against one of his allies, Basuki Tjahaja Purnama, who replaced Jokowi as the governor of Jakarta in 2014. The Chinese Indonesian politician wished to compete in the 2017 Jakarta gubernatorial election to secure his second term as the governor. But while receiving support from a large number of *pribumi* political elites and activists, his decision to run in the above election also induced massive resistance from an equally large group of the *pribumi*. Some of these groups even resented his inauguration as the governor early in 2014. The anti-Chinese nationalism that appeared in late 2015 and through the year 2016 might be explained in relation to the opposition movements against Purnama. The suspicion that the Chinese from China might migrate to Jakarta and be mobilized to vote for Purnama was heard in that period. So was the concern regarding the political rule of the Chinese Indonesians, who up to the present have been regarded as a group that dominates the Indonesian economy.

9.6   Conclusion

The previous sections of this chapter have provided a discussion on how China has been perceived by members of Indonesian elites today. As observable in the discussion, the perceptions of China—and of that country's relationship with Indonesia—amongst the Indonesian elites are divided. Some of the elites have a positive perception of China, but many more harbor a negative view of that country. Furthermore, critical views of China are dominant amongst the non-government elites, particularly amongst those who are critical of Jokowi.

The prevalence of the negative views of China is worth further analysis. While the concerns raised by members of the elites relate to the phenomena emerging in recent years, the belief that such concerns are based is arguably old. Except for the concern regarding the negative impacts that the coming of the new migrants has on the Indonesian blue-collar workers, most concerns are based on the suspicion that China may use its migrant workers to infiltrate Indonesia, encourage its people to populate some areas in Indonesia, have the intention to control some of the Indonesian strategic infrastructures through its investments and expand its relationship with the Chinese Indonesians for its interest. The root of the above suspicion may be traced back to the perception of China that existed in the pre-New Order as well as during the New Order period, that is, the view of China as an expansionist power, the perception of China as a threat, and the concern regarding the ethnic Chinese' role as the fifth column for China's sake. Thus, the negative views of China that are widespread amongst certain groups of the Indonesian elites today are a reproduction of the old perceptions in new forms. As discussed in the last section of this chapter, the reemergence of such negative views of China may also be seen as a result of China's recent international behavior, including the emergence of several incidents near the Natuna Islands, as well as of the recent developments in Indonesian internal politics. The former is particularly important because it may be perceived as China's demonstration of power by some groups of the Indonesian elites, and as a result strengthens their perception of China as a threat.

But regardless of its causes, the spread of the above negative perception of China amongst members of the Indonesian elites, as well as its parallel in the Indonesian public, should be seen as a significant phenomenon due to its potential effects on the government's policy toward China. Criticism against China's increased participation in the Indonesian development project potentially forces the key decision-making elites to seek a solution that prevents any backlash from happening. In the view of Dewi Fortuna Anwar, diversifying sources of investment and loans and avoiding becoming too dependent on any one country is one of the strategies that the Indonesian government should continue to apply. The adoption of such a strategy is by no means new, as it is consistent with the Indonesian foreign policy philosophy which was developed in the early years of the country's independence: *mendayung di antara dua karang* (rowing between two reefs).

Acknowledgements This work is based on research that was conducted from early 2016 to mid-2017 with support from ISEAS Yusof Ishak Institute, Singapore. I thank the institute for generously allowing me to use the data for this article. My special gratitude also goes to Dr. Hui Yew-Foong, the coordinator of the ISEAS Yusof Ishak Institute's Indonesia Study Program, for his significant contribution to the formulation of the research and interview questions, as well as the scope of the project.

References

Anwar, D. F. (2019). Indonesia-China relations: Coming full circle? *Southeast Asian Affairs, 145–161*.

Boulding, K. (1959). National images and international systems. *Journal of Conflict Resolution, 3*(2), 120–131.

Brown, C. (2003). *A short history of Indonesia: The unlikely nation?* Allen & Unwin.

Coppel, C. A. (1983). *Indonesian Chinese in crisis*. Oxford University Press.

Cottam, M. L. (1994). *Images and intervention: U.S. policies in Latin America*. University of Pittsburgh Press.

Fitriani, E. (2018). Indonesian perceptions of the rise of China: Dare you, dare you not. *Pacific Review, 31*(3), 391–405.

Fossati, D., Negara, S. D., & Hui, Y. F. (2017). *The Indonesian national survey project: Economy, society and politics* (Trends in Southeast Asia No. 10). ISEAS – Yusof Ishak Institute.

Herlijanto, J. (2013). *Emulating China: Representation of China and the contemporary critique of Indonesia* (Unpublished doctoral dissertation). Vrije Universiteit Amsterdam.

Herrmann, R. K., Voss, J. F., Schooler, T. Y. E., & Ciarrochi, J. (1997). Images in international relations: An experimental test of cognitive schemata. *International Studies Quarterly, 41*, 403–433.

Koran Tempo. (2009, June 12). *Ada Cina di antara Jawa dan Madura* [There is China between Java and Madura]. https://koran.tempo.co/read/ilmu-dan-teknologi/167890/ada-cina-di-antara-jawa-dan-madura

Liu, H. (2011). *China and the shaping of Indonesia, 1949–1965*. NUS Press

Mietzner, M. (2017). Indonesia in 2016: Jokowi's presidency between elite consolidation and extra-parliamentary opposition. *Asian Survey, 57*(1), 165–172.

Mozingo, D. (1976). *Chinese policy toward Indonesia, 1949–1967*. Cornell University Press.

Novotny, D. (2010). *Torn between America and China: Elite perception and Indonesian foreign policy*. ISEAS

Oppermann, K. (2011). The public images of Britain, Germany, and France in the United States. *Journal of Transatlantic Studies, 9*(4), 305–325. https://doi.org/10.1080/14794012.2011.622932

Pattiradjawane, R. (2016, March 23). Maritime colonialism with Chinese characteristics. *The Jakarta Post*. https://www.thejakartapost.com/news/2016/03/23/maritime-colonialism-with-chinese-characteristics.html

Schofield, C. (2016). Untangling a complex web: Understanding competing maritime claims in the South China Sea. In I. Storey & C. Y. Lin (Eds.), *The South China Sea dispute: Navigating diplomatic and strategic tensions* (1st ed., pp. 21–46). ISEAS Publisher

Storey, I., & Lin, C. Y. (2016). Introduction. In I. Storey & C. Y. Lin (Eds.), *The South China Sea dispute: Navigating diplomatic and strategic tensions* (1st ed., pp. 1–20). ISEAS Publisher

Sukma, R. (1999). *Indonesia and China: The politics of a troubled relationship*. Routledge.

Sukma, R. (2009). Indonesia's response to the rise of China: Growing comfort amid uncertainties. In Jun Tsunekawa (Ed.), *The Rise of China: Response from Southeast Asia and Japan* (1st ed., pp 139–155). National Institute for Defence Studies.

Suryadinata, L. (1990). Indonesia-China relation: A recent breakthrough. *Asian Survey, 30*(7), 682–696.

Suryadinata, L. (2017). *The growing "strategic partnership" between Indonesia and China faces difficult challenges* (Trends in Southeast Asia No. 15). ISEAS—Yusof Ishak Institute.

Suryadinata, L., & Izzuddin, M. (2017). *The Natunas: Territorial integrity in the forefront of Indonesia-China relations* (Trends in Southeast Asia No. 5). ISEAS—Yusof Ishak Institute.

Taylor, C. (1963). Indonesian views of China. *Asian Survey, 3*(3), 165–172.

Vickers, A. (2005). *A history of modern Indonesia*. Cambridge University Press.

Zhou, T. (2019). *Migration in the time of revolution: China, Indonesia, and the Cold War*. Cornell University Press.

Johanes Herlijanto is a senior lecturer at the Department of Communication, Pelita Harapan University (Indonesia). Johanes holds a Ph.D. in Anthropology from Macquarie University (Australia) and Vrije Universiteit (the Netherlands), under a cotutelle scheme. He also holds an M.Sc. in Sociology from the University of Indonesia (Indonesia). Johanes' works over the last ten years have been focused on how the phenomenon of the rise of China has been perceived by Indonesians, as well as on the political participation of the ethnic Chinese in Indonesia.

Part III
China's Acceptance as a Function of Partner Country's Structural Features

-

Chapter 10
China's Colombia Conundrum: From Warm Reception to Failure, Apathy and Prejudice

Sabrina van den Bos

Abstract The China-Colombia relationship began as any other between the People's Republic of China and most Latin American states after the turn of the twenty-first century. Two-way trade went from zero to multibillion dollars within a decade. However, despite its apparent successes and a host of widely publicized diplomatic initiatives, the initial bilateral relationship is ultimately a story of failure. Chinese petroleum companies failed to win a single bid for the development of Colombian oil fields. Bilateral Free Trade Agreement talks proved futile. Colombia received almost no overseas foreign direct investment from China, despite a crying need for infrastructure development. For China, Colombia became a Latin American anomaly. This chapter argues that it was Colombia's uniquely antistatist approach in the promotion of its liberal values complemented by a deep aversion to left-wing politics that left little room for government-backed initiatives. It draws on political theory, original interviews and survey results to bring to light new structural and ideational factors which better define state capacity and reveal the historical sources of modern Colombian constraints.

Keywords China · Colombia · Bilateral Relations · Foreign Policy Analysis · Petro Diplomacy

Abbreviations

ANH	Agencia Nacional de Hidrocarburos (National Hydrocarbons Agency of Colombia)
BIT	Bilateral investment treaty
CAF	Corporação Andina de Fomento (Development Bank of Latin America)
CCCIC	Cámara Colombo China de Inversión y Comercio (Colombian Chinese Chamber of Investment and Commerce)
CDB	China Development Bank

S. van den Bos (✉)
Sydney, Australia
e-mail: sabrina@alumni.lse.ac.uk

© The Author(s), under exclusive license to Springer Nature Singapore Pte Ltd. 2022
T. Tudoroiu and A. Kuteleva (eds.), *China in the Global South*,
https://doi.org/10.1007/978-981-19-1344-0_10

Ecopetrol	Empressa Colombia de Petróleos (Colombian Petroleum Company)
FARC	Fuerzas Armadas Revolucionarias de Colombia (Revolutionary Armed Forces of Colombia)
FDI	Foreign direct investment
FTA	Free trade agreement
IDB	Inter-American Development Bank
LAC	Latin America and the Caribbean
MOU	Memorandum of understanding
PRC	People's Republic of China
SOE	State-owned enterprise

10.1 Introduction

Over the last two decades, the People's Republic of China (PRC) has grown from maintaining only a paucity of projects in Latin America and the Caribbean (LAC) the largest trading partner and the lender of choice for the region. The scholarship first analyzing this phenomenon focused on China's economic and political strategies and the potential for cooperation or competition with each nation according to its economic strengths and weaknesses. Much less literature covers the foreign policy of LAC nations towards China. This demands a deeper analysis of both the LAC nations' agency and structure and how these have altered the course of relations. This chapter examines the Colombian response and highlights where Colombian agency shapes the trajectory.

The Sino-Colombian relationship began as any other between China and most Latin American states in the early 2000s, a period when two-way trade went from zero to multibillion dollars within a decade. The PRC's opportunities in Colombia were the same as or greater than they were in other nations. Early diplomatic efforts appeared promising. Colombia enthusiastically received Chinese state officials and China equally welcomed successive Colombian presidents on state visits. After these enthusiastic first steps, however, many of China's strong suits found no traction in the Andean republic. "For Latin America, the history of the region can be structured as a series of 'landings' (*desembarcos*) that shaped different encounters between those arriving (foreigners and foreign powers) and those already living in the region (indigenous peoples and the vast array of those who arrived, stayed and became local)" (Strauss, 2012: 2). Colombia's response to China's *desembarco* was unique amongst its neighbors.

The initial bilateral relationship is ultimately a story of failure. Chinese petroleum companies failed to win a single bid for the development of Colombian oil fields. Bilateral Free Trade Agreement talks proved futile. Colombia received almost no foreign direct investment (FDI) from China, despite a crying need for infrastructure development. In the wake of these early failings, mutual distrust and prejudices abounded. The PRC's approach to Colombia was no different to that taken with other countries. For China, Colombia became an anomaly. Colombia's uniquely antistatist approach in the promotion of its liberal values complemented by a deep aversion to left-wing politics left little room for government-backed initiatives spearheading this first approach. Examining the trajectory of relations reveals structural constraints due to both material and ideational factors.

This chapter draws on Hillel Soifer's (2015) work, *State Building in Latin America*, to identify the historical sources of modern Colombian constraints. It also draws on David Welch's (2005) *Painful Choices*, which seeks to both explain and anticipate foreign policy change. Where Soifer provides context for Colombia's inertia to engaging the PRC, Welch provides a theory which would not only predict such inertia but also one against which subsequent change can be tested. With the turn of a new decade, change did come. The bilateral relationship in 2020 saw a flurry of renewed diplomatic efforts along with a surge in Chinese investment in Colombia for the first time ever.

This chapter and the following provide two examples of smaller economies where trade with China started from next to nothing and did not take off until well into the twenty-first century. Sino-Colombian relations began in the 1990s with trade figures hovering around zero and two-way migration equally low. By 2012, trade increased by billions. Few other countries in the world had started so late and with so little in trade and migration.

The Colombian case is rare and reveals a greater diversity of responses to China's landing. The differences explored in this chapter from those of the Primorye case explored in the following reveal local actors' agency and the structural and ideational differences that shaped by them. Both examine the response within a heterogenous state, one diverse by virtue of geography and design and the other by the sheer vastness of its territory. Where the Primorye case explores the failings of heavy-handed top-down authority to promote a cohesive China strategy in its furthermost regions, Colombia shows the breakdown of initiative in a universally hesitant state with little capacity for unified national action.

10.2 Surface-Level Success

At the time of China's *desembarco*, Colombia was—and is—rich in natural resources for export, in particular oil, coal, and minerals. Fresh from signing a bilateral FTA with the US, Colombia was also poised to import cheap Chinese materials to which its industries could add value and then ship, tax free, on long-established trade routes north. It eagerly welcomed China's interest. For its part, the PRC approached Colombia with a proven track record of speedily deepening new ties. China needed oil—be it for equity or its own use—with an economy running primarily on coal and in demand of iron and steel for its continued growth. It came flush with inexpensively manufactured goods to sell and an eagerness to expand its Latin American presence.

Within two decades, bilateral trade went from close to zero in 1990 to $10.6 billion by 2011 (Devlin, 2008; Ludeña, 2012).[1] In 2002 Colombia had a GDP of

$97.93 billion (World Bank, 2013). Trade with China was less than $543 million (IMF, 2012). By 2012, Colombia's GDP nearly tripled and trade with China grew by 20-fold to almost $13 billion, making China Colombia's second largest trading partner.

Colombia's bilateral trade with China was roughly commensurate with an increase in Colombia's world trade. Colombia ranked 40th in the world when considering the actual dollar increase of trade with China as well as the proportional increase of two-way trade as a share of world trade. China's share of Colombia's foreign trade increased by just under 9%. Globally, the median increase of China's share of foreign trade between for each country in the world was roughly 5% during the same period (IMF, 2012, author's calculation).[2]

In politics, towards the close of the first decade of the twenty-first century and following in the footsteps of many, the rate of high-level deals between Chinese and Colombian business and government officials picked up pace. These deals covered a range of economic activities, not least of which included infrastructure development opportunities.

In April 2005, Colombian President Uribe travelled to Beijing for his first state visit. His entourage "included several cabinet ministers, businesspeople and university presidents, which he said, 'demonstrated the strong desire' of the Colombian Government to develop a relationship with China" (Xinhua, 2008). He returned with five documents for cooperation, three agreements and two memoranda of understanding (MOUs) (Xinhua, 2008). More visits and agreements ensued. Colombia was enthusiastically welcoming this new partner in trade with both diplomatic—from local mayors through to the president of the country—military, and industry arms open.

In 2011, the Colombian Senate approved a Bilateral Investment Treaty (BIT) with China. Throughout successive administrations, Colombia demonstrated a strong preference for free trade agreements, an attribute that made it well suited for Chinese interest. By 2016, Colombia had signed five BITs that were in force, seven bilateral FTAs in force, and six partial preferential agreements and twelve regional FTAs (Organization of American States, 2016). The BIT with China was a promising start for two countries with proven track records of successful trade agreements.

By May of 2011, China displaced Venezuela as Colombia's second largest trading partner and the *Financial Times* reported the announcements of two major Chinese-funded investments: a "dry canal" or railway connecting its Atlantic and Pacific Coasts and Nueva Shenzhen, a Chinese purpose-built regional business hub and international airport to be built from the ground up with China Development Bank (CDB) and China Railway Group funding to the tune of $7.6 billion (Rathbone & Mapstone, 2011). One year later, China and Colombia signed another nine agreements in the extractive industries (Gómez, 2015), CDB opened its first office in Colombia and several Chinese state-owned enterprises (SOEs) expanded their presence through joint ventures and acquisitions.

While there was markedly greater progress in the petroleum industry, there was potential for more partnerships to develop. Government-backed deals could help diversify Colombian exports to include the country's rare earth minerals, such as coltan, they could open direct trading channels by eliminating a host of tariffs in a bilateral FTA and could, in principle, provide a boost to Colombia's struggling farmers by opening access to the vast Chinese market. This surface-level analysis of trade and diplomatic advances, however, fails to consider deeper structural issues which would impede further progress.

To put these deals and shift in the trade tables in context, the pioneering scholarship on Sino-Latin American relations tended to group Latin American countries into "winners" and "losers" (González, 2008: 155; Jenkins et al., 2008: 245). "Losers" are those whose sectors compete with an influx of cheap Chinese goods at home and in third markets, termed this "the dragon in the room" when specifically addressing LAC manufacturing exporters who were outcompeted by their Chinese counterparts (Gallagher & Porzecanski, 2010: 1). The "winners" are those blessed with primary resources in high demand. Recent data has born this out as an undeniable canon. Colombia's engagement with the People's Republic, however, highlights the limitations of such a binary formulation.

Apart from Mexico, most LAC exports to China were composed of natural resources and articles thereof. Trade was highly concentrated. Despite accounting for a plethora of distinguishing national characteristics ranging from geography to political organization, ethnic makeup and natural resources, a clear trend emerged. China's primary purpose in Latin America was to secure natural resources. Colombia was therefore poised to benefit. Primary materials dominated its exports while its "threatened" export industries did not face as big a threat from the PRC as some of their peers.

Lall and Wess (2004) were among the first researchers to examine the Chinese competitive threat to the region. Despite many ominous assessments, the authors note two key aspects of competition from China: first, "countries like Guatemala and Colombia appear to place PRC under threat, because they gain market share in primary products where PRC is a small exporter and is losing market share" (Lall & Wess, 2004: 16) and that "the trade structure of most of LAC is generally more complementary than competitive with that of PRC" (Lall & Wess, 2004: 22). Colombia's economy then grew large enough to be grouped with the "LAC Big 3" driven by a boom in natural resource extraction. Colombia was destined to be a winner.

Scholars first examining the negative impact of China's going out policy in the region feared for the textile industry specifically (Feenstra & Kee, 2007; González, 2008), and manufacturing in general (Gallagher & Porzecanski, 2010). Colombia's manufacturing sector, however, was never the backbone of its economy.[3] Moreover, competitive threats from China in other markets did not necessarily equate to economic loss since "Closer trade ties between LAC and PRC may also lead to trade creation through increased bilateral trade and at least in principle this may compensate for losses in markets where these economies compete" (Lall & Wess, 2004: 20). China did not present a clear threat to Colombia's most significant sector—energy— in its most significant market, the US. Here, China posed more of an opportunity than a threat to Colombian industry. However, the Colombian case did not fit neatly into this overall pattern of relations.

While Jenkins et al. (2008: 21) promoted the "winners and losers" paradigm, the authors failed to account for the Colombian case. Noting that Mexico and Colombia were "the only large economies in the region where the terms of trade did not improve" after China's landing, they only explain Mexico, whose manufacturers suffered in third markets. Venezuela was a "winner" because its primary export was oil. Why then was primarily fuel-exporting Colombia, with a booming economy and little by way of manufacturing, not a "winner"? Colombia's balance of trade with China was *negative* by close to $6 billion while its balance of trade with the US was positive by $8.7 billion. China's initial overtures to Colombia appeared at that stage to have failed: bilateral trade had grown, but it remained deeply imbalanced and investments abysmal.[4]

Throughout this time, Colombia was uniquely under-resourced in one area. It simply had not experienced Chinese immigration. There were no Chinatowns in Colombia,[5] the only LAC country with over 10 million people without one. In 2012, Colombia still lacked diasporic connections to China (Armony, 2012; Jiang, 2012; World Politics Review, 2012). This reveals the utter lack of experience both China and Colombia had in working with each other.

10.3   Theoretical Considerations

This chapter draws on three distinct works which provide the theoretical underpinnings for an analysis of Colombia's unique reaction to China's *desembarco*. They deal with state building capacity, the construction of identity through foreign policy and, finally, foreign policy change.

The first, Hillel Soifer's *State Building in Latin America* (2015), examines a state's capacity to carry out the most fundamental affairs of a nation, from education to infrastructure. While Soifer's main thesis is that state building progresses most in times of prosperity (and not because of war), here it serves as a precision tool to gauge state capacity for engaging the PRC. It includes a chronicle of the development of the Colombian nation showing the evolution of the structural and ideational factors which were firmly in place at the point of China's *desembarco*. These factors played decisive roles in the bilateral relationship and distinguish Colombia from its like-minded neighbors.

The second work, David Campbell's *Writing Security* (1992), dives deeply into the role of foreign policy in identity formation. Campbell's insights into the development of American identity through the foreign policy of the Cold War period emerge from a human security approach looking at internal threats to security as well as the external, and in so doing takes a more nuanced approach to the classic constructivist understanding of the "other". As much of the initial discourse emerging out of Colombia focused on Communism, Colombia's own internal enemies of the state were important in determining the ideological factors that shaped the Colombian response to China.

Finally, David Welch's *Painful Choices* (2005) assesses the capacity for a nation to alter and adapt its foreign policy at critical decision-making moments. Welch provides a tool for analyzing when and how a nation's foreign policy changes. China's *desembarco* was a point of critical change for Colombia, and Colombian foreign policy underwent a series of stages in its response.

Together, these works provide a means for addressing the following questions: What accounts for Colombian inertia in adapting to its new partner? When likeminded countries such as Chile and Peru completed ambitious deals and projects with the PRC, why did Colombia hesitate despite initially warm overtures to the Chinese? What structural or ideational factors underpinned this response? And, finally, what was the framework laid at the turn of the century for how the relationship could develop into the future?

10.3.1 Methodology and Research Design

This chapter draws on key economic and trade data and 81 interviews conducted in both China and Colombia with foreign policy decision-makers in 2013 and 2014. Elite interviews are at the heart of this research. The decision-making process behind Colombia's evolution in foreign policy was impossible to gauge without first engaging the primary foreign policy actors. The agenda setters and authors of the agreements between the two countries, the businesspeople tapped to accompany Colombian officials in meetings in China and so on, those with their sleeves rolled up, at the very least, witnesses who could provide first-hand accounts of the events under investigation. The timing of this research renders elite interviews critical as they covered events in the recent past (Beckmann & Hall, 2013: 198). The results provide details of the sequence of events as Sino-Colombian relations unfolded and of the decision-making process itself.

The initial stage of research, including those conducted in China in 2013, began with semi-structured interviews used to "identify the key political actors" (Tansey, 2007: 765). The focus was on the key three challenges subjects saw in bilateral relations.

The second stage of research includes a survey completed in 2014 of 35 members of the Cámara Colombo China de Inversión y Comercio (CCCIC) or the Colombian Chinese Investment & Commerce Chamber. The CCCIC was founded in 2010 to create a political and economic bridge between China and Colombia. CCCIC events, such as one in 2015, have included addresses by the Chinese ambassador to Colombia and sponsorship from the large multinational Spanish banking group, Banco Bilbao Vizcaya Argentaria, S.A. By the end of 2014, the CCCIC had 110 members ranging from small consulting companies and law firms operating in niche markets to regional government investment promotion agencies to the largest company in Colombia, Ecopetrol, as well as large Chinese multinationals like Lenovo, and other foreign firms such as the British multinational Deloitte & Touche (CCCIC, n.d.) (Fig. 10.1).

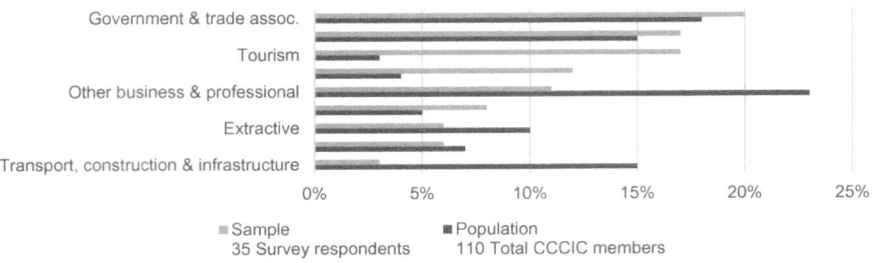

Fig. 10.1 CCCIC Total membership & survey sample by sector, June 2014

The goal of the survey is to examine the prevailing attitudes, assumptions, knowledge, challenges, and priorities of those at the forefront of the China-Colombia relationship. It took a threefold approach to identify key concepts, sources of support, and key international actors in bilateral relations. All survey interviews, barring two by phone, were conducted in person. Interviews were conducted in English, Spanish, and Mandarin. In addition, I interviewed 13 government officials and employees in the Chinese Embassy in Bogotá, the Colombian senate, and various ministries.

The research also draws from media reports, out-of-print joint venture real estate development plans, official trade data reports, internal government memos, the official state visit agenda for then-Vice President Xi in Colombia in 2009, the full text of the initial bilateral agreements, as well as official government statements and press releases. Interviewees also provided internal memos to the Colombian president with the details of Chinese investment and trade with Colombia, figures which are hard to come by and often misreported. These documents were crucial for corroborating the facts reported in interviews and the interviews compensated for "the lack and limitations of documentary evidence" (Davies, 2001, cited in Tansey, 2007).

10.4 Analysis and Key Findings

10.4.1 The President's Ugly Diplomacy

> *Somos la nova fea.*
> We are the ugly girlfriend.
> —David Barriga, Chairman of Asia B Consulting, Bogotá, 2014.

While well-positioned Colombians can imagine—and publicly declared—that increased trade and relations with China would be advantageous, few considered the logistics. Moreover, their stated reasons for not pursuing deeper ties are, on face-value, irrational (Chimienti & Creutzfeldt, 2017). Colombian foreign policy and its own brand of what may best be termed "ugly diplomacy" towards China cannot be understood with economics alone. It requires knowledge of the history as well as the unique geographical and political situation shaping Colombia's culture and priorities today. Its failure to capitalize further on China's growing interest in the region have led one Colombian businessman to call the country China's "ugly girlfriend in Latin America". Here, "ugly diplomacy" is used to describe the behavior of a smaller state in its refusal to "dress up" for the larger power in demand of its resources. If Beijing's first "Policy Paper on Latin America and the Caribbean" in 2008 can be seen as a formal invitation to engage each country in the region, then the immediate enthusiastic "Yes!" from Bogotá may in fact be interpreted as, "It sounds great, but we haven't considered the logistics, and we aren't inclined to." The initially warm Colombian response is evident in the acts of two former Colombian presidents and their respective ministers who signed the flurry of agreements which were widely publicized and even debated in the US Congress (*Economist*, 2011) along with Colombian businessmen who acknowledged the overall appeal of China's demand for agricultural and energy resources as a good match for what the Colombian economy can produce.

For over 60% of those surveyed in the CCCIC as well as a host of others interviewed prior to the survey, the president plays a determining—if not the determining—role in directing the bilateral relationship. Several frame the relationship in terms of the two Colombian presidents who held office as bilateral trade increase, either directly or by reference to what each administration has done. President Álvaro Uribe held office between August 2002 and August 2010. His successor, Juan Manuel Santos followed in 2010 for another two terms in office. Overall, these two administrations appear to represent the two main actions that Colombia has taken in its approach to China: it enthusiastically accepted China's invitations to deepen ties, but then failed to follow through. In some cases, this has meant that Colombia has launched talks that resulted in little to no action once the meetings concluded. As several interviewees have been at pains to highlight, even when Colombia showed up to the party, it just did not know "how to dance" with China.

10.4.2   Rebuffs

Colombia has a long history of bilateral FTAs, most of which entered into force just a few years after signing, and most signings occurred soon after initial talks. However, over a decade since China and Colombia penned their agreement to explore a bilateral FTA, there is little to no mention of making it happen. Interviews conducted at the Ministry of Trade and the Colombian Embassy in Beijing revealed that the Colombians themselves take full responsibility for this failure. They chose not to pursue the FTA. "It's crazy how they just one day threw away negotiations with China," said one Colombian businessman based in Beijing in 2013, "Right now FTAs are a very hot topic, and Colombian agriculture is going through a bad time…our exports [could] soar." Still, China's highest-ranking diplomats were rebuffed (Table 10.1).

Table 10.1 List of Colombia's international trade agreements

	Agreement	Type	Signed	Entry into force
1	Andean Community (CAN)	Customs Union	5 December 1987	25 May 1988
2	Canada–Colombia	FTA	21 November 2008	15 August 2011
3	Chile–Colombia	FTA	27 November 2006	8 May 2009
4	Colombia–Mexico	FTA	13 June 1994	1 January 1995
5	Colombia–Northern Triangle	FTA	9 August 2007	12 November 2009
6	EFTA–Colombia	FTA	25 November 2008	1 July 2011
7	EU–Colombia and Peru	FTA	26 June 2012	1 March 2013
8	Global System of Trade Preferences among Developing Countries (GSTP)	Partial Scope Agreement	13 April 1988	19 April 1989
9	Latin American Integration Association (LAIA)	Partial Scope Agreement	12 August 1980	18 March 1981
10	US–Colombia	FTA	22 November 2006	15 May 2012
11	Costa Rica–Colombia	FTA	22 May 2013	n.d
12	CAN–MERCOSUR (ACE 59)	FTA	18 October 2004	18 October 2006
13	Colombia–Nicaragua (AAP 6)	Partial Scope Agreement	2 March 1984	1985
14	Colombia–Cuba	Economic Complementation Agreement No. 49	22 June 1905	10 July 2001
15	Colombia–Venezuela	Partial Agreement on Commercial	28 November 2011	19 October 2012
16	Colombia–CARICOM	Agreement on Trade, Economic and Technical Cooperation	24 July 1994	1 January 1995
17	Pacific Alliance	Multilateral agreement / Trade Bloc	10 February 2014	1 May 2016
18	Colombia–Korea	FTA	21 February 2013	15 July 2016
19	Colombia–Panama	FTA	20 September 2013	

(continued)

Table 10.1 (continued)

	Agreement	Type	Signed	Entry into force
20	Colombia–Israel	FTA	30 September 2013	

World Trade Organization: rtais.wto.org; Colombian Ministry of Industry & Tourism: www.tlc. gov.co; Author's calculations

The Chinese forays into Colombia's petroleum sector also faced substantial setbacks. Attempts to build up projects from government-to-government relations failed. Chinese companies consistently failed to win bids in the competitive bidding process to develop new Colombian fields. While several petroleum company acquisitions seemed promising, they were in fact signs of a greater failure at entering the China's traditional means of petroleum engagement. The acquisitions had become a last resort and their small stature belie the immense effort behind previous attempts. The Chinese petroleum SOEs were rebuffed.[6]

After Xi Jinping's 2009 visit to Colombia, the plans which had been discussed for Nueva Shenzhen on the Caribbean Coast, built by Chinese companies and with Chinese financing, all but vanished. After Santos' May 2012 visit to China and the subsequent flurry of agreements, the Colombian government decided not to pursue further action. "It was just a PR trip," concluded another Colombian businessman who then pointed out that the Colombian Ambassador during the trip left his post shortly after. In his own way, the Colombian President had rebuffed his Chinese counterparts.

Even at international trade fairs there were setbacks. Several diplomatic and business leaders involved with Colombia's pavilion at the 2010 Shanghai Expo have spoken to the botched attempts at representing their country. The initial impetus to join, according to one interviewee, was spurred on by Xi's persistent comments to Uribe over Colombia's decision not to go at all. Under this pressure, "at the last minute," Colombia put together what was a comparatively weak showing for the expo. Where industry leaders from the best of Chile and Argentina's agricultural sector made an appearance, each with their own tables, Colombia had just one table representing them all.

Finally, Colombia's export promotion agency and numerous members of the Colombian Congress focused their efforts on securing wins for agricultural exports, but their setbacks stemmed from both sides of the Pacific. Restrictions on agricultural imports to China remained painstakingly high and agonizingly slow to surmount, and when Colombian farmers did have opportunities to fill sudden gaps in supplies to China, they failed to take them.

Just at the time when bilateral trade with China was reaching its place as second largest for Colombia, Colombian flower producers had a window of opportunity to fill a large gap in the Chinese market. They shrugged it off to maintain trade as usual with their US clients (former Proexport employee, personal communication, November 25, 2013). Banana sales provide another example. While China was one of the top producers of bananas in the world, it was also an importer of the fruit, and Colombian was one leading exporters of bananas in the world (Caracol, 2013). Trade, however, never took off. In 2014, Colombia's top agricultural export to the US was Cavendish bananas (Ministerio de Agricultura y Desarrollo de Colombia (MinAgricultura), n.d.). Despite the work of Colombia's own export promotion agency in Beijing, Colombian farmers and distributers remained resolute in choosing to deal with the US over China. Even in agriculture, Chinese overtures were rebuffed.

There were numerous reports in 2012 that, "A pact that Colombian state oil company Ecopetrol inked with the Sinochem conglomerate and CDB invites the energy-hungry Asian country to participate in a pipeline project linking central Colombia to the Pacific coast" (Rathbone & Mapstone, 2011), but one year later Ecopetrol projected only a modest increase in its exports off the Pacific Coast and no further reported plans for the pipeline.

The CDB's main financing project at the time was at Bogotá's El Dorado Airport, but the total loan was only $390 million. The airport was also financed with the Inter-American Development Bank (IDB) and the Development Bank of Latin America (CAF), so total financing appears to be paltry compared to their work in other nations (Milbank, Tweed, Hadley McCloy LLP, 2012). The CDB closed its Colombian office soon after.

Perhaps most tellingly, CDB signed an MOU with a Colombian company in May 2015 (China Gezhouba Group Co., Ltd. CGGC 2015) to have a better chance of winning the competitive tender process for the current 4G Road Project in Colombia. By then it was clear that independent initiatives had failed.

It is also now clear that CDB failed in its initial Colombian mission because their rates simply were not competitive (J. A. Jiménez Valderrama, personal communication, October 23, 2013; Gallagher & Irwin, 2017). CDB had set regional rates, so that Colombia was given the same lending rate as neighboring Venezuela and Ecuador. Later research showed that for Colombia's neighbors these rates were, in fact, below those of the private market. Ecuador had defaulted on its sovereign debt in 2008 and Venezuela had turned away private investors (Gallagher & Irwin, 2017) through a series of new projects purposefully requiring potential investors to be state-owned. This was seen as a move expressly against the US in the petroleum sector, as no American oil companies are state-owned. Colombia, however, had neither defaulted on its debt nor alienated private investors. Colombia could get better rates elsewhere. China's largest lender was rebuffed.

10.4.3 Communism in Colombia

Over the course of several weeks in October 2013, the Secretary General of the Commission on Ethics and Statutes assisted with securing interviews for this research with her colleagues in the senate. Among the most common impromptu responses as to why Sino-Colombian relations had not progressed further was, "But they're Communist." Diego Gonzalez, the Secretary General of the Second Commission and Gustavo Amado, the Secretary General of the Fifth Commission, both made this statement on record. These spontaneous responses were often echoed in off-record discussions with other government officials. After an interview with at the Ministry of Trade, Industry and Tourism, one staff member made small talk while walking out to the elevator, saying, "They're Communist, why would we work with them?" And, finally, a Colombian-based Chinese Manager in Shandorg Kerui Petroleum Equipment Co., Ltd., discussed the difficulties he and his Chinese staff had in securing their Colombian visas, suggesting, "Maybe because we're Communist" (personal communication, October 22, 2013). In 2013, the assertion that Colombia could not deepen ties with a Communist country was often followed by the explanation that Colombia works with the US instead. Such assertions clearly establish Colombia's chosen reference point regarding its relations with China.

The Colombian response was similar across industries and sectors. Government workers largely held similar views and attitudes as private sector workers. Only a few key individuals were passionate about promoting ties, but no one office, sector or industry made a concerted effort in the same way Moscow's central authority promoted a "turn to the East" policy, as explored in Chap. 11.

There are two interpretations of, "We're not communist". The most direct interpretation sees this phrase as a firm stance against communist ideology and those who espouse it. Such a stance taken by members of the Colombian senate speaks to Colombia's domestic politics first and foremost but with clear implications for its foreign policy. A second interpretation sees it as against the left more broadly. This speaks to Colombia's position within Latin America at the time of China's *desembarco*.

In the first interpretation, the greatest threat to Colombia's peace, economic progress and stability has been its ongoing conflict between the official state government, military groups, and guerrilla rebels. Global media outlets often discuss Colombia's conflict in the following terms: "Colombia has for decades struggled to reduce crime linked to the drug trade, waging a US-backed war against Marxist rebels, right-wing paramilitary groups and cocaine cartels" (H. Murphy & Bocanegra, 2013). The Colombian conflict began soon after its civil war, which ended in 1957. The largest guerrilla group, the Revolutionary Armed Forces of Colombia (FARC) was initially composed of members of the Colombian Communist Party (Murillo, 2004: 58). Even as this was among the longest-running conflicts in the world, the Colombian state's markedly anti-communist stance was developed and fortified through its close cooperation with the US. Only a few years later, the type of communism and fighting strategy that the FARC espoused featured Maoist elements. As late as 2001, onlookers noted that "active Maoist-oriented insurgent groups remain in the likes of Colombia" (Marks, 2002). Maoist insurgencies served as the foundation for groups that the central government still views as the greatest threat to its peace and stability today. While the threats to the United States—both real and perceived—posed by the spread of communism largely ended with the end of the Cold War in 1991, a brief examination of Colombia's history reveals that communism as a concept takes on a more rooted meaning in the present-day Colombian ethos.

Simply stated, "Throughout the post-World War II period, Colombia's international stance was based on consistent support of the United States against the Soviet

Union and its allies" (Library of Congress Federal Research Division 1988). Colombian military officers trained alongside other Latin American officers at what is now known as the Western Hemisphere Institute for Security Cooperation. The school would later become a central training ground for some of Latin America's most notorious dictators, however its focus at the start of the Cold War was to fight communism. Despite widespread attendance, only Colombia had joined the US to fight Korean, Russian, and—notably—Chinese troops in the Korean war of 1950–1953 (Bushnell, 1993: 212). Over 5,000 Colombians joined the war (Saldaña, 2013) with the US military counting over 1,000 Colombian troops in Korea on the day the Armistice Agreement was signed (USFK, n.d.). Colombia would become the only country in Latin America to fight Chinese soldiers under US tutelage.

On the one hand, Colombia's struggles with entrenched inequality and the continued conflict with rebel groups explain why bilateral relations with China have failed to become a priority for the Colombian government. They were too busy. Three years into China's Going Out Strategy, guerrilla groups occupied just under a third of all Colombian municipalities. On the other hand, some of the most clear-cut solutions to Colombia's longstanding inequality involve processes which would directly benefit from Chinese involvement, namely in infrastructure. Lack of adequate infrastructure exacerbates the impoverished conditions facing the Colombian regions outside of its major cities (Sales, 2013) and remained a top priority for the central government and a consistent point of reference throughout the interviews conducted in both nations.

The statement against communism reveals Colombia's agency as it navigates between two world powers and is also a marker of Colombia's regional positioning. In 2013, former President Uribe made a statement to the US Representatives' Subcommittee on the Western Hemisphere entitled, "Challenges to Democracy in the Western Hemisphere". In the same breath when Uribe highlights the devastation wreaked by guerrilla and paramilitary attacks, he denounced the governments of neighboring countries. He made clear that, "Marxist guerrillas" thrive, and the "pace of democratic progress" slows with "the rise of radical populist governments" going further to list these governments, in particular order: "Venezuela, Bolivia, Ecuador, Nicaragua, and, of course, Cuba" (Uribe, 2013). The distinctions Uribe drew between Colombia's stance on democracy and that of its neighbors resonates deeply in the discourse surrounding China and Colombia's bilateral relationship. "We are not Communist" was often interchangeable with, or even followed by, "We are not Venezuela," or "We are not Ecuador".

Around the same time, the work of Paula Garzón (2013 and 2014) details how roughly 80% of Ecuador's debt was held by just two Chinese banks by 2012 as the former president moved to shirk American ties. There, Chinese oil companies had distinct advantages over American ones: strong integration with overall Chinese foreign policy, government-backed lending, and as an alternative buyer and lender to the US amidst "anti-gringo" sentiment. Colombia did not have this "strength".

10.4.4   Petro Diplomacy

With these ideational factors strongly at play, perhaps nowhere more than in the number one source of the bilateral trade advancement—the petroleum sector—have Colombian structural characteristics posed the greatest constraints to the development of bilateral relations.

China's energy engagement in Latin America follows on the heels of widespread global success in promoting government-to-government deals, urged on by China's need to diversify from the oil supplies flowing through the Strait of Malacca (Bo Kong, 2010). While Latin America was a comparably insignificant source of energy for the Chinese, the unprecedented gains Venezuela and Colombia both made to rank among China's top ten crude oil suppliers by 2014 showed the undeniable importance of the sector (Office of the Secretary of Defense, 2015).

For its part, the PRC's decades-long process of extreme centralization of its petroleum industry followed by decentralization and significant government-led shake ups left China's energy companies at an important juncture. The strategic role China's SOEs grew to play in China at the time of its *desembarco* was best illustrated in Erica Downs' (2011) work *Inside China, Inc.* on the role of the China Development Bank's cross-border energy deals. Employing EBLs as powerful tools, CDB became the lynchpin driving China's energy engagements overseas, making it profitable for China's SOEs to follow the government's foreign policy priorities.

By default and by design, the Colombian oil industry is entirely different. On the surface, the industry is like that of China's, dominated by a large SOE, Ecopetrol, with a strong profit motive. Beyond that, however, the liberalization of the political, legal, and regulatory environment has led to radical differences. These differences—and the lack of clarity both China and Colombia mutually share on the way each industry operates—proved to be obstacles which direct bilateral government engagement was unable to overcome.

From its very first field, Colombian oil has been wholly owned by the Colombian government, leaving the state in charge of shaping the entire industry. According to the Colombian constitution of 1886, the national government owns all subsoil and the minerals contained therein, regardless of who owns the land above. Natural hydrocarbon reservoirs are therefore the property of the nation, belonging exclusively to the Republic of Colombia, no matter how far below the land or seabed they reside (Baker & McKenzie, 2012; Olavarría & Vicioso, 2013).

Such a fact alone would bode well for large Chinese SOEs seeking to enter the country through top-down government-to-government initiatives. However, to develop these resources, the Colombian government put in place a system which would entice a different type of foreign investor than the Chinese SOEs in the early 2000s. From the onset, most of Colombia's contract concessions for the development of oilfields went to private multinational companies primarily based in the US. These included Shell, Chevron, and the Colombian Petroleum Company (a US-owned and operated company, despite the name) (Echeveria et al., 2008).

Since the inception of the state-owned oil company, Empressa Colombia de Petróleos, now known as Ecopetrol, Bogotá has maintained ownership but developed and altered the rules of engagement in favor of Western policies and firms. In the early 1990s Colombia "liberalized and embraced the policies of the Washington Consensus, i.e., free market policies coupled with directives designed to reduce governmental intervention" (Holmes et al., 2010: 27). Where Deng Xiaoping ushered in the Open Door Policy in 1978, then-President Gaviria ushered in the *apertura* or economic opening in the 1990's. Broad-sweeping deregulation measures entailed the privatization of major sectors, including banking and telecommunications (Holmes et al., 2010: 42). Ecopetrol therefore remained a government-owned entity within an increasingly laissez-faire economy.

In a later bid to make Ecopetrol more competitive after a serious decline in production in 2003, the Colombian government freed the company of its regulatory functions, transferring them to a new and—notably—independent oil and gas regulator, the Agencia Nacional de Hidrocarburos (ANH) or the National Hydrocarbons Agency. This "released the Company from the State functions as the administrator of the oil source" (Ecopetrol, 2014). In further moves to liberalize and privatize the industry, then-President Uribe oversaw the partial privatization of Ecopetrol, creating a mixed-system public company in 2006 (Gómez & Sciabica, 2014) with shares on the Colombian, New York, and Toronto Stock Exchanges (PwC, 2014). Ecopetrol was to remain a large SOE, but it was to act increasingly like a private firm.

Throughout its *aperatura*, the Colombian government consciously structured its industry differently. Where China had developed many SOEs which, while not puppets of the state, nonetheless operate under the CPP working as a lynchpin between government policy and business action, Colombia had one SOE, and over time it showed that the central government—and the president, in particular—did not, in fact, have final say over who ran the company (A. Ossa Cárdenas, personal communication, October 24, 2013). Moreover, the Colombian government did all in its power to pattern the development of its SOE after private firms while it liberalized industries throughout the country. It forced Ecopetrol to compete on equal footing with all other companies for the rights to develop new oil fields. Even though the new fields remained relatively small compared to the ones Ecopetrol had already developed, this is nonetheless a significant structural move that introduced into the market an entity, complete with an independent regulator, with which the Chinese players were wholly unfamiliar.

Not only was Colombia following the industrial preferences and policies of the Washington Consensus, but its physical infrastructure remains entirely Western facing with marginally little ready for export to the Orient. Four of Colombia's six major oil pipelines connect to just one export terminal, Covenas, on the Atlantic coast. Only one pipeline, TransAndino, leads to the Pacific, and it transports oil from just one field, Orito, which in 1992 made headlines when 300 rebel insurgents carried out a surprise attack, killing 26 of the policemen guarding the drills (*New York Times*, 1992). From this standpoint alone, the on-the-ground prospects for Chinese companies sourcing Colombian crude for shipment to China were never ideal.

Given the historical development behind Chinese and Colombian petroleum policies, respectively, when the two countries "met" each other, their courtship included quickly signed contracts indicating goodwill on both sides and promises for a long-term relationship. Soon after this honeymoon phase, however, they faced barriers which neither could overpass.

In the beginning, this was a relationship just promising enough to incite US jealousy. In 2002, in addition to the flurry of agreements with China, Uribe also promoted the prospect of developing Colombia's palm oil for the Chinese market for both food and biodiesel, at which point others concluded that, "economic relations thus far are still exploratory" (Londoño Penilla, 2005: 52), but the good will stated on both sides was clear; Uribe had taken concrete steps. Ten years later, both Presidents Hu Jintao and Juan Manual Santos publicly promoted continued investment by Chinese state-owned energy companies in Colombia. In May 2012, Sinochem along with CDB signed a declaration of cooperation with Colombia's Ecopetrol in the presence of both leaders concerning the development of Colombia's pipeline project along its Pacific Coast (PetrolWorld, 2012). That year the American media reported that, "A pact that Colombian state oil company Ecopetrol inked with the Sinochem conglomerate and the … [CDB] invites the energy-hungry Asian country to participate in a pipeline project linking central Colombia to the Pacific coast" (Agencia EFE, 2012). The US Embassy in Bogotá immediately issued a warning in May 2012 about the threat of diverting American supplies (US Embassy Bogotá, 2012). Later, researchers from the US looked on with alarm and concern over further discussions of a dry canal (Ellis, 2014: 77).

However, US onlookers had little cause for concern. Despite promises, years later Ecopetrol projected only a modest increase in its exports off the Pacific Coast and there was no further mention of a pipeline or dry canal, but this has been the fate of many Chinese-backed projects in Latin America. "Many declared projects are never actually completed, such as the 'dry canal' across Colombia, a new interoceanic canal across Nicaragua or the transcontinental railroad linking Brazil's Atlantic coast with Peru's Pacific coast" (Farnsworth, 2019).

Colombian infrastructure does not support export to China not only because just one pipeline ends at the Pacific Coast but also because of the high cost of freights coming out of underdeveloped ports. The primary Pacific port of petroleum exports frequently serves as a target for guerrilla rebel attacks. In contrast, Venezuela, whose economy in 2013 was closer to the size of Colombia's, received over $50 billion in Chinese lending, including several billion for oil-related construction and purchases (Gallagher & Irwin, 2017).

While largely divorced from each other, where Colombia's Ecopetrol and the Colombian government's strategies and incentives have most clearly aligned is on their China strategy: neither of them had one. Ecopetrol's own presentation touting the greatness of the Chinese market and clear signs of demand mirrored that of Colombian Presidents touting the benefit of heightened cooperation. They included sweeping statements without any details or specifics. In 2013, Ecopetrol shared a 30-slide PowerPoint presentation on its "commercial strategy" and "approach to China" to a group of companies and organizations interested in bilateral relations. The PRC is mentioned on just three slides. The slide entitled, "China: a great market to develop", lists statistics for Asian—rather than Chinese—GDP growth and crude oil demand without any mention of country specifics. The four slides on "Transportation and Logistics", show that only one of the six pipeline projects planned for development through the year 2018 would run towards the Pacific Coast.

Despite the Ecopetrol presentation's assertion that, "Asia (mainly China) will remain as the main importing region of crude oil in the world", the bulk of Colombian exports to Asia must therefore leave the Atlantic Coast and pass through the Panama Canal rather than leaving Colombia's Pacific shores to head directly across the Pacific Ocean. Ecopetrol is a dues-paying member of the Colombian Chinese Investment & Commerce Chamber, but it would not consider the logistics of developing the Asian market, and instead chose the closest market and the most familiar faces (Colombian government official, personal communication, November 15, 2013).

To illustrate such early petroleum engagement, the former Colombian Commercial Attaché in Beijing, Alejandro Ossa, discussed arranging a meeting with the then-VP and later President of the large Chinese SOE, Sinochem. The first question Ossa fielded was "Where is Colombia? I know it's in the Americas, but I don't know exactly where it's located." Then:

> We started to share information with [Sinochem]. Once they evaluated that info, they decided to come to Colombia. We organized a very comprehensive agenda: they met Ecopetrol, the operators, the ANH, and they said they liked the framework, the overall legal framework of Colombia. [So, we said,] "Let's do this!". (A. Ossa Cárdenas, personal communication, October 24, 2013)

But bid after bid, Sinochem failed to make headway. The Colombian system would have unforeseen and crippling consequences for future Chinese firms trying to enter the country, even though Ossa himself led a team working to coach the likes of Sinochem on the Colombian rounds system. The Colombian structure and legal processes set in motion were ill suited for Chinese engagement on several fronts.

First, all firms—even Ecopetrol itself—would be subject to the same bidding process, a process in which the Chinese oil companies had little experience.

Second, the legal framework that emerged out of Colombia's recent boom had been tailored to small, independent ones and large Western publicly traded ones. Chinese SOEs fit neither category. An analysis of the concessions offered from the first Colombia rounds through to the 2012 rounds reveals that of the 53 total blocks offered and 27 companies involved as either operators or partners, Ecopetrol is the only SOE on the list (OpenOil, 2013; author's calculations). Chinese firms baffled Colombian regulators.

Third, the Colombian government did not control Ecopetrol enough to direct its relationship with any Chinese SOE, no matter how lucrative the possibilities. "Ecopetrol became a business oriented company, with a legal framework closer to private law" (Baker & McKenzie, 2012: 62).

Even with Ossa's support—a rare win for consultant-shy companies—Sinochem continued to falter. The bidding process proved to be impossible. The problems concerning legal issues and paperwork were largely a result of mutual ignorance.

On the part of the Chinese firms, what took a day for an American or European firm to complete would take a Chinese firm two months, and when they did, the completed forms were often inaccurate with certain documents still in their original Mandarin (anonymous, personal communication, October 18, 2013). For their part, Colombian regulators were wholly unfamiliar with the financial structuring of Chinese SOEs and could not decipher which entity they were dealing with (D. Sanchez Galvis, personal communication, October 18, 2013; A. Ossa Cárdenas, personal communication, October 24, 2013).

Beyond distrust of lawyers and the struggle to understand Colombian rules regarding registration, another hurdle in the legal realm was that China is not a member of The Hague Apostille Convention. Colombia, along with the US and a host of other trading partners, has signed onto an agreement which allows for a legal document in one country to be recognized by any of the other signatories (HCCH, 2016). Without being party to the treaty, Chinese firms faced an additional legal hurdle that firms from most other countries against whom they competed for bids—primarily European and North American ones—did not. Together, these issues serve as an example of the structural hurdles towards greater bilateral energy engagement.

That Chinese SOEs eventually succeeded in penetrating the Colombian market reveals that the ideational and structural factors which stymied bilateral engagement were not insurmountable. To be sure, they were insurmountable obstacles to *direct* bilateral government engagement. Moreover, Colombia's ideas about China and its structure favoring all but Chinese-styled firms did not change or alter, no matter how lucrative such changes could be. Engagement proceeded via a different route altogether.

In bidding, acquisitions and direct sales, China-Colombia petroleum relations found their only successes by involving other countries. The only successful bids on the part of Chinese companies in Colombia have been in partnership with a third party from another country, such as those of Mansarovar, a joint venture between two Chinese and Indian SOEs. The same has been true for Chinese acquisitions. Sinopec and Sinochem, who remained helpless in the Colombian bidding process, eventually acquired European companies' stakes in Colombian oil fields. They did not acquire Colombian companies, which may have stoked fears of foreign takeovers, but rather acquired the operations of other foreign companies who had a well-established foothold in the Colombian market. Even when a Colombian diplomat—along with his government-run export-promoting office—was guiding the efforts of interested Chinese firm, the Chinese company was only able to gain headway by buying out a British company's assets followed by a French one. Success was possible, but not through any change or amendment in Colombian ideas or structures.

10.5 Survey Results and Analysis

Beyond the long-entrenched structural barriers in the petroleum industry, nimbler industries still made little headway. A decade into a boom in trade, Colombian industries continued to struggle in their relations with China, which begs the question: Why? In order to address this issue, to find out why, as one Colombian diplomat explained, a Colombian businessman would rather take a plane to Europe and lose 10% of his potential profits than try to understand how to conduct business in China, an analysis of the perceptions of the members composing the China-Colombia Chamber of Commerce and Investment led to extensive data on the top challenges, fears, concerns, and, finally, opportunities and potential future for these struggling industries.

10.5.1 "What comes to mind when you hear the word, 'China'?"

The question, "What are the first words that come to mind when you hear the word, 'China'?" provides insight into each respondent's conceptions of China before being exposed to the lists of organizations and ideas throughout the rest of the survey. Nearly one-third of respondents (10 of the 33) said, "opportunity". The next most cited response was "culture" followed by "big", "culture clash", and "dynamism" (Table 10.2).

Table 10.2 Compilation of replies to "What comes to mind when you hear the word, 'China'?"

Words	Occurrences
Opportunity	10
Culture	6
Big	4
Culture clash	4
Dynamism	3
The food	3
Aggressive	2
Future	2
Market	2
Businesses	2
Culturally different	2
Difficult	2
Innovation	2

Author's calculations based on CCCIC survey responses

Fig. 10.2 World cloud depicting responses to "What comes to mind when you hear the word 'China'?" Where size corresponds to occurrence. Author's calculations based on CCCIC survey responses

The concept of cultural differences emerged as the most salient.[7] The following word cloud is an alternate means of portraying the same data. Here, the words "clash" and "big" and even "difficult" loom larger than "work" (Fig. 10.2).

Most respondents associated China with both an opportunity as well as an immense challenge. Table 10.3 presents another means of analyzing the responses. Here, answers are tallied under five broader categories.

Just over two-fifths of respondents thought of opportunity and potential when considering the other country while half thought about how dissimilar and even strange the other country was.

The third most salient concept that emerged from the data was China's immensity across multiple dimensions: its population, its market, its demand, its manufacturing capacity, and the overall phenomenon of its rise in the world. This word grouping includes the word "monster", *monstruo*, which in English can also directly translate to a "phenomenon" associated with either a "freak" of nature or an individual whose talents or skills make them the type of phenomenon that is associated with "genius" (WordReference.com, 2016).

Taken together, the above concepts highlight China's size, scale and scope, its rapid development and enormous potential dominated the impression of the Colombian respondents. China was seen as a large, potentially grand place to conduct business, but it was also a wholly unknown entity that struck them as thoroughly different from their own culture.

Table 10.3 Categorization of answers to "What comes to mind when you hear the word, 'China'?"

Cultural differences	23
Aggressive, Culture, Culturally different, Culture clash, Exotic, The food, Loyal, [The method of] cleaning your nose, Mysterious, Respect for ranks, Way of doing business	
Opportunity & potential	**16**
Infinite investment potential in Colombia, Opportunity, Boundless thought, Unfulfilled, Unrealized great potential	
Large Scale and size	**10**
Big, Huge, Market volume, Population, Volume, Manufacturing giants, Monster	
Rapid change & growth	**9**
Growth, Progress, Development, Speed, Unrealized great potential, Unfulfilled, Dynamism	
Manufacturing	**5**
Low cost manufacturing, Manufacturing giants, Good price, Industrial park of the world, Reputation for cheapness	

Author's calculations based on CCCIC survey responses

10.5.2 China in Latin America: Alternative Market or Hegemonic Threat?

The Concepts portion of the survey included words and phrases taken from the literature on Sino-Latin American relations as well as the diplomatic initiatives such as China's first Policy Paper on the region. They include alternative market (López & Ramos, 2010: 114), threat (Heine, 2008), harmonious world and peaceful development (People's Republic of China, 2008), multipolar world (Torres, 2014), solidarity and South-South cooperation (People's Republic of China, 2008), regional stability (Makeham, 2013) and hegemony (Armony, 2012: 179) (Fig. 10.3).

Nearly everyone associated China's role in the region with "development", but far fewer would call it, "South-South cooperation".

While the least popular concept, a whopping four out of ten dues-paying members of the Chamber tasked with promoting bilateral engagement perceived China to be a threat to the Latin America. More people strongly agreed with the applicability of "threat" to Sino-Latin American relations than "solidarity" or "regional stability". Moreover, half of those who perceived China as a threat *strongly* held that view.

These replies can be triangulated with responses to one of the final questions of the survey. Subjects chose one of five cartoons which "best represents China's personality" (Fig. 10.4).

While each image affords room for interpretation, the first one is of a yellow squid engulfing the globe taken from World War II-era anti-Japanese propaganda, selected as the most negative, with the generations' old racist undertones of "yellow peril". Though fear-based and directly racist in origin, one of the 11.4% of respondents who selected this first image chose it because, "China is everywhere!". No other image portrayed China's global reach (Figs. 10.5 and 10.6).

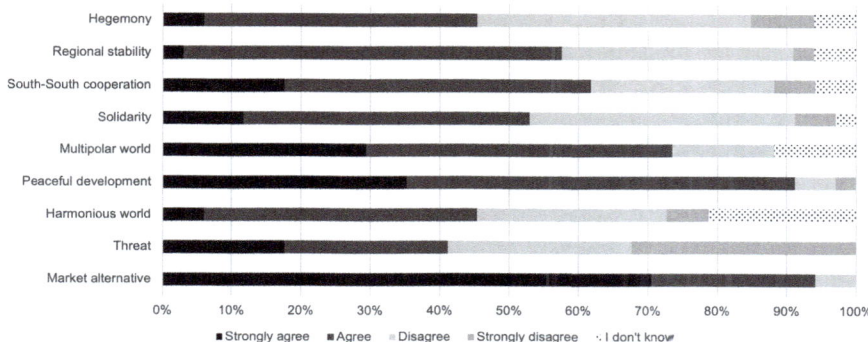

Fig. 10.3 "Which concepts are closer to the reality that China presents ir its relations with Latin America?" Listed according to the greatest number of "Strongly agree" replies. Author's calculations based on CCCIC survey responses

Fig. 10.4 Yellow peril: possible reply to, "Which cartoon best represents China's personality?". Schilling (1935)

Fig. 10.5 Sino-Colombian handshake. Quetzalcoatl1

The other two images showed a dragon consuming a city and a weary dragon carrying the continent of South America on its back. Combined with the first, the two resource-sucking portrayals of China composed nearly one-third of the replies (Fig. 10.7).

In total, an alarming proportion of respondents held a negative view of China's role in their world. In global terms, based on responses to the cartoons, 31% of respondents saw China in a resource-hogging. In regional terms, 41% saw China as a threat. In national terms, 39% saw China's impact as negative. In sum, roughly one-third of all respondents were negative about China's role.

10.5.3   The Top Three Challenges: Ignorance, Cultural Differences and Getting a Foothold in the Market

Respondents then listed what they felt to be the top three challenges facing the bilateral relationship. Here, survey results combined with semi-structured interviews posing the same question gave a total of 41 individuals who provided answers to "What are your top three challenges in your work with China/Colombia?" Not

Fig. 10.6 Panda eating. Zakowski

Fig. 10.7 Distribution of responses to, "Which Cartoon best represents China's Personality?". CCCIC survey data; author's calculations

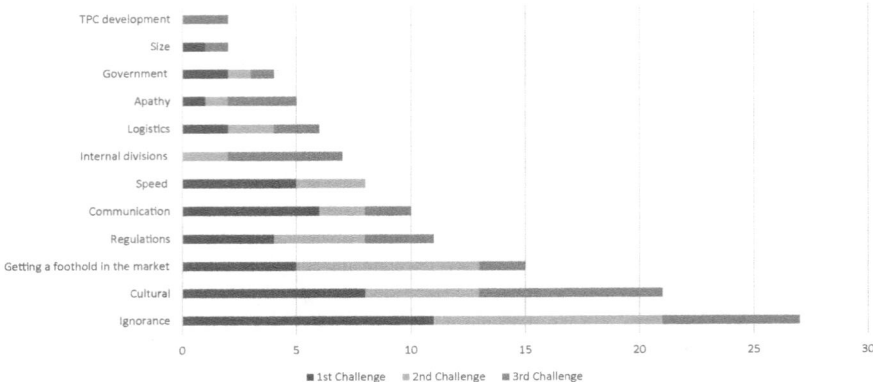

Fig. 10.8 Tally of top three challenges facing industry leaders in the China-Colombia relationship. CCCIC survey data and personal interviews; author's calculations

all individuals listed three complete challenges and some interview subjects only mentioned one. The chart here tallies 118 challenges (Fig. 10.8).

One reason ignorance emerges as the predominant challenge is because the category encompasses a long list of issues. For example, both Colombian coffee exporters and importers of Chinese goods lamented customer ignorance—including those in the middle of the supply chain and not just the end-user, such as Ecopetrol in its search for oil well machinery—and the inability to distinguish their quality products. Chinese consumers were unaware of Colombian brands and how to gauge the quality of coffee. Colombian consumers dismissed Chinese products as low quality even though Chinese manufactured goods cover the full range of quality options. These challenges made "getting a foothold in the market" difficult. Those listing "communication" included both Chinese and Colombian respondents who lamented the lack of language skills and cultural understanding behind the use of certain expressions even when they shared a common language. As one Colombian respondent lamented, "We keep offending them!".

In total, the top three challenges were all associated with a lack of mutual experience with each other's cultures, regulations, and products.

10.5.4 The Top Problem Solvers: The Pacific Alliance, the Colombian Government and ProExport

Answers to further questions reveal that out of eight possible entities from the national to the international arena, members of the CCCIC looked to Proexport as "the most helpful in promoting the China-Colombia bilateral relationship". Over 80% of respondents agreed the export promotion agency—renamed in 2014 as ProColombia

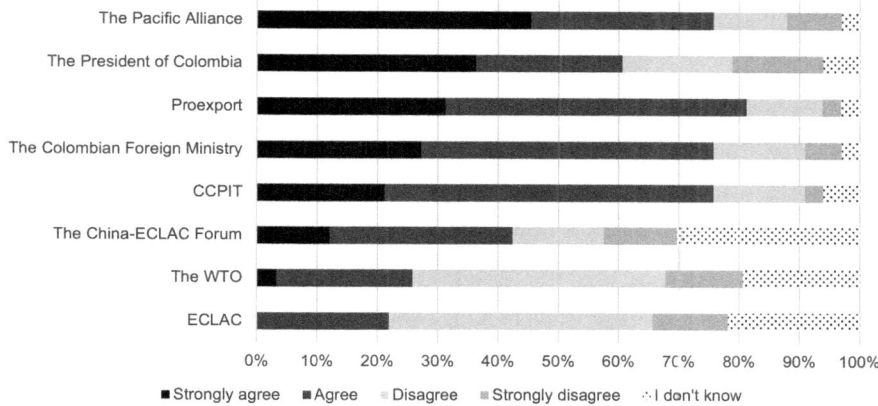

Fig. 10.9 CCCIC survey replies to, "Which is the most helpful in promoting the China-Colombia bilateral relationship?". CCCIC survey data and personal interviews; author's calculations

(CEPRI, 2014)—would be the most helpful. However, the entity with the most enthusiasm behind it was the Pacific Alliance. The numbers favoring the alliance would be even more impressive if factoring in the response of government officials to earlier questions prior to the survey.

The survey responses here are ranked in descending order of the percentage of "strongly agree" responses (Fig. 10.9).

Most respondents suggested that the Colombian government, from the President to the Foreign Ministry and Proexport, was the solution. What all but a small handful of them knew, however, was that the Colombian government had already worked to develop a project to promote deeper ties with China, designing it from the ground up and accounting for Colombia's own domestic needs, its desire to connect with its neighbors through better infrastructure whilst exploiting China's desire for a gateway into the region. The Colombian courts, however, blocked the final land acquisition for the project. Colombia's structural constraints were as difficult to surmount as the ideational ones highlighted in response after response to the survey questions above.

10.5.5 Campbell

That Colombia could easily benefit from Chinese investment in infrastructure and yet failed to capitalize on such prospects at the outset of their relations suggests that ideational and structural factors, rather than the obvious material prospects, determined the course of the relationship. The survey and other interview results reveal the shared ideas representing the identities and interests of the "purposive actors" that are not just naturally found, according to Alexander Wendt's tenets of constructivism (1999: 1). Here, an analysis of state identity is rooted in human associations rather than the more obvious material conditions.

If there was one overarching theme which could convey the sentiments associated with China, it is one of "othering" (Gabriel & Griffiths, 2008; Wendt, 1992). In an example of "othering" in foreign policy analysis, Suzuki's (2007) "The importance of 'othering' in China's national identity," highlights China's own "ambiguous social position within International Society, where it is often viewed with suspicion as the 'Other' which is at odds with International Society's rules and values" (p. 24). This China-branded distinction is an important one shared by many Colombian politicians and businesspeople interviewed. The specific factors contributing to this perception become clear when looking at the top three challenges each interview subject identified in their work with China.

The process of "othering", while important for identity formation (Wendt, 1998), is almost always associated with uncooperative behavior. At its worst, it is dehumanizing and can lead to genocide (Snow & Su, 2011). In economic, educational, and business realms, it can be a destructive response to group dysfunction as part of a stereotyping blame game when the group fails at its tasks (Gabriel & Griffiths, 2008). In each example provided in the literature, lack of the recognition of the other's humanity or basic rationality (Rorty, 1993) negates an essential prerequisite to cooperation which, in turn, hinders progress and development. "Othering" is dangerous.

In the constructivist foreign policy literature, however, "othering" is more than a barrier to engagement, it is a crucial means of the identify formation for the state itself. Identity shapes foreign policy and the practice of foreign policy, in turn, shapes identity. According to David Campbell:

> Foreign Policy, understood as one of the practices that contingently constructs through stylized and regulated performances the identity of the state in whose name it operates, is more obviously dependent on discourses of fear and danger .... A notion of what 'we' are is intrinsic to an understanding of what 'we' fear and, moreover, that "the social space of inside/outside is both made possible by and helps constitute a moral space of superior/inferior, which can be animated in terms of any number of figurations of higher/lower". (1992: 85)

By this notion, Colombia's initial reaction to China's overtures is not only a reflection of its identity but also one in which Colombian identity was shaped. Throughout this process, an important tenant of the Colombian state's hierarchy has been the distinction between (higher) liberal democratic practices and (lower) communist threats that emanate not just from foreign powers, as in Colombia's fight alongside US soldiers against the Chinese in the Korean War, but more significantly within itself against domestic insurgents. Campbell's work on the Cold War has been instrumental in bringing to light how "foreign" or "other" is not just beyond the geographic borders of a country but, in the words of another, it "is about national identity itself: about the core elements of sovereignty it seeks to defend, the values it stands for and seeks to promote abroad" (Wallace, 1991: 65). To state, again and again, that "We're not communist," was to embark on an iterative process of identity formation domestically and regionally while also determining a continued course of action.

10.5.6 Soifer

Colombia's unique response to China follows a history of exceptionalism within the region. Colombia developed a distinctive set of norms and governance policies long before the PRC's *desembarco*. Compared to its Pacific Alliance partners—namely Peru, Chile, and Mexico—Colombia was always unique. Liberal like these peers but staunchly antistatist, Colombia emerged as a remarkably weak state.

Beginning with state building efforts during Latin America's "Liberal era", from the mid-19th to the early twentieth centuries, a period of independence from colonial powers coupled with the needed economic growth and comparative political stability to undertake state-building projects, Soifer shows that failed projects then mean weak states now. In analyzing these failings, he finds that the first and main constraint on a nation's ability to develop was the degree of urban primacy which a capital city held.

Soifer's work provides a precision tool for tracing the development of ideational and structural factors that distinguish the Colombian state. Soifer determined that state building efforts in Latin America depended on the degree of urban primacy their capitals held. A strong state requires a dominant capital city. During the Liberal era, no Chilean city could compete with the likes of Santiago, Lima was the standout in Peru as was Mexico City in Mexico. In Colombia, however, a "nation of nations", each region maintained its own strong capital. No one regional capital was strong enough to dominate the others. One reason for this is geography. Mountains and impassable jungles divide these regions so that it is easier for a businessman in Medellín to develop foreign trade out of the Port of Buenaventura on the Pacific Coast than deal with his fellow countrymen on the Atlantic coast.

Under these conditions, Colombia's subnational regions each took on nation-state roles to a mystifying degree. They negotiated and signed their own treaties with other nations (Soifer, 2015: 54), imported their own weapons while the national army remained "vestigial at best" (Soifer, 2015: 213) and even collected taxes while "As of 1850, the Colombian state collected no direct taxes" (Soifer, 2015: 168). The Colombian nation state of the Liberal era was nearly non-existent.

Throughout Colombia's development, Colombian elites maintained staunchly antistatist views within a laissez-faire policy framework. When there were opportunities for strengthening the central state, they refused them. Bogotá would never be endowed—by dint of both geography and design—with the same powers as every other national capital in Latin America.

This accounts for many of the idiosyncrasies in Colombia's response to China's *desembarco*. No Colombian president would have the power to follow through on any initiative facing China without the backing of numerous other actors. Even though, by other metrics, the Colombian executive appears relatively unencumbered, Soifer shows that this branch of government faces unique constraints Colombia is an outlier in this regard. All other Liberal states, and specifically Mexico, Chile, and Peru, have stronger central governments with greater capacity to enact change. Colombia emerged to be as strongly liberal, like its Pacific Alliance partners, as it is antistatist.

These factors made Colombia ill-suited for the top-down approach of its authoritarian communist partner.

10.5.7 Welch

One of the foremost thinkers on foreign policy change in a "low-politics" case—i.e., one that does not involve war or similar crises—is David Welch who applies his theory of foreign policy change to the negotiations of the US-Canadian Free Trade Agreement. Welch establishes two central tenants. First, that inertia is the default state in foreign policy decision-making. Second, when change does occur, it is by and large to stave off loss. Given this Nobel-prize-winning fact of economic behavior (an individual will spend more to prevent loss than to realize gain) Welch posits that foreign policy decision-makers will change foreign policy primarily motivated by a fear of loss rather than an expectation of gain. From this, he delineates the "signs of change" based on regime type, leaders' perceived policy failures, and leaders' perception of loss vs. gains. These signs are his hypotheses (Welch, 2005, 45).

Hypothesis 1 states that foreign policy change is less frequent in highly bureaucratic states with democratic regimes. He draws on the Polity project[8] with yearly scores of the POLITY variable for nations, ranging on a scale of total autocracy, -10, to "fully institutionalized democracy", $+6$ to $+10$. One variable which contributes to this score is "Executive constraints", XCONST. It reveals how much "accountability groups", such as the military or an independent judiciary, can constrain executive action. Welch uses it as a "proxy for degrees of bureaucratization" (Welch, 2005, 63).

Long before China's landing, from 1995 through to 2018, Colombia maintained a POLITY score of $+7$ (where $+6$ to $+10$ are fully institutionalized democracies). Colombia had an XCONST score of 6 (on a scale from 1 to 7 where 7 is a highly constrained executive or strong bureaucracy). In comparison, China's POLITY score was -7 (where -10 is a total autocracy) and has an XCONST score of 3. Figure 10.10 plots regime and state characteristics (POLITY and XCONST) following Welch's method of displaying the data (2005: 220).

Hypothesis 1 would predict that change would by highly unlikely in Colombia, although more likely than any of its Pacific Alliance partners.

By these metrics, the Colombian executive is more unencumbered than its liberal partners in the region. However, Soifer shows that the Colombian executive is, in fact, significantly *more* constrained. He quickly determines that Colombia has a remarkably *weak* executive. The polity score fails to account for the unique aspects of the Colombian system that pose great barriers to enacting change.[10] Soifer's work suggests that, by these metrics, the Colombian regime type is amongst the least likely to create foreign policy change because the central state lacks both the capacity and the willpower. Welch's metrics of state capacity require an amendment in the Colombian case.

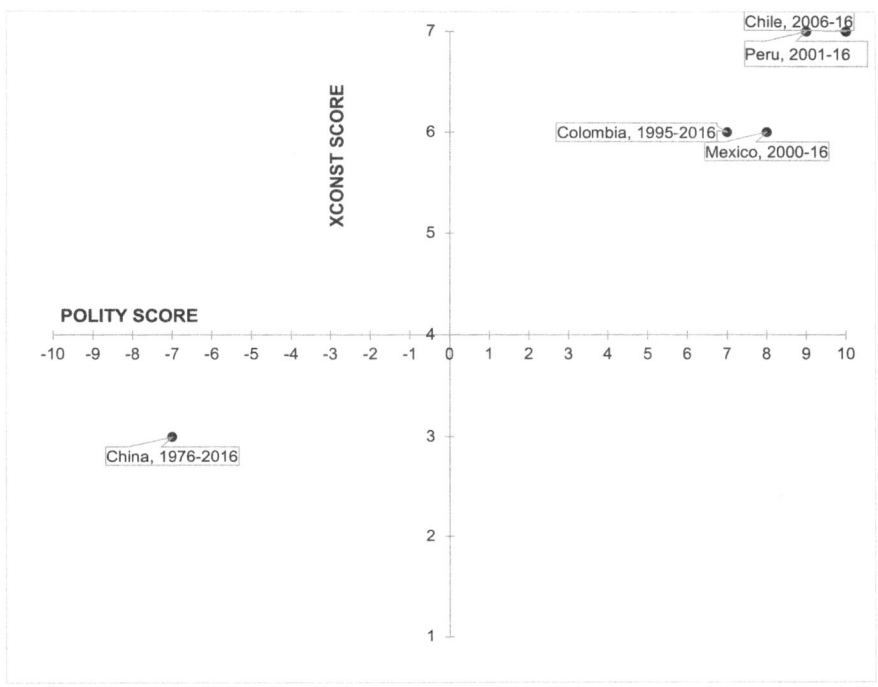

Fig. 10.10   Regime and state characteristics[9]. Author's calculations

Hypothesis 2: Failure feared or repeated. Here Colombian ideational factors come to bear. None of the Colombian government's initial China-facing projects succeeded. The *respice polum* doctrine—follow the North Star, the US—appears to have been as deeply entrenched in small tradesmen and local farmers as it was in Colombian statesmen. However, neither the farmers nor most government officials viewed these as failures, nor were they afraid of "losing opportunities". Such fears were left to a few members of the export promotion agency and some businessmen.

The fear of failure found no place in Colombian deliberations because they never *perceived* or cared about their failures. Welch's theory here requires an amendment: the *perception* of failure feared or repeated is more important than actual failures. Hypothesis 2 would, under this amendment, predict a resistance to change.

Hypothesis 3: The prospect-theory-inspired prediction. Colombian decision makers were either largely unconscious of the failures of bilateral engagement, or, put simply, apathetic. There can be no doubt of Colombian preferences in this case—the reference point of continued trade and diplomatic relations and subsequent strategies were all in favor of remaining with the US. It is also clear that the gains from further dealings with China seemed minimal in comparison. Hypothesis 3 would predict a resistance to change.

Despite the amendments necessary for the first two hypotheses, Welch's overall theory would clearly predict Colombian inertia to China's *desembarco*.

10.6 Conclusion

The predictions against Colombia's willingness to change and adapt to their new partner were accurate, but only in one respect. Until recently, Colombian foreign policy did not change. The structural and ideational factors that were well established at the time of China's *desembarco* proved to be lasting constraints in the development of the relationship, but the relationship did progress.

Chinese SOEs in the petroleum sector never succeeded at mastering the Colombian tendering process, but they found other avenues of success. For their part, Colombian businessmen, despite professed ignorance and fear of "the other", moved with alacrity into new dealings with the Chinese when partnered with their like-minded peers throughout the Pacific Alliance. The repeated failings on both sides to make deals work—be they over flowers, land development or oil production—were often the failings of bilateral government-to-government workings. Once other countries, familiar to both parties, became involved, fear and hesitation dissipated, and structural barriers began to give way. Once joining the Pacific Alliance, Colombian groups slowly began to partner with or parallel the more successful structures of their Alliance peers. Colombia's ProExport became ProColombia to fall in step with ProChile, ProMexico and Promperú. With these structural changes instigated by Colombia's own banding together with other countries with whom it shared ideational affinity, new discernible pathways to rapprochement emerged. Colombia would deal with China, but it would be in its own way, on its own terms, and alongside trusted partners.

Moreover, regional governments would lead the way, as they had when first formed in the Liberal Era by Soifer's account. The proof of these alternate pathways of success was definitively proclaimed when "2019 was the year in which Chinese companies finally made their way into Colombia, the Latin American country that had perhaps been most sceptical about investment from the region's second largest trading partner" (Bermudez Liévano, 2019). It was the governments of Bogotá and Medellín—not the national government—that opened the door for large Chinese infrastructure investment.

The 2019 deals together highlight two important structural factors and one ideational one that have each have shaped Sino-Colombian relations.

First is the strength and continued primacy of Colombian substate actors. The City of Bogotá awarded contracts to large Chinese companies for the construction of the Bogotá metro and an electric commuter train to the city's suburbs. Medellín and Cali both turned to Chinese companies for securing new electric bus fleets. The only deal in which the national government played a hand was for the construction of a long-troubled highway in the south of the country. However, there was no further sign of development after the initial announcement, which itself came only after the Latin American companies originally tasked with the project faced corruption scandals and bankruptcy (Bermúdez Liévano, 2019). This is in stark contrast to the Primorye case explored in the following chapter, where regional elites were excluded from the development decision-making process in Sino-Russian relations. Where the Colombian case highlights the influence of regional authorities, the Primorye case may show the opposite.

The second important structural aspect is that when these successful substate deals occurred, they were through a competitive bidding process rather than through direct government-to-government negotiations. China's infrastructure companies proved themselves more capable of winning competitive tenders than their compatriots in the extractive industries.

Recently, when a Chinese company, Zijin Mining, did make great strides into the mining sector, it came through acquiring another foreign company, Canada's Continental Gold, thus continuing the pattern of Chinese firms gaining ground in the extractive industries only through partnering with or acquiring a third—and decidedly foreign—party. One foreign firm acquiring another foreign firm does not raise the same alarm on an ideational level as it would had a Chinese firm overtaken a Colombian one.

Beyond initial headlines with surface-level success, more recent data shows more material shifts. Having secured almost zero Chinese FDI since 2017, Colombia became one of the main recipients of Chinese FDI in 2020 (Dussel Peters, 2021: 7). For Colombia, FDI amounts remained a minuscule proportion of Chinese investments regionally, but the employment generated by this FDI in Colombia accounted for nearly 60% of the total employment generated by Chinese investment throughout LAC (Dussel Peters, 2021: 7).

In the first stage of China's *desembarco*, China's large, publicly owned companies were at the fore, particularly in the energy sector (Dussel Peters, 2021: 8). This chapter highlights their repeated failings in the Colombian market. In this second wave of engagement, however, China's private companies are leading the way. Privately-owned Chinese companies generated 23,201 jobs in Latin America in 2020 compared to just 1,343 jobs generated by public ones (Dussel Peters, 2021: 9). This new development is better suited to Colombian tastes and abilities, its ideational and structural makeup.

Such trends have been accompanied by a new wave of government initiatives on both sides. In March of 2020, the two countries were "finalizing an agreement" related to China's Belt and Road Initiative (Fieser & Jaramillo, 2020). Colombia was the only Latin American country yet to join the BRI. The following year, China sent multiple batches of Sinovac vaccines to Colombia with a special video message by President Xi Jinping (CGTV, 2021).

Perhaps the biggest challenge to Colombia's status quo, however, is the tectonic shift in energy markets. The Colombian people and economy suffered immensely because of the global pandemic while its largest employers and contributors to GDP, coal, and petroleum, saw their traditional customers shift to renewables and shale gas. Europe and the US no longer demand Colombian extractive products as they once did. Thus, where this case and the Primorye one are perhaps most alike is in the fact that the greatest cooperation with China does, in fact, result after a "crisis in relations with the West rather than a strategic choice" (Kuteleva and Ivanov).

Colombia has no great proven oil reserves for the future and coal is rapidly going out of favor globally. While the varying—but often high—cost of freight has made Colombian coal more expensive than what China can secure elsewhere, China remains a large and untapped market amid the Colombian government's scramble to save the economy. While the structural constraints highlighted by Soifer's work remain in place, in terms of Welch's theory, the reference point for Colombia is rapidly shifting, and with it change is ripe. In terms of Campbell, the Colombian state may soon find that it can no longer afford to promote the exact same ideational factors in its foreign policy. China may no longer remain the "other".

Notes

1. According to Devlin (2008: 113), Colombia's 1990 export and import figures were both zero, based on the United Nations Statistics Division's Comtrade database. However, the IMF's Direction of Trade Statistics report $2,081,500 in exports to and $1,844,590 in imports from China in the same year.
2. This is based on 181 countries in the IMF Direction of Trade Statistics which excludes countries like Namibia, listed as having 0 foreign trade, and South Sudan, which did not exist in 2002 for this comparison.
3. At its peak, Colombian manufacturing contributed less than 25% of GDP, consistently below the overall manufacturing value added for LAC (Mesquita Moreira 2007: 8).
4. From 2000–2009, Colombia's founding member partners of the Pacific Alliance, Chile and Peru, both maintained positive balances of trade with China, with 28% and 17%, respectively (Mesquita Moreira 2010: 9).
5. This fact simply illustrates the lack of exposure to China, its people and its languages. It does not suggest that Chinatowns hold the key to deeper ties with the PRC because its residents' political leanings may make this impossible.
6. Even after penetrating the market, Chinese companies faced both kidnappings and public accusations that they had been bribing FARC rebels (Chimienti & Creutzfeldt, 2017).
7. Where some respondents said, "culture", others said, "culture clash", or "culturally different", so that a total of 14 respondents listed words or phrases with "culture" in them.
8. Specifically, the Polity IV Project, Integrated Network for Societal Conflict Research (INSCR) Program, Centre for International Development and Conflict Management (CIDCM) at the University of Maryland, College Park.
9. The figure follows the formatting in Welch (2005), Figure 6.1 (220).
10. In 2010 the FARC controlled 40% of the Colombian territory and held 4,000 Colombian citizens as political prisoners (Marshall, Gurr & Jaggers, 2010). The Polity project did not register the FARC or other groups like the ELN as an "accountability group", but its constraints on the executive are severe. Even if Colombia was a complete autocracy, the executive could only exert influence over half the state.

Acknowledgements This work was partially supported by the École française d'Extrême-Orient (EFEO) who generously funded fieldwork and provided a central office space in Beijing, China. Preparation for fieldwork in China was also supported by funding from the School of Oriental and African Studies language grant program.

References

Agencia EFE. (2012, May 9). China, Colombia agree to boost oil cooperation. *Fox News Latino*. http://latino.foxnews.com/latino/politics/2012/05/09/china-colombia-agree-to-boost-oil-cooperation/

Armony, A. C. (2012). A view from Afar: How Colombia sees China. *China Quarterly, 209*, 178–197.

Baker & McKenzie. (2012). *Latin America Oil & Gas Handbook—2012*. Baker & McKenzie International.

Beckmann, M. N., & Hall, R. (2013). Elite interviewing in Washington, DC. In L. Mosley (Ed.), *Interview Research in Political Science* (pp. 196–208). Cornell University Press.

Bermúdez Liévano, A. (2019, December 19). The year of Chinese transport infrastructure in Colombia. *Diagolo Chino*. https://dialogochino.net/en/infrastructure/32249-the-year-of-chinese-transport-infrastructure-in-colombia/

Bo Kong. (2010). *China's International Petroleum Policy*. Praeger Security International.

Bushnell, D. (1993). *The making of Modern Colombia: A Nation in spite of itself*. University of California Press.

Campbell, D. (1992). *Writing security: United States Foreign Policy and the Politics of Identity*. University of Minnesota Press.

Caracol. (2013). Colombia pasó del primer al tercer lugar en exportación de plátano en el mundo. *Caracol*. www.caracol.com.co/noticias/economia/colombia-paso-del-primer-al-tercer-lugar-en-exportacion-de-platano-en-el-mundo/20130528/nota/1906125.aspx

CEPRI. (2014, November 14). *Proexport avanza y se convierte en PROCOLOMBIA*. Press Office of the President of Colombia. http://wsp.presidencia.gov.co/cepri/prensa/2014/noviembre/Paginas/20141114_01-es-InvExp-Esp.aspx

CGTN. (2021, March 21). *Xi Jinping hails friendship between China, Colombia as Chinese vaccines arrive in Bogota*. https://news.cgtn.com/news/2021-03-21/President-Xi-Jinping-delivers-speech-to-Colombian-people-via-video-YOl5lYYiFa/index.html

Chimienti, A., & Creutzfeldt, B. (2017). Who wants what for Latin America? Voices for and against the China-backed extractivist development model. In M. Myers & C. Wise (Eds.), *The political economy of China–Latin America relations in the New Millennium*. Routledge.

China Gezhouba Group Co., Ltd. (CGGC). (2015). *CGGC signed Columbia Bogota Tramcar MOU*. www.cggc.cc/2015-05/25/content_20845956.htm

Colombian Ministry of Industry & Tourism. (n.d.). www.tlc.gov.co

Devlin, R. (2008). China's Economic Rise. In R. Roett & G. Paz (Eds.), *China's Expansion into the Western Hemisphere* (pp. 111–147). Brookings Institution Press.

Downs, E. (2011). *Inside China, Inc*. John L. Thornton China Center at Brookings.

Dussel Peters, E. (2021, March 31). *Monitor of Chinese OFDI in Latin America and the Caribbean 2021*. RED ALC-China. https://www.redalc-china.org/monitor/images/pdfs/menuprincipal/DuselPeters_MonitorOFDI_2021_Eng.pdf

Echeverry, J. C., Navas, J., Navas, V., & Gomez, M. P., (2008). Oil in Colombia: History, Regulation and Macroeconomic Impact (Spanish). *SSRN Electronic Journal*, 1–28. www.ssrn.com/abstract=1486129

Economist. (2011, February 17). Colombia and the United States, Trade disunion; Santos's China card. *Economist: The World in 2015*.

Ecopetrol, S. A. (2014). Ecopetrol About: Our History. *Ecopetrol*. www.ecopetrol.com.co
Ellis, E. (2014). *China on the Ground in Latin America*. Palgrave Macmillan.
Farnsworth, E. (2019, April 12). Why Washington is right to be concerned about China in Latin America. *Americas Quarterly*. https://www.americasquarterly.org/article/why-washington-is-right-to-be-concerned-about-china-in-latin-america/
Feenstra, R. C., & Kee, H. L. (2007). Trade liberalisation and export variety: A comparison of Mexico and China. *World Economy, 30*(1), 5–21.
Fieser, E., & Jaramillo, A. (2020, March 4). *China looks to boost investment, strengthen ties with Colombia*. Bloomberg. https://www.batimes.com.ar/news/latin-america/china-to-invest-in-colombia-the-us-closest-ally-in-latin-america.phtml
Gabriel, Y., & Griffiths, D. S. (2008). International learning groups: Synergies and dysfunctions. *Management Learning, 39*(5), 503–518.
Gallagher, K. P., & Irwin, A. (2017). China's economic statecraft in Latin America: Evidence from China's Policy Banks. In M. Myers & C. Wise (Eds.), *The Political Economy of China–Latin America Relations in the New Millennium*. Routledge.
Gallagher, K. P., & Porzecanski, R. (2010). *The dragon in the room: China and the future of Latin American industrialization*. Stanford University Press.
Garzón. (2013, October 29). Inversiones Chinas en América Latina: ¿Existen Reglas de Juego? In *discussion held at Asociación Ambiente y Sociedad, organised by the Instituto Latinoamericano para una Sociedad y un Derecho Alternativo (ILSA) and la Red por la Justicia Ambiental en Colombia*. https://pt.slideshare.net/rosaluxandina/inversiones-chinas-en-amrica-latina-existen-reglas-de-juego-paulina-garzn-panel-1
Garzón. (2014, December 21). El sueño chino: ¿pesadilla ecuatoriana? *Plan V investigación*. www.planv.com.ec/investigacion/investigacion/el-sueno-chino-pesadilla-ecuatoriana
Gómez, C., & Sciabica, S. (2014, August 4). Mexico's Energy Reform: Lessons from Colombia and Brazil. *Americas Quarterly*. http://americasquarterly.org/content/mexicos-energy-reform-lessons-colombia-and-brazil
Gómez Peña, N. (2015). *Chinese Investments in Colombia: Revision of cooperation agreements between Colombia and China*. Asociación Ambiente y Sociedad. www.ambienteysociedad.org.co/wp-content/uploads/2016/01/Chinese-Investments-in-Colombia.pdf
González, F. (2008). Latin America in the economic equation—Winners and losers: What can losers do? In R. Roett & G. Paz (Eds.), *China's Expansion into the Western Hemisphere* (pp. 148–169). Brookings Institution Press.
Hague Conference on Private International Law (HCCH). (2016). *FULL TEXT 12: Convention of 5 October 1961 Abolishing the Requirement of Legalisation for Foreign Public Documents*. Hague Conference on Private International Law. www.hcch.net/en/instruments/conventions/full-text/?cid=41
Heine, J. (2008, July 25). *China's Claim in Latin America: So far, a partner not a threat*. Council on Hemispheric Affairs, Research Analysis. www.coha.org/2008/07/china's-claim-in-latin-america-so-far-a-partner-not-athreat
Holmes, J. S., de Piñeres, S. A. G., & Curtin, K. M. (2010). *Guns, drugs, and development in Colombia*. University of Texas Press.
International Monetary Fund (IMF). (2012, October). *Direction of Trade Statistics*. UK Data Service. https://doi.org/10.5257/imf/dots/2012-10
Jenkins, R., Dussel Peters, E., & Mesquita Moreira, M. (2008). The impact of China on Latin America and the Caribbean. *World Development, 36*(2), 235–253.
Jiang S. (2012). Las relaciones de China con Colombia. In B. Creutzfeldt (Ed.), *China en América Latina: Reflexiones sobre las relaciones transpacíficas* (pp. 279–296). Universidad Externado de Colombia.
Lall, S., & Wess, J. (2004). *People's Republic of China's Competitive Threat to Latin America*. (LAEBA) Latin America/Caribbean and Asia/Pacific Economics and Business Association.
Londoño Penilla, M. (2005, April 29). Colombia's Uribe Tours China, Japan. *Executive Intelligence Review*, 51–53.

López, A., & Ramos, D. (2010). The Argentine Case. In *China and Latin America: Economic relations in the twenty-first century* (pp. 65–158). German Development Institute / Deutsches Institut für Entwicklungspolitik (DIE).

Ludeña, M. P. (2012). Is Chinese FDI pushing Latin America into natural resources? *Vale Colum* (63). http://academiccommons.columbia.edu/catalog/ac:145554

Makeham, H. F. (2013). Chinese perspectives on the feasibility of an Asia Pacific Community. *The Chinese Journal of International Politics, 6*(4), 365–399. https://doi.org/10.1093/cjip/pot012

Marks, T.A. (2002). *Colombian Army Adaptation to FARC Insurgency*. Strategic Studies Institute. www.strategicstudiesinstitute.army.mil/pubs/download.cfm?q=18

Marshall, M. G., Gurr, T. R., & Jaggers, K. (2010). *Polity IV country report 2010: Colombia*. Center for Systemic Peace. https://www.systemicpeace.org/polity/Colombia2010.pdf

Mesquita Moreira, M. (2007). Fear of China: Is there a future for manufacturing in Latin America? *World Development, 35*(3), 355–376.

Mesquita Moreira, M. (2010). *Ten years after the take-off: Taking stock of China-Latin America and the Caribbean economic relations*. Inter-American Development Bank.

Milbank, Tweed, Hadley McCloy LLP. (2012). Milbank Represents Lenders in $1.2B Expansion of the El Dorado Int'l Airport in Bogotá, Colombia. *Milbank*, 1–2. www.milbank.com/news/milbank-represents-lenders-in-1-2-billion-expansion-of-the-el.html

Ministerio de Agricultura y Desarrollo de Colombia (MinAgricultura). (n d.). *Reporte de Destino de las 20 exportaciones del sector agropecuario*. Ministerio de Agricultura y Desarrollo de Colombia. www.agronet.gov.co/www/htm3b/excepcionesNuke/cargaNet/netcarga123.aspx?cod=123&fechaF_year=2014&submit=Ver%20Reporte&reporte=Destino%20de%20las%20exportaciones%20del%20sector%20agropecuario%20por%20pa%EDs&file=200692911517_200696121457

Murillo, M. A. (2004). *Colombia and the United States: War, Unrest, and Destabilization*. Seven Stories Press.

Murphy, H., & Bocanegra, N. (2013, March 10). Money laundering distorts Colombia's economic comeback. *Reuters*. www.reuters.com/article/us-colombia-moneylaundering-idUSBRE94R03E20130528

New York Times. (1992, November 8). Colombia Rebels Attack Oilfield, Killing 26. *New York Times*. www.nytimes.com/1992/11/08/world/colombia-rebels-attack-oilfield-killing-26.html

Office of the Secretary of Defense. (2015, April 7). *Annual Report to Congress: Military and Security Developments Involving the People's Republic of China 2015*. Department of Defense, United States of America. www.defense.gov/Portals/1/Documents/pubs/2015_China_Military_Power_Report.pdf

Olavarría, L. & Vicioso, C. (2013). Ten things to know—Investing in the Colombian oil and gas industry. *Norton Rose Fulbright*. www.nortonrosefulbright.com/knowledge/publications/108814/ten-things-to-know-investing-in-the-colombian-oil-and-gas-industry

OpenOil. (2013). *Colombia Oil Almanac: An OpenOil Reference Guide*. http://openoil.net/?wpdmact=process&did=MTQuaG90bGluaw==

Organization of American States. (2016). *Foreign Trade Information System (SICE)*. www.sice.oas.org/ctyindex/COL/COLagreements_e.asp

People's Republic of China. (2008). Full text: China's Policy Paper on Latin America and the Caribbean. *Xinhuanet*. www.news.xinhuanet.com/english/2008-11/05/content/_10308117.htm

PetrolWorld. (2012, May 10). Columbia: Ecopetrol Signs Deal with China's Sinochem. *Petrol-World*. www.petrolworld.com/latin-america-headlines/columbia-ecopetrol-signs-deal-with-chinas-sinochem.html

Productos de Colombia com S.A.S., Colombian Flowers. (n.d.). *Products of Colombia*. www.productsofcolombia.com/main/Colombia/Flowers.asp

PwC (PricewaterhouseCoopers). (2014). *Colombia Oil & Gas Industry 2014: An Overview*. PricewaterhouseCoopers.

Quetzalcoatl1. Shutterstock. https://www.shutterstock.com/image-vector/handshake-two-flags-colombia-china-flat-1962492184

Rathbone, J. P., & Mapstone, N. (2011, February 13). China in talks over Panama Canal rival. *Financial Times.* https://www.ft.com/content/7e14756c-37a9-11e0-b91a-00144feabdc0

Rorty, R. (1993). Human rights, rationality, and sentimentality. *Wronging Rights?: Philosophical Challenges for Human Rights,* 167–185. https://doi.org/10.1017/CBO9780511625404.010

Saldaña, J. (2013, April 2). Colombia's legacy with Korea. *The City Paper.* http://thecitypaperbog ota.com/features/colombias-legacy-with-korea

Schilling, E. (1935, January 27). The Japanese "Brain Trust". *Simplicissimus, 44*(39), cover.

Secretariat of the United Nations Conference on Trade and Development (UNCTAD). (2005). *Trade and Development Report, 2005.* United Nations.

Snow, D. A., & Su, Y. (2011). Criminology, racial dehumanization and the crime of genocide in Darfur. *Contemporary Sociology: A Journal of Reviews, 40*(1), 10–12.

Soifer, H. D. (2015). *State Building in Latin America.* Cambridge University Press.

Sales, M. (2013, November 5). Colombia's infrastructure; one of Latin America's worst. *Colombia Politics.* www.colombia-politics.com/infrastructure-2/

Strauss, J. C. (2012). Framing and claiming: Contemporary globalization and "going out" in China's rhetoric towards Latin America. *The China Quarterly, 209,* 134–156.

Suzuki, S. (2007). The importance of 'Othering' in China's national identity: Sino-Japanese relations as a stage of identity conflicts. *The Pacific Review,* 20.

Tansey, O. (2007). Process tracing and elite interviewing: a case for non-probability sampling. *PS: Political Science & Politics, 4*(40), 765–772.

Torres R., A. (2014, June 7). China afianza su estrategia en Ecuador. *El Comercio,* June 7. www.elc omercio.com/actualidad/china-ecuador-negocios-prestamos.html

Uribe, A. (2013, September 10). *Challenges to Democracy in the Western Hemisphere* Committee on Foreign Affairs. U.S. House of Representatives. https://www.govinfo.gov/content/pkg/CHRG-113hhrg82761/html/CHRG-113hhrg82761.htm

U.S. Embassy Bogotá. (2012, May 10). *Today's Business Opportunities.* U.S. Embassy Bogotá Blog. http://usbusiness-opportunities-embassybogota.com/2012/05/10/colombia-and-china-a-growing-economic-partnership/

U.S.F.K. (n.d.). *United Nations Command.* United States Forces Korea. www.usfk.mil/About/Uni ted-Nations-Command/

Wallace, W. (1991). Foreign policy and the national identity of the United Kingdom. *International Affairs, 67*(1), 65–80.

Welch, J. (2005). *Painful choices: A theory of foreign policy change.* Princeton University Press.

Wendt, A. (1992). Anarchy is what states make of it: The social construction of power politics. *International Organization, 46*(02), 391–425.

WordReference.com. (2016). monstruso. *WordReference.com.* Retrieved June 3, 2013, from www. wordreference.com/es/en/translation.asp?spen=monstruo

World Bank. (2013). Data: Countries and Economies. *World Bank Open Data.* http://data.worldb ank.org/?display=default

World Politics Review (WPR). (2012, May 24). Global Insider: Colombia Jumps on the China Bandwagon, Interview with Benjamin Creutzfeldt. *World Politics Review.*http://www.worldpoli ticsreview.com/trend-lines/11988/global-insider-colombia-jumps-on-the-china-bandwagon

World Trade Organization (WTO). (n.d.). *Regional Trade Agreements (RTAs) Database.* rtais. wto.org

Xinhua. (2008, November 23). China, Colombia agree to strengthen cooperation. *People's Daily Online.* http://news.xinhuanet.com/english/2008-11/23/content_10397902.htm

Zakowski, I. Shutterstock. https://www.shutterstock.com/image-vector/cartoon-illustration-giant-panda-bear-89019337

Sabrina van den Bos is an independent researcher based in Sydney, Australia. She received her PhD from the Department of Politics and International Studies at the School of Oriental and African Studies, University of London. She also holds a dual-master's degree with an MPA from the London School of Economics and an MIA from the School of International and Public Affairs at Columbia University in New York. She has been working, observing and researching international affairs for nearly 20 years. Starting at age 17 in Niamey, Niger, she has gone on to complete projects on six continents. Her research focuses on foreign policy change and identifying new mechanisms of cooperation which can overcome local prejudices and politics.

Chapter 11
The Sino-Russian Rapprochement Through the Prism of the Development of the Russian Far East: Identity Contestations and Conflicting Representations of China in Russian Eastern Frontiers

Anna Kuteleva and Sergei Ivanov

Abstract This chapter examines intersections between Russia s China policy and the Far Eastern development strategy, with a focus on Primorye. Primorye is a particularly interesting venue for a case study of Sino-Russian interactions because it is both far from and important to Moscow. The distance between Vladivostok, the capital of Primorye, and Moscow spans seven time zones and 5,770 miles. China, on the other hand, is right on Primorye's doorstep. In the mid-2000s, Primorye and, specifically its capital Vladivostok, became a showcase for Russia's "turn to the East." Drawing on the case of Primorye, the chapter illustrates contingencies, complexities, challenges, and paradoxes that underpin the development of Sino-Russian relations and identify the implications of closer ties between Beijing and Moscow for the development of the Far East. Drawing on interviews and extensive fieldwork conducted between 2014 and 2021, we show that the "turn to the East" promotes political rapprochement between Moscow and Beijing but does not facilitate establishing harmonious relations between communities along the Sino-Russian border and hardly facilitates the modernization of the regional economy. Overall, Russia's inconsistent attitudes towards China reveal the fragile foundation of Sino-Russian friendship as well as complex internal identity contradictions that prevents Russia's Far Eastern provinces from fully embracing the opportunities that China's rise might offer them.

Keywords Sino-Russian relations · Russian Far East · Development · National identity

A. Kuteleva (✉)
School of International Regional Studies, National Research University
Higher School of Economics, Moscow, Russia
e-mail: a.kuteleva@gmail.com

S. Ivanov
Palacký University Olomouc, Olomouc, Czechia

Abbreviations

APEC   Asia-Pacific Economic Cooperation
FDI   Foreign Direct Investment
NOCs   National Oil Companies
US   United States

11.1   Introduction

China and Russia share a land border of more than 2,600 miles, whose particulars were formally agreed upon only in the mid-2000s. Rivers and an interminable stretch of forests separate the Russian Far East from Northeast China (Heilongjiang, Jilin, and Liaoning). While Beijing and Moscow are more than 3,600 miles apart, the distance from Changchun and Harbin to Vladivostok, Khabarovsk, and Birobidzhan is less than 600 miles. As the ties between the Far East and the outside world revitalized after the collapse of the Soviet Union, the research on contemporary interactions between China's and Russia's frontier regions revived too for a brief period between the mid-1990s and the early 2000s (Alexseev & Troyakova, 1999; Cotton, 1996; Iwashita, 2004; Larin, 2006; Wishnick, 2000). As for the most recent studies, despite some notable exceptions (Jia & Bennett, 2018; Kuhrt, 2012; Savchenko & Zuenko, 2020; Zuenko et al., 2019), the large cosmopolitan community of scholars of Sino-Russian relations, as well as Russian and Chinese cohorts, tend to concentrate overwhelmingly on interactions between Moscow and Beijing.

Studies that explore the issues related to the history of Russian expansion to the Pacific and Sino-Russian cross-border interactions in the late 19th and the early 20th centuries (e.g. Sablin & Sukhan, 2018; Urbansky, 2020), cultural studies (Adda, 2020), and anthropologists' research on informal cross-border interactions and economies (e.g., Holzlehner, 2018; Ryzhova, 2018; Stern, 2015) approach Sino-Russian relations from a different angle. These scholarship shows that actors across the China-Russia border and inside either of these enormously complex states experience the relations between Moscow and Beijing differently and thus respond to the recent rapprochement between the two states in distinctive ways. Drawing on these interdisciplinary insights, we examine the development of Sino-Russian relations in the 2010s through the prism of Russia's eastern frontier. Specifically, we consider how Sino-Russian interactions play out in Primorye (Primorsky Krai) and its administrative center Vladivostok.

The distance between the capital of Primorye, Vladivostok, and Moscow spans seven time zones. China, on the other hand, is right on Primorye's doorstep. The province's strategic location near the key Asian markets, coupled with its three major ice-free ports, and valuable natural endowments, determine its special place in Moscow's China policy. For the central authorities concentrated in Russia's European heartland, Primorye is a distant periphery and, simultaneously, a gateway to the

Asia Pacific region (Kuhrt, 2012). Unsurprisingly, in the early 2010s, Primorye and, specifically Vladivostok, became a showcase for Russia's "turn to the East" on both domestic and international levels.

Our analysis is based on "thick" constructivist and poststructuralist theorizing of the relationship between foreign policy and identity. First, we discuss the role of identity in foreign policy design and implementation. Further, drawing on this theoretical framework, we position Russia on the border between the Global South and the Global North and contextualize Sino-Russian relations in Russia's ongoing identity crises. In the second part of the analysis, we map the evolution of Russia's Far Eastern development strategy from the early 2000s to the late 2010s to determine the role that the Russian state assigns to the region in its China policy. Finally, using ethnographic research and interviews collected between 2014 and 2021, we conduct an in-depth case study of the development of Sino-Russian relations on the regional level and provide a nuanced understanding of perceptions of China in Primorye. Our analysis shows that the scope and intensity of the regional cooperation with China take different forms than Russian central authorities and experts in Moscow have anticipated, which highlights miscalculations in both the "turn to the East" policy and the new Far Eastern development strategy.

11.2   Identity as a Structure and as a Practice

Identity contestations and reconciliations reveal unique ontologies of the international and are significantly affecting politics and policy in the states as well as its external interactions. As Ted Hopf (1998: 172–173) puts it, "a world without identities is a world of chaos, a world of pervasive and irremediable uncertainty, a world much more dangerous than anarchy." Indeed, identities tell us who "we" are and how "we" should interact with "them." Dynamic renegotiations of national identities shape foreign policies and have a profound effect on relations between states. In this sense, all international politics begins at home (Hopf, 2002), and to understand how a state perceives others we first need to understand how it defines itself in the framework of the international.

Following Lene Hansen (2006), Iver Neumann (2016), and other "thick" constructivists and poststructuralist scholars, we examine identity as a dynamic and relational discursive system. As Hansen (2006: 6) specifies, "representations of identity place foreign policy issues within a particular interpretative optic, one with consequences for which foreign policy can be formulated as an adequate response." In this conceptual framework, identity has some characteristics of a causal variable but still does not cause an action. Instead, identity explains normative rationalities of actions.

Usually, analysis of the relationship between identity and foreign policy focuses on a homogeneous national "we" (e.g. Kaczmarski, 2019; Tsygankov, 2018; Wilson, 2019; Wishnick, 2017). In contrast, we show how dominant identity constructions travel across a vast heterogenous state and how new identity representations emerge in the process of discursive mobilization when the state presents and implements foreign policies and geopolitical visions on the regional level. Approaching identity as a structure and as a practice, we show how Russia's complex and contradictory self-representations along the line of the North–South dichotomy influence relations between its European heartland and eastern periphery and how, in turn, this problematic domestic dynamic plays out in Sino-Russian relations. Overall, we examine Sino-Russian relations as a practice and a discursive achievement on national and regional levels, answering three interrelated questions: (1) How does Russia define itself vis-à-vis China and how does it envision the development of its eastern frontier in the context of China's rise? (2) What is the socioeconomic impact of the recent Sino-Russian rapprochement on Primorye? (3) How do the residents of this territory experience Sino-Russian relations? Our case study illustrates contingencies and paradoxes that underpin the development of Sino-Russian relations and identify the implications of closer ties between Beijing and Moscow for the development of the Far East.

The first part of the study draws on a discourse analysis of a heterogenous collection of texts, including official statements and speeches, reports of governmental institutions and policy-making agencies, strategic policy documents, and international and intergovernmental agreements. All these sources were collected from the official websites of individual institutions and through archival research. Further, we present a qualitative study of the socioeconomic impact of the recent Sino-Russian rapprochement on Primorye based on 25 interviews and series of fieldwork observations conducted between 2014 and 2021 in different parts of Primorye.

11.3   Russia on the Border Between the Global South and the Global North

Arif Dirlik (1996: 31) argues that as a "metaphoric reference" the Global South designates "the marginalized populations of the world." Similarly, Walter Mignolo (2011: 166) specifies that the Global South should be understood as "an ideological concept" that captures "the economic, political, and epistemic dependency and unequal relations in the global world order, from a subaltern perspective." Accordingly, the notion of Global South challenges Eurocentric master narratives and implies "the mutual recognition among the world's subaltern of their shared condition at the margins of the brave new neoliberal world of globalization" (López, 2007: 1). Thereby, the concept travels well across different contexts and can accommodate even deviant cases, such as Russia.

Russia is and always has been an empire that proclaims itself a great power and strives to be treated accordingly by both its partners and competitors. In this sense, Russia has little in common with other countries discussed in this volume. However, Russia is a heiress of the Second World that disappeared in the early 1990s leaving behind "one hegemonic power, and one hegemonic ideology: neoliberalism" (Dirlik, 2007: 13). As a result, Russia's inclusion to and interactions within the neoliberal system dominated by the Global North are tainted by the failure of the hegemonic socialist project. Russia has never been colonized, yet it is located at the very margins of the Eurocentric modernity and struggles to be recognized as equal among equals in the Global North. Overall, complex and profoundly contradictory identity constructions push Russia on the porous border between the Global South and the Global North.

Political elites construct Russia's "greatpowerness" (*velikoderzhavnost'*) as an inborn characteristic that belongs to Russia by the virtue of its enormous size, vast natural resources, and rich culture (Lauruel, 2007; Urnov, 2014). Russia carries its greatpowerness by legacy, as a descendant of the Russian Empire and the Soviet Union. After the collapse of the Soviet Union, the notion of greatpowerness becomes tied to the state's ability to control its territory (Svarin, 2013: 131), as well as the so-called "Russian world" (*Russkyi Mir*) (O'Loughlin & Talbot, 2005) and the "near-abroad" (*blizhnee zarubezhe*). The revived great power identity is tightly bound with the concepts of sovereignty, statehood, and independence that continue imperial patterns the modern Russia inherited from the Russian Empire and the Soviet Union. Hence, this identity is best understood in Partha Chatterjee's terms as the "imperial prerogative," a self-claimed right of an empire to declare the colonial exception within its spheres of influence (2005). In this sense, proclaiming its greatpowerness, Russia emphatically associates itself with the Global North. However, Russia's relations with the countries traditionally designated as the Global North are turbulent and marked by waves of friendship and confrontation.

Russia has complex and contradictory relations with European intellectual and cultural hegemony. It perceives the United States and the core Western European countries as developmental ideals to work toward. The dominant discourses interpret Russia's greatpowerness as a sign of parity with the West, and hence force Russian political elites to seek from the West a recognition of Russia's special status in international relations (Kuteleva, 2021: 71–74). On the other hand, Russia never identified itself and was never identified by others as a Western country without a stipulation for some uniquely Russian developmental path (Morozov, 2015; Neumann, 2016). In the words of Viatcheslav Morozov (2015: 101–102), Russia is "a subaltern empire in a Eurocentric world" that is "fully locked in an unequal relationship with the global capitalist core" and internalized "its subaltern position in its own national identity discourse."

Russia's subaltern position in relation to the core countries of the Global North and recurring conflicts with them accentuate Russia's non-Western self-representations and particularly its "Asian state" identity (Kaczmarski, 2019; Wishnick, 2017). However, Russia's Eurasianism, as Mark Bassin (1997: 565) puts it, "was founded on the radical assertion that Russia formed a part of neither Europe nor Asia, but rather represented an autonomous continent and civilization unto itself." Both real and perceived differences between Russia and its various non-Western Others— including Russia's East Asian neighbours (Curanović, 2012; Morozov, 2015)—reinforce and solidify Russia's understanding of self as being distinct from them and thus detached from the Global South.

As any other imperial project Russian one is inherently Orientalist and renders other non-Western societies as inferior. For Madina Tlostanova (2008: 3), Russia is the "Janus-faced empire," because "often the negative characteristics associated with Orientalism were projected by the Russians onto the interpretation of other empires deeds while the native material was not coded in the Orientalist terms." In this sense, the historical and sociocultural differences that separates Russia from Asian powers are more significant than those that separate it from the West. Moreover, the legacies of the peculiar relations between the Soviet Union and postcolonial states (Ermarth, 1969) do not allow Russia to treat the countries that used to be designated as the Third World as its equals. The ideological commitment to the socialist revolution in the Third World was an important component of Soviet foreign policy. In this framework, postcolonial states were portrayed as backward, vulnerable, and dependent and thus in need of assistance, guidance, and protection. Finally, as Morozov (2015: 71) emphasizes, Russia has a "peripheral position vis-à-vis the global capitalist core," which today includes not only the West but also most of East Asia. Being a subaltern "in a rather special way" (Morozov, 2015: 101) and striving to be recognized by the international community as a great power in the changing international hierarchy, Russia willfully disassociates itself with the Global South.

Defending its supposedly unique development path, Russia juxtaposes itself to the Western modernity. Development experiences of the past three decades and strong non-Western identities bring Russia closer to the Global South. Yet, Russia conceives itself not as a subaltern but as a state destined to be a great power (if not a super-power) and attempts to behave as such by initiating diverse colonial projects. Russia's peculiar position in-between the Global North and the Global South influences the development of Sino-Russian relations significantly, and the interplay of identities is even more evident when we look at interactions between the two in the eastern frontier of Russia's vast empire, the Russian Far East.

11.4 The Politics of Development in the Russian Far East and Russia's China Policy

Since the accession of the southern Far East in the mid-19th century, the region was variously a distant periphery, a colony sustained by state subsidies, and a mighty fortress. Overall, the Far East remains an appendage and a subaltern subject of the Russian empire. Describing the relationship between Russia's European heartland and the eastern frontier, Mark Bassin (1991: 766) emphasizes that "the simple circum-stance of territorial contiguity with the metropolis" coupled with the "large and long-established Russian population" turned the Far East into a "continuation or extension of the zone of Russian culture and society." According to him, such an image of the eastern frontiers parallels "not European colonial domains but America's perceptions and myths of its own frontier, the Wild West" (Bassin, 1991: 766). Indeed, the vast and varied territories that extend eastward from the Ural mountains across northern

Asia to the Pacific affirms Russia's greatpowerness by legitimizing narratives of its unbounded wealth and symbolizing its perpetual development potential.

Yet, the Russian Far East denotes not only Russia's greatness but also its vulnerabilities. The proximity of the Russian Far East to China, Japan, and Korea both determines its value for the empire and presents a permanent security threat. The region has gone through long periods of securitization interrupted by shorter periods of increased autonomy that allowed its elites to pursue regional interests and accumulate capital by intensifying trade with Asian neighbors (Sablin, 2018: 62–72). These periods of relative freedom coincided with the contractions of Russia's imperial power. In the face of existential challenges, the inherently Eurocentric empire chose to leave its eastern frontier to itself. To allow the region to survive on its own, the central authorities gave it greater economic and political autonomy and implemented liberalized development policies, including deregulating trade and stimulating foreign investment.[1] However, once the empire regained its powers and started recovering, the state did its best to maintain a firm grip on the Russian Far East, controlling and restricting foreign interactions along the borders.

Following the collapse of the Soviet Union, the Russian Far East entered into yet another period of freedom from the heavy metropolitan control. The authoritarian bureaucracy and the Communist Party structures that tied the Russian Far East to the Soviet center have fallen apart. As soon as the Russian Far East was reopened after being isolated since the mid-1930s (Zaitsev, 2008), the cross-border trade bloomed and the regional cooperation renewed. The Russian Far East reverberated with autonomist and self-reliance discourses demonstrated that the local residents understand all advantages of their geographic location and, if need be, are ready to integrate into the Asia–Pacific economy without the help of the central authorities. However, as sociologist Zhanna Zayonchkovskaya (2005: 72) summarizes it, the "real migration explosion" and an "unexpected invasion" of Chinese merchants and entrepreneurs in the Russian Far East revived the ghosts of the "yellow peril" in the early 1990s (Dyatlov, 2012). Very soon many experts became suspicious about and taken aback by China's proactive economic interest in Russia's eastern frontier (e.g., Bogaturov, 2004: 95; Bystritsky & Zausaev, 2007: 223). These interrelated tendencies forced Moscow to seriously reassess the state of its Russian Far Eastern regions as well as their role in her China policy.

Since Putin rose to power in 1999, Moscow has started to rhetorically compensate for the loss of the "external periphery" in Eastern Europe, Central Asia, and the Caucasus following the collapse of the Soviet Union by emphasizing the importance of internal colonies in the Russian Far East. Striving to preserve and increase its power and the special status of an "Europe-Asian" empire (*Yevro-Aziatskaya*

---

[1] The duty-free regime (the so-called porto franco) introduced in the 1860s brought to the region a new wave of settlers from Europe and Asia, stimulated the development of Russian and foreign businesses, and contributed to the thriving rise of Vladivostok, Khabarovsk, and Blagoveshchensk. The state abolished the duty-free regime (first in 1900–04 and ultimately in 1909), yet the regional development continued thanks to the Trans-Siberian Railway. During the tumultuous half-decade between 1917 and 1922, regional elites established a semi-autonomous polity that in 1920 institutionalized into a short-lived buffer-state, a nominally democratic and capitalist Far Eastern Republic.

imperiya), Russia designated the Russian Far East as its gateway to the Asia–Pacific region and the Asian century. In other words, the rejuvenation of the eastern frontiers became an important part of Putin's project of rebuilding Russia's power and prestige in the international arena. Responding to various development challenges, Putin's regime combined the revived and upgraded narratives of Russia's greatpowerness with condensed market reforms and began forging close relations with China.

Referring to China as Russia's "respected and beloved neighbor," Putin made it clear that the effective and mutually beneficial Sino-Russian cooperation is one of the key conditions of the successful development of the Russian Far East (e.g., Kremlin.ru, 2002b). As with many other challenges, Putin's solution for both rejuvenation of the Russian Far East and rapprochement with China was a systematic centralization of power. In 2004, China and Russia resolved three-century-long border disputes and transformed the friendship statements made back in 1996 into practical cooperation agenda (Voskresenski, 2015). Putin unequivocally dismissed popular concerns about China's ultimate designs on the Russian Far East. He made it clear that if the Russian ethnic population would ever start speaking Chinese, Korean, or Japanese languages, it would be the fault of local authorities rather than a result of the ill intentions of Russia's neighbors (Kremlin.ru, 2003). Putin and the central government openly blamed local authorities for the overflow of Chinese labor immigrants in the border regions (e.g., Kremlin.ru, 2003) and uncontrollable exports of raw materials (specifically, unprocessed wood) to China (e.g., Kremlin.ru, 2002a, 2007). As the ties between Beijing and Moscow were growing stronger, the central authorities regained control over trade flows and continued to tighten immigration policies, ignoring regional elites as agents of development in their own right. Local governors, politicians, strongmen, landlords, and influential businessmen— portrayed as helpless at best and selfish at worst—were rendered as incapable to contribute meaningfully to the design of the regional development policy and build mutually beneficial relations with China and other Asian powers.

In 2007, reaffirming itself as an Asian power, Russia took the opportunity to chair the APEC (Asia–Pacific Economic Cooperation) forum in 2012 and announced that it will host the CEO Summit in Vladivostok. This high-profile event gave impetus to new round of development initiatives in the Russian Far East. Preparing Vladivostok for APEC Summit, the central authorities invested in its complex reconstruction and launched several grandiose infrastructure projects, including the conference site on Russky Island and the longest cable bridge in the world that linked it to the rest of the city. These projects were designed to symbolize Russia's ambitious plans to both rejuvenate the Russian Far East and strengthen ties with the Asia Pacific. According to Putin's (2012) article in *The Wall Street Journal*, the APEC summit was supposed to demonstrate to hundreds of high-ranking guests from the 21 nations of the Pacific Rim that "Russia is a nation of broad opportunities and ready to join forces with our neighbors to advance our common creative goals." Following Putin, many Russian officials presented Vladivostok as Russia's Pacific capital and suggested flattering comparisons with Hong Kong, Singapore, and Busan. The original symbolism associated with the APEC summit, however, has rapidly evolved into a disappointment as Moscow's promises and ambitions went astray in the vast eastern wastes (Adda, 2014:

25–28; Zubarevich, 2016: 102). A year after the summit, Russia's federal authorities acknowledged the dismal economic failure of the Russian Far Eastern modernization projects of the late 2000s, including the expensive makeover of Vladivostok, and announced yet another upgrade of regional development policies.

In the mid-2010s, Russia's Asian policy was increasingly boiling down to a China policy. Returning to the presidency, Putin announced that Russia will strive for an even closer friendship with China and designated the Russian Far East as the key tool and, simultaneously, the major beneficiary of Russia's gaining momentum "turn to the East." In 2013, Putin (Kremlin.ru, 2013) declared the socioeconomic rise of the Russian Far East "the national priority for the entire twenty-first century," promising to redesign regional development policies accordingly. In 2015, the federal authorities launched Russia's own annual international discussion club in Vladivostok, the Eastern Economic Forum, and over the following years consolidated and expanded regional development programs, including special economic zones, investment regimes, a liberalized regional visa regime, and land redistribution programs. Yet, "the market-driven social and spatial transformation never took place and the new project just refashions direct state interventions" and the state still perceives the Russian Far East as a space that has to be protected and tightly regulated (Kuteleva et al., 2021).

The "turn to the East" is designed by bureaucrats in Moscow and powered by oil and gas giants such as Rosneft, Sibur, and Gazprom, as well as powerful monopolies, like Russian Railways. These state-owned companies launch new or revive old large-scale infrastructure projects, using massive loans from Chinese banks. Choosing loans over direct investment, Russian companies prevents the Chinese from getting access to the Russian Far Eastern and Siberian resources and infrastructure. To a certain extent such a system is similar to a colonial economy and, therefore, is prone to the drain of wealth.

Federal authorities demonstrated that all international matters, including foreign investments and loans, are better arranged in Moscow than in Vladivostok, Khabarovsk, Blagoveshchensk, or elsewhere in the Russian Far East. Putin himself on multiple occasions emphasized that high-level dialogue and traditional statist diplomacy are the most effective tools in promoting regional cooperation. As a case in point, during a plenary session of the 2017 Eastern Economic Forum, Putin cited the efforts of China's government to stimulate regional cooperation and invest in the Russian Far East as an example for Japan, Mongolia, and South Korea (Kremlin.ru, 2017).

Over decades, Moscow's attention to its far-flung eastern territories has oscillated from indifference and neglect to obsessive control. The surge of interest in the development of the Russian Far East in the mid-2000s and the 2010s is based on the opportunities offered by its location about the world's most dynamic economies and, particularly, China. The state implements development projects across the Russian Far East within the statist, rigid, and centralized political system where it can control the region's relations with its neighbors (Kuteleva et al., 2021). As a result, the main beneficiaries of Russia's turn towards China are the state gas and oil giants.

In the mid-2000s, Rosneft and Transneft, major Russian oil companies, received generous loans from Chinese state-owned banks to launch the Eastern Siberia-Pacific Ocean oil pipeline. In 2016, Gazprom secured a $2.2 billion investment from the Bank of China in the Power of Siberia pipeline, a 3,000 km pipeline that runs from the gas fields of eastern Siberia to the Chinese border in the south-east. In 2019, Gazprom received another $4.2 billion from Chinese investors to construct a gas processing plant in the Amur region. Only a tiny part of this Chinese money remained in the Russian Far East and went to regional budgets (Bliakher, 2014). In the active phase of a large-scale infrastructure project, the oil and gas giants headquartered in Moscow open local offices, hire local subcontractors, provide employment to the locals, and pay taxes to the local municipalities. However, these revenues drain rapidly. Giant infrastructures such as oil and gas pipelines are poorly linked with the local economy and use fly-in fly-out workforce regimes. For example, as an official at Mikhaylovsky District attests, Gazprom's pipeline project brought his district a short-term budget surplus, but the company left behind roads destroyed by heavy construction equipment and promises to come back, whereas the district's budget quickly "fell into a hole again" (Interview, Primorye, 01.08.2014).

Consequently, rebuilding itself as a Europe-Asian great power and ambitiously claiming a respectable place among the countries of the Global North, Russia embarks on colonial projects inside and outside its borders. A former member of the Legislative Assembly of Primorye, argues that the "turn to the East" on the domestic level equals to "an offensive of the big Russian capital" (Interview, Primorye, 01.06.2018). Like many other Russian Far Eastern politicians, he sees the fact that the capital from Russia's European heartland dominates the region's economy as a disregard for the interests of local populations. As another former official from Primorye summarizes, the hands-on experience and expertise of interaction with China that he and his colleagues have are not in demand because the central authorities want to single-handedly manage the province's relations with its neighbors (Interview, Primorye, 15.11.2015).

In practice, nevertheless, the metropolitan control over exchanges of people, goods, and services across the long Sino-Russian border is not—and has never been—absolute. For instance, even in the 1970s during the Sino-Soviet split, unofficial interactions at the local level continued (Urbansky, 2020, 236–239). In this sense, contacts between the local populations and the Chinese have never been interrupted and today like decades ago the residents of the Russian Far East are tightly connected to China. The next section scrutinizes the dynamics of formal and informal cross-border cooperation and examines the socio-economic impact of the recent Sino-Russian rapprochement on Primorye.

11.5 The Dynamics of Formal and Informal Cross-Border Cooperation

The evaluations of China's socio-economic impact on Russia's eastern frontier are blurred by the imperial imaginations, the questionable success of neoliberal development policies, the domination of the state in the realm of formal bilateral cooperation, as well as informal cooperation invisible to official statistics. The mixture of gross misperceptions and persistent informality of Sino-Russian interactions in the Russian Far East results in inconsistent and uneven integration of the Russian Far East into the regional and global economy. In this context, only a qualitative inquiry based on interviews with various local stakeholders and fieldwork observations can allow us to understand how the residents of the Russian Far East experience Sino-Russian relations.

11.5.1 Investment and Trade

Since the early 1990s, the structure of Chinese exports to Primorye has shifted from agricultural raw materials and food products to higher value-added products like machinery and equipment. In the regional exports to China, the development was quite the opposite. Since the early 1990s, Primorye has been exporting mainly raw materials, and their share has increased notably over the past three decades squeezing the share of higher value-added exports and especially that of machinery and equipment. In the 2010s, the fluctuations in oil prices and the dynamic of Sino-Russian energy relations explain the fluctuation in exports between Primorye and China. Kozmino port located near Nakhodka is Russia's second most important channel for oil exports to China. Between 2013 and 2015, the share of oil and petroleum products in the total Primorye's exports to China (41–63%) even exceeded exports of seafood and timber, the two export categories that traditionally dominated Primorye's export portfolio. However, after 2015 sales of oil and petroleum products dropped significantly, making up less than 25% of the total exports in the following years. In 2019, fish, timber, and oil constituted 55, 21%, and 9% of the province's export to China respectively.

Compared to the sizable trade flows, Chinese investment in the Russian Far East remains low. According to the Central Bank of Russia, 67 enterprises registered in Primorye received foreign direct investment (FDI) in 2019, with 14 of them having Chinese investors. The key industries that attract Chinese investment in Primorye are forestry, fishing, and agriculture. However, the official records do not include several significant regional businesses owned by Chinese entrepreneurs and joint-ventures with Russian companies (Zuenko et al., 2019: 106). Both the federal government and local authorities tend to focus on Chinese big businesses and state-owned corporations. Consequently, the actual volume of Chinese FDI in Primorye exceeds the official statistics.

Overall, Chinese investments in Primorye are primarily driven by the availability of natural resources. The Chinese invest in the processing only when they want to avoid restrictions on raw materials export imposed by the Russian state. In this sense, they are no different from Chinese investments elsewhere. Public opinion often relates Chinese investment in the Russian Far East to China's food security challenges, the quest for energy resources, scarcity of arable land, and overpopulation. However, large Chinese loans did not increase economic and political influence of Chinese state-owned companies in the Russian Far East, as it happened in many other places (see for example Tudoroiu and Ramlogan's chapter on Trinidad and Tobago in this volume). For instance, despite generous Chinese loans to Russian NOCs for modern- ization of the Eastern Siberia—Pacific Ocean oil pipeline system that runs through Primorye and many other parts of the Russian Far East Chinese companies did not build the pipeline new sections on Russian territory (Kuteleva, 2021, 76–77). Conse- quently, in the case of Primorye, it is Russian state-owned companies but not Chinese ones benefit most from Chinese loans. A substantial number, if not the majority, of Chinese investors in Primorye are private entities, whether individuals or enterprises (Zuenko et al., 2019). These investors are disparate and unorganized and invest in businesses with low capital intensity. Their major goal is essentially to make a profit rather than support the state's development goals and security concerns. The forestry sector of Primorye is a case in point.

Forestry is one of the key targets of Chinese investors in the Russian Far East, which is not surprising given that Russia's timber reserves account for a quarter of the world's total, and trade in timber makes up for more than 10% of the total Sino- Russian trade. Chinese timber imports from Russia quadrupled between 1993 and 2007 from an estimated 12.5 thousand to 31.5 million m3. Timber imports peaked in 2007 when Russia supplied 90% of China's total softwood roundwood imports (Forest Trends, 2017: 5), and then declined rapidly after Russia instituted a hefty log export tax (by 2009 the tax increased to 25%). At the same time, hardwood lumber imports from Russia increased by 600% after 2007 and nearly 100% after 2013, making Russia China's third-largest supplier of this product (Forest Trends, 2017: 13). Even though nearly all of the recent growth in Russian timber exports to China has been in processed logs, there are still few opportunities for local employment in timber-exporting regions of the Russian Far East, including Primorye. Chinese entrepreneurs are not motivated to invest in value-added timber processing facilities in Russia because they are less efficient than those in Northeast China. In addition to this, the local consumer demand is low because of the small size of its population. Consequently, Russian Far Eastern wood is more valuable if processed elsewhere rather than in the Russian Far East. Despite attempts of the government to stimulate domestic production of lumber by creating tariff barriers for unprocessed log exports, most Russian wood is imported to China after minimal processing that is required to declare it as lumber at customs and is processed into manufactured products at Chinese factories (Forest Trends, 2017).

According to Vladimir, a director of a forestry complex in the Chuguevsky District of Primorye, Chinese own about 80 sawmills in his district, each with a capacity of 500 cubic meters of wood per month. However, only three or four of those sawmills are officially registered. Before 2013, Vladimir's company also engaged in sawmilling but abandoned this line of business being unable to compete with the Chinese. He explains that his company works in full compliance with the existing regulations, whereas Chinese sawyers often use shortcuts. Local authorities regularly close Chinese illegal sawmills, but the next day they reappear in a new location. Vladimir admits that the fight against Chinese sawyers is a rather complicated issue because they provide jobs to the locals. In the Chuguevky District, where the forestry industry is the main source of income for the local population, the closure of all Chinese illegal sawmills will lead to high unemployment (Interview, Primorye, 16.09.2015).

Estimates of the extent of illegal logging in the Russian Far East range from 15 to 70% of the total, depending on the definition and methodology used (Newell & Simeone, 2014, 49–51). According to the interviewees, the Chinese "are afraid" to engage in illegal logging themselves but create demand for it. As an owner of a timber facility in the Terneysky District of Primorye explains, Chinese sawyers buy illegally harvested trees from the locals and break them into cants (unfinished logs to be further processed) and flitches (unfinished planks) that are further exported to China for further processing.

While Chinese experts and officials see these trade patterns as both natural and promising because of the "strong complementarity" of national economies (Pan, 2015: 109–113, 118; Zhao & Tang, 2018), their Russian counterparts diagnose a "deep division of fundamental developmental interests" that complicates bilateral relations (Korolev & Portyakov, 2019: 51). Russian authorities introduce various protectionist measures to constrain Chinese imports and restrain exports of raw materials. The Russian Far Eastern custom champions the all-Russian statistics of lawsuits against trading firms (Larin, 2017: 322–325). However, as the case of the forestry sector indicates, despite the government's attempts to influence the dynamic of bilateral trade between the Primorye and China, it still follows the patterns established in the mid-1990s: Russians sell commodities, whereas the Chinese export is gradually moving from labor-intensive to capital-intensive products.

11.5.2   Informal Cross-Border Economy

Chinese products ranging from cucumbers to car carburetors dominate wholesale markets in all major cities of Primorye. In the early 1990s, the cross-border trade with China developed rapidly in Primorye, but it often took illegal and spontaneous forms. Chinese consumer goods were coming through shuttle trade (*chelnochnaya torgovlya*), while Russian timber, fish, and other bio-resources were smuggled to China. This informal economy generated high and fast revenues for the residents of Primorye, cushioning the shocks of economic transition after the collapse of the Soviet Union. In the late 2000s, the Russian government introduced new restrictions on the border crossing and new customary rules; however, shuttle traders and smugglers creatively adapted to the new rules, and the informal economy still flourishes in Primorye in various forms (Holzlehner, 2018).

Both Chinese and Russian suppliers and retailers abuse flexible cross-border tourism policies. Thousands of so-called *chelnoki* or *pomogaiki*[2] travel daily visa-free from Vladivostok and Ussuriysk to Suifenhe and Mudanjiang in organized commercial groups and bring back up to 50 kg (25 kg after 2019) of goods free from import taxes. The sharp devaluation of the Ruble in the second half of 2014 did not stop the development of the shuttle business but strengthened the trends that had already emerged in the late 2000s. For example, today the majority of *pomagaiki* bring to Russia goods not for market wholesalers but for customers of online shops.

The shuttle trade belongs to a grey zone. Even though the shuttle trade is illegal, the state does not securitize it and, as a result, the customs make little effort to restrict it. Poaching as well as illegal wildlife trade and logging, in contrast, are way more complex and controversial issues. Illegal trade in rare plant and animal species in demand in East Asian markets, including tiger (Miquelle et al., 2010, 418–420), trepang (sea cucumber), and wild ginseng root (Baeg & So, 2013), is currently at conspicuous levels for use as medicine, luxury foods, and curios. Local Russian authorities turn a blind eye to illicit harvesting and gathering of various high-valued animals and plants, but poaching of critically endangered species, specifically Amur tigers, is increasingly securitized.

Estimating the level of the shuttle and illegal trade is, by their very nature, extremely difficult. In the case of Sino-Russia relations, it is specifically challenging. The principal techniques of detecting illegal trade, such as the partner country data comparison method (Morgenstern, 1963), are not efficient because of the gaps in China's trade statistics. For instance, China itself suffers from "missing imports" (Fisman & Wei, 2004; Kar & Freitas, 2013). Thus, while estimating the level of Sino-Russian shadow trade in Primorye has not previously been attempted, the evidence from interviews and fieldwork observations suggests it is alive and thriving.

11.5.3   Chinese Tourists in Vladivostok

The steady increase of intra-regional tourist flows has long been identified as one of the main targets of regional development programs. However, as the former head of the International Relations and Tourism Department of Vladivostok claims, obsolete infrastructure was the main barrier to tourism development (Interview, a local official, Primorye, 25.02.2015). According to him, the city administration was ready to invest in a "Disneyland" but ignored matter-of-fact problems, such as worn-out roads and outdated sewerage systems. Indeed, tourists from China, Japan, and South Korea came to Primorye only after the massive renovations related to the 2012 APEC summit held in Vladivostok.

---

[2] *Chelnoki* (literally translates as a "shuttle") travel backwards and forwards in and out of the country buying goods and then selling them within the country. *Pomogaiki* (translates as "helper") are courier help traders for a small fee to mover goods across the border. Shuttle trade originated during the perestroika and spread across many border regions in the post-Soviet space.

According to statistics of the Department of Tourism of the Primorye, more than 778 thousand foreigners visited the province in 2018, and a half of them were Chinese citizens. It is the most popular destination for Chinese tourists in the Russian Far East and their number doubled between 2014 and 2018. The federal and regional governments present these figures as an important indicator of the efficiency of the new development projects and predict that as the number of Chinese tourists increases, operating income and revenues from tourism and hospitality industry will boost too. However, as our fieldwork observations and interviews with local stakeholders in October 2019 indicate, growing share of Chinese tourism in the Russian Far East is out of reach of taxation, legal control, public regulation, and licensing, and thus it generates only a small economic impact on local businesses and communities.

The vast majority of Chinese tourists come to Russia in organized groups, which exempts them from obtaining individual visas at consulates.[3] Local entrepreneurs complain that, except buying Russian chocolate and vodka in local supermarkets, these holidaymakers spend their money in China. Coming to Vladivostok for a short vacation, they travel to and around the city on a Chinese bus with a Chinese driver and a Chinese guide, stay in a Chinese-owned hotel prepaid in China, and eat at Chinese-owned restaurants with their meals often being a part of the package they bought in China too. Primorye's residents blame the federal and regional authorities for the weak regulatory framework and non-existent licensing requirements for tourist guides, tour managers, interpreters, and other professionals involved in the tourist industry. As one of the prominent regional business owners emphasizes, "we need to squeeze the Chinese out of the tourist sector and start earning ourselves, and to do so we need a comprehensive licensing system like Thailand and Italy" (Interview, 06.11.2019).

Another issue is the reasons that attract Chinese tourists to the Russian Far East. Some Russian officials and representatives of the tourist industry hope that the Russian Far East will attract Chinese communist heritage tourists[4] and environmental tourists, which, in turn, will bring revenues to regional museums, culture centers, and recreation facilities (RG 2017, Primorsky.ru 2017). The case of Primorye, nevertheless, proves that the majority of Chinese holidaymakers are not interested in the Soviet historical sites or unique natural beauties. Vladivostok that became the epicenter for Chinese tourism in the Russian Far East does not have any landmarks of the Great October Socialist Revolution and is not the birthplace of a popular proletarian leader. It is not a prominent sight for eco-tourism either. Vladivostok's growing popularity among the Chinese is explained by market rationales. These tourists cannot afford a trip to Paris or Rome and settle for an exotic taste of Europe in just a few hours by bus from their hometowns in Jilin and Heilongjiang.

As the Russian ruble lost more than 50% of its value against the US dollar in the aftermath of the Ukrainian crisis, the "zero-fare" group tours to Vladivostok are

---

[3] In 2018, the Russian government simplified the procedure, reducing the minimum group size to three people and increasing the duration of the stay to 21 days. Chinese citizens are also eligible for electronic visas for visiting the territory of the special investment regime Free port Vladivostok.

[4] Also referred to as "red tourism," see Li et al. (2010) and Gao and Guo (2017).

becoming increasingly popular among Chinese tourists. The "zero-fare" group tours are a peculiar phenomenon in China's rapidly developing tourist market (Chen et al., 2011). These tours are cheaply packaged and heavily skewed towards shopping. Tourists usually pay a minimal fee that often barely covers the full cost of their travel, while travel agencies arrange tourist shopping at designated outlets and receive generous commissions from them to pay for tour operations and profits. Even though China's first tourism law explicitly banned "zero-fare" tours in 2013 (Tourism Law of the PRC, 2017, Article 35), shopping-subsidized tours to Vladivostok are still available and widely advertised online. As a result, crowds of Chinese tourists come to Vladivostok to buy cheap chocolate, premium alcohol, luxury perfume, jewelry, or even the most earthly goods such as flour and sunflower oil. They strop by the major historical landmarks advertised in the brochures of travel agencies to take a couple of pictures and rarely visit local museums or engage in other cultural activities.

Although there are significantly fewer Korean tourists in Vladivostok, they are more visible. Local businesses put signs and provide services in the Korean language, Korean restaurants are occupying the best locations downtown, and local tourism companies advertise Korean-speaking guides. Unlike Chinese tourists, most Koreans come to Vladivostok not in groups but individually using the new visa options (Kim & Kim, 2020). Not being controlled and restricted by inbound tour operators, they book accommodations via international hospitality websites, such as Booking.com and Airbnb.com, and spend money in local coffee shops and restaurants. While it is too early to assess the economic effect of the growing inbound tourism flow from Korea, it is already clear that holidaymakers from Korea are more welcomed in Vladivostok than those from China. As the local experts point out, "Koreans get an inexpensive and interesting vacation just two hours from Seoul, while Vladivostok residents gain access to a developed air traffic network and a service industry boom" (Zuenko, 2018).

11.5.4 The Myth of Chinese Takeover of the Russian Far East

As Russia's relations with the West rapidly deteriorated in the mid-2010s, China became the closest thing to a strategic ally for Russia. Against this backdrop, Russian representatives in one voice proclaimed that the relations between the two states are at their peak and are more developed than at any time in their long and turbulent history. The majority of the Russian public supports this official thesis, clearly identifying China as one of Russia's best friends. According to Sinophone Borderlands Europe Survey,[5] almost 59.5% of respondents have positive attitudes towards China, and 31% claim that their sentiments towards China improved over the past decade. In comparative terms, China scores as favorably as Germany (57.9%) and France (56.1%) and significantly overtakes in popularity the United States (36.3%) and the

---

[5] The survey was supported by the European Regional Development Fund Project "Sinophone Borderlands - Interaction at the Edges," CZ.02.1.01/0.0/0.0/16_019/000079.

United Kingdom (45.7%). Russians see China as a rising power with a strong military and sound economy and find it culturally attractive. The vast majority of respondents believe that China is important for Russia's development (76.5%), support trade with China (73.3%), and welcome Chinese investment (59.1%). Surveys conducted in Russia's Pacific regions in 2017 show the attitudes of local residents are in line with the national trends, and, as the authors highlight comparing the 2017 survey data with previous studies, the number of respondents with a positive attitude towards China has been growing consistently since the mid-1990s (Larin & Larina, 2018: 12). However, the results of these surveys might be misleading and should be taken with a grain of salt. Popular attitudes towards China to a large extent depend on perceptions of Russia's relations with the West and ultimately on perceptions of Russia's greatpowerness.

After the annexation of Crimea and the war in Ukraine, Russian media has started to portray the West—personified mainly by the United States and Western Europe—as Russia's adversary, seeking to prevent it from rebuilding its greatpowerness (Tolz & Teper, 2018: 219–220). On the contrary, the media presents China as Russia's friend and essential partner (Kuteleva & Vasiliev, 2020: 16–18). Anna Efimova and Denis Strebkov's (2020: 106) research shows that swings in public opinion correlate with shifts in the media coverage: "The worse the people's attitudes towards the US, the EU and Ukraine, the better they were towards China, and vice versa." Studying opinions of students at a major university in Russia known for its liberal stance, Joanna Szostek (2018: 70) came to the paradoxical conclusion that these students "expressed both distrust and/or distaste towards Russian state television" but "spontaneously reproduced the overarching narrative which Russian state television conveys regarding the causes and optimal solutions of East–West discord."

In this context, it is unsurprising that overall favorable attitudes towards China coincide with the anxiety over Chinese presence in Russia's eastern frontier.[6] According to the Sinophone survey, many respondents believe that China laid eyes on the Russian Far Eastern arable lands (47.1%) and vast natural resources (39.3%). Despite the support for trade with China and Chinese investment, more than half of respondents (56.8%) think that Chinese businesses operating in the Russian Far East pose a threat to the local environment. Importantly, a substantial number of respondents assume that China has plans to annex Russian territories in the medium future (37%) and believe that the Chinese represent a significant part of the population in the Russian Far East (36.6%). Similarly, Victor Larin and Liliia Larina (2018: 20–21) argue that more than half of Primorye's residents believe that China threatens their region and, especially, its territorial integrity and economic independence. They

---

[6] In Russian geopolitical imagination, China is the opposite of Russia. However, the Russians focus on China's demographic and socio-cultural features and are less concerned with ideological and political differences. According to the Sinophone Survey, when asked about their first associations with China, Russians most often answer that it is a country with a large population. Respondents from countries with a strong Russian population—Latvia, Serbia, and Slovakia—give similar answers, whereas the most popular answer for residents of Western and Central European countries was COVID-19, while the large population featured only after dictatorship and communism.

are suspicious of Chinese investment in the region, seeing them as an unwelcomed competition (Larin & Larina, 2018: 18).

The regional authorities' attitudes towards China are no less controversial. As our analysis above shows, the metropole excludes regional elites from development decision-making and limits their opportunities to influence Sino-Russian relations. Nevertheless, seeking to integrate themselves into Moscow's hegemonic discourse, the regional authorities reiterate Putin's welcoming messages to Chinese neighbors. The quest for generous Chinese investors ready to fund the modernization of the Russian Far East has been a political obsession for Primorye's governors throughout the 2000s and the 2010s. However, the local authorities can invite foreign investors only to the sectors unclaimed by Russian state-owned companies affiliated with Moscow. Consequently, projects they propose to the Chinese are often unprofitable or difficult (and even outright impossible) to accomplish, because of the scarce population, poor infrastructure, high transport costs, or deficient public services. As a result, Chinese private entrepreneurs are hesitant to reach out for a partnership with their Russian neighbors, lacking in incentives and success stories.

Nonetheless, for many locals informal and often illegal business with the Chinese is the only means of survival. While Moscow tries to restrict and regulate the "grey" cross-border economy, the local authorities often accept it as a necessary evil and even themselves engage in semi-formal cooperation with the Chinese. Almost all districts of Primorye struggle with budget deficits and receive substantial subsidies from the federal authorities. Mayors of declining frontier towns confess that they would host a military base or two as they used to back in the Soviet times rather than engage with a bunch of Chinese agriculture entrepreneurs (Interview, a local official, Primorye, 28.07.2014). The reason of such nostalgia for the Soviet militarization is a programmatic rational. District authorities value military personnel as domestic state-affiliated taxpayers. They also lack experience of working with private investors but find themselves at the front line of the cross-border economy. They lease available municipal land plots and properties, oversee environmental law enforcement, and control many other aspects of the local business environment. In the Russian context, these administrative functions convert into leverage on entrepreneurs. For example, the local authorities can organize different types of audits for unaccommodating business owners (Yukhanaev et al., 2015: 329–330). In all seven districts of Primorye that we surveyed between 2014 and 2019, each and every company with Chinese capital (co)funds various social programs or cultural events. Such compulsory social responsibilities of business range from providing financial support to local sports teams and celebrations of national holidays to paying for road repair and social infrastructure. As a case in point, Chinese entrepreneurs paid for the construction of a health care center in the Mikhalovsky district, which the local authorities were tasked to build after Putin's annual Direct Line press conference in 2014 (Interview, Primorye, 01.08.2014).

11.6 Conclusions

China's rapid and powerful rise accentuates Russia's precarious position on the border between the Global South and the Global North and stirs up Russia's internal identity conflict about its own status on the international stage. Defining Russia vis-à-vis a rising China, Putin's regime actualizes imperial discourses and practices, seeking to centralize resources to disassociate itself from the Global South and re-emphasize Russia's greatpowerness. Despite official proclamations of enduring Sino-Russian friendship, the Russian state feels vulnerable. Having lost its "external periphery" in Eastern Europe, Central Asia, and the Caucasus following the collapse of the Soviet Union, the state became anxious about the future of its internalized colonies in the Russian Far East. Hence, the state follows the logic of the "imperial prerogative" and securitizes its eastern borderlands.

The central authorities recognize that the Russian Far East faces serious development problems and try to stimulate its economic recovery by welcoming FDI. However, they are not ready to deregulate and liberalize regional development and, specifically, the cooperation across the Sino-Russian border. Moscow treats the Russian Far East as Russia's internal raw-material base. Statist rent-seeking policies slow down the development of borderland provinces, whereas corruption and malfeasance sustained by these policies further hinder local economic modernization and diminish the region's chances to integrate into the Asia Pacific economy. Against this backdrop, Moscow limits engagements with China to state-to-state contacts centered on energy exports. Since the mid-2000s, one of the key principles of Putin's policy has been that the Russian Far East can only benefit from China's rise if its interactions with China are managed by Moscow. The Russian Far East in this framework is merely a transit zone but not a willing, reflexive, and active agent of Russia's pivot to China.

Putin's "turn to the East" supports positive readings of the expanding Sino-Russian cooperation, presenting it as one of the paths to secure Moscow's developmental agenda in the eastern frontier and, ultimately, enhance Russia's greatpowerness. Russia is an imperial power in its own right, yet its official discourses are essentially similar to anti-colonial discourses that produce positive representations of Chinese FDI in Papua New Guinea, Trinidad and Tobago, and other formerly colonized states of the Global South (see for Xiang's, Szadziewski's, and Tudoroiu and Ramlogan's chapters in this volume). Russian leaders portray China as a partner and an ally in the struggle against the Western hegemony. However, these official discourses of Sino-Russian friendship contradict the reality, which is particularly obvious on the regional level. As the case of Primorye vividly shows, Putin's "turn to the East" promotes political rapprochement between Moscow and Beijing but does not facilitate establishing harmonious relations between communities along the Sino-Russian border and hardly benefit local economies. The balk of investment comes to the province from Moscow through state-owned companies, whereas opportunities for Chinese and Russian private entrepreneurs to launch join ventures are few. Despite the government's attempts to influence the dynamic of bilateral trade between the

Primorye and China, it still follows the patterns established in the early 1990s: the Russian sides sells commodities, whereas the Chinese export switch from labor-intensive to capital-intensive products. The locals are missing out on the opportunity to cash in on the "turn to the East" because protectionism is bizarrely juxtaposed with a lack of regulation. As the case in point, the state fiercely protects the forestry sector, limiting legal opportunities for productive cooperation between the Russians and the Chinese. In contrast, the development of the tourist sector and more broadly service industries connotes poorly with Moscow's great power logic and thus receives little, if any, attention from the authorities. As a result, the money of Chinese visitors to Primorye stays in China. Driven by the great power ambitions, Moscow rhetorically shifts the focus of the regional development from trade and resource extraction to industrialization, expecting local entrepreneurs and Chinese investors to animate an export-led growth model. Yet, such articulations of development priorities create a three-fold contradiction. Firstly, exercising its "imperial prerogative," Moscow transfers regional resources to almighty state monopolies, which ensures their domination in the regional economy and subsequently preserves the rigid and centralized economic order. Secondly, transport bottlenecks, high costs of electricity, and the low demand for Russian consumer goods in Asia make manufacturing in Primorye unprofitable, and thus many local entrepreneurs envision Primorye as a trade hub rather than an industrial center. Thirdly, Chinese entrepreneurs, just like their Russian counterparts are hesitant to invest in the industrial sector of the Russian Far East. The local political elites reiterate the official narrative of the strong Sino-Russian bond but, lacking the agency in economic decision-making, can only welcome Chinese investors to the least profitable industrial sectors and thus are still forced to rely mainly on subsidies from the center.

In sum, the Russian state reluctantly opens up its Russian Far Eastern provinces for interactions with Chinese neighbors. As the case of Primorye shows, the cooperation along the Sino-Russian border is a result of Russia's response to China's rise and a crisis in Russia's relations with the West rather than a strategic choice based on regional development aspirations. Russia's inconsistent attitudes towards China reveal the fragile foundation of Sino-Russian friendship as well as complex internal identity contradictions that prevent the Russian state from fully embracing the opportunities China's rise might offer for the development of its eastern frontier.

Acknowledgements We wish to thank Iacopo Adda (Université de Genève) who took the time to read our first draft and gave many helpful suggestions for its improvements. Our work was supported by the National Research University Higher School of Economics (Moscow) and the European Regional Development Fund Project "Sinophone Borderlands - Interaction at the Edges," CZ.02.1.01/0.0/0.0/16_019/0000791.

References

Adda, I. (2014). *L'Extrême-Orient russe: un acteur central dans le glissement de la Fédération de Russie à l'Est* (Doctoral dissertation, University of Geneva).

Adda, I. (2020). Sino-Russian relations through the lens of Russian border history museums: The Nerchinsk treaty and its problematic representations. *Eurasian Geography and Economics, 62*, 1–25.

Alexseev, M. A., & Troyakova, T. (1999). Watching out for regional separatism in the Russian Far East: Ideological cueing of territorial security, economic incentives and cultural identity. *Geopolitics, 4*(3), 120–144.

Baeg, I. H., & So, S. H. (2013). The world ginseng market and the ginseng (Korea). *Journal of Ginseng Research, 37*(1), 1.

Bassin, M. (1991). Inventing Siberia: Visions of the Russian East in the early nineteenth century. *The American Historical Review, 96*(3), 763–794.

Bassin, M. (1997). History and philosophy of geography. *Progress in Human Geography, 21*(4), 563–572.

Bliakher, L. (2014). *Iskusstvo nepravlyayemoy zhizni: Dal'niy Vostok [The Art of Uncontrollable Life: The Far East]*. Izdatel'stvo Evropa.

Bogaturov, A. (2004). Rossiyskiy Dal'niy Vostok v novykh geoprostranstvennykh izmereniyakh Vostochnoy Yevrazii [Russian Far East in the new geospatial dimensions of Eastern Eurasia]. *Mirovaya ekonomika i mezhdunarodnyye otnosheniya,* (10), 90–98.

Bystritsky, S. P., & Zausaev, V. K. (2007). *Rossiya–Severo Vostochnaya Aziya. Dal'nevostochnyy ekonomicheskiy most na rubezhe epokh [Russia–North East Asia. The Far Eastern economic bridge at the turn of eras]*. The Gaidar Institute for Economic Policy.

Chatterjee, P. (2005). Empire and nation revisited: 50 years after Bandung. *Inter-Asia Cultural Studies, 6*(4), 487–496.

Chen, Y., Barry, M., & Guo, Y. (2011). 中国 "零团费" 旅游: 事实表述与分析框架. ["Zero-Fare" group tours in China: An analytic framework] *Journal of China Tourism Research 7*(11), 425–444.

Cotton, J. (1996). China and Tumen River cooperation: Jilin's coastal development strategy. *Asian Survey, 36*(11), 1086–1101.

Curanović, A. (2012). Why don't Russians fear the Chinese? The Chinese factor in the self-identification process of Russia. *Nationalities Papers, 40*(2), 221–239.

Dirlik, A. (1996). The global in the local. In R. Wilson & W. Dissanayake (Eds.), *Global/local: Cultural production and the transnational imaginary* (pp. 21–45). Duke University Press.

Dirlik, A. (2007). Global South: Predicament and promise. *The Global South, 1*(1), 12–23.

Dyatlov, V. (2012). Chinese migrants and anti-Chinese sentiments in Russian society. In F. Billé, G. Delaplace, & C. Humphrey (Eds.), *Frontier encounters* (pp. 71–88). Open Book Publishers.

Efimova, A., & Strebkov, D. (2020). Linking public opinion and foreign policy in Russia. *The International Spectator, 55*(1), 93–111.

Ermarth, F. (1969). The Soviet Union in the third world: Purpose in search of power. *The Annals of the American Academy of Political and Social Science, 386*(1), 31–40.

Fisman, R., & Wei, S. J. (2004). Tax rates and tax evasion: Evidence from "missing imports" in China. *Journal of Political Economy, 112*(2), 471–496.

Forest Trends. (2017, August 2). *China's forest product imports and exports 2006–2016: Trade charts and brief analysis.* https://www.forest-trends.org/publications/chinas-forest-product-imports-exports-2006-2016/

Gao, Z., & Guo, X. (2017). Consuming revolution: The politics of red tourism in China. *Journal of Macromarketing, 37*(3), 240–254.

Hansen, L. (2006). *Security as practice: Discourse analysis and the Bosnian war*. Routledge.

Holzlehner, T. (2018). Economies of trust: Informality and the state in the Russian-Chinese borderland. In C. Humphrey (Ed.), *Trust and mistrust in the economies of the China-Russia borderlands* (pp. 65–86). Amsterdam University Press.

Hopf, T. (1998). The promise of constructivism in international relations theory. *International Security, 23*(1), 171–200.

Hopf, T. (2002). *Social construction of international politics: Identities and foreign policies, Moscow, 1955 and 1999*. Cornell University Press.

Iwashita, A. (2004). *A 4,000 kilometer journey along the Sino-Russian border*. Hokkaido University.

Jia, F., & Bennett, M. M. (2018). Chinese infrastructure diplomacy in Russia: The geopolitics of project type, location, and scale. *Eurasian Geography and Economics, 59*(3–4), 340–377.

Kaczmarski, M. (2019). Convergence or divergence? Visions of world order and the Russian-Chinese relationship. *European Politics and Society, 20*(2), 207–224.

Kar, D., & Freitas, S. (2013). *Russia: Illicit financial flows and the role of the underground economy*. Global Financial Integrity, 13 February 2012. https://gfintegrity.org/report/country-case-study-russia/

Kim, B., & Kim, J. (2020). The rise of a new tourism destination: How did Vladivostok become the closest Europe for Korean tourists? *Journal of Eurasian Studies, 11*(2), 117–132.

Korolev, A., & Portyakov, V. (2019). Reluctant allies: System-unit dynamics and China-Russia relations. *International Relations, 33*(1), 40–66.

Kremlin.ru. (2002a). *Speech at a meeting on the social and economic development of the far eastern federal district*. President of Russia. http://kremlin.ru/events/president/transcripts/21694

Kremlin.ru. (2002b). *Speech at a meeting on the social and economic development of the far eastern federal district*. President of Russia. http://kremlin.ru/events/president/transcripts/21694

Kremlin.ru. (2003). *Excerpts from the president's live television and radio dialogue with the nation*. President of Russia. http://kremlin.ru/events/president/transcripts/22256

Kremlin.ru. (2007). *Transcript of press conference with the Russian and foreign media*. President of Russia. http://kremlin.ru/events/president/transcripts/24026

Kremlin.ru. (2013). *Presidential address to the Federal Assembly*. President of Russia. http://kremlin.ru/events/president/news/19825

Kremlin.ru. (2017). *Plenary session of the Eastern Economic Forum*. President of Russia. http://kremlin.ru/events/president/news/55552

Kuhrt, N. (2012). The Russian Far East in Russia's Asia policy: Dual integration or double periphery? *Europe-Asia Studies, 64*(3), 471–493.

Kuteleva, A., & Vasiliev, D. (2020). China's belt and road initiative in Russian media: Politics of narratives, images, and metaphors. *Eurasian Geography and Economics, 62*, 1–25.

Kuteleva, A. (2021). *China's energy security and relations with petrostates*. Roughtledge.

Kuteleva, A., Chernilevskaya, K., Salnikova, P., & Shevchuk, E. (2021). *Russia's actually (non-)existent neoliberalism: The development of the Russian Far East as discourse and practice*.

Larin, V. (2006). *V teni prosnuvshegosya drakona: rossiysko-kitayskiye otnosheniya na rubezhe XX-XXI vekov* [In the shadow of the Dragon awaken: The Russian-Chinese relations on the boundary of the 20th—21st centuries]. Dalnauka.

Larin, V. (2017). *Tikhookeanskaya Rossiya v integratsionnom nachale Severnoy Patsifiki v nachale XXI veka: opyt i potentsial regional'nogo i prigranichnogo vzaimodeystviya* [Integrating Pacific Russia into the North Pacific region: Experience and potential of regional and cross-border cooperation in the beginning of 21st century]. IHAE FEB RAS.

Larin, V. L., & Larina, L. L. (2018). Kitay v obshchestvennom mnenii zhiteley Tikhookeanskoy Rossii (po itogam oprosa 2017 g.) [China in the public opinion of in Pacific Russia (the results of a survey in 2017)]. *Russia and Asia-Pacific, 2*(100), 5–33.

Lauruel, M. (2007). *La quête d'une identité impériale: Le néo-eurasisme dans la Russie contemporaine*. Petra.

Li, Y., Hu, Z. Y., & Zhang, C. Z. (2010). Red tourism: Sustaining communist identity in a rapidly changing China. *Journal of Tourism and Cultural Change, 8*(1–2), 101–119.

López, A. J. (2007). Introduction: The (post) global south. *The Global South, 1*, 1–11.

Morozov, V. (2015). *Russia's postcolonial identity: A subaltern empire in a Eurocentric world*. Springer.

Mignolo, W. D. (2011). The Global South and world dis/order. *Journal of Anthropological Research, 67*(2), 165–188.

Miquelle, D. G., Goodrich, J. M., Smirnov, E. N., Stephens, P. A., Zaumyslova, O. Y., Chapron, G., Kerley, L. L., Murzin, A. A., Hornocker, M. G., & Quigley, H. B. (2010). The Amur tiger: A case study of living on the edge. In D. Macdonald & A. Loveridge (Eds.), *Biology and conservation of wild felids* (pp. 325–339). Oxford University Press.

Morgenstern, O. (1963). *On the accuracy of economic observations*. Princeton University Press.

Neumann, I. B. (2016). *Russia and the idea of Europe: A study in identity and international relations*. Taylor & Francis.

Newell, J. P., & Simeone, J. (2014). Russia's forests in a global economy: How consumption drives environmental change. *Eurasian Geography and Economics, 55*(1), 37–70.

O'Loughlin, J., & Talbot, P. F. (2005). Where in the world is Russia? Geopolitical perceptions and preferences of ordinary Russians. *Eurasian Geography and Economics, 46*(1), 23–50.

Pan, X. (2015). China's approach to China-Russia cooperation in the development of Russia's Far East and Siberia. In J. Huang & A. Korolev (Eds.), *International cooperation in the development of Russia's Far East and Siberia* (pp. 99–122). Palgrave Macmillan.

Putin, V. (2012, September 6). An Asia-Pacific growth agenda. *Wall Street Journal*. https://online.wsj.com/article/SB10000872396390443847404577629312716242648.html

Ryzhova, N. (2018). Invisible trade: Sovereign decisions on the Sino-Russian border. In A. Horstmann, M. Saxer, & A. Rippa (Eds.), *Routledge handbook of Asian borderlands* (pp. 334–344). Routledge.

Savchenko, A. E., & Zuenko, I. Yu. (2020). Dvizhushchiye sily rossiyskogo povorota na Vostok [The driving forces of Russia's pivot to the East]. *Comparative Politics, 11*(1), 111–125.

Sablin, I. (2018). *The rise and fall of Russia's far eastern republic, 1905–1922: Nationalisms, imperialisms, and regionalisms in and after the Russian empire*. Routledge.

Sablin, I., & Sukhan, D. (2018). Regionalisms and imperialisms in the making of the Russian Far East, 1903–1926. *Slavic Review, 77*(2), 333–357.

Stern, D. (2015). 'Nado Minimum!': Mediating respectability at informal markets on the Russian-Chinese border. *Inner Asia, 17*(1), 5–30.

Szostek, J. (2018). News media repertoires and strategic narrative reception: A paradox of dis/belief in authoritarian Russia. *New Media & Society, 20*(1), 68–87.

Tlostanova, M. (2008). The Janus-faced empire distorting orientalist discourses: Gender, race and religion in the Russian/(post) Soviet constructions of the 'Orient.' *Worlds and Knowledges Otherwise, 2*(2), 1–11.

Tolz, V., & Teper, Y. (2018). Broadcasting agitainment: A new media strategy of Putin's third presidency. *Post-Soviet Affairs, 34*(4), 213–227.

Tsygankov, A. P. (2018). The sources of Russia's fear of NATO. *Communist and Post-Communist Studies, 51*(2), 101–111.

Urbansky, S. (2020). *Beyond the steppe frontier: A history of the Sino-Russian border*. Princeton University Press.

Urnov, M. (2014). 'Greatpowerness' as the key element of Russian self-consciousness under erosion. *Communist and Post-Communist Studies, 47*(3–4), 305–322.

Voskresenski, A. D. (2015). Rossiysko-kitayskiye otnosheniya v kontekste aziatskogo vektora rossiyskoy diplomatii (1990–2015) [Russian-Chinese relations in the context of the Asian vector of Russian diplomacy (1990–2015)]. *Sravnitel'naya Politika/comparative Policy, 1*(18), 32–52.

Wilson, J. L. (2019). Russia's relationship with China: The role of domestic and ideational factors. *International Politics, 56*(6), 778–794.

Wishnick, E. (2000). Chinese perspectives on cross-border relations. In S. Garnett (Ed.), *Rapprochement or rivalry? Russia-Chinese relations in a changing Asia* (pp. 227–256). Carnegie Endowment for International Peace.

Wishnick, E. (2017). In search of the 'Other' in Asia: Russia-China relations revisited. *The Pacific Review, 30*(1), 114–132.

Yukhanaev, A., Fallon, G., Baranchenko, Y., & Anisimova, A. (2015). An investigation into the formal institutional constraints that restrict entrepreneurship and SME growth in Russia. *Journal of East-West Business, 21*(4), 313–341.

Zaitsev, Yu. (2008). Kontrrazvedyvatel'nyye meropriyatiya po zashchite ob"yektov voyennoy infrastruktury na Dal'nem Vostoke SSSR (1930-ye gg.) [Counterintelligence measures to protect military infrastructure in the Far East of the USSR (1930s)]. *Russia and Asia-Pacific, 2*, 128–138.

Zayonchkovskaya, Z. (2005). Pered litsom immigratsii [In the face of immigration.] *Pro et Contra, 9*(3), 72–87.

Zhao, J., & Tang, J. (2018). Industrial structure change and economic growth: A China-Russia comparison. *China Economic Review, 47*, 219–233.

Zubarevich, N. (2016). Crises in post-Soviet Russia: Regional projection. *Regional Research of Russia, 6*(2), 96–104.

Zuenko, I., Ivanov, S., & Savchenko, A. (2019). Kitaiskie investitsii na rossiiskom Dal'nem Vostoke [Chinese Investment in the Russian Far East]. *Mirovaya ekonomika i mezhdunarodnye otnosheniya, 11*(63), 105–113.

Zuenko, I. (2018, March 28). The Yuan's Russian vacation: Why Chinese tourism barely benefits Russia's budget. *Carnegie Moscow.* https://carnegie.ru/commentary/75921

Anna Kuteleva is a post-doctoral research fellow at the School of International Regional Studies at the National Research University Higher School of Economics in Moscow. Anna received her PhD in Political Science from the University of Alberta (Canada) in 2019. Previously, she obtained a Master's degree in World Politics (Shandong University, 2010) and a Master's degree in Comparative Politics (Peoples' Friendship University of Russia, 2010). Her research is located in a broad constructivist tradition of IR and focuses on the nexus between politics and sociocultural contexts in international relations, with particular interests in politics of security and international energy politics.

Sergei Ivanov obtained his PhD in history at Irkutsk State University (Russia, Irkutsk). He began China research at the Institute of History, Archaeology and Ethnology (Russia, Vladivostok) and taught several courses on China and East Asia at Far Eastern Federal University. His research interests cover Chinese entrepreneurship in the Russian borderlands, Sino-Russian cross-border cooperation, and regional development strategies in East Asia. Sergei joined the Sinophone Borderlands project at Palacký University Olomouc in December 2019 to contribute to research on Chinese farming in the Russian Far East.

Part IV
Conclusion

Chapter 12
Normative Power China, Subnational Agency, and Structural Factors in the Global South

Theodor Tudoroiu

Abstract The concluding chapter constructs a unifying conceptual framework for China's multifaceted impact on the Global South illustrated by the contributions to this volume and uses it to analyze their findings. I explain the Chinese growing influence in the developing world as a projection of normative power that uses a specific set of norms to shape understandings of "what is normal" in accordance with Beijing's views and interests. However, this is not a one-way, unopposed action. Political elites in power do align their views—and their states' policies—with Chinese local, regional, and global interests. This is the consequence of a very effective process of Chinese international socialization based on normative suasion and role playing. But numerous other socio-economic groups in the target countries are not socialized and resist Beijing's actions that are detrimental to their own, independently constructed interests. Furthermore, cognitive and institutional structural factors in target countries may influence the acceptance or rejection of Chinese actions as much as the agency of subnational groups. The chapter's conclusion is that the future of the complex relationship between China and the countries of the Global South is open and local actors can influence it significantly.

Keywords China · Global South · Normative power · Subnational actors · Agency

12.1 Introduction

This final chapter constructs a unifying conceptual framework for China's multi-faceted impact on the Global South illustrated by the contributions to this volume and uses it to analyze their findings. The editors' intention in bringing together these very diverse topics was to show the impressively wide range of interactions between the Middle Kingdom and the developing world. From informal trade in Vladivostok to Spanish language TV programs in Argentina, Beijing impacts the Global South in so many ways that the multidisciplinary approach adopted in this volume was

T. Tudoroiu (✉)
The University of the West Indies, St. Augustine, Trinidad and Tobago
e-mail: theodor.tudoroiu@sta.uwi.edu

© The Author(s), under exclusive license to Springer Nature Singapore Pte Ltd. 2022   259
T. Tudoroiu and A. Kuteleva (eds.), *China in the Global South*,
https://doi.org/10.1007/978-981-19-1344-0_12

almost inevitable. From Development Studies to Anthropology, almost all fields of Social Sciences are concerned. Diversity, however, does not prevent coherence. The assertive leadership of President Xi was instrumental in the creation of a strategy supported by a vast institutional mechanism that explains the impressive success of China's Global South enterprise. Its best illustration may be the positive reception of the Belt and Road Initiative in the developing world and the southern and eastern peripheries of the European Union. Still, observers fail to reach an agreement on the exact nature of this strategy. Libraries have been written by economists to explain the geoeconomic logic of China's expansion. Their views are rejected by International Relations (IR) scholars and analysts who prefer to see a geopolitical construct. In this chapter, I argue that the Chinese presence in the Global South represents a projection of normative power; the geoeconomic and geopolitical dimensions are hardly negligible, but they represent only its consequences. Equally important, Beijing's efforts to shape understandings of "what is normal" internationally in accordance with its views and interests do not represent a one-way, unopposed action. Target states are not turned into passive recipients of Chinese norms, which are internalized and uncritically followed. This internalization does happen, but only in the case of specific subnational groups that prominently include political elites in power. Case studies in this volume typically show such elites aligning their views—and their states' policies—with Chinese local, regional, and global interests. This alignment is the effect of a very effective process of international socialization based on normative suasion and role playing. Numerous other socio-economic groups in the target country, however, are not socialized and resist Beijing's actions that are detrimental to their own, independently constructed interests: civil society reactions against Chinese extraction enterprises in Papua New Guinea, for example, "can be viscerally negative" (see the chapter by Szadziewski in this volume). Overall, there is no uniform acceptance of China's influence. It is the goal of this book in general and this chapter in particular to emphasize the importance of agency that leads to very diverse perceptions and responses. Furthermore, both book and chapter do not ignore the structure-agency debate that has marked the development of the IR theory preferred by this volume's editors, Constructivism. Part III of this volume deals precisely with the influence of cognitive and institutional structural factors in target countries, which may influence the acceptance or rejection of China as much as the agency of subnational groups. Ultimately, it is the triangular interaction between Chinese normative power, local agency, and structural factors that I analyze in this chapter.

With respect to methodology, I acknowledge the fact that abundant literature exists that covers most of the issues dealt with in the following pages. However, I conceived this chapter as a conclusion to the present volume, not a standalone piece. Accordingly, whenever possible, I base my statements on the empirical information and analytical findings of previous chapters instead of using other sources. This approach also has the advantage of illuminating unexpected convergences between case studies that, at first view, may seem to have nothing in common. To repeat myself, diversity does not prevent coherence.

The chapter is structured as follows. The next section introduces the concept of normative power, presents the features of Normative Power China, and scrutinizes the Chinese socialization of political elites in the Global South. Section 12.2 presents the numerous negative reactions to the Chinese presence visible at subnational level and analyzes them as consequences of the weaknesses of China's persuasion efforts, subnational agency, and structural factors. The last section summarizes and further analyzes the chapter's findings.

12.2 Normative Power China as Socializer of Elites

12.2.1 Defining Normative Power

It was Ian Manners who introduced the concept of normative power in a 2001 paper and a seminal 2002 article (Manners, 2001, 2002), which triggered "a neo-normative turn in theorising the EU's international presence" (Whitman, 2013: 171). In his study of the European Union, this scholar defined normative power as the "ability to shape conceptions of normal" in world politics; this "is, ultimately, the greatest power of all" (Manners, 2002: 240, 253). By combining François Duchêne's "civilian power" with Johan Galtung's "ideological power" (Whitman, 2013: 172), Manners depicted Normative Power Europe "as a foreign policy actor intent on shaping, instilling, diffusing – and thus 'normalising' – rules and values in international affairs through noncoercive means" (Tocci, 2007: 1). Back in the early 1970s, Duchêne had already studied the adoption of "amilitary" values by the European Economic Community that was transforming this group of states into a new type of international actor. It exerted essentially civilian forms of power (Diez, 2005: 617) and "aim[ed] to 'civilize' international politics in the sense of making war a non-acceptable instrument" (Diez, 2013: 197). In his upgrading of the concept, Manners further argued that a normative power "binds itself to international norms, whether they are in its interest or not"; its impact "is not merely through non-military (mostly economic) means, but through the force of ideas" (ibid.). Because normative powers are able to "define what passes as 'normal' in world politics" (Persson, 2018: 194) based "on ideas and conscience" (Diez & Manners, 2007: 175), this type of power is different from and "greater" than relational or structural power (Manners, 2002: 253). As it concerns itself with the importance of norms, the "normative power argument has a distinctly social constructivist ring to it" (Diez, 2005: 616). Target states experience the "palpable constitutive effects" of normative power as their perceptions, attitudes, and identities change. Critically, states modify their behavior but "do not perceive to be following somebody else's goals, but their own" (Kavalski, 2014: 305). Normative power "in its ideal or purest form" is an ideational concept that should be totally separate from the use of material incentives or physical force (Manners, 2009: 2). However, the experience of normative powers shows that there is no such incompatibility. Often, economic incentives and even military capabilities underpin normative power (Diez, 2005: 616; Diez & Manners, 2007: 176). Different from the case of civilian power, military force can be used to spread normative values (Diez & Manners, 2007: 180). Similarly, it is difficult to clearly divide great powers into normative and non-normative ones. The first stage in the process of transformation into a normative power is to become a normative actor (which involves action trigger, policy processes/structures, and performance structures). But the final stage of normative power is reached only when the normative foreign policy of that actor effectively shapes its international environment (He, 2016: 93). Establishing *when* this happens is quite difficult due to the diversity and continuous evolution of actors' instruments and objectives, as well as the divergence of their normative understandings and interpretations. Therefore, "the issue is really less *whether* a nation is a 'normative power', but *the degree* to which it is one" (Hamilton, 2008: 77–78; emphasis in the original). Consequently, the number of generally acknowledged normative powers is surprisingly high. In addition to the European Union, there is the United States, which has used normative power to construct and maintain the present international order (Diez, 2005); but also China, Japan, India, Brazil, Russia, Turkey, and the ASEAN (Tudoroiu, 2022: 27). Interestingly, the patterns they follow in exercising normative power are very different. The European Union has adopted a model based on rules. That of China is relationship-based (see the next subsection). Japan centers its normative actions on responsiveness to the needs of its partners. India, on its old civilization. These differences are important, but in all cases "the expression of what is 'normal' invokes certain agenda and entails power relations" (Kavalski, 2014: 306, 324). As shown in the following sections, this applies fully to the case of China's projection of normative power in the Global South.

12.2.2 China's Relationality-Based Normative Power

Before scrutinizing the actual work of Normative Power China in the Global South, it is important to discuss the peculiar features of its normative power profile that "prioritize sociality, personalization, and reciprocity" (Kavalski, 2017: 155). China "understand[s] that a position of leadership cannot be inflicted upon others (by force or through domination), but needs to be earned (in the process of interaction)", which has led to the development of a specific type of normative power that emphasizes dialogue (Kavalski, 2014: 313). Beijing's international interactions are strongly marked by the "harmonious respect for the other" (Kavalski, 2018: 94). In practical terms, this "cardinal virtue" translates into "an intense and skilful diplomacy of respect" (Womack, 2008: 21). Small or large, weak or powerful, all states are the target of China's 'flattering diplomatic demarche' (Bernal, 2016: 3162). President Xi himself "lavishes attention on the[ir] leadership" (Womack, 2008: 21). "Instead of Western 'lessons' and criticism of bad governance and corruption, [these leaders] have their real or imaginary merits praised in eulogistic speeches that present their states as peers of the Middle Kingdom" (Tudoroiu and Ramlogan in this volume). Chinese leaders do not fail to travel to remote poor and tiny states or to offer red carpet treatment to their counterparts invited to Beijing (French, 2014: 10). The logic of appropriateness of the rule-based normative model of the European Union is replaced with a very different model that relies on practices of interaction and the logic of relationships. Instead of optimizing transactions, China optimizes relationships. Instead of using superior power to maximize benefits, it chooses to stabilize beneficial relations. Instead of bargaining, it tries to unilaterally accommodate the perceived needs of its partners. The Chinese norms presented in the next subsection are not defined as rights and obligations. Rather, they represent behavioral standards that partners accept in the process of interaction (Womack, 2008: 20–21; Kavalski, 2014: 313–314). Relevantly, a major Chinese IR author, Yaqing Qin, has created a theory of International Relations whose basic unit of analysis is represented by relations. Emphasizing the Confucian concept of relationality (*guanxi*), he even defined power as the ability to manage relations. Due to the complementary nature of rationality and relationality, this approach perceives international cooperation as based on the level of intimacy and importance of the relationship instead of self-interest calculations (Qin, 2016; Qin, 2018; Summers, 2019: 210; Demir, 2017: 98). Using this original form of normative power, Beijing is "altering the suspicion and bias from past interactions and opening up opportunities for new relationships", which benefit from "the affective feeling produced by the process of repeated interactions" (Kavalski, 2017: 154). Actors commit to the interaction while exercising self-restraint. In both cognitive and affective terms, ethical obligations mediate and shape action and agency: "the relational normativity of China's global outreach is embedded in the very practices through which ideas of sociality are shared" (ibid., 155). It should be added that *guanxi* is a Confucian-inspired "tradition of nuanced balancing of relationships within the family, society, the state, and the international community" (ibid., 151) that applies to many domains. Even "Chinese capitalism is guanxi capitalism" (Nyíri, 2005: 170). Relationality has the merit of committing actors of various social interactions to appropriately respond to social expectations and demands through the creation of networks associated with "the practice of unlimited exchange of favours and underpinned by reciprocal obligations, assurances, and mutuality" (Kavalski, 2017: 151). Yet, *guanxi* is hardly perfect. Unfortunately, it "implies both a propensity and a capacity for living *with* and *in* ambiguity". A "negative flavour of *guanxi* comes from its association with graft" (Kavalski, 2018: 91, 95). As discussed in Sect. 12.3, in the absence of EU-type rules, Chinese actions in the Global South ignore and, in many cases, are detrimental to the respect of the rule of law, financial responsibility, transparency, and openness. Often, the support of political elites in power is obtained through methods—such as the secretive negotiation of undisclosed government-to-government bilateral agreements on prestige infrastructure projects—that severely damage good governance. Moreover, Western social scientists have studied relationality outside China under the form of "social exchange" or "diffuse reciprocity" and, more generally, as related to the exchange of favors and gifts. They have come to the conclusion that such practices create vulnerability to exploitation. "Indebtedness engineering" is one of its forms of manifestation (Vuving, 2019: 224). Indeed, Chinese "debt-trap diplomacy" actions that resulted in the taking over of Sri Lanka's Hambantota port provide a good example of how *guanxi* can be very beneficial to China while resulting in clearly negative outcomes for its partners. Despite appearances, relationality does not necessarily bring harmony.

12.2.3   Chinese Norms

Any normative power has "a unique identity featured by a group of norms that it is committed to both domestically and internationally" (He, 2016: 94). The normative core is essential to both its identity and its interactions with and recognition by other states. Indeed, it is through the content of their norms that great powers acquire the legitimacy needed to be accepted as normative powers by other states (Kavalski, 2014: 303, 305, 308–309, 322). This subsection presents the particular set of norms that define China as a normative power in the Global South. It is important to note that these norms are not enforced in all of Beijing's external interactions. Shortly after assuming power, President Xi adopted the so-called "peripheral diplomacy". At the Work Forum on Peripheral Diplomacy in 2013 and the Central Conference on Foreign Affairs in 2014, he replaced the Western-centered foreign policy of his predecessors with a strong focus on "contact zones with less powerful actors" (Vangeli, 2019: 82). Since then, the Global South and the southern and eastern peripheries of the European Union have represented the main targets of China's external actions. This is well illustrated by the geography of the Belt and Road Initiative, which avoids strong and potentially dangerous actors such as the United States or the Franco-German axis. Accordingly, Beijing does not use the same set of norms when interacting with the developing world or Washington. This being a book about China in the Global South, I present in this chapter only the Chinese norms relevant to this region. Another important aspect is related to the relationality that defines China's normative power. Unlike the European Union, this is not a rule-based approach. Consequently, norms represent only instruments of order, not its embodiment (Paltiel, 2007: 236). Some of them are not even explicitly formulated: "they are implicitly present in its *guanxi* practice and have to be deduced from actual policies and actions" (Tudoroiu, 2022: 31). In fact, the explicit ones are limited to the Five Principles of Peaceful Coexistence first mentioned in the Sino-Indian treaty of 1954: "mutual respect for each other's territorial integrity and sovereignty; mutual non-aggression; mutual non-interference in each other's internal affairs; equality and cooperation for mutual benefit; and peaceful co-existence" (Panda, 2014). These norms define China's famous "win–win" cooperation formula and support its "altruism narrative" and "ideology of brotherhood" (see the chapter by Mock in this volume). They also legitimate "China as a builder of world peace, a contributor to global development, and an upholder of international order", to quote President Xi (see the chapter by Xiang in this volume). However, the Five Principles represent only a part of the norms that actually define Normative Power China in the Global South. Some implicit and more pragmatic ones have to be added. They include a general norm and three specialized normative subsets: political, economic, and social. The former is probably more important in cognitive than normative terms. It states that "cooperation with China needs to be established and developed as it is genuinely beneficial to the target country in general and its elites in particular" (Tudoroiu, 2021: 41). It significantly contributes to the process of Chinese socialization of political elites presented in the next subsection as it tries to convince them that "China's rise is inevitable; there are rich rewards for those who co-operate with it; resistance is futile" (*The Economist*, April 17, 2019). The political subset requires: (a) the diplomatic non-recognition of Taiwan; (b) the rejection of any contact with the Dalai Lama; (c) the non-criticism of China's lack of democracy and infringement of human rights; (d) the non-criticism of Beijing's repressive policies and practices in Tibet, Xinjiang, and Hong Kong; (e) support for China's position in international fora that debate these issues; and (f) a Chinese-friendly attitude in international and multilateral institutions, conferences, and public debates (Tudoroiu, 2021: 41). The economic normative subset is intended to support the activities of Chinese firms in the developing world. Its norms state that a) the activity of Chinese firms should encounter no obstacle; b) a political, economic, legal, and informal framework of interaction as favorable as possible to these firms should be set up with the assistance of the target country's government; and c) whenever possible, a business pattern should be adopted that circumvents traditional bidding processes, which are to be replaced with government-to-government agreements (ibid., 42). It should be added that the latter agreements are often secretively negotiated while their text is not made public (see the chapter by Tudoroiu and Ramlogan in this volume). The last, social normative subset contains only one norm that prevents governments in the Global South from regulating the inflow or economic activities of Chinese entrepreneurial migrants (ibid., 43). As explained by Fred Mutesa, a former Zambian finance minister,

> whenever his government sent delegations to Beijing for talks, in at least one session they would be leaned upon to maintain relaxed immigration policies toward Chinese. The language, he said, wasn't particularly subtle either; something along the lines of: We are making so many friendly gestures to your country, building roads and stadiums, etc. We would consider it a friendly gesture if you did not enforce such strict immigration controls on our citizens. (French, 2014: 83)

In certain countries or regions (the Commonwealth Caribbean is a good example), some or all of the three normative subsets have been turned into actual conditionalities (Tudoroiu, 2020). More importantly, the entire normative set is used in China's projection of normative power in the Global South. Its most visible and effective form of manifestation, the process of socialization of political elites in power, is presented in the next subsection.

12.2.4 The Chinese Socialization of Political Elites

As already mentioned, case studies in this volume typically show Global South political elites in power as enthusiastic supporters of the Chinese presence in their countries. Often, this is contrasted with the negative perception of other socio-economic groups, which point to the detrimental impact of this presence. Political elites choose to see the "win–win" side of the relationship with the Asian rising partner for a very good reason: they have been socialized by China, which deeply affects the way they construct their interests individually and as a group. In theoretical terms, international socialization is a "process by which principled ideas held by individuals [or agents] become norms in the sense of collective understandings about appropriate behaviour which then lead to changes in identities, interests and behaviour" (Park, 2014: 337; see Risse et al., 1999: 11; Checkel, 1999: 548; Johnston, 2001: 494). Through social interaction, normative understandings are internalized and lead to new definitions of interest, which are independent of external material constraints (Johnston, 2003: 108). Importantly, identity—which can be defined as relatively stable, role-specific understandings and expectations about self that represent "a property of international actors that generates motivational and behavioral dispositions" (Wendt, 1999/2003: 224; Flockhart, 2006: 94–97)—changes, too. Furthermore, new identities of actors can result in interactions conducive to a different Wendtian 'culture' of international anarchy. Various processes of international socialization have been studied. They include socialization by hegemons (Ikenberry & Kupchan, 1990) or by great powers such as the Soviet Union and Russia (Tudoroiu, 2015). Two different types of international socialization target the political elites and the society, respectively (for a discussion see Tudoroiu, 2021: 24–36; Tudoroiu, 2022: 49–52). The former are defined as "individuals and small, relatively cohesive and stable groups with disproportionate decisional power to affect … national outcomes" (Körösényi, 2018: 41; Higley, 2018: 27; Best & Higley, 2018). They have the significant advantage of controlling the state, which allows them to align its policies with the norms they internalize and, consequently, with the interests of the socializer. "Socializing the elites also means socializing the state" (Tudoroiu, 2021: 8). Moreover, the socialized elites act as norms entrepreneurs conveying norms learned from the external socializer to the local society. They institutionalize these norms, which eventually influence the entire population. China prefers this top-down "elite learning" strategy to the more difficult "upward mobilization from the masses, a bottom-up change in attitudes from individuals, citizens, and civil society" (ibid., 24). Moreover, Beijing is satisfied with the socialization of the political elites in power and shows little interest in extending the reach of this process to all elites or the society. This is due to the fact that governing politicians and top bureaucrats control or influence key state institutions and political parties. Their support is therefore sufficient for the adoption of China-friendly policies required by the leadership in Beijing. The latter is also satisfied with a limited degree of socialization. Various scholars have proposed up to four such degrees (Park, 2014: 340; Risse et al., 1999; Wendt, 1999/2003), but—at least in my opinion—Jeffrey Checkel's two-stage model remains the reference. His Type I, role playing socialization refers to material rewards that incentivize targets to learn a role. They can disagree with this role, but in order to get material benefits, they do act in accordance with expectations associated with it. In the case of Type II socialization, material incentives become irrelevant. This is a more advanced process where targets accept new norms as the right thing to do. Instrumental calculation is replaced by the "taken for granted" logic of appropriateness (Checkel, 2005: 804). Of course, reaching Type II socialization takes time and is much more difficult. Doing it on the scale of the entire Global South would represent a Herculean task. Consequently, China has adopted a low-cost strategy limited to the Type I socialization of political elites in power. In special cases such as the Commonwealth Caribbean, Type II socialization is contemplated, at least in the long run (Tudoroiu, 2020; Tudoroiu & Ramlogan, 2019). But efforts to achieve it are seldom justified, and this is equally true when the socialization of the entire society is concerned. The successful Type I socialization of political elites in power has been sufficient for turning China into a close partner of most states in the developing world. It is through this process of socialization that Beijing projects its normative power. The Chinese norms presented in the previous subsection are not fully internalized by target elites because only Type I, role playing socialization is achieved. But these elites do learn to behave as if they had internalized the norms. In practical terms, the difference is not that important.

The Chinese socialization is the result of two mechanisms. On the one hand, there is the micro-process of persuasion that pertains to the process of normative suasion. The latter "involves changing attitudes without use of either material or mental coercion" (Flockhart, 2006: 97) and has a constitutive effect: it is able to modify both the interests and the identity of the socializee (Acharya, 2011: 2). Through ongoing, iterative interactions, the micro-process of persuasion ensures norm-consistent behavior without coercion (Flockhart, 2006: 97; Johnston, 2001: 499; Park, 2014: 338). Global South political elites have to be convinced that China's norms are right and should influence their own behavior. Once this happens, "new courses of action [will be] viewed as entirely reasonable and appropriate" (Johnston, 2003: 113–115; 2008: 25). Chinese persuasion is at work during the numerous meetings and visits organized by Beijing that allow for interpersonal interactions between Global South political elites, on the one side, and officials, diplomats, and various agents of the Chinese state and state-owned enterprises, on the other. Secret diplomacy—typically represented by the secretive negotiation of government-to-government agreements on infrastructure projects (see the chapter by Tudoroiu and Ramlogan in this volume)—is extremely effective (Terhalle, 2011: 353). As part of the "logic of relationships" associated with Chinese relationality, "China's flattering diplomatic demarche" that appeals to the "variable of vanity" is particularly important: it allows politicians from peripheral countries "for a fleeting moment to live the illusion of respect" (Bernal, 2016: 3162, 3230–3241). During his first year in power, President Xi visited Port of Spain, the tiny capital of a nation numbering less than 1.4 million people. Eventually, all Trinidadian Prime Ministers were his honored guests in Beijing (Tudoroiu and Ramlogan in this volume). The effect of this "diplomacy of respect" is enhanced by the South-South solidarity discourse that frames the relationship between China and developing countries in terms of partnership, friendship, brotherhood, sameness, and common victimization and marginalization at the hands of hostile Western powers (see the chapter by Mock in this volume). This *guanxi* strategy is indeed conceived to prioritize relationships instead of transactions, and contributes to the preception of China as a harmony-seeking, benevolent socializer (Kavalski, 2014: 313–314; Womack, 2008: 20–21). Various propaganda means are also employed all over the Global South to "tell stories about China well", in President Xi's words.

The "dramatic internationalization" of China's outbound media—which includes the creation of the media center in Nairobi and the Spanish language TV channel of CGTN (see the chapters by Xiang and Morales in this volume)—contributes to China's persuasion efforts through the intended creation of a common "weltanschauung legitimated within speeches, newspaper editorials, magazines, and advertisements" (Mock in this volume). This strategy "seeks to improve [China's] international image, shape perceptions around the globe and ultimately create positive public sentiment in its advantage" (Morales in this volume). Such actions may target a general audience, but the use of "carefully curated images of the PRC" created for Global South consumption (Mock in this volume) often has narrower, elites-related objectives: "the constructive approach of CCTV's journalistic practice … is aimed to manufacture the consensus between Chinese and African elites to embrace Chinese investment"; the "Chinese government dedicates to obtaining the support of African elites for China-Africa cooperation. And one way to achieve that is to foster the young generation's intimacy with China" (Xiang in this volume). Overall, "China's prime target remains the top elites" (Shen quoted in Tudoroiu and Ramlogan in this volume).

However, even in their case, persuasion alone is not sufficient. To give a relevant example, political elites in Moscow have constantly been targeted by China's "flattering diplomatic demarche" but did not replace rational choice with socialization. They do cooperate with their counterparts in Beijing, but this is due to common geopolitical interests and, in a non-negligible measure, fear (see the chapter by Kuteleva and Ivanov in this volume). The cause is the absence of the second, more effective mechanism of Chinese socialization. This is the micro-process of role playing or mimicking (Johnston, 2008: 24), which pertains to the process of cognitive role playing that, as shown earlier in this subsection, was associated by Jeffrey Checkel with Type I socialization. Actors internalize not the norms but the obligation to pretend that they follow them; this is often done due to "social incentives to accept another actor as a behavioral exemplar" (ibid.; Simmons, 2013: 371). China's instruments that contribute to this acceptance are remarkably diversified. They include "corruption, support for authoritarian regimes, military cooperation, exploitation of ideological affinities, party-to-party relations, taking advantage of the liberalization imposed by Western creditors, trade dependency, and political influence activities", and are customized to local conditions (Tudoroiu, 2021: 252; 2022: 54). However, the most important one consists of prestige infrastructure projects loan-financed and constructed by China. Beijing rather inappropriately describes them as development assistance and typically offers them as tied aid (see the chapter by Tudoroiu and Ramlogan in this volume). Their real objective is to provide political legitimacy and electoral support to recipient political elites in power; hence their enormous popularity among these elites leading to the effectiveness of micro-processes of mimicking conducive to Type I socialization. Empirical data indicate that the "socialization of … political elites has relied more on material incentives resulting in cognitive role playing than on normative suasion" (Tudoroiu, 2021: 251). This explains Beijing's aforementioned failure to socialize the political elites in Moscow. Rosneft, Transneft, and Gazprom have used Chinese loans to construct oil and gas pipelines in Siberia (see the chapter by Kuteleva and Ivanov in this volume), but President Putin hardly perceives this financing as essential to his political survival. Things are different in poorer countries. The 2017 completion of the *Madaraka* railway was an electoral campaign promise of Kenya's President Uhuru Kenyatta. He didn't care that the project absorbed more than five percent of his country's GDP; getting reelected was more important. It is hardly surprising that, "like many leaders across Africa, [he] has long heralded the benefits of Chinese-led projects" and hailed *Madaraka* as marking "a new era of autonomous rule on the continent" (Mock in this volume). In Trinidad and Tobago, Prime Minister Patrick Manning inaugurated the National Academy for the Performing Arts 'with much fanfare' in 2009, some months before early general elections. It was irrelevant that the quality of the Chinese loan-financed and constructed building was so poor that it was soon closed for two years for repairs. One month before the 2015 general elections, Prime Minister Kamla Persad-Bissessar similarly opened the Couva children's hospital that the Chinese construction firm had in fact not completed. Two years later, the roadway and the hospital's cooling tower collapsed; the building started to be used only in 2020 as a Covid-19 quarantine facility. But, again, these were irrelevant details when compared with the much higher objective of staying in power. Both Trinidadian Prime Ministers had good reasons to accept China's incentives and norms (see the chapter by Tudoroiu and Ramlogan in this volume). In Indonesia, numerous specific factors have made a large part of the society, the political elites not in power, and even peripheral members of the current administration adopt very critical attitudes toward China. However, during his first presidential term, President Joko Widodo focused on improving connectivity between the country's regions. A Chinese loan was essential for the completion of a prominent project, the Jakarta-Bandung high-speed railway; various other projects similarly benefited from Beijing's support. Unsurprisingly, "Indonesia's warm relationship with China developed further and, as a prominent Indonesian political scientist put it, has 'come full circle'". The Indonesian leader shared the same degree of Chinese socialization as his Kenyan and Trinidadian counterparts (see the chapter by Herlijanto in this volume). The Papua New Guinea case illustrates a variation of the same pattern that is specific to the "infrastructure for resources" deals promoted by China in many parts of the Global South. A Chinese company owns 85% interest in the Ramu Mine, which represents China's largest investment project in Oceania. In exchange, one of the two policy banks in Beijing, China Development Bank, has provided loans for a US $3.5 billion road project, a US $4 billion industrial park in Sandaun Province, and the improvement of water supply in the Eastern Highlands Province. There is little need to comment on the electoral value of this financial package for the political elites in power in Port Moresby and its effectiveness in ensuring their Chinese socialization (see the chapter by Szadziewski in this volume). Many similar examples can be found all over the developing world. They show that the main engine of Chinese socialization, role playing, has much to do with the "power-centered, interest-driven, and often corruptible nature of poli-cymaking processes" (Vangeli, 2019: 79). Instead of a rational-instrumentalist logic that benefits the public, Global South political elites choose a strongly utilitarian approach that benefits their group. As an effect, they "could be rather complacent" and show an "uncritical understanding of the matters at stake" in their interactions with Chinese partners (ibid., 80). Overall, Beijing's skillful use of persuasion and mimicking has led to the successful Type I socialization of political elites in power in many Global South countries.

12.2.5 Changed Perceptions: A Historical Example

This triumph of Normative Power China is well illustrated by the case of admiral Zheng He, a historical figure frequently employed in Beijing's image construction efforts presented in this book (see the chapters by Mock and Herlijanto). Zheng was a Muslim eunuch in the service of the early Ming dynasty who led seven large naval expeditions in South East Asia and the Indian Ocean between 1405 and 1433. Today, China uses this historical episode as "an armature connecting the navigator's contributions to China's narrative of 'longstanding', 'anti-colonial' friendship and partnership with Africa" (Mock in this volume), Sri Lanka, and various South East Asian states. Making reference to one of the exotic animals brought by the fleet to the court in Nanjing, the Chinese Ambassador in Nairobi, Liu Guangyuan, wrote in 2010 in a local newspaper about the "friendship between China and Kenya [that] started almost 600 years ago with a beautiful and elegant giraffe" (ibid.). In 2015, Chinese Foreign Affairs Minister Wang Yi stated at the 15th Lanting Forum that the Ming ships "brought to Africa ... silk and porcelain, and friendship and goodwill. They did not grab an inch of land. Nor did they ever take back one single slave" (ibid.). That same year, the Chinese Prime Minister Li Keqiang similarly claimed that, unlike Westerners, "Zheng He engaged in nothing like plundering, expansion or colonization. Instead, he became known for his goodwill and moves of peace, for which people still keep a fond memory" (The State Council of the People's Republic of China, 2015). Technically, the colonization-related statement is true. Historians agree that Zheng He's enterprise was not colonial in nature. Rather, it was proto-colonial as it did not rely on the long-term occupation of territory. What it imposed under "the pretext of ushering in a harmonious world order under the Chinese Son of Heaven" was the control of key nodes and networks in the Indian Ocean, a strategy replicated by the Portuguese less than one century later (Sen, 2014; 2018: 382, 387; Wade, 2005: 51, 55). Like their Lusitanian successors, the Chinese were rather muscular in their enterprise. In order to weaken Majapahit, a Hindu maritime empire centered on Java that represented the main regional power in South East Asia, Zhen He intervened in its internal affairs in 1407 (Sen, 2014). He captured and replaced with Ming protégés the leader of Aceh and the King of Palembang in Sumatra (both places were strategic maritime nodes). Also in Sumatra, the Chinese intervened in a civil war and captured Su-gan-la, the head of the Samuderan camp, accusing him of being a bandit; and, in 1407, abducted Chen Zuyi, the ethnic Chinese leader of Old Port, who was portrayed as a pirate, taken to Nanjing, and publicly executed. He was replaced with a Ming pawn. During this raid alone, Zheng He's forces killed 5,000 people, burned ten ships, and captured seven (Herlijanto in this volume; Sukma,

1999: 53; Sen, 2014; 2018: 387; Wade, 2005: 47; 50). In the Western Indian Ocean, the Chinese fleet made "use of force or the threat of force to establish tributary relations with kingdoms along the East Africa Coast" (Mock in this volume; Wade, 2005; Snow, 1988). But it is in Sri Lanka that the best-documented intervention took place. During his third expedition, Admiral Zheng simply kidnapped Alakesvara, the ruler of Kotte (a place that is today a suburb of Colombo and Sri Lanka's legislative capital) and his family and court, "bringing back to our august capital, their women, children, families and retainers, leaving no one; cleaning out in a single sweep those noxious pests, as if winnowing chaff from grain" (Peebles, 2006: 34;Sen, 2018: 386; Wade, 2005: 50). The generous Chinese emperor nevertheless spared the lives of "these insignificant works, deserving to die ten thousand times over, trembling in fear". In response, "they humbly kowtowed, making crude sounds and praising the sage-like virtue of the imperial Ming ruler" (Sen, 2018: 386). In his wisdom, the latter nominated the "virtuous and worthy" Yebanaina as tributary king of Kotte as proposed by the Ministry of Rites (ibid., 387; Wade, 2005: 50).

The reader will agree that, against this harsh historical background that is well known locally, it is a bit surprising to see the Sri Lankan government gratefully accepting a gold-plated statue of the Chinese admiral from China's International Tour Management Association, which used it as a symbol of "ancient commercial and peaceful relations between China and Sri Lanka" (Sen, 2014). South Africa's President Jacob Zuma also recalled the friendly Sino-African exchanges promoted by Zheng He. The latter's stone image was installed on the platform at the inauguration of the *Madaraka* railway by Kenya's President Uhuru Kenyatta despite the fact that, six centuries earlier, the admiral's fleet had compelled African kingdoms on the coast to pay tribute to the Ming emperor. The most interesting case is that of Indonesia. In the early 1970s, Zheng He's expeditions were used as "example[s] of China's aggressive and expansionist nature". In the early twenty-first century, however, they were "regarded as friendly" (see the chapter by Herlijanto in this volume; Sukma, 1999: 53). This situation is paradoxical only at first view. Unlike five decades ago, political elites in Sri Lanka, South Africa, Kenya, Indonesia, and much of the Global South have been successfully socialized by China. The fact that they now perceive the recycled image of a historical enemy as a symbol of friendship and cooperation shows the effectiveness of the Chinese socialization process. In much of the developing world, the political elites in power have become enthusiastic followers of China's norms, aligning their states' policies with Chinese interests and thus contributing to China's geoeconomic and geopolitical advancement. Zheng He's new perception is just one of the many elements indicative of these elites' uncritical reconstruction of the national interest that is ultimately engineered in Beijing.

However, an analysis stopping at this point would necessarily be incomplete. All over the Global South, there are numerous subnational actors that criticize vocally the impact of the Chinese presence and strongly reject the political elites' orientation. Their case is scrutinized in the next section.

12.3 Persuasion, Subnational Agency, and Structural Factors

12.3.1 An Ocean of Criticism

In principle, China's comprehensive public diplomacy strategy that makes use of instruments such as CGTN or Confucius Institutes "seeks to improve its international image, shape perceptions around the globe and ultimately create positive public sentiment in its advantage" (Morales in this volume) at both elites and society levels. All Global South people are "spoon-fed" the "curated messages of *brand-China*" centered on partnership, friendship, brotherhood, and sameness as China "insinuates itself" into the "origin, evolution, and eventual fate" of the developing world (see the chapter by Mock in this volume). And yet, out of 91 articles about the Chinese ownership of the Ramu nickel mine in Papua New Guinea, 48 were positive and 30 negative. This mirrors the "vigorous public debate" between pro-Chinese state officials and the, at times, "viscerally negative" civil society (see the chapter by Szadziewski in this volume). In Indonesia, Beijing-friendly views are popular only among government elites and supporters of President Jokowi. "Critical views of China are rampant" among common people, as well as elites opposing the government or taking a neutral stance (see the chapter by Herlijanto in this volume). In Trinidad and Tobago, there is no single anti-Chinese politician. Members of the opposition might criticize the use of Beijing's loans made by the government, but once in power, they hurry to get their own Chinese-financed and constructed prestige infrastructure projects. Among local contractors, laborers, and the society at large, however, there is "a high degree of frustration and discontent" related to these projects (see the chapter by Tudoroiu and Ramlogan in this volume). Globally, the most frequent criticism concerns the Chinese migrant workers brought by China's contractors to build infrastructure projects or work in natural resources extraction. Until recently, this was not the case in Indonesia, a populous country where their presence was less visible. But when Chinese labor was imported for the construction of the Jakarta-Bandung high-speed railway, the public became aware of the fact that 30.000 to 50.000 "new Chinese migrants" were employed by Chinese construction and mining companies, thus "taking job opportunities from the Indonesian workers". Large-scale criticism ensued (Herlijanto in this volume). In Papua New Guinea, such criticism can be very brutal: "forget the promised 1000 plus job—its rubbish, breadcrumbs, bullshit—as the majority of the workforce will be Chinese again—people whole don't speak a word of English" [*sic*] (Szadziewski in this volume). Trinidad and Tobago has a population of less than 1.4 million inhabitants, which makes the impact of migrant workers on the construction labor market difficult to ignore. Despite the reassuring statements of pro-Beijing Prime Ministers claiming that foreign workers are not "boxing bread out of the mouths of the citizens of Trinidad and Tobago", trade unions and professional associations have organized various forms of protest. Common people generally believe that "Chinese nationals were coming in, they were living in squalid conditions, they wouldn't contribute to the national economy, they took jobs away from us". Moreover, dissatisfied citizens are aware of the fact that, because most of the workers' wages are sent to China, Trinidad ceased to represent a net receiver of remittances for the first time in its history (Tudoroiu and Ramlogan in this volume). In all developing countries, the negative perception is further aggravated by the massive inflow of Chinese entrepreneurial migrants who set up convenience stores, Chinese restaurants, groceries, gambling rooms, and casinos. Some of them are in fact former contract workers who decide to exploit local opportunities. Due to better connections in China, they outcompete and bankrupt local small traders, which further increases unemployment and frustration among the local society. Ensuing hostility leads to various—and, often, extravagant—rumors. To give just one of the numerous possible examples, to many Indonesians, the Chinese migrant workers are either spies or "criminals who are meant to be banished"; there is also a "Chinese migration strategy" of relocating people to Indonesia "to solve the population issue that [China] has been facing" (Herlijanto in this volume). In many parts of the Global South, this has led to Sinophobia, protests, individual cases of violence, and even riots. The migrant-related criticism is ultimately derivative of China's economic and social normative subsets, which prevent the socialized elites from limiting the inflow and economic activities of both Chinese firms and entrepreneurial migrants. The former, which are mainly but not exclusively state-owned enterprises, are also criticized by rival local companies for being given contracts without bidding (see the chapter by Tudoroiu and Ramlogan in this volume); and by local employees for low pay, difficult work conditions, and non-recognition of trade unions—practices that, in most cases, reflect the situation in China (French, 2014: 179). More generally, their "clumsiness" in terms of social responsibilities, business sustainability, and environmental issues gives them a very bad image locally and internationally (Lau, 2019). It would be difficult to expect Papuans to ignore the 2019 Ramu project spill of 200,000 L of toxic slurry that changed the color of the ocean to bright red and stained the coast of Madang province (Szadziewski in this volume). The poor quality of many projects can be added. In the words of a Trinidadian respondent, "I think they have lost the battle in terms of the public opinion. There is generally extraordinarily negative viewpoint of Chinese firms" (Tudoroiu and Ramlogan in this volume).

Aspects of the Chinese presence are also criticized that may not be general but are particularly impactful in specific countries or regions. Indonesia's society, for example, responds very negatively to China's expansion in the neighboring South China Sea and its efforts to impose the famous nine-dash line. Incidents in the waters of the Natuna Islands involving Indonesian patrol vessels, Chinese illegal fishing boats, and China's coast guard vessels have "sparked public outcry". The alleged relationship between citizens of Chinese origin and China's embassy is regarded with suspicion by no less than 47.6% of Indonesians, who believe that "Chinese Indonesians will help the Chinese from China in their effort to infiltrate Indonesia". Only 17.9% think that the Chinese minority does not harbor loyalty toward Beijing. Massive investment from China is considered to be motivated by the interest to control strategic locations such as the Sunda Strait. Large loans for projects that may well incur financial losses are perceived as Hambantota-style debt traps due to which "our [Indonesian] economy will be completely under their [China's] control" (Herlijanto in this volume). Suspicions and disputes of this kind make China unpopular among the societies of many Global South states that, officially, maintain excellent bilateral relations with Beijing.

The chapters on Indonesia and Papua New Guinea are illustrative of another widespread criticism of the Chinese presence in the developing world that is located at the border between the aforementioned "extravagant rumors" and the less speculative analysis of the center-periphery pattern that characterizes Beijing's relationship with its Global South partners. Fears of Chinese "neocolonialism" are explicit in many Indonesians' views of loans potentially associated with debt-traps: "I worry if China has the ambition to colonize other countries." This may be a loan-based, "modern form of colonization which, unlike in the past, is characterized by political, rather than by physical domination". In addition, Beijing's South China Sea ambitions suggest a complementary "maritime colonialism with Chinese characteristics" (Herlijanto in this volume). Neocolonialism is also invoked in Papua New Guinea, at times in association with very crude terms. In the words of a villager from Mindere, close to the Ramu mine, "the Chinese are unscrupulous. ... They are raping our country" (Szadziewski in this volume). There is a vast literature on this issue, reflecting the irreconcilable views of anti- and pro-Chinese camps. A possible response is that "China hardly wants to colonise, but it has immense mercantilist ambitions" (Rotberg, 2008: 1). However, the debate itself is less relevant than the fact that many people in the developing world perceive Chinese neocolonialism as a real threat.

A somewhat related criticism targets explicitly the Trojan horse role played by socialized political elites in their unconditional support of the Chinese presence: "Hon. Tuke [Papua New Guinea's Minister of Mining], come out straight and say you got bribe money from the Chinese company operating the Mine. ... When will we change our attitude of benefiting and living luxuriously at the expense and suffering of the people and the country?" (Szadziewski in this volume). "The general Trinidadian population is extraordinarily weary of whether the Trinidad and Tobago government is selling out the country to the Chinese" (Tudoroiu and Ramlogan in this volume). Actual corruption, however, is not always invoked. Beijing-hostile citizens and activists fully understand the more subtle but ultimately similar role played by the prestige infrastructure projects. In Trinidad and Tobago, the numerous scandals related to the poor quality of Chinese-made constructions drew attention to the fact that Beijing has systematically imposed one specific Chinese contractor—often, of dubious repute—for each project it loan-financed. China Harbor Engineering Company was well-known for fraud and corruption in other Global South countries. Shanghai Construction Group had a record of poor work in Trinidad itself. They were nevertheless selected during secretive government-to-government negotiations resulting in undisclosed agreements. Ensuing project failures were associated by the media and the public with the lax conditions likely stipulated in these inaccessible agreements (ibid.). This is a general Chinese practice. Beijing's foreign lending "contracts contain unusual confidentiality clauses that bar borrowers from revealing the terms or even the existence of the debt" (Gelpern et al., 2021: 2). A 2021 study that scrutinized 100 such contracts in 24 developing countries revealed the scale of this practice. The Chinese loans are provided by two policy banks, China Development

Bank and China ExIm Bank. The former's contracts have always included these confidentiality clauses. Only 43% of the latter's loans did, but this is due to the situation before a 2014 policy change. Previous to it, ExIm seldom imposed such clauses. Since 2014, all its contracts have been secretive. It is important to note that sovereign debt contracts of other lenders impose confidentiality obligations on the lenders. China, which seldom discloses economic data, imposes them on the borrowers. Typically, they "commit the debtor not to disclose any of the contract terms or related information unless required by law"; and few recipient countries have such laws (ibid., 6, 22). Even government experts are unaware of the exact content of documents signed by their ministers (Oosterveld et al., 2018: 16–24). Consequently, the Chinese side and the socialized elites involved in negotiations are free to set whatever contractual conditions they find appropriate from their self-interested point of view. This obviously "endanger[s] existing policies and practices of public transparency and accountability, thus negatively affecting the [recipient] country's good governance" (Tudoroiu and Ramlogan in this volume). Citizens are not blind to this situation. In Papua New Guinea, some of them rhetorically ask "When is somebody going to stand up and say – Enough is enough???? Since when did we become a colony of China so that they can push us to bypass our set processes?" (Szadziewski in this volume). The sequence of statements made by respondents in Trinidad and Tobago is relevant: "the problem lies with the official policies of Caribbean states 'for not being strategic or protective'"; this is "the fault of [political leaders] who were involved in the exercise"; in turn, "this is due to 'the political system that gives these leaders too much room to act against the national interest:' the constitutional system lacks 'robust checks and balances'"; therefore, the ultimate cause is "the immaturity of the state" (Tudoroiu and Ramlogan in this volume). What these citizens say is that China takes advantage of governance weaknesses in their countries to promote its interests at the price of further worsening the already less-than-perfect governance.

The existence of so many critical views among the societies of developing states that have established close partnerships with China suggests that Beijing's image construction efforts are far from perfect. The causes of this failure are examined in the next subsection.

12.3.2 Weaknesses of China's Persuasion Efforts

Observers with a positivist mindset may argue that, objectively, there are good reasons that explain large-scale dissatisfaction with China's actions. Preventing construction workers from getting jobs or spilling chemicals that turn the ocean red are hard facts that cannot be hidden. A Constructivist, however, would point to the fact that political elites see the same "hard facts" very differently. To them, Chinese workers "are not boxing bread out of the mouths of the citizens of Trinidad and Tobago". Papua's Prime Minister did not seem to be very concerned by the toxic slurry spill. Type I socialization—i.e. the internalization of the need to play a China-friendly role—explains the pro-Beijing reconstruction of elites' understandings. For its part, the society at large was not the target of a similarly well-conceived effort. As explained in Sect. 12.2, China's "low-cost strategy" is not compatible with the huge resources needed to incentivize the entire population of the Global South, which would be required in order to make the process of mimicking effective. Persuasion alone has been at work, and the impossibility to use important instruments such as secret diplomacy has diminished its effectiveness. But even under such conditions, the "carefully curated images of the PRC" created for Global South consumption and the associated legitimating discourse (see the chapter by Mock in this volume) should have "improve[d] [China's] international image, shape[d] perceptions around the globe and ultimately create[d] positive public sentiment in its advantage" (Morales in this volume). I argue that this did not happen—or only happened on a disproportionately small scale—within target societies for three reasons: inbuilt weaknesses of the Chinese actions, the agency of subnational actors in target countries, and, in certain cases, unfavorable structural factors.

I remember a Caribbean respondent particularly impressed by the effectiveness of China's bureaucracy he had interacted with in an official capacity. Yet, severe incompetence is one of the root causes of Beijing's failure to impose a positive image of its actions in the Global South. The situation of Confucius Institutes depicted in Chapter 6 is both dramatic and absurd. These numerous and costly educational institutions are conceived as a key part of an "instrumental strategy to 'win hearts and minds' by exerting 'soft power'". They are welcomed by local audiences offered the opportunity "to glimpse into Chinese society and culture" and eventually find a job within the ecosystem of Chinese firms in their country. What students actually encounter, however, is an ideologically motivated representation of Chinese culture that is problematic even for the Chinese instructors; and, more importantly, a shockingly poor organization of the teaching process. "Instructors lack proper training in local languages, pedagogical methods, and cultural awareness" (see the chapter by Zhang in this volume). They are unable to communicate effectively: in Madagascar, they do not speak Malagasy or French. Teaching is limited to "writing Chinese vocabulary on the blackboard with English or French translations, and students writing down notes and reading the words out loud after the instructor". Students learn Chinese songs, but do not understand the lyrics. The poorly prepared Chinese instructors are not allowed to interact with students outside the classroom, and when they do they can only use their very limited knowledge of English, which is not one of the local languages. Worse, "their lack of cultural awareness about local social etiquette often leaves them unconscious of their behavior deemed rude in the eyes of local people". Unsurprisingly, only ten percent of registered students show up for the final exam (ibid.). It should be noted that Confucius Institutes represent one of the key instruments of China's charm offensive in the Global South.

Another one is China Global Television Network (CGTN). The quality of its Spanish language service presented in Chapter 5 is so terrible that the huge majority of Mexican and Argentinean students in *International Relations*—who are likely to be much more interested in such issues than the average citizen—are not even aware of its existence. Language, again, is a formidable obstacle. Often, the Chinese presenters' command of Spanish is perceived by Latin American viewers as "very bad" or even "terrible". Some words are difficult to understand. The occasional audience gets easily distracted by the foreign accent, does not pay attention to the content, and switches over to a different channel. Moreover, the way of talking is boring. The channel is a product of the Chinese media system that has not been shaped to play a "role at a transcultural level and [to] fit within the media systems in Latin America and their regional and/or national variations". Unable to "navigate cultural differences", the Chinese TV station cannot be expected to favorably and significantly impact Spanish-speaking target audiences (see the chapter by Morales in this volume). This situation is particularly strange because the same CGTN has set up a media center in Nairobi that "made a point of recruiting prominent and highly competent African anchors and reporters" to attract African audiences (Xiang in this volume). One would have expected the Latin American section to get some inspiration from the more successful African experience of the same TV station. This did not happen, which raises serious questions about the competence of China's image-building apparatus.

A second explanatory level concerns features of the Chinese persuasion effort that, unlike TV presenters, cannot be easily changed. The first is "the association to the Chinese government" that undermines the credibility of CGTN and other propaganda instruments. State media in general and those controlled by authoritarian regimes in particular "instill distrust about their reliability". "Pre-conceived images of China and its censorship system appeared to influence the participants' first impressions of CCTV by undermining its credibility" (Morales in this volume). Given the increasingly tight control of Chinese media under President Xi, these "preconceived" images are unlikely to change. Instead of promoting generally shared journalistic values, CGTN is perceived as accomplishing the task of "disseminat[ing] a particular vision of the country in line with PR activities of self-promotion". Moreover, when it criticizes the human rights situation in the United States while not saying a word about the large-scale infringement of the same human rights in Xinjiang, Tibet, or Hong Kong, Latin American viewers—most of whom happen to live in democratic states—unsurprisingly tend to think of "hypocrisy" (ibid.). In Africa, viewers are similarly critical of the fact that "the frictions between Chinese actors and African society [are] left out of the CCTV news" while, unlike remote Xinjiang, they represent "a lived reality for African audiences" (Xiang in this volume). Moreover, despite being "spoon-fed" images of "sameness", they have serious and well-justified reserves with respect to Beijing's effort to "conflat[e] vastly different African and Chinese experiences as equally post-colonial". Critically, this effort "elides differences and overlooks the complexities of power relations" between China and Africa (Mock in this volume) in ways that are indicative of a self-interested manipulatory Chinese strategy.

The example of the Confucius Institute reveals another counterproductive feature of China's persuasion efforts in the Global South. As briefly mentioned earlier in this subsection, its educational activities rely on an ideologically motivated representation of Chinese culture that is problematic even for Chinese instructors. The "thickness and vibrancy" of the contemporary Chinese culture are "wiped out by CI's tendency to treat 'culture' as a static and bounded entity" that exclusively emphasizes its traditional elements "such as Kung Fu, Tai Ji, paper-cutting, dumpling making, singing and dancing". This is not an accident. It is a direct consequence of the "revival of Confucianism in and outside of China [that] is closely related to the hegemonic representation and the strategic use of 'culture' in China's state agenda". Confucianism is employed to reinforce the authoritarian "socialist spiritual civilization" and "the state promotion of social cohesion against the threat of Westernization". Within China, this allows the Communist Party to take advantage of "a national cultural ethos encapsulated by Confucianism". But in the Global South, it indicates "a new cultural nationalism" (Zhang in this volume) that does in no way enhance the acceptance of Beijing's sameness-based discourse (Mock in this volume).

More generally, the overall Chinese message to the developing world is too China-centered. CGTN in Latin America is "perceived as being unapologetically focused on China and Chinese news"; viewers describe it as "auto-referential" (Morales in this volume). CGTN Africa is much more localized and tries "to disguise its Chineseness and to be more international". Yet, despite this effort, "the subjective perspective is on China instead of on African countries"; its "framing is consistent with a 'China rising' narrative instead of an 'Africa rising' narrative" (Xiang in this volume). Chinese loan-financed and constructed prestige projects also play "a role symbolic of the strength of the Chinese state and its global ambitions". "Although *Madaraka* [railway] was a Kenyan possession, it was still very much Chinese owned". Moreover, its inauguration was mirrored by China's 2018 Spring Festival Gala, a highly popular TV show that featured "Chinese actors in blackface, caricaturing the vagaries of Kenyan life", and "a solidarity Africana actor donning a monkey costume" (Mock in this volume; *BBC*, February 16, 2018; YouTube, 2018). This latter attitude resonates with the overtly condescending views of a Confucius Institute instructor in Madagascar:

> I do not really care about learning the [Malagasy] culture and language here, and I do not want to communicate much outside of my classroom. I have already read a lot about the geography of this country and it should be enough. … [The possible closing of the Confucius Institute in this university] is not a big deal because there are so many institutions that desperately want to work with CI. Anyhow, learning Chinese is already an irresistible trend in the world. Chinese is such a beautiful, musical, and sophisticated language! (Zhang in this volume)

If all these features of China's persuasion efforts in the Global South are taken into consideration, it would be unrealistic to expect outstanding results. Moreover, the actual outcome has been further affected by the agency of subnational actors in the target countries.

12.3.3   Subnational Agency

As explained in the chapter by Tudoroiu and Ramlogan in this volume, China defines development assistance as a much wider set of interactions than those accepted by the Development Assistance Committee of the OECD. This means that more domains are concerned by the fact that "the aid relationship between donor and recipient is an extremely asymmetric power relationship" (Stokke, 1995, 2006: 33). Indifferent of Beijing's win–win, South-South cooperative discourse, all "foreign aid represents an intervention in the recipient country that significantly influences the resources and power position of various social groups, which are turned into beneficiaries or losers based on the donor's choice" (ibid., 34; Tudoroiu and Ramlogan in this volume). For reasons presented in Sect. 12.2, China always uses its widely defined development assistance, as well as all other forms of economic interaction, to place the political elites in power in the category of beneficiaries. Other socio-economic groups are, at best, unaffected and, at worst, detrimentally impacted by the various negative consequences of the Chinese economic and social normative subsets. The abundant criticism reviewed earlier in this section shows that the number of losers is hardly negligible. Many groups incur actual losses that may seriously affect their socio-economic situation. Chinese actions that damage public goods—such as environmental degradation—are matters of concern for the entire society. Accordingly, as revealed by the example of Papua New Guinea, "criticisms are expressed in defending grounded interests … and not just an absorption of overseas narratives outlining a vague 'China threat'" (Szadziewski in this volume). These interests far overweight the effects of Beijing's poorly organized persuasion efforts targeting the local society. Due to the absence of an effective form of socialization, rational choice is at work that explains the very visible agency of subnational actors.

Papua New Guinea provides a good example of how "civil society and sub-national actors meaningfully exert agency on PNG's interactions with China". The socialized political elites in power present Chinese investment as supportive of national self-reliance because it decreases dependence on former colonial powers. But there is a "negative reflexive response in civil society towards China and [the] national government": civic activists also target self-reliance, but they critically engage Chinese investment by expressing serious concerns over violations of environmental and labor standards, restricted employment opportunities, and inadequate compensation to landowners. Their discourse is centered on the "rejection of China's 'neocolonial' attitude towards Papua New Guinea's natural resources". Interestingly, another subnational actor is involved, in a somewhat different way, in the national debate: provincial governments act on the basis of their own interests to advocate for more local benefits. "These processes indicate degrees of agency in relations with Chinese investors", thus justifying Henryk Szadziewski's call for analyses of the Chinese presence in Oceania that take into consideration local conditions and substate actors (see the chapter by Szadziewski in this volume). Agency is not always the effect of economic factors. As shown by Yu Xiang in her chapter, given the promising career prospects of Chinese-educated Africans, one may expect a clear "correspondence between being an African student in China and supporting the hegemony of China in Africa". In fact, the "less rosy reality" they experienced during their studies—which includes racism and the shocking discrimination faced during the epidemic—made them realize "the misalignment between real-life encounters and the official discourse of reciprocity and egalities". In turn, this has "create[d] room for [an] alternative reading" of their own position; their consent for China's hegemony "remains open for negotiation [and] even resistance" (Xiang in this volume).

Moreover, subnational agency is not necessarily anti-Chinese. Hundreds if not thousands of demonstrations against Chinese workers depriving locals of jobs, Chinese firms receiving contracts without bidding, environmental degradation, harsh work conditions, and so on are held every year all over the Global South. However, the Colombian case study shows that, after the failure of China's first *desembarco*, "it was the governments of Bogotá and Medellín—not the national government—that opened the door for large Chinese infrastructure investment". The former chose Chinese contractors for the construction of the metro network and an electric commuter train to the suburbs. Medellín and Cali bought new electric bus fleets from companies in China (see the chapter by van den Bos in this volume). The agency of regional authorities is also visible in Russia's Far East. President Putin's systematic centralization of power has resulted in tight controls on cross-border interactions with China, which excluded regional elites from development decision-making. The Russian "'turn to the East' is designed by bureaucrats in Moscow and powered by [state-owned] oil and gas giants such as Rosneft, Sibur, and Gazprom, as well as powerful monopolies, like Russian Railways". They are the only ones to benefit from massive Chinese loans. Just a tiny part of this money goes to regional budgets. "Governors, politicians, strongmen, landlords, and influential businessmen … were … incapable to contribute meaningfully to the design of the regional development policy and build mutually beneficial relations with China". As a result of this Russian "colonial project", the Far East "is merely a transit zone but not a willing, reflexive, and active agent of Russia's pivot to China" (Kuteleva and Ivanov in this volume). And yet, there is local agency. Back in the early 1990s, cross-border shuttle trade enacted by petty "suitcase traders" developed tremendously. In the late 2000s, the government in Moscow imposed restrictions on border crossing, as well as new customs rules; "however, shuttle traders and smugglers creatively adapted to the new rules, and the informal economy still flourishes in Primorye in various forms". Local authorities do their best to show absolute loyalty to the leadership in Moscow. Still, they retain their agency within local business networks and, in a certain measure, are able to adjust and realign Moscow's China strategy on the ground. They accept the "grey" cross-border informal economy "as a necessary evil and even themselves engage in semi-formal cooperation with the Chinese". Moreover, they use their leverage on Chinese entrepreneurs in innovative ways: "each and every company that has Chinese capital (co)funds various social programs or cultural events". Such firms have been compelled to finance sports teams, national holiday celebrations, road repairs, and social infrastructure (ibid.). This looks very much like extortion, but it does reveal an undeniable form of subnational agency.

A somewhat similar phenomenon has been noted in Ghana with respect to the local treatment of Chinese entrepreneurial migrants. Two decades ago, President John Agyekum Kufuor initiated a partnership with China that has led to the socialization of Ghanaian political elites in power and the ensuing development of a close and multidimensional relationship between the two countries, which includes the construction of large infrastructure projects such as the US \$622 million Bui dam. In this context, a large number of Chinese entrepreneurial migrants have moved to the African country and got involved in mainly trade-related activities. Surprisingly, they perceive themselves as highly vulnerable despite the "widely publicized image of a 'powerful China in Africa'" (Lam, 2015: 10): half of them have gone bankrupt. In part, this is due to competition from local traders and poor relations with Ghanaian employees; but the main reason is large-scale harassment and extortion by corrupt local officials. In Ghana, public office is a means of private enrichment. "The informality and corruption characteristic of neopatrimonialism remains predominant over legal-rational structures" (Crawford & Botchwey, 2017: 444). But the newly arrived Chinese are disproportionately targeted by such practices. Upon request or voluntarily, they have to pay bribes in order to bypass exaggerated bureaucratic delays. Immigration, revenue, and municipal officials make frequent inspections intended "to extract unofficial and often unjustified payments" (Mohan & Lampert, 2013: 109). Visas, taxes, and fines for non-declared business profits have to be negotiated, usually with the help of well-connected intermediaries. Newly arrived Chinese are "surprised by the levels of corruption relating to everyday micro-administrative procedures" (Lam, 2015: 17–19). Scholars studying this phenomenon have come to the conclusion that it "is reflective of negative African social agency at lower non-state levels of people-to-people interaction" (Chipaike & Bischoff, 2018: 1012). Much of the criticism presented at the beginning of this section is valid in the Ghanaian case and has led to widespread anti-Chinese views in the local society (for details see Tudoroiu, 2022: 144–148). Given the pro-Beijing attitude of socialized political elites, the negative views of societal actors cannot translate into anti-Chinese policies. The harassing of China's entrepreneurial migrants by corrupt officials is a response to this blockage: "the strong China / weak Ghana contrast is replaced at individual level by the opposition between weak Chinese and strong Africans" (ibid., 129). Ultimately, this is "African agency by African actors against the Chinese to advance their own interests and aspirations" (Lam, 2015: 11).

The conclusion is that China's presence in the Global South is impacted in many ways by the agency of subnational actors that explicitly or implicitly reject the cooperative pattern visible in the case of socialized elites. But this is not the only major element that shapes significantly China's projection of normative power. Structural factors are also at work.

12.3.4 Structural Factors

These factors can be divided into two categories: cognitive and institutional. At times, the former may pass unnoticed; but even then they do influence the reception of Beijing's persuasion efforts. For example, in Mexico and Argentina, there is "a rather negative pre-conceived image of China among [respondents], proved to be undermining the effort of making the country attractive to the eyes of viewers". The target audience of CGTN in these countries knows about Chinese authoritarianism and censorship; the expectation that the TV channel "inevitably reproduce[s] state interests" is so strong that it discourages potential viewers (Morales in this volume). In Indonesia, the 1965 communist coup attempt contributed to the development of the "China threat" discourse that was dominant during the 1966–1998 New Order period. China was regarded with suspicion while Indonesians of Chinese ethnic origin were accused of being Beijing's agents. Today, government elites around President Jokowi have been socialized by China and perceive it as a friendly power. But other elites and much of the society preserve the old "view of China as an expansionist power, the perception of China as a threat, and the concern regarding the ethnic Chinese' role as the fifth column" (Herlijanto in this volume). In Colombia, due to local causes, the heritage of Cold War anti-communism is so strong that it led to the failure of China's first *desembarco*. From 2005, two Presidents and their ministers traveled to Beijing and received prominent Chinese officials. They signed a flurry of agreements that even included plans for a "Nueva Shenzhen on the Caribbean Coast, built by Chinese companies and with Chinese financing". But ultimately this was a "story of failure. Chinese petroleum companies failed to win a single bid for the development of Colombian oil fields. Bilateral Free Trade Agreement talks proved futile. Colombia received almost no overseas foreign direct investment (OFDI) from China" (van den Bos in this volume). The explanation was simple—and puzzling: "But they're Communist". The deep aversion to left-wing politics inherited from the Cold War era and kept alive by the internal conflict with Marxist guerillas represented a powerful structural factor that delayed with 15 years the taking off of the economic relationship with China (ibid.). In Russia, the opposite situation is visible: "popular attitudes towards China to a large extent depend on perceptions of Russia's relations with the West" (Kuteleva and Ivanov in this volume). More than a decade and a half ago, President Putin chose to increase his domestic legitimacy through the adoption of an anti-Western foreign policy line. This change responded to popular frustrations related to the dramatic post-Soviet decline of living standards and the loss of superpower status. With the West as an enemy, nominally communist China became a positive reference by default: "59.5 percent of respondents have positive attitudes towards China, and 31 percent claim that their sentiments towards China improved over the past decade". Despite the anxiety over the Chinese presence in Russia's eastern periphery, Russians believe that "China is important for Russia's development (76.5 percent), support trade with China (73.3 percent), and welcome Chinese investment (59.1 percent)" (Kuteleva and Ivanov in this volume). Accordingly, all Russian actors are eager to cooperate with Chinese ones as long as central authorities do not block such initiatives.

This latter aspect takes the discussion to the category of institutional structural factors. Once more, the Russian example is relevant. As shown by Anna Kuteleva and Sergei Ivanov in their chapter, historically, episodes of contraction of the Russian imperial power have alternated with periods of restoration and expansion. After the fall of both the Tsarist Empire and the Soviet Union, the "inherently Eurocentric empire chose to leave its eastern periphery to itself". For a short period in the early 1990s, provinces were granted greater economic and political autonomy that included deregulation of trade and stimulation of inward foreign investment. To survive economically, elites pursued regional interests by intensifying trade with China and other Asian neighbors. These periods of increased autonomy and agency came to an end as soon as the central power was fully restored. As shown in the previous subsection, this has happened under President Putin. Decision- and money-making accordingly moved from Vladivostok to Moscow (ibid.). Regional actors may still find ways to manifest their agency; but, for the decades to come, structural factors are in place that severely constrain their actions. The opposite situation exists in Colombia. Due to the peculiar history of this country, a "uniquely antistatist approach" developed that led to the construction of "a remarkably weak state". The weakness of the executive "made Colombia ill-suited for the top-down approach" that has considerably contributed to China's economic expansion elsewhere in the Global South (van den Bos in this volume). The secretive government-to-government negotiations resulting in undisclosed agreements that give contracts to Chinese firms without bidding cannot be imagined in this country. "No Colombian president would have the power to follow through on any initiative facing China without the backing of numerous other actors". Even the national oil company, Ecopetrol, is subject to the same bidding processes as private firms. In this unfamiliar environment, the state-owned Chinese oil companies systematically failed to win contracts despite the political support of the Colombian executive. The belated success of the second wave of Chinese engagement after 2020 was not due to the disappearance of these structural factors. They continue to be effective and limit the entry of China's state-owned firms, particularly in the energy sector. The change took place on the Chinese side: today, "private companies are leading the way" as they fit local conditions better. In other words, institutional structural factors have significantly shaped the dynamic and nature of the Chinese presence in Colombia.

Overall, it can be concluded that both cognitive and institutional structural factors add to the agency of subnational actors in shaping responses to China's projection of normative power in the Global South. This complex relationship is further analyzed in the next section.

12.4 Conclusion

The understanding of the overall Chinese interaction with the developing world proposed in this chapter has the advantage of avoiding the trap of narrow geoeconomic or geopolitical approaches, which are poorly equipped to appropriately take into consideration the numerous and diverse subnational actors visible in this volume. Some of these actors are affected by Chinese economic activities. Some are influenced by Beijing's geopolitical plans. But all are directly impacted by Normative Power China, simply because its norms have succeeded to significantly shape their states' policies. This is done through the socialization of political elites in power based on well-conceived and conducted micro-processes of persuasion and mimicking. The latter is highly effective due to the systematic use of prestige infrastructure projects. As an effect, the elites align their views with Chinese local, regional, and global interests; and uncritically reconstruct the national interest and ensuing policies in line with these interests. Behind this harmonious picture, however, lies an ocean of frustration and criticism that affects many socio-economic groups. Their incentive-based socialization would be too costly. Therefore, it is only through persuasion that Beijing tries to gain their sympathy. This frequently fails due to reasons that include, unexpectedly, severe incompetence, and, more predictably, elements associated with China's authoritarian and self-centered nature. Consequently, rational choice reasoning has the upper hand. Subnational actors resist Chinese actions that are detrimental to their own, independently constructed interests.

One theoretical aspect needs to be mentioned here. As explained in Sect. 12.2, top-down "elite learning" socialization processes do not necessarily rely on the external socializer in order to convince the society to accept new norms. Much or all of this work is normally done by the already socialized elites, which act as norms entrepreneurs. By institutionalizing the norms they have accepted, the political elites in power convey them to the local society. Eventually, the entire population "learns" them. This is not happening in China's case for a reason that has much to do with the "power-centered, interest-driven, and often corruptible nature" of national elites' pro-Beijing role playing. Instead of serving the public, these elites center their interaction with the socializer on a strongly utilitarian approach that, even when actual corruption is absent, still benefits their group in terms of increased political legitimacy and electoral support. Even citizens whose personal interests are not directly affected by the negative consequences of Beijing's economic and social normative subsets realize, with frustration, that China takes advantage of governance weaknesses in their countries to promote its interests at the price of further worsening the already less-than-perfect governance. Against this negative background, it would be naive to expect the state hijacked by the pro-Chinese elites to successfully convey China's norms to discontented citizens.

In the absence of inhibiting factors such as socialization, anti-Chinese agency emerges when groups incur actual losses due to Chinese actions that may seriously affect their socio-economic situation. But such agency is not always the effect of economic factors. As illustrated by the case of African students in China, psychological elements related to "the misalignment between real-life encounters and the official discourse of reciprocity and egalities" (Xiang in this volume) can equally be at its origin. Extreme forms of manifestation include Sinophobia, protests, individual cases of violence, and even riots. Perhaps the least expected one is the large-scale harassment and extortion of Chinese entrepreneurial migrants by corrupt Ghanaian officials that "is reflective of negative African social agency at lower non-state levels of people-to-people interaction" (Chipaike & Bischoff, 2018: 1012). China's projection of normative power also has to face cognitive and institutional structural factors. As illustrated by Colombia's anti-communism, they can prevent the taking off of the bilateral relationship despite the active support of the target country's political leadership. In a way, structural factors are more important than the agency of subnational actors. Against the latter, Beijing can always use the socialized political elites that control the state and have a reasonable chance of defending Chinese interests. When cognitive or institutional configurations intervene—"But they're Communist"!—there is little that even a China-friendly President can do. Still, not everything is hostile to Chinese interests. In certain cases, both agency and structure actually work in Beijing's favor. Among subnational actors, regional administrations such as those in Colombia and Russia's Far East did their best to bring the Chinese in (even if, in the Russian case, friendly efforts were slightly extortion-scented). Similarly, Moscow's anti-Western stand represents a structural factor that is highly beneficial to China's interests.

Overall, the triangular interaction between Chinese normative power, subnational agency, and structural factors is too complex to be captured in a simplified pattern. Normative Power China has a clear advantage due to its influence over socialized elites. But its interactions with the countries of the Global South are far from representing a strong and stable patron-client relationship. Their future is open and local actors can influence it significantly.

References

Acharya, A. (2011). *Asian regional institutions and the possibilities for socializing the behavior of states* (ADB Working Paper Series on Regional Economic Integration No. 82). Asian Development Bank. Retrieved May 28, 2021 from https://www.adb.org/publications/asian-regional-institutions-and-possibilities-socializing-behavior-states

BBC. (2018, February 16). *Lunar New Year: Chinese TV gala includes "racist blackface" sketch.* Retrieved May 28, 2021 from https://www.bbc.com/news/world-asia-china-43081218

Bernal, R. L. (2016). *Dragon in the Caribbean: China's global re-dimensioning - Challenges and opportunities for the Caribbean* (Rev. and Updated ed.). Kindle ed. Ian Randle Publishers.

Best, H., & Higley, J. (Eds.). (2018). *The Palgrave handbook of political elites.* Palgrave Macmillan.

Checkel, J. T. (1999). Social construction and integration. *Journal of European Public Policy, 6*(4), 545–560.

Checkel, J. T. (2005). International institutions and socialization in Europe: Introduction and framework. *International Organization, 59*(4), 801–826.

Chipaike, R., & Bischoff, P. H. (2018). A challenge to conventional wisdom: Locating agency in Angola's and Ghana's economic engagements with China. *Journal of Asian and African Studies, 53*(7), 1002–1017.

Crawford, G., & Botchwey, G. (2017). Conflict, collusion and corruption in small-scale gold mining: Chinese miners and the state in Ghana. *Commonwealth & Comparative Politics, 55*(4), 444–470.

Demir, E. (2017). The Chinese school of international relations: Myth or reality? *All Azimuth, 6*(2), 95–104.

Diez, T. (2005). Constructing the self and changing others: Reconsidering "normative power Europe". *Millennium: Journal of International Studies, 33*(3), 613–636.

Diez, T. (2013). Normative power as hegemony. *Cooperation and Conflict, 48*(2), 194–210.

Diez, T., & Manners, I. (2007). Reflecting on normative power Europe. In F. Berenskoetter & M. J. Williams (Eds.), *Power in world politics* (pp. 173–188). Routledge.

Flockhart, T. (2006). "Complex socialization": A framework for the study of state socialization. *European Journal of International Relations, 12*(1), 89–118.

French, H. W. (2014). *China's second continent. How a million migrants are building a new empire in Africa.* Alfred A. Knopf.

Gelpern, A., Horn, S., Morris, S., Parks, B., & Trebesch, C. (2021, March 31). *How China lends: A rare look into 100 debt contracts with foreign governments.* Peterson Institute for International Economics, Kiel Institute for the World Economy, Center for Global Development, and AidData at William & Mary. Retrieved May 28, 2021 from https://www.aiddata.org/publications/how-china-lends

Hamilton, D. S. (2008). The United States: A normative power?. In N. Tocci (Ed.), *Who is a normative foreign policy actor? The European Union and its global partners* (pp. 76–155). Center for European Policy Studies.

He, J. (2016). Normative power in the EU and ASEAN: Why they diverge. *International Studies Review, 18*(1), 92–105.

Higley, J. (2018). Continuities and discontinuities in elite theory. In H. Best & J. Higley (Eds.), *The Palgrave handbook of political elites* (pp. 25–39). Palgrave Macmillan.

Ikenberry, G. J., & Kupchan, C. A. (1990). Socialization and hegemonic power. *International Organization, 44*(3), 283–315.

Johnston, A. I. (2001). Treating international institutions as social environments. *International Studies Quarterly, 45*(4), 487–515.

Johnston, A. I. (2003). Socialization in international institutions: The ASEAN way and international relations theory. In G. J. Ikenberry & M. Mastanduno (Eds.), *International relations theory and the Asia-Pacific* (pp. 107–162). Columbia University Press.

Johnston, A. I. (2008). *Social states: China in international institutions, 1980–2000.* Princeton University Press.

Kavalski, E. (2014). The shadows of normative power in Asia: Framing the international agency of China, India, and Japan. *Pacific Focus, 29*(3), 303–328.

Kavalski, E. (2017). Normative power Europe and normative power China compared: Towards a relational knowledge-production in international relations. *Korean Political Science Review, 51*(6), 147–170.

Kavalski, E. (2018). Chinese concepts and relational international politics. *All Azimuth, 7*(1), 87–102, 155–156.

Körösényi, A. (2018). Political elites and democracy. In H. Best & J. Higley (Eds.), *The Palgrave handbook of political elites* (pp. 41–52). Palgrave Macmillan.

Lam, K. N. (2015). Chinese adaptations: African agency, fragmented community and social capital creation in Ghana. *Journal of Current Chinese Affairs. China Aktuell, 44*(1), 9–41.

Lau, S. (2019, April 7). Greece's ancient civilisation was once a lure for China's leaders. Now It could prove their nemesis. *South China Morning Post.* Retrieved May 28, 2021 from https://www.scmp.com/news/china/diplomacy/article/3005031/greeces-ancient-civilisation-was-once-lure-chinas-leaders-now

Manners, I. (2001). Normative power Europe: The international role of the EU, paper presented at the *European Community Studies Association Biennial Conference*, Madison.

Manners, I. (2002). Normative power Europe: A contradiction in terms? *Journal of Common Market Studies, 40*(2), 235–258.

Manners, I. (2009, May). *The concept of normative power in world politics* (DIIS BRIEF). Danish Institute for International Studies. Retrieved May 28, 2021 from https://pure.diis.dk/ws/files/68745/B09_maj_Concept_Normative_Power_World_Politics.pdf

Mohan, G., & Lampert, B. (2013). Negotiating China: Reinserting African agency into China-Africa relations. *African Affairs, 112*(446), 92–110.

Nyíri, P. (2005). The "new migrant": state and market constructions of modernity and patriotism. In P. Nyíri & J. Breidenbach (Eds.), *China inside out: Contemporary Chinese nationalism and transnationalism* (pp. 141–175). Central European University Press.

Oosterveld, W., Wilms, E., & Kertysova, K. (2018). The Belt and Road Initiative looks East. Political implications of China's economic forays in the Caribbean and the South Pacific. *The Hague Centre for Strategic Studies.* Retrieved May 28, 2021 from https://hcss.nl/report/belt-and-road-initiative-looks-east

Paltiel, J. T. (2007). *The Empire's new clothes: Cultural particularism and universal value in China's quest for global status.* Palgrave Macmillan.

Panda, A. (2014, June 26). Reflecting on China's Five Principles, 60 years later. *The Diplomat.* Retrieved May 28, 2021 from https://thediplomat.com/2014/06/reflecting-on-chinas-five-principles-60-years-later/

Park, S. (2014). Socialisation and the liberal order. *International Politics, 51*(3), 334–349.

Peebles, P. (2006). *The history of Sri Lanka*. Greenwood

Persson, A. (2018). "EU differentiation" as a case of "normative power Europe" (NPE) in the Israeli-Palestinian Conflict. *Journal of European Integration, 40*(2), 193–208.

Qin, Y. (2016). A relational theory of world politics. *International Studies Review, 18*(1), 33–47.

Qin, Y. (2018). *A relational theory of world politics.* Cambridge University Press.

Risse, T., Ropp, S. C., & Sikkink, K. (Eds.). (1999). *The power of human rights: international norms and domestic change.* Cambridge University Press

Rotberg, R. I. (2008). China's quest for resources, opportunities and influence in Africa. In R. I. Rotberg (Ed.), *China into Africa. Trade, aid, and influence* (pp. 1–20). Brookings Institution Press.

Sen, T. (2014, September 23). Silk Road diplomacy – Twists, turns and distorted history. *YaleGlobal Online.* Retrieved May 28, 2021 from https://yaleglobal.yale.edu/content/silk-road-diplomacy-twists-turns-and-distorted-history

Sen, T. (2018). Serendipitous connections: The Chinese engagements with Sri Lanka. In B. Schnepel & E. A. Alpers (Eds.), *Connectivity in motion. Island hubs in the Indian Ocean world* (pp. 369–395). Palgrave Macmillan.

Simmons, B. A. (2013). International law. In W. Carlsnaes, T. Risse, & B. A. Simmons (Eds.), *Handbook of international relations* (pp. 352–378). Sage.

Snow, P. (1988). *The star raft: China's encounter with Africa.* Weidenfeld and Nicholson

Stokke, O. (1995/2006). Aid and political conditionality: Core issues and state of the art. In O. Stokke (Ed.), *Aid and political conditionality* (pp. 1–87). Frank Cass.

Sukma, R. (1999). *Indonesia and China: The politics of a troubled relationship.* Routledge.

Summers, T. (2019). A relational theory of world politics. By Yaqing Qin, Book review. *International Affairs, 95*(1), 210–211.

Terhalle, M. (2011). Reciprocal socialization: Rising powers and the West. *International Studies Perspectives, 12*(4), 341–361.

The Economist. (2019, April 17). *Hope remains for Western solidarity. Look at embassies in Beijing.* Retrieved May 28, 2021 from https://www.economist.com/china/2019/04/20/hope-remains-for-western-solidarity-look-at-embassies-in-beijing

The State Council of the People's Republic of China. (2015, November 23). *Historic admiral heralded goodwill of China.* Retrieved May 28, 2021 from http://english.www.gov.cn/premier/news/2015/11/23/content_281475240492252.htm

Tocci, N. (2007, December). *Profiling normative foreign policy: The European Union and its global partners* (CEPS Working Document No. 279). Centre for European Policy Studies, Brussels. Retrieved May 28, 2021 from https://www.ceps.eu/ceps-publications/profiling-normative-foreign-policy-european-union-and-its-global-partners/

Tudoroiu, T. (2015). The reciprocal constitutive features of a Middle Eastern partnership: The Russian-Syrian relation. *Journal of Eurasian Studies, 6*(2), 143–152.

Tudoroiu, T. (2022). *China's globalization from below: Chinese entrepreneurial migrants and the Belt and Road Initiative.* Routledge

Tudoroiu, T., & Ramlogan, A. R. (2019). China's international socialization of Caribbean state–society complexes: Trinidad and Tobago as a case study. *Asian Journal of Political Science, 27*(2), 157–176.

Tudoroiu, T., with Ramlogan, A. R. (2020). *The myth of China's no strings attached development assistance: A Caribbean case study.* Lexington Books.

Tudoroiu, T., with Ramlogan, A. R. (2021). *China's international socialization of political elites in the Belt and Road Initiative.* Routledge.

Vangeli, A. (2019). A framework for the study of the One Belt One Road Initiative as a medium of principle diffusion. In L. Xing (Ed.), *Mapping China's 'One Belt One Road' initiative* (pp. 57–89). Palgrave Macmillan.

Vuving, A. L. (2019). Emilian Kavalski. (2018). The guanxi of relational international theory. London: Routledge. 129 ISBN: 978-1-138-08878-8, Book review. *Journal of Asian Security and International Affairs, 6*(2), 221–224.

Wade, G. (2005). The Zheng He voyages: A reassessment. *Journal of the Malaysian Branch of the Royal Asiatic Society, 78*(1), 37–58.

Wendt, A. (1999/2003). *Social theory of international politics.* Cambridge University Press.

Whitman, R. G. (2013). The neo–normative turn in theorising the EU's international presence. *Cooperation and Conflict, 48*(2), 171–193.

Womack, B. (2008). *China as a normative foreign policy actor* (Working Document No. 282), Brussels: Centre for European Policy Studies. Retrieved May 28, 2021 from https://papers.ssrn.com/sol3/papers.cfm?abstract_id=1337618

YouTube. (2018, February 16). *2018 – China – CCTV's lunar New Year TV gala showcase "racist blackface" african sketch – 15/2/18.* Retrieved May 28, 2021 from https://youtu.be/siEPxHafx-4

Theodor Tudoroiu is a Senior Lecturer at the Department of Political Science of the University of the West Indies, St. Augustine campus. He earned his Ph.D. in Political Science from the Université de Montréal and an M.A. from the College of Europe in Bruges, Belgium. His China-related publications include *The Myth of China's No Strings Attached Development Assistance: A Caribbean Case Study* (Lexington Books, 2020), *China's International Socialization of Political Elites in the Belt and Road Initiative* (Routledge, 2021), and *China's Globalization from Below: Chinese Entrepreneurial Migrants and the Belt and Road Initiative* (Routledge, 2022).

Printed by Printforce, the Netherlands